China and Inner Asia

From 1368 to the
Present Day

MORRIS ROSSABI

THAMES AND HUDSON · LONDON

© 1975 Thames and Hudson Ltd, London

PRINTED IN GREAT BRITAIN
BY WESTERN PRINTING SERVICES LTD,
BRISTOL

CHINESE HISTORY AND SOCIETY

General Editors: W. J. F. Jenner
and E. P. Wilkinson

China and Inner Asia

CONTENTS

MAPS

Preface

The areas lying between the People's Republic of China and the Soviet Union together form what scholars refer to as Inner Asia. They have been the scenes of several clashes between Chinese and Soviet troops during the past ten years. There is no doubt that both China and the Soviet Union prize these territories and are willing to fight for them, as various states have been prepared to do over the past six hundred years. In this book I propose to describe the great impact which these lands have exerted on one state, China, since the fourteenth century. The book is a survey of Chinese relations with Inner Asia throughout this period. I have written it for the general reader, but hope that the specialist will find certain sections useful. Few general accounts based on the latest research are available, and these tend to emphasize the period of Russian interest in Inner Asia and seek to explain Sino-Russian and Sino-Soviet conflicts in the region. My intention is different, however, for I seek to describe and analyse traditional and modern Chinese foreign relations with Inner Asia. A consideration of Sino-Inner Asian contacts before Russian expansion in the East is essential for this purpose. Thus, approximately one-quarter of the book is devoted to Ming relations with Mongolia, Manchuria, and Central Asia – that is, to the time immediately before Russia first became seriously involved with Inner Asia. I have tried to provide a general overview of Chinese diplomatic and commercial relations with Inner Asia; for maps and specific detail I have drawn extensively on my own research and published writings.[1]

Despite the declared views of imperial Chinese officials, which have been accepted by some modern scholars, I believe that Inner Asia was extremely important to China. It was strategically vital to the defence of China, and Chinese officials, despite their frequent denials, needed and coveted trade with the region. In modern times, it has, if possible, gained in importance in the defence and economy of China. In short, relations with Inner Asia have been and are highly significant for Chinese economic and political life.

Due to space limitations, this book focuses on political and economic relations between China and Inner Asia and omits other equally interesting and valuable subjects that are peripheral to the central concern. Thus, discussion of mutual cultural and religious influences between the Chinese and their neighbours in the north and north-west is generally excluded. Domestic political and economic issues within China or Inner Asia that do not bear directly on the conduct of foreign policy are passed over, and Russian relations with areas in Central Asia that have had only minimal contacts with China are ignored.[2] I have dealt principally with those of the numerous religious, racial, and language groups in Inner Asia whose relations with China demand most attention. The Buryat Mongols in the Lake Baikal region and the Uzbeks of Russian Central Asia, for example, are only occasionally mentioned, but the Kazakhs and Uighurs of Sinkiang, whose paths repeatedly crossed those of the Chinese, are frequently cited.

The general reader will, I hope, consider this book a sufficiently detailed introduction to a long and complicated story. I have provided selected references to more specialized studies on the various subjects touched upon in these pages, and draw the reader's attention to my forthcoming book, *Inner Asia: A Critical Bibliography*, commissioned by the American Council of Learned Societies. This will contain a more complete, graded, and annotated enumeration of the principal studies in this field.

It is necessary to define the well-established but unsatisfactory term 'Inner Asia' as used in this book. If there is an Inner Asia, one may ask, where is Outer Asia? To avoid this illogicality, Denis Sinor, of Indiana University, has suggested the use of the term 'Central Eurasia' to describe the area that 'lies beyond the great sedentary civilizations of Eurasia' and includes the non-European minorities of the Soviet Union, the minorities of northern and western China, and the peoples of Tibet and Mongolia.[3] 'Central Eurasia' more clearly designates the role of this area as an intermediary between Europe and Asia and its importance in both continents. The term has not gained wide currency, however, and so I will use the unsatisfactory but more common concept 'Inner Asia'. But my focus is only on those regions in Inner Asia that had extensive dealings with China; these include Manchuria, Mongolia,

Sinkiang, and parts of Soviet Central Asia. Tibet is generally not covered because it did not pose a military threat to China during this time, because it had hardly any role in Sino-Russian territorial conflicts from the seventeenth to the twentieth centuries, and because, due to its uniqueness and its special relationship to China from the Ming dynasty to the present, it deserves a separate study. I have, nonetheless, devoted some space to the influence of Tibet on Inner Asian politics and to the impact of Tibetan Buddhism on Mongolia and China.

Inner Asia has great contemporary relevance. Newspapers and periodicals in Western Europe and the United States often publish reports on developments in the region, and in the past decade the number of such accounts has increased significantly. I have not attempted to give an account of all the changes that have occurred over the last few years. The available information is strongly biased in one way or another, and few independent observers have visited and written about the parts of Inner Asia under Soviet and Chinese control. I have thus tried principally to portray the general patterns of Sino-Inner Asian relations since the re-establishment of a unified state in China in 1949. As more reliable information becomes accessible, the changes in the area will be more comprehensible, and another chapter can then be added to this book.

The transcription of Oriental names always poses problems. It seems to me that consistency and familiarity in transcription are most important for the purposes of this book. For most Mongol names, therefore, I have chosen to follow the transcription system used in the well-known work *The Modern History of Mongolia* by Charles R. Bawden (New York and London, 1968). So I have written 'Tushetu Khan' instead of the phonetically more accurate 'Tüshiyetü Khan', 'Setsen Khan' instead of the more accurate 'Sechen Khan', 'Sain' instead of 'Sayin', and so on. I have used the commonly known term 'Dzungars' rather than the more correct 'Zunghars'. I have also romanized Mongel place-names (e.g. the familiar 'Kobdo' and 'Ulias-sutai' are used instead of the more accurate 'Khobdo' and 'Uliyasutai'). A scholarly controversy rages over the proper romanization of the name of the people who inhabited Manchuria before the Manchus. I have decided to write 'Jurched', rather than 'Jurchen', but I do not rule out the possibility that 'Jurchen' may prove to be more accurate. In these circumstances, it is reasonable to expect that it may be necessary to adopt a different policy with regard to transcription in my other works.

My principal debt in the writing of this work has been to my wife Mary Jane. While teaching, pursuing her own research, and helping to raise a family, she has found the time to edit and vastly improve all of my writings. Without her good cheer and her assistance, I would certainly not have completed the work with dispatch. Whatever merit the book possesses is in no small measure due to her criticisms and suggestions.

I would like to thank Dr Endymion Wilkinson and Mr W. J. F. Jenner for inviting me to write this work and my good friend Professor Joseph Fletcher for his help and advice over a number of years. I am also grateful to Dr Gerald Bunker, Professor Herbert Franke, Professor L. C. Goodrich, Mrs Deborah Kramer, and Professor Denis Sinor for various kindnesses offered during the preparation of the book.

Introduction

Late in the year 1413, the Yung-lo emperor of the Ming dynasty ordered Ch'en Ch'eng, an official in the Ministry of Personnel, to lead an expedition to Central Asia. Accompanied by another civil servant, a eunuch, and an unspecified number of escorts and pack animals, Ch'en left the protection of the Great Wall at Su-chou in north-western China on 3 February 1414 and started the four-thousand-mile journey to Herat, the capital of Tamerlane's son Shāhrukh Bahādur. Ch'en kept a diary and itinerary of his travels and wrote a report on the flora and fauna, the customs, and the products of the oases, towns, and states which he visited.[1] Though often vague and unilluminating, these accounts are still invaluable for their revelations of Chinese knowledge of, and attitude towards foreigners and for their delineation of the main trade route from China to Central Asia. One scholar, in fact, describes them as 'the most important sources for the situation in Central Asia during the early Ming period'.[2]

After performing sacrifices to the gods of the Western Regions, Ch'en and his party left Su-chou. They followed the traditional so-called 'silk route', heading directly for the town of An-hsi. Here they took a sharp detour to the north and now faced the severe test of crossing a section of the Gobi desert, where, fortunately, water was available almost every other day. They had completed a particularly dangerous and arduous part of the journey once they reached the town of Hami, and they remained there almost a week before continuing their travels. Their principal objective was to avoid the inhospitable Taklamakan desert, which travellers from the earliest days of the silk trade between China and the Roman empire had sought to bypass. Ch'en's embassy proceeded north of the Taklamakan through Hami, Karakhojo, and Turfan (see the map on pages 48–49). Ch'en mentions

13

innumerable halting places, many of which have not yet been identified. It is clear from his descriptions, however, that he skirted Lake Issyk-kul and visited in quick succession Sairam, Tashkent, and Samarkand, the capital of Tamerlane's grandson, Ulugh-Beg. He was impressed by Samarkand's conspicuous prosperity, its highly skilled craftsmen and its magnificent bazaars which displayed products from all of the known world. Leaving this fabulous city after a ten-day sojourn, he passed through Kesh and completed his journey in Herat, almost exactly ten months after his departure from China proper.

The embassy was not harassed by bandits and looters who might have stolen the gifts for the rulers of the seventeen states and oases to be visited. Showered with lavish gifts, these potentates accorded the envoys a fine reception. Some even dispatched men to welcome and escort the embassy. This was no accident. The Yung-lo emperor had cultivated good relations with the Central Asian states and had amply rewarded rulers and envoys who reached the Chinese capital.[3] Tamerlane's abortive invasion of China in 1404–1405 was the only untoward incident in the generally amicable relations of the Ming emperor and what the Chinese called the 'Western Regions'.

The security of Ch'en's embassy, however, required more than the co-operation of a few oases and towns. Perhaps equally important were several institutions devised as early as the first century BC to facilitate travel and trade between China and Central Asia. The system of military bases known as guards (*wei*) created by the Chinese beyond the Great Wall were the most important of these institutions in Ming times (see page 28). The men stationed there were occasionally Chinese soldiers but were more often Mongols, Uighurs, or other non-Chinese who often performed valuable services for the Ming dynasty. They used smoke and flag signals to warn of dangers or unusual occurrences. They ran hostels, served as suppliers of water and other necessities, and indicated the distance to the next resting place. A second institution that promoted travel was the postal station. Though the primary objective of the postal stations was the speedy conveyance of government documents, they also encouraged travel, for many of them lay on major trade routes. Each station had a specified number of horses, mules, ox-drawn carts, camels, or sedan chairs. Travellers found food, water, beds, and washing facilities for themselves and fodder for their animals in the stations. They also received valuable information about weather, terrain, and possible hazards.[4] A third institution, the caravanserai, was located primarily in the Middle East and Persia and was run by Arabs and Persians. Like the guards and the postal stations, the caravanserais offered supplies and rest for men and animals. They were, in addition, easily defendable and provided refuge and security for weary travellers.[5]

Even with these conveniences, trips from China to Central Asia were hazardous. Ch'en, like many other voyagers, noticed skeletons of numerous horses, camels, and even humans along the main trade routes.[6] He and his men lost their way in a blinding snowstorm; they travelled along rugged mountain paths where one wrong step by man or animal would have been fatal; they erected makeshift bridges in order to cross turbulent streams; they went without drinking water for days, melting down chunks of ice when thirsty. The roads they traversed were primitive. 'Trails' might be a more appropriate term for most of the paths on their route.

Still another difficulty was the enormous expense required for the embassy. Supplies for the travellers and their animals, gifts for foreign rulers, and maintenance of the postal stations and guards en route were costly. The Ming court, nonetheless, bore the financial burden of this and other embassies dispatched during the Yung-lo period. The emperor sent emissaries to Korea, South-east Asia, Mongolia, Persia, and other states because he was confident that China would ultimately profit from this policy, despite its cost.[7]

The Chinese explanations for the dispatch of the Ch'en Ch'eng embassy are logical, if limited. The court, according to the official account, was merely responding to tribute missions from Herat, Samarkand, Turfan, Karakhojo, and Kashgar that reached the Chinese capital in 1413. It sent Ch'en to reward the rulers of those states for their loyalty to the throne. It further sought to reassure Herat and Samarkand, the two capitals of the empire inherited by Tamerlane's descendants, that Tamerlane's incursions had been forgotten and that peaceful and mutually beneficial relations were now possible. The court deliberately failed to mention other perhaps even more pressing reasons for its willingness to subsidize the embassy: one likely motive was its need for information about Central Asian states.

Chinese officials valued Ch'en's report on his travels so highly that they inserted it into the court records. Though they appreciated his accounts of the etiquette, clothing, medicine, food, architecture, religion, marital and burial customs, festivals, and education of Herat and the other states, they concentrated on his descriptions of the legal system, commercial practices, and monetary transactions. Such data were invaluable not only for Chinese merchants but also for the court. Ch'en scarcely refers to military matters in his written account, but he doubtless proffered strategic information in conversations with government officials. He was certainly on the alert for hints of aggressive intentions on the part of Central Asian rulers and reported on such dangers to the court.

A second unstated objective of his mission was to encourage the Central Asian states to send trade and tribute embassies to China. Despite official pronouncements to the contrary, the Ming needed and desired certain foreign products. It did not at this time attempt to prohibit the entry of foreign emissaries as long as they followed Chinese regulations.

Ch'en's embassy did indeed stimulate the arrival of missions from the Central Asian states. The embassy sent by Shāhrukh Bahādur of Herat in 1419, the most renowned of the missions in the early Ming period, met with a generally cordial reception at the court. An account of its travels and experiences is extant. Written by a painter named Ghiyāth al-Dīn Naqqāsh, this account affords a rare and invaluable glimpse of the Ming attitude towards and treatment of foreigners. Some of the incidents and figures cited in the work appear unreliable or exaggerated, but most confirm and are, in turn, confirmed by the traditional Chinese accounts.[8]

The embassy left Herat on 24 November 1419 and by mid-August 1420 had reached a Chinese outpost approximately ten days away from Su-chou. A few Chinese officials met the envoys there and prepared a feast and entertainment for them. The officials requested and received a list of the names of the 150 men in the embassy and then accompanied the embassy to Su-chou; 'thereafter whatever requirements the envoys had as regards horses, food, drink, and bedding were all provided'.[9] They obtained, according to their rank, food and drink at each postal station en route to the capital and were accorded banquets in the major cities. Some of the envoys apparently had the leisure and freedom to sightsee, for Ghiyāth al-Dīn offers detailed descriptions of Chinese houses, temples and gates. The envoys reached their destination in Peking early on 14 December and were granted the unusual honour of an immediate audience with the emperor. Most foreign embassies spent days, if not weeks and months, practising the proper rituals in preparation for their meeting with the emperor, but the escorts for this mission ushered Ghiyāth al-Dīn and the other envoys into the palace on their very first day in Peking. On entering the palace complex, they noticed that 'there were about 300,000 people, both men and women, gathered in that open space [main square], while nearly two thousand musicians stood singing in concert and chanting the praises of the Emperor in the Chinese language'. Then the emperor appeared, accompanied by two girls who jotted down whatever might fall from his lips on that particular day.[10] The emissaries waited until the emperor had sentenced some criminals and then a court official read a statement in Chinese explaining the nature and purposes of the embassy. When he had finished, a Muslim interpreter employed by the Chinese ordered the envoys to kowtow to the emperor and to present the letters and gifts of their prince to a eunuch who in turn handed them to the Ming ruler. The emperor asked them some polite questions about their own ruler and then dismissed them.

An official from the Ministry of Rites (Li-pu) guided the embassy to the College of Interpreters (Hui-t'ung-kuan), a government hostelry where Ghiyāth al-Dīn and his fellow envoys resided for five months. The Chinese now imposed limitations on their freedom of movement. They could neither travel freely around the city nor meet with individual Chinese without permission. There were, however, compensations for these restrictions. The envoys received provisions from the Chinese: each person was daily granted flour, a bowl of rice, two large loaves of sweets, a pot of honey, garlic, onion, vinegar, salt, a selection of vegetables, two jugs of beer, and a plate of desserts, and each group of ten secured a sheep, a goose, and two fowl. Servants, 'endowed with great beauty and ever on their feet from morning to evening and from evening to morning',[11] catered for their needs. The emperor invited them to several banquets; one of these, held during the New Year festivities, was attended by all the foreign envoys in China. The lavish entertainments consisted of music, acrobatics, and dancing. The emperor rewarded the envoys and their ruler with silk robes, undergarments, hawks, paper money, and other goods, giving particularly elaborate presents to those tribute bearers who offered fine horses: the horses of Central Asia had been coveted by China's rulers for a millennium. He permitted the envoys to trade with Chinese merchants at the College of Interpreters for three to five days under the supervision of Chinese officials. He even invited them to participate in a hunt with him and his entourage, which almost ended badly for them. The emperor complained that 'I mounted for chase one of the horses which you brought me, and it being extremely old and feeble fell down throwing me off. Ever since that day my hand is giving me pain and has become black and blue.'[12] Fortunately for the envoys, the emperor restrained himself and did not punish them.

Restrictions and controls characterized Chinese policy towards embassies from Inner Asia. For example, when the envoys reached the Chinese border on their way back to their native land, frontier officials searched their baggage for contraband and checked their names on the list compiled on their entry into China. The Chinese court enforced regulations on these missions for its own pecuniary, military, and political gain. It sought to impose its own view of international relations on its neighbours, believing that if it failed, its image of itself, its confidence, and its superior economic and political position would all be subverted. These restrictions were also vital to the defence of China's northern borderland.

THE CHINESE VIEW OF FOREIGN RELATIONS

China's curious view of international relations derived from centuries-long experience with the Inner Asian peoples. It appears that this view originated as early as the Han (206 BC–AD 220) dynasty. Some scholars have accepted at face value the traditional Chinese exposition of this attitude, but I will show that part of this is a self-serving myth.

China was always concerned about its northern and western borders. It feared the raids or invasions of the frontier peoples, and the construction of the Great Wall across northern China was one attempt to curb such attacks. As Owen Lattimore has observed, the Chinese army had a decidedly disadvantageous position in battles with the border tribes.[13] Its cavalry was no match for that of the Mongols or the Central Asian peoples, and its supply lines could not sustain deep incursions into enemy territory. Even if Chinese troops secured a major victory over the border tribes, the latter could easily retreat into the steppes, nearby oases, or forests, regroup, and then continue hostilities. Long wars damaged the Chinese economy but did not exhaust the nomadic or oasis economies of most Inner Asian peoples. Various dynasties throughout Chinese history, however, persistently attempted to conquer and control the borderlands. When these costly expeditions occasionally resulted in temporary territorial expansion, the natives were still not pacified and large Chinese garrisons were required. The court would eventually abandon the new territories, partly because of the expenses incurred in maintaining a residual force and partly because of the demoralization and decline in military skills of its troops. Even the most powerful dynasties in pre-modern times, the Han and the T'ang (AD 618–907), could not permanently govern Mongolia, Manchuria, or Central Asia.

According to Lattimore, Chinese efforts at colonization in these territories generally proved fruitless, as did most attempts by steppe peoples to establish Chinese-style agriculture. Farmers found most of the land unsuitable for the Chinese style of intensive agriculture.[14] They also faced stiff competition from pastoral peoples for the marginal land that appeared to be cultivable. Wars in Inner Asia thus often erupted in response to Chinese expansionism. Such difficulties discouraged individual colonization and reduced the possibility of peaceful penetration of Chinese influence. On the other hand, the style of life of the foreigners often attracted Chinese frontier farmers. Many fled across the border to join the nomads when the reigning dynasty either imposed onerous taxes and services or was too weak to be effective on the borderlands. Similarly, border officials and soldiers also defected under the same conditions. The nomadic peoples frequently accorded these defectors a cordial reception, for they possessed highly valued skills unavailable in Inner Asia. They served as translators, scribes, envoys, and craftsmen, or taught agricultural and metallurgical techniques.

The Chinese, dismayed by the defection of their own people and by the spread of their technology, and fearful of invasion, devised several methods of dealing with Inner Asia. The Han dynasty pursued the *ho-ch'in* policy, under which the court presented gifts and offered Chinese princesses in marriage to Inner Asian rulers in return for a pledge of peace. The same government also attempted to 'use barbarians to regulate barbarians' (*i-i-chih-i*). It sought through gifts and diplomacy to generate or exploit hostility among the tribal peoples, favouring first one group, then another. When disunity was created among the leading Inner Asian tribes, the hazard of large-scale assaults on China was minimized.[15] Though succeeding dynasties intermittently continued to employ these two tactics, as well as military methods, the policy that guided Chinese international relations from Han times until the end of the Ming period (1644) was the tribute system.

The proponents of the tribute system assumed that Chinese civilization was superior to the cultures of its neighbours. They believed that their literature, their Confucian ethics, their technology, and their magnificent cities and palaces, all of which the frontier peoples lacked, assured them a position of world leadership. They rejected international relations on the basis of sovereign equality. Instead, foreigners came to China as vassals of the Chinese emperor, the Son of Heaven. The emperor's virtue, compassion, and generosity would lead foreigners to acknowledge their inferiority, submit to the Chinese state, and employ Chinese rituals. They would, in Chinese terms, 'come and be transformed' (lai-hua).[16]

The Inner Asian rulers and the emperor each had clearly stated obligations in their relationship. The former adopted the Chinese calendar, used a Chinese seal in all official correspondence with the court, and received patents of appointment, noble ranks, and avuncular letters of advice from the emperor. The emperor, on the other hand, presented the so-called 'barbarians' with various honours and decorations, including caps, badges, and robes. He also invested new rulers with power and was supposed to furnish military or economic support in times of trouble.

The tribute embassy was the supreme expression of the mutual obligations of the emperor and foreign rulers. According to the official Chinese view, foreign potentates periodically sent embassies to offer tribute of native products to the emperor. The court prescribed the exact number of envoys, the frequency of embassies, and the point of entry for each tributary state. After several days of instruction interspersed with feasts and entertainment, the envoys finally went to the palace, performed the proper ceremonies, and offered tribute goods to the throne. The Chinese sovereign, in return, gave them valuable products for themselves and their ruler and permitted them to trade with Chinese merchants in additional goods which they had transported from their native lands. The Chinese, in effect, conducted international relations on their own terms. They limited the number of foreign visitors to China, regulated and closely supervised foreign envoys, and thereby minimized the possibility of spying. They also managed to limit contact between their own people and foreigners. This system further preserved the myth that the emperor and the Chinese people as a whole were culturally superior to the so-called 'barbarians'.

The official Chinese historians insist that the Chinese developed the tribute system primarily for defence, not for economic gain. Though the court permitted foreign envoys to trade at the College of Interpreters and operated markets on its north-eastern and north-western borders for commerce with frontier tribes, its principal objectives were to protect its territory and to pacify the more hostile and aggressive 'barbarians'. The Chinese provided the Inner Asian tribes with valued goods in return for peace. Similarly, they gained a measure of control by threatening to deny these foreigners essential products.[17]

The Chinese court, as reported by the official historians, frowned upon profit from commerce. It professed to consider trade a parasitic occupation and thus attempted to restrict the dealings of Chinese merchants with foreign envoys. The government sought to monopolize foreign goods in order to keep crafty merchants from cheating and thereby alienating the 'barbarians'. It repeatedly declared that it neither profited from nor needed trade and tribute and proclaimed its economic self-sufficiency so often that even so eminent a scholar as John K. Fairbank writes that 'there was little benefit to the imperial treasury in anything that a tribute mission might bring'.[18] Another modern writer asserts that 'Chinese statesmen, up to recent decades, hardly looked upon trade and tribute with the eye of an economist'.[19] The tribute offerings were generally luxuries designed to amuse and divert the emperor and his court, but they had scant economic significance. The gifts which the emperor presented to the tribute bearers and their sovereigns were more valuable and useful. The foreigners also obtained vital products from Chinese merchants.

The official Chinese historians offer several explanations of the toleration by the Inner Asian rulers of a system which treated them as vassals and inferiors. One is that the foreigners coveted Chinese goods and were even willing to submit to Chinese regulations in order to obtain them. Another is that investiture by the Chinese emperor doubtless enhanced the prestige of the tribal ruler among his own people and neighbouring tribes. Still another is that some of the strategically located tribes or oases could, on occasion, count on military or economic support from China.

In sum, the official historians attributed the origins of the tribute system to the Chinese fear of foreign attack. National defence is the most frequently cited objective of Chinese foreign policy. An important reason for the dispatch of envoys, for example, was the acquisition of military intelligence. Chinese officials discounted the value of trade as a motive. Yet, despite China's exaggerated claims of economic self-sufficiency, foreign trade was a major consideration in the minds of Chinese officials, and tribute was regarded as the prelude to trade. One recent student has observed that 'the early Ming court took Chinese commerce to the foreigners'.[20] A student of an even later period in

Chinese history notes that 'the Ch'ing state . . . found itself involved in a complex of co-operation with powerful merchants'.[21] The Chinese court needed certain foreign products, and it can be argued that the elaborate Chinese regulations on trade and the government's attempt to monopolize commerce served to secure a better bargaining position for the court in trade with foreigners. If the court was the only source for a particular commodity, it was only logical that the Inner Asian tribes would be forced to pay a higher price for it. The government, as we shall see, did not seek to abolish foreign trade, but tried to limit private enterprise and to control commercial transactions for its own profit.

I do not wish to discount the importance of defence in Chinese official policy towards the peoples of Inner Asia. Strategic considerations undoubtedly influenced Chinese officials in devising their policies and institutions for coping with the 'barbarians'. But the economic motives are often overlooked by historians of traditional China, and it is therefore part of my purpose to give them more emphasis than they have hitherto received.

1 Ming China and its neighbours

The Ming, a native Chinese dynasty, gained power in 1368, ending a century of Mongol control. Even before the Mongol conquest, inhabitants of Manchuria, Mongolia, and Central Asia had harassed and ruled Northern China for several centuries. The early Ming government was thus understandably xenophobic. On the other hand, the Mongol hegemony in Inner Asia in the thirteenth and fourteenth centuries had stimulated a tremendous upsurge in East–West commerce and travel. The caravan trade, which had been generally dormant for three hundred years, revived, merchants and missionaries travelled without hindrance from Europe through Asia; and crafts, techniques, and inventions were transmitted from one part of Asia to another. The Ming were unwilling completely to renounce these gains, so profit as well as defence shaped their policy towards Central Asia, Manchuria, and Mongolia.

MING CHINA AND CENTRAL ASIA

Ming China dealt most frequently with those Central Asians who lived in the oases along the Tarim River basin as well as the nearby pastoral tribes. Envoys from as far away as the Persian cities of Shiraz and Isfahan and the Timurid centres of Herat and Samarkand also reached the Chinese capital. The neighbouring towns on the fringes of the Taklamakan desert and the nomadic communities on the Dzungarian steppes, however, were clearly of most concern to the Chinese.

The lack of rainfall determined the economy of these regions. Only the T'ien Shan (Heavenly Mountains), which divided Dzungaria and the Tarim River basin, made possible the existence of the oases. Conservation of the waters descending from the T'ien Shan permitted the

23

inhabitants to sustain a subsistence agriculture. The local peoples, with the aid of carefully constructed irrigation works, cultivated a variety of food crops, but their style of farming differed considerably from the intensive agriculture of the Chinese. They also raised domestic animals and collected jade and other gems, and relied on trade with the nomadic peoples in the nearby hills and mountains for meat, wool and other clothing materials, and milk.

Hami was representative of the oases in Central Asia. It lay along the southern foothills of the T'ien Shan and was surrounded by deserts. The strongest Chinese dynasties, the Han and the T'ang, and the Mongol rulers of the thirteenth century sought and achieved control of Hami and other oases in the Tarim River basin. It is no accident that these were the times when the volume of trade through Inner Asia was greatest. When bandits threatened Hami or when internal disputes racked the town, trade declined. The inhabitants of this area were extremely heterogeneous. During the Han dynasty, there was a strong Iranian and Indian influence in the region, and Buddhism was probably introduced at this time. Later, in the eighth century, Islam first appeared in the oasis and the surrounding regions. Turks, Uighurs, and Mongols, in succession conquered Hami, and these diverse groups coexisted in the oasis. Ghiyāth al-Dīn reports that 'in this town [Hami] Amir Fakhru'd-Din had built a magnificent mosque, facing which they had constructed a Buddhist temple of a very high size'.[1] Hami's cosmopolitan character doubtless promoted and facilitated trade, for foreign merchants could often find inhabitants who spoke the same language or practised the same rituals. The town had flourishing bazaars which displayed the merchandise of numerous peoples and states.

Hami, like most of the other oases in the region, was only fertile in the small area where water from the melting snows of the T'ien Shan made agriculture possible. A census of the eighth century counted approximately ten thousand people in the area, while the Ming emissary Ch'en Ch'eng, who stayed in the oasis from 27 February to 4 March 1414, wrote that 'the population numbered several hundred households'.[2]

Hami was clearly neither a source of military manpower nor an important market for Chinese or Inner Asian products. Nor did it possess rich natural resources that other states coveted. The inhabitants of the oasis and the immediately adjacent lands bred horses and camels, extracted jade, cultivated wheat, millet, peas, and jujubes, and raised the so-called 'long-tailed sheep'.[3] The Chinese prized the horses of Hami, but they had other sources for most of the other goods produced in Hami. Hami owed its significance primarily to its location. It lay along the main trade route from Central Asia to China and was an important resting place for travellers and caravans crossing the desert to China. As Marco Polo noted, its inhabitants were cheerful, loved to sing and dance, and were hospitable to the point of lending their wives to weary travellers.[4] Geography ensured that Hami would remain vital in trade to China. In addition, since invading armies and roving groups of bandits from Central Asia needed to pass through Hami to reach China, it could, if on good terms with the Chinese, serve to warn the Middle Kingdom of impending dangers.

In the fifteenth and sixteenth centuries, as during much of its earlier history, Hami had powerful and occasionally hostile neighbours. The Oirats or Western Mongols lay directly to the north. These pastoral nomads roamed with their flocks through western Mongolia and Dzungaria, uniting around several charismatic leaders and frequently raiding or invading Hami, neighbouring towns or oases in Central Asia, and even China from the fifteenth until the middle of the eighteenth centuries. The Eastern Moghuls were Hami's closest western neighbours. These Muslim peoples, with a capital originally in Bishbalik (modern Urumchi) and later in Turfan, sought to expand their territory at the expense of Hami. Their rulers wished to conquer Hami in order to gain control of the trade routes to China. As a result, their relations with the Chinese had become increasingly hostile by the late Ming period.

It should be noted that most of our knowledge of Ming relations with Hami derives from the Chinese sources. Similarly, the Ming chronicles are the principal sources on the Mongols and the Jurched because the majority of the Inner Asian peoples developed written languages relatively late in their histories. The Chinese historians interpret events in Inner Asia in the light of their inherited concepts of foreign relations, making it extremely difficult for the modern historian to obtain a clear and relatively unbiased view. Much of what follows is thus of necessity based on the Chinese sources, though the interpretation varies considerably.

In early Ming times the Chinese court pursued a defensive policy in its dealings both with the nearby oases and with the distant empires of Central Asia. The first emperor, who reigned from 1368 to 1398, offered a historical parallel as an explanation for this policy:

The ancients have a saying: 'The expansion of territory is not the way to achieve enduring peace, and the overburdening of the people is a cause of unrest.' For example, the Sui Emperor Yang (600–618) sent his forces to invade Liu-ch'iu (Ryūkyū Islands), killing and injuring the foreign people, setting fire to their palaces and homes, and taking several thousand of their men and women as prisoners. Yet the land which he gained was not enough to furnish him with supplies and the people he enthralled could not be made to serve him. For vain glory he exhausted China.[5]

His justification was purely pragmatic. He believed that military conquest and control of restive and unco-operative 'barbarian' tribes was burdensome and expensive. He failed to mention that the Chinese had not the means to occupy Hami and the oases along the Tarim River basin. Caravans from Chinese territory took approximately three weeks to reach Hami, the nearest oasis, and it was clearly prohibitively expensive for the court to maintain a supply line of that length free from harassment by bandits. Chinese troops could temporarily control Hami but could never become permanent occupation troops. The court had difficulty in supplying soldiers from within its own borders and often recruited merchants to transport grain, clothing, and other necessities to frontier troops. On the other hand, it could not adopt a purely *laissez-faire* attitude, for an unco-operative government in Hami might disrupt the profitable trade and tribute system that the Chinese envisioned. Equally critical, the conquest of Hami by a hostile and aggressive Central Asian emperor might pose a military threat to China, as advance guards and armies could use Hami as a base for raids and incursions on Chinese soil. So the court needed to develop a forceful policy towards Hami, which would not, however, tie down too many troops.

But the Mongols diverted the attention of the first emperor. Though many of the Mongols left China in 1368, the Ming court had not destroyed Mongol opposition. The emperor did not finally defeat the last Mongol ruler of China until 1388, and even then remnants of the latter's forces continued to raid Chinese border villages. The descendants of the Mongol ruling family of Hami were also hostile to the new Ming court and only terminated their attacks on China after an impressive show of force by Ming troops in the last decade of the fourteenth century. By 1400, there was thus no effective working relationship between China and Hami.

Nor had China evolved a satisfactory relationship with the great empires of Central Asia. The chronicles of the first Ming emperor record the arrival of several embassies from Tamerlane. That great ruler, though not a descendant of the Mongol ruling family of Central Asia, had seized power in 1369, and from his base in Samarkand had set forth on a series of conquests in Persia, the Middle East, northern India, and other areas. It seems only natural that he should have turned his attention at some time to the populous and prosperous Chinese empire, but he was preoccupied with other projects until the early fifteenth century. Thus these early embassies were not led by official emissaries, but consisted merely of Central Asian merchants who represented themselves as Tamerlane's envoys in order to gain access to China. One such embassy reached the court in October 1394 with two hundred horses as tribute and a letter purportedly written by Tamerlane. The letter, which was undoubtedly forged by a Central Asian merchant, extolled the emperor for his superior virtue and acknowledged his supremacy in the world. It is inconceivable that Tamerlane, who aspired to world conquest, could have written such a fawning, self-deprecatory missive. A modern scholar notes that 'there is nothing in the Muslim conqueror's character to make one suppose that Temür would have acquiesced knowingly in any infidel's "mandate of Heaven" to rule the world'.[6] The Ming emperor was, nonetheless, so enchanted with the 'submission' of the great Muslim conqueror that in 1395 he dispatched an embassy of fifteen hundred men, led by a certain Fu An, who is identified as an Interpreter (*t'ung-shih*), and Liu Wei, a eunuch, to Tamerlane's capital at Samarkand. The emperor's letter to Tamerlane, in which he referred to the latter as a vassal, enraged the Central Asian ruler, who immediately seized Fu An and the rest of the embassy. In 1397, the Chinese court, anxious about the fate of its envoys, sent a second embassy, which Tamerlane again detained.[7] The first Ming emperor died the very next year, and the rebellion which followed his death precluded further action. Meanwhile Tamerlane laid plans for an invasion of China once he had pacified other parts of his empire.

Though China's relations with the oases adjacent to its north-western border and with Tamerlane were chaotic and unstable, an underlying Chinese foreign policy may be perceived. The first emperor acknowledged that China was neither powerful enough to overwhelm the Mongols, Uighurs, and other peoples on the frontier nor wealthy enough to maintain large garrisons outside its borders. The court sought to preserve the territorial integrity of the nearby oases in order to prevent more powerful states from engulfing them. If the Chinese failed, a great Central Asian empire could not only threaten the security of China's borders but could also control the trade and tribute road to China. And China in the early Ming period did wish to extend its trade and tribute relations.

It was left to the Yung-lo emperor, the first emperor's son, who ascended the throne in 1403, to initiate relations with other states. He dispatched the eunuch Cheng Ho on naval expeditions to Southeast Asia, the rim of the Indian Ocean, and the Persian Gulf, and the official Ch'en Ch'eng to Central Asia to stimulate the rulers of that area to send trade and tribute missions. He took the initiative in establishing diplomatic and economic contacts with the Oirat Mongols, Tibet, Thailand, and the Jurched of Manchuria, and concluded a commercial and tributary agreement with Japan.[8] He was generous to foreign ambassadors, their retainers, and their sovereigns. In 1407 he established the College of Translators (Ssu-i kuan) to train specialists who could provide readable and accurate translations of foreign documents.[9]

It is not surprising then that he actively attempted to promote good relations with Hami. In the first year of his reign, he sent an embassy to inform Hami's rulers of his enthronement and to stimulate them to offer tribute to China. Hami responded with a mission that presented horses to the emperor. The emperor, in turn, gave the envoys paper money, silk robes brocaded with gold, and lined garments of fine silk, and bestowed silk and silver on their ruler. Hami, encouraged by the Yung-lo emperor's cordial reception of its embassy, sent a total of forty-four missions during the emperor's reign, which lasted for twenty-one years.

The emperor borrowed a Mongol military institution, the *wei*, or guard, to regulate Ming relations with Hami. A guard, in theory, consisted of 5,600 soldiers divided into five battalions of 1,120 men, who were, in turn, composed of ten companies of 112 men. The court created guards either within or just outside the Chinese borders; they were intended to defend Chinese territory from 'barbarian' attacks. The guards located beyond the border differed from those in areas directly subject to Chinese authority. Henry Serruys, a distinguished scholar of Chinese relations with foreigners during the Ming period, describes them as 'protectorate territories',[10] but this term is misleading. As he himself states, the establishment of a guard did not imply Ming political control. The princes of Hami, for example, still ruled their oasis, and though the guards were presumably part of the Chinese military system, the participation of Hami in Ming campaigns was extremely rare. The Ming court granted the princes Chinese military titles, but, as Serruys remarks, 'neither the Hung-wu [first] emperor nor his successors intended to force [them] upon the road of rapid sinicization'.[11] The Ming did not govern Hami and the surrounding territories. The princes of Hami collected and kept taxes. They administered justice, raised their own armies, and generally resolved questions of succession on their own. In sum, the guards in Hami and neighbouring areas neither guarded the borders nor obeyed the dictates of the Ming government. The creation of the guards did not represent an intermediate step to full control by the Chinese government. Their function was to ensure that no other power should have that control.

On one occasion, however, the Yung-lo emperor attempted to impose Chinese rule on Hami. He had in his court a man related to the Hami ruling family named Togto (T'o T'o). The Chinese had captured this young prince during the Ming campaigns against Hami in the 1390s. They had apparently tutored him at the court and prepared him to be the ruler of his native town. Earlier Chinese dynasties had set a precedent for keeping the sons of foreign rulers as hostages who could be sinicized and prepared for future roles as client kings. In 1404, a perfect opportunity to achieve the Ming's aims arose when the reigning prince of Hami died, leaving no heirs. The emperor immediately enfeoffed Togto as the new prince and tried to bribe several powerful chieftains in Hami to accept Togto as the new ruler. But on Togto's arrival in Hami his own paternal grandmother joined with the leading chieftains to expel him, and it was only because of the emperor's threat to intervene that Togto was reinstated.[12]

The emperor's policy was a political disaster. He failed to realize that the Chinese court was a poor training ground for a boy who was to rule illiterate shepherds, farmers, and merchants living in small, separate, and sometimes hostile tribal units, deprived of the amenities of a sophisticated urban environment. He had apparently not foreseen the difficulties of such a transition for Togto. Even the Chinese sources reveal that Togto fared poorly on his return to Hami. The official Ming History (*Ming shih*) accused him of drunkenness, lack of interest in government affairs, and rudeness to Chinese envoys.[13] His oppressiveness and corruption precipitated rebellions and created hostility towards China. Fortunately for the court, Togto died in 1411. The Yung-lo emperor made no further attempts to replace him with his

29

own candidate, though it is clear that he attached great significance to Hami both for defence and trade.

A policy of not interfering in Hami's domestic affairs proved to be more beneficial to Chinese interests. Togto's successor, left to his own devices, cultivated good relations with the Chinese. He offered tribute once a year to the emperor, permitted emissaries from distant Central Asian states to pass through his land unhindered, and sold fine horses to the Chinese at frontier markets. In addition, he reported on military and political developments in Central Asia and occasionally ordered his own people to translate diplomatic documents sent by Central Asian rulers to China. The Chinese established good relations not only with him but also with chieftains of outposts closer to China and with rulers of the other oases around the Tarim River basin. Khotan, the prime source of jade, Kashgar, the site where the two routes around the Taklamakan meet, and Turfan, the principal supplier of a dye used in the production of Ming blue and white porcelains, dispatched trade and tribute missions to China from the early days of the Yung-lo reign.

The Timurid empire was at first hostile but eventually a good relationship developed between it and the Yung-lo emperor. The latter, perturbed that the envoys sent by his father had still not returned, sent yet another embassy which Tamerlane once again detained and humiliated. Ruy González de Clavijo, the Spanish ambassador to the Timurid empire, observed:

> Those lords now conducting us began by placing us in a seat below that of one who it appeared was the ambassador of Chays Khan, the emperor of Cathay. Now this ambassador had lately come to Timur to demand of him the tribute, said to be due to his master, and which Timur year by year had formerly paid. His Highness at this moment noticed that we, the Spanish ambassador, were being given a seat below that of this envoy from the Chinese Emperor, whereupon he sent word ordering that we should be put above, and that other envoy below.[14]

Tamerlane intended to avenge himself on the infidel Chinese emperor who had dared to treat him as a vassal. He may perhaps have planned to convert the Chinese to Islam, particularly on hearing the untrue story that the Chinese had executed a hundred thousand Chinese Muslims. He undoubtedly knew of the resources and wealth of China and was eager to add it to his empire. In fact, when he started on his invasion of China, he was accompanied by a descendant of the Mongol khans, whom he presumably planned to enthrone as his client on the throne of China. From 1398 on, he prepared for a major assault against the Chinese by sending soldiers eastward to build forts and to farm the land so that his forces would be well supplied. In December 1404, he set forth with two hundred thousand troops for China. The Chinese were totally unprepared to counter this invasion by the greatest military figure of the era, and, in fact, were oblivious of the gravity of the threat. Fortunately for the court, Tamerlane died en route on 18 February 1405, and the succession crisis that followed his death aborted the planned invasion.[15]

Shāhrukh, Tamerlane's son and eventual successor, was less of a conqueror than his father. He sought to trade with the Chinese and apparently believed that wars with them would be expensive and wasteful. Unlike his father, he did not have the evangelical zeal to convert the Chinese to Islam. Nor was he determined to avenge himself on the Chinese emperor for treating him as a vassal. He had also moved his capital westward from Samarkand to Herat, another indication that he had no designs on Chinese territory. He placed his own son Ulugh-Beg, a man with great intellectual curiosity but with little interest in conquest, on the throne of Samarkand, and neither he nor his son attempted or even contemplated an invasion of China. In conformity with this policy of peace, Shāhrukh finally released the Ming envoys detained by his father and exchanged trade and tribute missions with the Chinese.

The Chinese emperor, in turn, took extraordinary steps to promote good relations with the Central Asian monarch. He amply rewarded Shāhrukh's envoys and treated them to lavish banquets. He dispatched several embassies, including three led by Ch'en Ch'eng, to bestow Chinese products on Shāhrukh and his family. Most important, he dealt with Shāhrukh as his equal, not as a vassal. In 1418, he wrote a letter which, according to one scholar, 'reveal[s] the inconsistency between Ming doctrine and practice and challenge[s] some widely held notions about Chinese foreign relations'.[16] The emperor lavished praise on Shāhrukh, noting that the Timurid ruler was 'enlightened, perceptive, knowing, mature, sensible, and greater than all the Muslims'.[17] He expressed gratitude for the excellent reception that Shāhrukh had accorded his envoys and avoided any claim of world domination or any implication of divine right. Instead, he referred to Shāhrukh as a political equal. He repeatedly announced his desire that 'envoys and merchants should constantly come and go, and there

31

should be no interruption'.[18] In attempting to encourage trade and to establish peaceful relations, he willingly abandoned the myth of superiority over other sovereigns and states.

Shāhrukh responded favourably to the emperor's initiatives. He sent the embassy of which Ghiyāth al-Dīn wrote his renowned account, as well as nineteen other missions between 1407 and 1424. The envoys offered horses, camels, sheep, and jade, all of which the court coveted. The court reciprocated with silk and paper money. It obtained desirable products at little cost, for its gifts placed no great burden on the Ming economy. The Central Asian state, on the other hand, received valuable goods for its own use and for trade with countries further to the west. This mutually beneficial relationship between the Timurid and the Ming courts encouraged more distant states to dispatch embassies on the long road to China. Envoys from as far away as Tashkent, Shiraz, and Isfahan reached the capital during the Yung-lo reign.

The Yung-lo emperor attained his principal objectives in Central Asia. He established working relationships with Hami and the neighbouring oases. These oases remained independent, and the Chinese engaged in profitable commerce with them. The relatively numerous embassies from distant Central Asian states and the safe passage accorded them by the oases reflected the good feelings between the Ming court and the rulers of those towns. The Yung-lo emperor clearly defused the military threats from those areas closest to the border. He further reduced tensions between the court and the Timurid and other Central Asian and Persian empires. The caravan trade across Asia flourished, and commerce and tribute missions flowed without interruption. Though the frontier markets handled a greater volume of goods, the long-distance trade also expanded during this period. The government limited and regulated its own merchants and, as a result, garnered most of the profit from this Central Asian trade.

The death of the Yung-lo emperor in 1424, however, disrupted this previously beneficial arrangement. It ushered in a period of retrenchment in Chinese foreign and military enterprises. The court discontinued the far-flung naval expeditions of Cheng Ho within a short time; Vietnamese rebels defeated a large Chinese force and reasserted their independence; and the Mongols, along with the peoples of Manchuria, threatened Chinese positions on the border.[19] The military forces of the Ming, partly because of corruption and demoralization, declined considerably following the termination of the Yung-lo emperor's expansionist campaigns. The government acknowledged that 'on one occasion in the 1420s . . . of 15,716 men conscripted in Shansi province . . . 1,713 had deserted. . . .' Agricultural colonies, which had formerly supplied Chinese troops on the borders, deteriorated, and the court had to transport grain, clothing, and other necessities to its soldiers, often an arduous, if not impossible task. One scholar has observed that 'during the fifteenth century the military colonies decayed . . . Frontier colonies were exposed to barbarian attack. It was even argued that farming and pasturing animals "beyond the frontiers" tended to provoke these attacks.'[20]

As the military power of the Ming waned, its economic difficulties increased. Its control over Chinese merchants became less effective. The merchants evaded government regulations and traded illegally with foreigners. Smuggling flourished, and foreign rulers, who could now more readily obtain Chinese products, were less willing to comply with government rules. Their envoys often refused to accept gifts of inflated paper money from the Chinese emperors and made unprecedented demands for such valuable goods as silver, porcelain, drugs, and copper coins. They requested and frequently received higher prices than they had obtained when the court monopoly of commerce was more effective. The Central Asian rulers dispatched more missions and with larger entourages. Court expenditure for maintaining the envoys consequently increased. The inhabitants along the ambassadors' route often bore the burden of supplying the emissaries. Many embassies used false credentials to gain entry into China and sought primarily to profit from trade, not to pay homage to the emperor. The envoys occasionally maltreated or took advantage of the Chinese population; they traded for such contraband goods as weapons and metal tools; they resided in the capital for inordinately lengthy stays; and they often offered defective or inferior products in tribute, frequently presenting more luxury and fewer essential goods than in earlier times. The Ming system, which relied on stringent regulations and government monopolies, was badly shaken. Chinese economic relations with Central Asia became costlier and less beneficial to the court.

Numerous irritating incidents hindered relations between China and Hami and the neighbouring oases, and the rise of a powerful and hostile figure in the Mongol steppes truly exacerbated these tensions. Esen (Yeh-hsien), who became chief of the Oirat or Western Mongols

33

in the Altai, north of Hami, in *c.* 1440, united the different factions among his people and started to expand his power. He resented Chinese maltreatment of some of his envoys and the inadequate, even paltry, gifts and payments which the court offered him in return for his tribute. He repeatedly asserted that Chinese merchants and officials short-changed his people in commercial transactions and that the court unfairly lowered its price for his horses. On the other hand, the court complained bitterly about the excessive number of envoys on his tribute embassies, their rude and occasionally criminal behaviour, and the poor quality of the tribute. Before Esen's accession, the majority of Oirat missions consisted of fewer than a hundred men, but he dispatched 2,302 in the missions of 1442, 1,867 in 1444, and over 2,000 in 1449.[21] China's expenditure in feeding, transporting, and providing gifts for these people was burdensome, and local officials frequently reported that the envoys consumed vast quantities of grain, fruit, meat, and liquor. Court officials protested that the Oirat tribute horses were 'mostly emaciated, small, and unfit'.

These economic difficulties led to tensions on the border between Esen's forces and Ming soldiers. In the early 1440s, Esen started to conduct raids on Hami and other towns in the Tarim River basin. The Ming court, whether aware of its military deficiencies or because its forces were already committed elsewhere, provided scant assistance to those areas, so that by 1446 Esen easily overwhelmed the oases adjacent to China's north-western border. In 1449, when Esen appeared ready to launch an invasion of China, the Chinese emperor personally led an ill-fated campaign to counter the threat of the Oirat chieftain. At the end of the year, Esen captured the hapless emperor, and only his indecisiveness and a quick Chinese regrouping of forces prevented his occupation of the Chinese capital. Fortunately for China, power struggles among the Oirats led to the assassination of Esen in 1454 and to the temporary dissolution of the Oirat confederation.[22]

Hami and the other oases along the Tarim River basin regained their independence after Esen's death, but the earlier harmonious relations of the Yung-lo era were never restored. The Chinese complained of the inferior or defective tribute goods offered by Hami's officials and merchants and occasionally refused to accept products, such as jade and horses, of poor quality. They objected to the greater frequency and size of the embassies that reached the Chinese border. Hami's envoys were, according to Ming sources, rude, had drunken brawls with

34

ordinary Chinese, and demanded undeserved military titles or promotion, expensive gifts, and such contraband as military supplies. Some traded with Chinese merchants illegally and obtained goods more cheaply than from the government. The court accused the inhabitants of Hami of robbing a Chinese envoy to Central Asia and of harbouring bandits who plundered the Chinese border communities.

The rise of the Moghul state of Turfan heightened China's difficulties with Hami and the nearby oases. Turfan was located north of the Taklamakan desert, only a short distance from Hami, and was a vital stop for caravans travelling from Persia and Central Asia to China. Like Hami, Turfan relied on carefully constructed irrigation works to sustain agriculture, but its importance was based upon its location along the main East–West trade routes. It too had a mixed population of Turks, Uighurs, Mongols, and others. It had been a peaceful, if not docile, area during the early Ming, but became increasingly hostile to the court from 1449 onwards. In the first part of the fifteenth century, it changed from a minor Buddhist principality to the capital of the powerful country of the Moghuls. By the 1450s, the rulers were Muslims and its land was dotted with mosques. It had annexed many of the towns and oases along the trade routes from China to Central Asia. Yunus Khan, its ruler, now sought to expand trade with China, while the Ming court attempted to limit commerce with foreign states. In 1465, the Minister of Rites, with the approval of the emperor, announced that only one mission from each of the neighbouring towns (Hami, Turfan, and others) would be permitted to enter China every three to five years and that it might consist of no more than two hundred men, only ten of whom would travel to the capital while the rest remained on the frontier.[23] Yunus apparently attempted to ignore the new regulations, but the court on occasion enforced the rules. His envoys met with several rebuffs. The Chinese refused entry to some of the larger embassies and rejected Yunus' requests for extravagant or forbidden goods.

Such incidents embittered relations between Yunus and the Ming court. Yunus had an excellent opportunity both to avenge himself on China and, incidentally, to enrich his state through neighbouring Hami. After the death of Esen and the retreat of the Oirats, the various minorities in Hami became embroiled in disputes over the succession to the throne. The Uighurs and a few Muslim groups were the main antagonists, but other tribesmen and mountain-dwellers also contributed to the chaotic political situation. In 1473, Yunus took advantage of the disunity within Hami to attack and occupy the town. The Chinese attempted to rouse the nearby oases to launch a counter-attack against Turfan (the old policy of 'using barbarians to regulate barbarians'), but the local chieftains were unable or unwilling to challenge Turfan. Yunus, noting that the Chinese failed to act, continued to occupy Hami for about a decade and made greater demands in his tribute embassies to the court. Surprisingly enough, even though he and the court remained hostile, tribute missions from Turfan continued to reach the capital and the envoys arrived more frequently and with entourages larger than was prescribed by Chinese regulations. One possible explanation for this is that the embassies still offered products which some Chinese coveted and the Chinese could not therefore afford to prohibit their entry into China.

Late in the 1470s, Yunus left Hami to pursue campaigns in the western part of his empire, allowing China, on that frontier, a peaceful interlude of about a decade. In 1482, Han Shen, the Uighur chieftain of Hami, profited from Yunus' absence to attack and reoccupy Hami, easily overwhelming the small contingent left behind by the Moghul ruler.[24] Han's triumph was short-lived, for Yunus' son and successor Ahmad, described as a 'true son of the steppes' and as 'The Killer' by contemporary writers, would not tolerate any diminution of Turfanese power in Hami and along the north-western borders of China. In 1488, he moved his forces to the outskirts of Hami and sent a letter to Han Shen proposing a marriage alliance. The latter unwisely permitted him and his troops to enter the town. Taking advantage of his successful ruse, Ahmad killed the Uighur chieftain and plundered Hami. The Chinese made several half-hearted attempts to recapture the town, but it was only when the rise of the Uzbeks, a new nomadic power in Central Asia, threatened the Moghuls from the west that a native prince was able to regain the throne of Hami. The Uzbeks' pressure forced Ahmad to march westward to repel their attacks, a campaign during which he was captured and lost his life in 1503. Even during the height of the hostility between the Chinese court and Ahmad, an average of one tribute mission a year, nonetheless, arrived in China from Turfan. The Chinese court apparently so coveted the products of Turfan that it did not stem the flow of tribute.

Mansur, Ahmad's son, finally detached Hami and the nearby oases from Ming influence. By means of promises of elaborate rewards and greater profits from trade, he persuaded the new chieftain of Hami to renounce his ties with China and to accept a position as prince in the

Moghul state. The newly enthroned prince moved to Turfan, and Mansur's troops occupied Hami by 1513. The court retaliated by prohibiting embassies from Turfan and Hami from entering China. Mansur, in turn, responded with raids and large-scale attacks on Chinese frontier communities, which almost immediately forced the court to relent and to allow his embassies to reach Peking. It recognized that it could no longer hold sway over the important oases on the caravan route to Central Asia. As a result, an uninterrupted flow of tribute missions from Turfan reached China until the end of the Ming dynasty in 1644. Despite the court's injunctions to border officials to examine scrupulously the credentials of foreign envoys before permitting them entry into China, 150 so-called 'princes' from Samarkand, Turfan, and Mecca arrived in the capital in 1536. The Ministry of Rites frequently issued proclamations limiting tribute missions from Turfan, but the ministry and border officials failed to enforce the rules.

Since the Chinese government could not carry out its own regulations, its previous pecuniary advantage was lost. Prices for Central Asian goods rose and smuggling flourished. Central Asian and Chinese merchants, not the court, obtained most of the profit from this commerce. The court could no longer count on the nearby oases as convenient buffers against foreign attacks and unwelcome embassies. Other tribes readily recognized China's weakness and detached more and more of its north-western border areas from Ming control. As its economic position worsened in the latter part of the fifteenth century, the Ming court had added more restrictions. The inhabitants of Turfan, who constantly sought an increase in the number of tribute and trade missions, chafed at the regulations, and their rulers clashed repeatedly with China until the court relented early in the sixteenth century, abandoned its claims to Hami and other towns in the Tarim basin, and allowed tribute embassies freely to enter China.

China's growing military weakness, as well as the economic and political difficulties with the nearby oases, led to disrupted relations with more distant Central Asian states. The route to China was no longer as safe as in the Yung-lo period. Some of the states that the Yung-lo emperor had gone to such lengths to induce to send tribute now lost touch with China. The Chinese themselves, due partly to the hazards of the journey, partly to the enormous cost, and partly to an attempt to limit the excessive number of embassies from Turfan and Hami, dispatched fewer emissaries to Central Asian states. Tensions and struggles within Central Asia accounted for a further reduction in the number of towns and states that appear in the court listings of tribute embassies. Turfan conquered many of these smaller principalities during its rise to power.

The Timurid empire too suffered severe setbacks in the latter part of the fifteenth century. The death of Shāhrukh in 1447, and the assassination of his successor Ulugh-Beg by his own son in 1449, marked the beginning of the empire's decline. Dynastic struggles and the decay of its military forces permitted nomadic communities to gain the upper hand over the urban centres of Samarkand and Herat.[25] The Uzbeks were the first such group, and they, along with the Safavid dynasty of Persia, dismembered the Timurid empire early in the sixteenth century. Later, the Kazakhs and the Kirghiz, offshoots of various Turkic tribes including the Uzbeks, threatened the sedentary peoples in Central Asia and the Moghul state of Turfan. It is not surprising then that Herat and Samarkand rarely dealt with the Chinese after the middle of the fifteenth century. The Ming annals record not a single tribute mission from Herat in the latter half of the fifteenth century.

Samarkand, under Ulugh-Beg, maintained excellent relations with the Chinese court. The Ming emperors particularly prized the fine horses offered as tribute by the Timurid ruler. They sent, in return, silks, satins, and, above all, porcelains, for which Ulugh-Beg built a beautiful pavilion in his palace.[26] Ulugh-Beg's death, however, interrupted this cordial and mutually beneficial relationship. The Ming annals of the late fifteenth century record an ever-growing number of unpleasant wrangles between Chinese officials and the envoys of Samarkand. The Chinese asserted that Samarkand sent poor, unworkable jade, and miserable nags. They further complained that the embassies from the Timurids often did not follow the prescribed routes of entry into China. The most scathing criticism of these embassies was that of a Minister of Rites who was infuriated by their gift of two lions in 1484. He noted bitterly that the lions consumed two sheep daily and required at least one keeper. In ten years, according to this outraged official, the court would have to provide over 7,000 sheep and about 3,500 man-days of labour! He suggested that the tribute be rejected and that the Chinese gifts not be offered in return. The emperor, fearing the repercussions of such a sharp rebuke of Samarkand, overruled him and accepted the lions.[27] This compromise failed to improve relations with Samarkand, for each party accused the other throughout the sixteenth century of economic chicanery.

From the middle of the fifteenth century until its fall the Ming dynasty was unable to attain its objectives in Central Asia. It could not rely on the oases close to the north-western border to help protect it against foreign invasions or even to warn of impending dangers. Nor could it regulate the flow of tribute and trade missions to ensure its own profits. The nations and tribes along the Chinese border could not be persuaded to accept Chinese suzerainty; they preferred to join with the hostile states of Central Asia in attacks on China.

MING CHINA AND MONGOLIA

The same problems that plagued Ming relations with Central Asia also afflicted its associations with the Mongols. The court feared the Mongols more than any other foreign nation, for it was the Mongols who had ruled China from the middle of the thirteenth century until they were ejected with great difficulty in 1368. The court's fears were confirmed as the Mongols frequently clashed with the Ming. The objectives of the two parties were incompatible. The Chinese sought secure borders and control of economic relations with the Mongols. The descendants of the Mongol emperors who had once governed China resented Ming efforts to restrict commercial and tributary transactions and were perturbed by the appearance of Chinese farmers in traditionally Mongol territories. Various Mongol groups inhabited a vast region stretching further north and north-west than Turfan in Central Asia eastward to the border of Manchuria. They thus came into contact not only with the Chinese but also with the Uighurs and Turks of Central Asia and the Jurched of Manchuria.

Scarcity of water shaped Mongol life. The low precipitation, the long cold and dry winters, and the excellent feed grasses made animal husbandry the natural basis of their economy. The Mongols raised principally sheep, goats, cattle, horses, and camels. Sheep were by far the most numerous and probably the most highly prized. The Mongols ate the flesh of the sheep, drank its milk, used its skin for clothing and its wool for the felt with which they made their tents. They obtained wool, meat, and milk from goats as well, but goats were not as vital to the Mongol economy. Many tribes also used cattle, including yaks, for food and milk and as draught animals, though cattle, like goats, were less important than sheep. Pasture-fed horses and camels served primarily for pulling and carrying. The Mongols also drank the milk and ate the flesh of horse and camel. Since the Mongols 'cut no hay and raised no grain for their animals',[28] they depended almost entirely on pasturage. After their herds had consumed the grass in one area, they moved to new pastures. Many Mongol families moved eight to ten times a year, and a few migrated as often as twenty-five to thirty times annually. Under such circumstances, a sedentary administration, bureaucracy, and government of the Chinese style were clearly out of the question.

The Mongols appeared economically self-sufficient, though in fact they were not. Owen Lattimore has argued that 'trade was not imperatively necessary'[29] for them. They produced their own clothing, meat, and shelter. They had horses, camels, and occasionally mules for transportation and obtained fuel from the dung of these animals. Their economy centred on their flocks and did not, in good times, require trade. Their dependence on animals, nonetheless, made them extremely vulnerable to climatic or natural catastrophes. They provided no shelter or dwellings for their herds even in the most severe weather. In winters when the snow was heavy huge numbers of animals died, for they could not reach the grass beneath the snow and the herdsmen had no reserves of grain or hay for them. Similarly, many animals starved to death during droughts. Mongol knowledge of animal diseases and of veterinary medicine was, by our standards, rudimentary, so that epidemics occasionally devastated their herds. Wolves and other predators also took their toll of the herds. Surprisingly enough, the Mongols rarely attempted to destroy wolves, or even to chase them away from their flocks.

Such hazards clearly made outside sources of grain and other foods necessary. In addition, certain foreign commodities (including tea, silk, clothing, salt, metals, medicines, and musical instruments), though not essential, were undeniably desirable. After the Mongols had been converted to Buddhism in the late sixteenth century, they also required tea for religious purposes. The Mongol princes doubtless reserved some silks and satins for ceremonial occasions, and some probably were traded with distant tribes who had no direct access to China. Mongols (both princes and commoners) wore cotton cloth, boots, and stockings from China. The Ming court attempted to prohibit the export of iron, fearing its use in the production of weapons. Chinese merchants and officials, however, supplied the Mongols with iron both for weapons and for farming tools, as a few Mongols living near the Chinese border practised a primitive form of agriculture. Mongol envoys frequently besought the court for gifts of the medicines which the Mongols had learned about during their occupation of China. Since the nomadic Mongol life offered few opportunities for the training and development of artisans, they relied on the Chinese for such articles as musical instruments. Many of the products which they requested and received from the Chinese were doubtless luxury goods. 'A parasol washed with gold', cosmetics, and 'one yellow-bodied flag [made of] the swimming bladder of a fish'[30] were certainly not vital, but more essential products usually accompanied these superfluous items.

The Mongols, in sum, required and desired trade with China. According to a leading student of Ming 'barbarian' relations, 'this need for Chinese manufactures was the most important single factor in Sino-Mongol relations'.[31] Ming attempts to deny the Mongols Chinese products inevitably created tensions and often provoked raids on Chinese border areas.

Though minor irritations and major military encounters character-ized the first half-century of Ming-Mongol relations, these relations were sometimes harmonious, at least from the Ming point of view. After the twenty years that it took the first Ming emperor to defeat the forces of the last Mongol ruler, it was left to his son, the Yung-lo emperor, to seek a peaceful and permanent arrangement with the Mongols. Even during the height of the hostilities, however, the first emperor permitted Mongols to settle in North China. Some did not migrate when the Ming ousted their ruler, and the emperor allowed them to remain unhindered in their homes. The court welcomed Mongols who surrendered voluntarily, employing some of them in the Ming army or creating special divisions within Chinese units for them. It also made provisions for Mongols dissatisfied with their uncertain and precarious mode of livelihood and eager for the more secure existence of a sedentary agricultural society. The Mongols generally migrated with their women and children and appear to have severed the ties with their native land. The court enticed them with offers of military titles and appointments, presents of food, robes, and housing materials, and occasionally annual subsidies of grain and paper money. In the early fifteenth century, it even gave them grants of farm land in an effort to assist them in the transition from nomadic pastoralism to sedentary agriculture.[32] In return, the Mongols served mostly as soldiers, envoys, and interpreters, though a few were simply civilians. The court initially permitted them to settle throughout the empire, including the capital, but also on the northern and north-western border. It often formed guards of Mongols in the strategic frontier areas.

The Chinese seldom regarded these resettled Mongols as a fifth column. A scholar who has examined the Ming records of the Mongols concludes that 'the central government never was unduly concerned about the number of Mongols in and around the capital'.[33] The first emperor and his immediate successors appeared confident that they could gain the allegiance of most of the Mongols in China and could isolate and control the few recalcitrant and hostile ones. They planned to sinicize the Mongols though they may not have realized that this would be a slow, tortuous process. Some Chinese officials, not sharing the generally optimistic view of the court, protested against the generous treatment of the Mongols. They asserted that they were untrustworthy and advised the emperor not to settle them on the northern borders but rather to scatter them throughout the empire. There is no doubt that Chinese bureaucrats and military men were jealous of the titles, salaries, and presents that the court granted the Mongol immigrants. Their objections, along with the court's real fear of an invasion following the capture of the Chinese emperor in 1449, persuaded the court, from the late fifteenth century onwards, to reject some of the Mongol requests for specific settlement areas in Peking and on the northern border.

Military clashes between the Chinese and the Mongols who remained in their native land were frequent in the early fifteenth century. The Yung-lo emperor attempted to reduce tensions with both the Eastern and the Western Mongols. In 1409, he dispatched an emissary to make an agreement with the Eastern Mongols. But their chieftain Arugtai killed the unfortunate envoy and eventually provoked the first of five major military campaigns led personally by the emperor. The emperor solicited and received the support of the Western or Oirat Mongols against Arugtai and proceeded to chase the Eastern Mongol chieftain into northern Mongolia. Though the Ming sources claim a victory for the Chinese, the Mongols apparently fled after a skirmish and the Chinese forces reluctantly turned back because their supply lines were not secure.[34] The emperor organized four other costly campaigns against the Eastern and Oirat Mongols. Most of these campaigns ended in futility and frustration, for, as Henry Serruys has noted, 'the extreme elusiveness of the Mongol cavalry made real contact with the enemy all but impossible'.[35] Though the emperor's troops on occasion came across and crushed a Mongol band, Arugtai of the Eastern Mongols and the leaders of the Oirats avoided capture and roamed freely in Mongolia.

The Ming practised a policy of 'divide and rule', attempting to fragment the various Mongol groups. For example, while the Yung-lo emperor pursued his campaign against Arugtai, he simultaneously cultivated good relations with the Oirats. A few years later, when he was at war with the Oirats, he bestowed a title on and granted elaborate gifts to Arugtai. The Mongols, due partly to this Chinese policy and partly to the internal discord, which it exploited, did not voluntarily unite, which certainly reduced the military problems of the Chinese.

The Ming also used economic inducements to control the Mongols. The Yung-lo emperor, for instance, permitted the Oirats to send nine tribute embassies over a fifteen-year period. The Mongols in this way obtained textiles, grain, and other essential goods and offered horses, camels, and furs to the Chinese. These bribes were not effective: the Yung-lo emperor still had to fight the Mongols and died while on a military expedition against them.

His successors were deterred from campaigning in Mongolia by the expense. According to the Ming records, one of the expeditions had consisted of over 200,000 men and about 100,000 wagons of supplies.[36] Even allowing for exaggeration, these campaigns still entailed vast government outlay. The court now decided to be conciliatory and to permit more Mongol tribute missions to reach China, so that their demand for Chinese products would not provoke incursions on Chinese frontier areas. The Mongols, in particular the Oirats, took advantage of this policy and dispatched an excessive number of embassies. The Oirats, who had sent nine in the twenty-one years of the Yung-lo reign, sent thirty-one in the twenty-one years following that emperor's death.[37]

Relations between China and the Oirats, like those between the court and the Central Asian states in the same period, became increasingly strained. Complaints about inferior goods, corrupt officials, and unmanageable envoys appear frequently in the Ming and Mongol chronicles. The rise of the Oirat chief Esen in the 1430s exacerbated the tensions between the court and the Western Mongols. Though he carefully refrained from claiming the title 'khan' and maintained a descendant of the original royal family as khan, Esen actually wielded power over the Western Mongols from the early 1430s until his death in 1454. Owen Lattimore suggests that because great Mongol leaders, such as Esen, attracted a huge following, in time they had a surplus of livestock which they needed to trade with sedentary societies if they expected to retain the support of their subordinates. Esen thus became enraged by China's frequent rejections of his demands for more trade and better commercial opportunities. He prepared for his revenge by conquering or forming marriage alliances with China's neighbours, including the peoples of Hami and the other north-western oases, the Eastern Mongols, and the Jurched of Manchuria.[38]

War erupted between his troops and the Chinese in 1449. The incident that precipitated the final break was the Ming court's refusal to give presents to the two thousand men in Esen's tribute embassy of 1448. In reply, Esen launched a massive attack on China in July 1449, and the emperor unwisely decided to conduct the campaign against the Oirat chieftain in person. Esen defeated the Chinese force sent against him and captured the emperor shortly thereafter. Fortunately for China, he inexplicably delayed exploiting his victory and did not head for Peking immediately. During this brief respite, the Chinese Minister of War calmed the panic-stricken inhabitants of the city and prepared its defences for an attack. Esen finally reached the Chinese capital two months later and laid siege to it. Surprised by the stiff resistance that he encountered, he lifted the siege after four days and withdrew when he learned that a Chinese relief force was approaching the city.

This defeat, together with Esen's dynastic ambitions, precipitated discords in the Oirats' domains, again preventing the Western Mongols from making a concerted effort against the Chinese. Esen, noticing that the Chinese had enthroned a new emperor, released the Chinese emperor in his hands in 1450, a move that did not meet with the approval of all of his subordinates. His dispute with the previously compliant khan led to a war, during which the latter was killed. Esen then proclaimed himself khan, an act that precipitated his downfall. Since he was not descended from the original Mongol ruling family and had no recognized claim to the title, this sudden proclamation aroused tremendous opposition. His subordinates rebelled, his empire started to crumble, and he himself met his death at the hands of the son of a man whom he had executed. His demise ushered in a lengthy period of disunity and inter-tribal warfare. The Western Mongols lacked unified leadership and thus did not pose a threat to China's security until the seventeenth century.[39]

Strong rulers of the Eastern Mongols, on the other hand, twice attempted during the remainder of the Ming period to reunify the Mongols. Batu Möngke (c. 1464–1532), whose royal title was Dayan

Khan, made the first effort in the late fifteenth and early sixteenth centuries. A recent biographer writes that Batu was 'probably ambitious to re-establish Mongol rule over China'.[40] He revived the Eastern Mongols and helped them to reassert the leadership which they had relinquished during Esen's heyday. He first unified his own realm, organizing his people into a left and a right wing, each composed of three units (*tümen*). He then overwhelmed his chief rivals in the west, defeated the Oirats, and pacified the peoples of northern, or present-day Outer, Mongolia. Feeling strong enough now to deal with China, he, like Esen, sought more favourable trading conditions and the right to offer tribute. The Chinese repeatedly denied his requests, and as a result, 'from about 1480 not a single year passed without some major Mongol raid across the Chinese north-western frontier'.[41] The court appeared powerless to prevent these incursions, but remained reluctant to grant concessions to Batu. Early in the sixteenth century, Yang I-ch'ing, the governor of the province of Shensi, attempted to strengthen China's northern defences, but he was too late. The military forces had deteriorated to the point that Batu could organize large-scale invasions of frontier areas with impunity.

Only the disunity and internal disputes among the Mongols, which had plagued Esen, frustrated Batu's efforts and saved China. Batu must bear some of the blame for discord within his ranks. He attempted to impose his own son as second in command (*Jinong*) of the Mongols, an extremely unpopular and unwise move. By the early sixteenth century disaffection had finally bred rebellion. Batu shifted many of his troops from foreign (that is, Chinese) campaigns to the preservation of domestic control. Though he continued to send his troops to raid Chinese border settlements, he no longer threatened the survival of the Ming empire in the last three decades of his reign.[42]

Batu's grandson Altan Khan posed a far greater threat to China's security. He too demanded tribute and trade privileges, demands which the court initially rejected. A series of devastating raids followed, which persuaded the court to revise its policy. In 1551, it consented to the establishment of border markets for the exchange of Mongol horses and Chinese silks. When the Mongols, after a few months, requested grain as a supplementary item of commerce, the court immediately cancelled the Mongols' trading privileges. It thus invited retaliation by Altan Khan's forces.[43] Wars plagued the Sino-Mongol border for the next two decades. The Chinese economy suffered, and the Mongols themselves were exhausted by the necessity of continual raids on Chinese frontier areas. The court, partly because of pressures exerted by border officials and by merchants and officials eager for Mongol products, finally relented and reached an agreement with Altan Khan in 1570. It opened several markets on the border for Sino-Mongol trade; it permitted Altan Khan to present an annual tribute of five hundred horses at the frontier and in return gave him Chinese goods; and it awarded him the hopeful title 'Shun-i Wang' ('Obedient and Righteous Prince'). His principal advisers were given other ceremonial titles.[44] There were a few disruptions, disagreements, and actual disasters, but on the whole the new agreements ensured peace and promoted trade on the northern borders until the end of the dynasty. The Mongols consequently obtained such varied goods as tea, grain, salt, silk, carpets, musical instruments, paper, drugs, drinking cups, and cosmetics, and the Chinese received horses and furs.

The only unresolved problem was that of the Chinese in southern Mongolia. A large number were prisoners of war, but many others had migrated voluntarily. When a Chinese dynasty declined and imposed higher taxes and stiffer military and labour obligations on its people, some Chinese on the frontier began to believe that the Mongol style of life was less restrictive and onerous and accordingly fled to southern Mongolia. They proved invaluable to the Mongols, for their expertise and knowledge were not available among the nomadic pastoral tribes. They served as secretaries, envoys, interpreters, spies, and informants, all occupations that required knowledge of the Chinese language. Chinese craftsmen designed and built boats, temples, houses, and palaces, and fashioned iron tools and weapons for the Mongols. The Mongol rulers valued the contributions of these Chinese artisans and frequently attempted to entice Chinese carpenters, painters, and metal workers to Mongolia. They even organized expeditions specifically to capture Chinese artisans. The Chinese immigrants whom the Mongols prized most highly were those qualified to instruct them in agricultural methods. The Mongols had previously traded for grain, but the Chinese farmers helped them to grow some of their own food, which made them less dependent on Ming China. The political influence of the Chinese grew as the Mongols recognized their economic and cultural value. Some became the principal advisers to the Mongol rulers.

Though the Mongols clearly valued and amply rewarded the Chinese immigrants, the Ming court was perturbed by the emigration of its subjects to Mongolia. It not only lost considerable tax revenue from the emigrants, but also inadvertently provided the Mongols with their expertise. Since the Chinese helped the Mongols to produce iron tools and weapons, Chinese officials doubtless viewed them as a dangerous force. Their potential for espionage further unnerved the court. Nevertheless, though the court prohibited its citizens from leaving China, the flow of Chinese into Mongolia continued.

The court had mixed feelings about the conversion of the Mongol rulers from their ancestral shamanistic religion to Buddhism. Though the Chinese and Mongol records indicate that there were Mongols of Buddhist faith early in the Ming period, it was Altan Khan's conversion that eventually resulted in the effective establishment of Buddhism in Mongolia. Altan probably had spiritual motives for turning to Buddhism, but the political implications of his move certainly did not escape him. He recognized that Buddhism was a fine vehicle for the unification of the Mongols. The primitiveness and the absence of formal organization of shamanism hindered the development both of a national religion and of political unity. Japanese and other East Asian rulers had used Buddhism at various times to strengthen the state and to foster political centralization. Altan Khan pursued the same ends and also linked Buddhism with past Mongol glory. Several of the Mongol rulers of China in the thirteenth and fourteenth centuries had been ardent Buddhists, and Altan Khan could thus link the religion to the golden era of Mongol history. Buddhism, with its copious written literature and its association with a broad cultural heritage, also appealed to the Mongol ruler and promoted his conversion.[45]

The Chinese court was pleased that Buddhism had attracted the Mongols, but it was less enthusiastic about some of the political aspects of the doctrine in Mongolia. The Buddhist disapproval of bloodletting, and emphasis on patience and acceptance in this life, may have encouraged the Chinese to believe that the Mongols would be less aggressive as Buddhists than as believers in shamanism. They believed too that they, as Buddhists, would share common interests and beliefs once Buddhism prevailed in Mongolia. On the other hand, the court recognized that the consequent political unification of the Mongols might pose a formidable threat to Chinese security.

The Ming court also feared, but was unable to prevent, contact between the Mongols and the Tibetan Buddhists. In 1577, Altan Khan invited a Tibetan lama to meet him. The two leaders reached an agreement at the meeting which they hoped would assure them

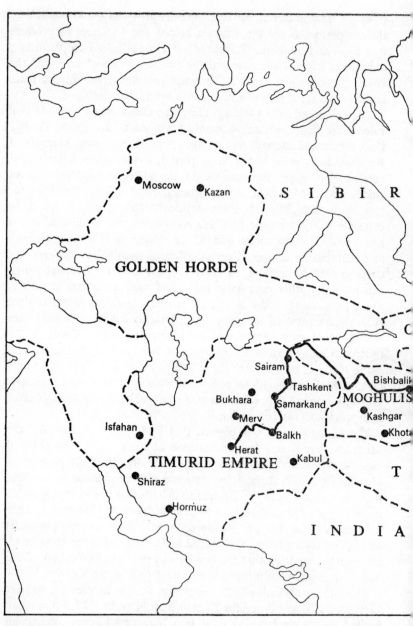

Ming China and Asia in 1413

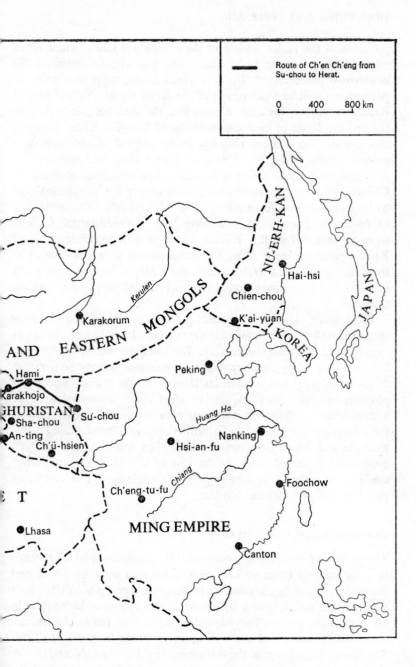

Route of Ch'en Ch'eng from
Su-chou to Herat.

0   400   800 km

NU-ERH-KAN

JAPAN

Hai-hsi

Chien-chou

K'ai-yüan

KOREA

Kerulen

Karakorum

EASTERN MONGOLS

AND

Hami

Peking

Karakhojo

GHURISTAN

Su-chou

Huang Ho

Sha-chou

An-ting

Ch'ü-hsien

Nanking

Hsi-an-fu

Chiang

Ch'eng-tu-fu

Foochow

T

MING EMPIRE

Lhasa

Canton

positions as the major leaders in their respective lands. Altan Khan gave the lama the title Dalai Lama, which he also conferred on the lama's two predecessors. The new Dalai Lama, eager to obtain the political support and patronage of the Khan for his Yellow Sect of Buddhism against his chief adversaries, the Red Sect, in turn proclaimed the Khan to be a reincarnation of Khubilai Khan. Through this entente, the Tibetan religious leader insured himself against a possible attack by the Mongols on northern Tibet, and also ensured his victory over the Red Sect of Lamaism. This agreement alarmed the Chinese, who were apprehensive of unity among the 'barbarians' and had continually pursued a policy of 'divide and rule'. The separation of Mongolia from Tibet had long been a fundamental Chinese strategic aim. When the Tibetan lamas in 1588 proclaimed Altan Khan's great-grandson to be the reincarnation of and successor to the recently deceased Dalai Lama, the Chinese became even more frightened of a possible union of spiritual and temporal power against them.[46]

Their fears, however, proved groundless. Buddhism did not instantly achieve wide popularity among the Mongols, and the lamas catered principally for the nobility. The Buddhist hierarchy identified itself with the ruling class because its monasteries became repositories of great property and wealth. Its lamas and the nobility exchanged political and religious titles, and its chief clerics consorted with the various khans. Buddhism did not unify the Mongols. Though many of the Mongol leaders of the late sixteenth century followed Altan Khan's example and became converts to Buddhism, the Mongols had not established a unified state by the end of the Ming dynasty. They could not therefore take advantage of the weakness of the later Ming rulers to conquer Chinese territory.

THE JURCHED OF MANCHURIA

The peoples of Manchuria, whom the Ming considered less dangerous than the various tribes of Mongolia, eventually engulfed China and toppled the Ming dynasty itself. The Jurched, a group associated with the Tungusic peoples, were the principal inhabitants of Manchuria in the early Ming period. They were descended from the Jurched whose Chin dynasty had ruled much of northern China from 1115 to 1234. The Mongols had ousted them from north China in 1234 and driven them into Manchuria, which they devastated. The Jurched used the period of Mongol hegemony in the thirteenth and fourteenth centuries to revive their economy and rebuild their land.

The territory of Manchuria clearly had more economic potential than Mongolia or Central Asia. The soil of southern Manchuria was rich and fertile, while northern Manchuria had vast forests with many valuable fur-bearing animals. In addition, northern Manchuria had a wealth of gold and other metals, and rivers with abundant fish. These rivers, however, were frozen for half the year, thus disrupting transport, communications and commerce with China. Transport was, in fact, the major problem in the development of the region. Roads were primitive and often impassable in the summer monsoons and the winter snows, dog-sleds being the only feasible means of transport in the winter months.

These difficulties of transport, together with other features of the topography, resulted in the development of at least three styles of life in Manchuria. The first was that of a group of Jurched who inhabited southern Manchuria, from the Liao River to the territory north and north-east of the Yalu River. The Ming sources describe this group as sedentary farmers who were 'skilled in spinning and weaving'.[47] Their customs, clothing, and food resembled those of the Chinese, and it appears that a sizeable number of Chinese lived in their land and contributed to the developing economy of the region. Their geographical proximity to Shantung and other north-eastern provinces of China made close relations and extensive trade possible. The second group, known to the Chinese as the Wild Jurched, hunted and fished along the Amur and Ussuri rivers in the forest regions of northern and eastern Manchuria known as Nurgal. The Chinese sources depict them as warlike and barbaric. They possessed neither a written language nor a structured government. They often attacked the other Jurched and occasionally harassed and robbed Chinese envoys. Since they were composed of numerous small groups who resided at a considerable distance from China and rarely sent tribute to the court, they appear only infrequently in the Chinese sources. A third and probably small group lived west of Kirin and bordered on Mongol territory. The nomadic life of this group in the western Manchurian steppes was similar to that of the Mongols and attracted some Mongols and Chinese who joined and aided them in seeking pasture for their flocks and herds.

The first Ming emperor concentrated on the Mongols and devoted scant attention to the Jurched. He did organize an expedition to drive

away the principal Jurched marauders of the Chinese border settlements. Unlike the Mongol rulers, however, he did not occupy
Manchuria. The Ming established a base in the Liaotung peninsula
and recruited some Jurched from southern Manchuria to their cause.
Though the Ming founded postal stations for transport and for
communications, they failed to create institutions for trade and
tribute with the Jurched. They did not govern the Jurched territories.
Individual Jurched leaders collected taxes, administered justice, and
raised their own armies. The court also faced difficulties in its relations
with the sinicized but fiercely independent state of Korea. The first
Ming emperor feared competition from the Koreans for influence and
control of the Jurched. The Koreans benefited from trade with the
Jurched and wished to be the sole supplier for the tribes of Manchuria.
They resented and sought to minimize Chinese relations and contact
with the Jurched.

It remained for the Yung-lo emperor to resolve some of these
problems and to initiate relations with the Jurched. The emperor had
five principal objectives in his policy towards these frontier peoples.
The first was to achieve peace and to secure China's north-eastern
border. The second was to replace Korea as the dominant influence
among the Jurched, a task that entailed frequent contact with these
'barbarians'. The third was to stimulate tribute and trade and to obtain
essential Jurched products. The fourth was to keep the various Jurched
groups from uniting and threatening China. The fifth was to encourage
the process of sinicization among the Jurched farmers, but this did
not receive a high priority. The emperor apparently agreed that the
adoption of agriculture, bureaucracy, and Confucianism by the
Jurched were splendid objectives, but felt that his prime concerns here,
as with the Mongols and Central Asians, were defence and trade.

The emperor first courted the sedentary Jurched. He dispatched
embassies with lavish gifts and titles for Jurched rulers in the hope of
wooing them to accept a peaceful relationship. The Jurched chiefs
responded with tribute missions and accepted their designations as
commanders in the Ming empire. The court created 179 guards (*wei*)
during the early years of the Yung-lo reign. This new relationship
encouraged many of the Jurched chiefs to seek Chinese, rather than
Korean, goods. The Koreans punished them by suspending the
border trade which had earlier supplied the Jurched with salt, oxen,
horses, and iron. This tactic boomeranged on the Koreans, for it made
the Jurched even more dependent on China.[48]

52

It is clear that the Yung-lo emperor initiated relations with the Jurched. Yet the Chinese sources fail to mention his numerous embassies to the north-eastern 'barbarians'; the Korean records are the sole authorities for these missions. Nonetheless, the sizeable number of embassies, which entailed effort and expense, clearly indicates that the early Ming court valued good political and commercial relations with the Jurched.

The emperor even sent missions to the Wild Jurched of northern Manchuria. In 1409, he ordered the eunuch Isiha, himself of Jurched ancestry, to lead an embassy to Nurgal. After two years of preparations, Isiha, leading an expedition of twenty-five ships and over one thousand men, departed from Kirin towards the north. He met little opposition and therefore generously rewarded the local chieftains, stimulating them to send their first tribute embassy to China. The emperor was so pleased that he again dispatched Isiha to reward the Wild Jurched. During this second expedition, Isiha built a Buddhist temple on the banks of the Amur River in honour of Kuan-yin, the Goddess of Mercy, and erected a stele to commemorate his success. The inscription briefly recounts the origin of the expedition and lists the names of the leading Chinese, Mongols, and Jurched who accompanied Isiha; they include a surprisingly large number of eunuchs.[49]

The emperor, still pursuing a policy of compromise, permitted some Jurched to settle within or adjacent to the Chinese border. In 1408, the court founded two communities, An-lo and Tzu-tsai, for the new immigrants. It provided them with robes, oxen, sheep, grain, and materials for the construction of houses. The immigrants repaid the Chinese by offering tribute and by acting as middlemen in trade with the Jurched in the north. They also served as translators and interpreters and often led Ming missions to the Jurched.[50]

While some Jurched moved into China and served the Ming court, a few Chinese simultaneously visited or resided in Manchuria and assisted the Jurched. Some Chinese merchants evaded the Ming prohibitions, crossed into Jurched territory, and illegally traded with the 'barbarians'. A number of Chinese farmers and soldiers living on the border, who were dissatisfied with the financial and military impositions of the government, emigrated to aid the more congenial Jurched peoples. There is no doubt that they contributed enormously to Jurched development. They guided and encouraged the Jurched to become farmers and taught their protégés the uses of agricultural tools and techniques. They worked as craftsmen, trained skilled artisans among the Jurched and advised the 'barbarians' on military technology and iron production. Some received appointments as envoys to China. These immigrants evidently played an important role in Ming-Jurched relations.

The Yung-lo emperor attained all his principal political objectives without recourse to arms. He established a peaceful relationship with the major Jurched groups, creating guards to pacify Jurched territory. His court and his officials replaced the Koreans as the dominant external force among the Jurched. Through his efforts, as well as those of the Chinese who assisted the north-eastern 'barbarians', the Jurched made significant strides towards sinicization. He permitted some of them to move into China, and those who did so presumably adopted various Chinese customs and institutions. He did not seek to impose punitive regulations on those Jurched living outside China, but the influence of the Chinese expatriates certainly accelerated the sinicization of the tribes.

The emperor also fulfilled his economic objectives. He dispatched numerous missions, partly in order to initiate a formal tributary and commercial relationship with the Jurched. The court incurred expenses in providing supplies, housing, and gifts for the Jurched emissaries. Yet, in the early years of the dynasty, the missions were not a drain on the Ming economy. Since the Jurched embassies consisted of small groups of people, the costs of food and lodging were not prohibitive. The gifts to the Jurched, usually silks, satins, boots, and stockings, were inexpensive and readily available. The arrangement generally served China's purposes.

The tribute system was economically beneficial during the Yung-lo reign because it supplied China with essential products. Because China was unable to breed its own war horses, Jurched tribute horses were essential. Though these ponies were not as sturdy or as powerful as the horses from Central Asia, the Chinese still needed and coveted them. Jurched furs were valuable and useful for the cold winters of North China. The Ming prized the camel, another frequent Jurched present, for transport of goods, movement of military supplies, and ploughing. Such other tribute goods as gerfalcons, walrus teeth, pearls, and gold and silver vessels were more exotic than useful. But nearly every tribute mission arrived with at least some of the important goods together with the luxury items.

The Chinese also acquired useful products through trade. The court permitted Jurched envoys to trade with Chinese merchants for three to five days at the College of Interpreters, and established border markets for trade with the Jurched. In 1406, the emperor founded a horse market and determined the prices to be paid for Jurched horses. He could preserve these prices only through rigid controls on private trade. If the Jurched obtained coveted Chinese products from merchants, they might be less willing to accept the relatively low prices offered by the government. The court was apparently able to enforce its regulations on private commerce during the Yung-lo reign, but merchants later evaded the restrictions and smuggled grain, textiles, and iron into Jurched territory. In this early period, however, the court obtained horses, ginseng, furs, and falcons in the border markets at a low cost.[51]

The death of the Yung-lo emperor disrupted the system of Ming-Jurched relations that he had devised. The Jurched sought greater profits from tribute and trade and were reluctant to accept the court's trade controls. The arrangement through which the court had earlier profited now became a liability to it. The Ming complained of the frequency and size of Jurched embassies. As the Jurched observed that each member of a mission received gifts, their missions grew larger and demanded additional presents. Some of the emissaries intimidated the Chinese populace and created disturbances on their journeys and in the capital. They even attempted to secure contraband goods. The Chinese accused them of trading for weapons, metal tools, and certain types of silk, all of which the court had refused to export to foreign peoples. The Jurched on occasion offered weak or diseased horses, fake or flawed pearls, and inferior furs.[52] Jurched abuses and demands therefore converted a previously profitable arrangement into an increasingly serious drain on Chinese resources.

The Chinese, for their part, took advantage of the Jurched. The Chinese sources repeatedly cite examples of officials who demanded and often received bribes for permitting emissaries to enter China. They also charge some officials with provoking Jurched attacks by reducing gifts to the 'barbarians' or by raiding their settlements. The Chinese texts further acknowledge that some Chinese goods were defective or inferior, particularly from the late fifteenth century onwards. Even silk so declined in quality that Jurched emissaries rejected it in favour of silver.

These disputes, together with dissatisfaction at the new court restrictions on commerce, made the Jurched more responsive to foreign invitations to join alliances against the Chinese. Many of the Jurched joined or passively co-operated with Esen in his attacks on China in the late 1440s. The court, its military forces declining, used economic sanctions to punish the rebellious Jurched. It closed the border horse markets in 1449, curtailed and occasionally cancelled elaborate banquets for envoys, and reduced the quantity of gifts to them and their rulers. Not unnaturally, the Jurched responded violently to these impediments to trade. Raids continued until 1466, when a joint Sino-Korean force of sixty thousand troops defeated and dispersed the main Jurched marauders. (The Koreans participated because they too had had commercial disputes with the Jurched which had resulted in attacks by the Jurched on Korea.) The Jurched, nonetheless, regrouped within a short time and started to raid border villages again.

The Chinese were themselves partly responsible for the deterioration of relations with the Jurched in the late fifteenth century. The most flagrant example of official abuse involved Ch'en Yüeh, the governor of Liaotung in the 1470s. Ch'en led several devastating attacks on previously friendly Jurched tribes and alienated others by maltreating them and then demanding lavish gifts from their tribute envoys. A young official submitted a report to the court, accusing Ch'en of corruption and murder. But the eunuch who was Ch'en's patron in the capital had him cleared of the charge and instead falsely alleged that it was because the young official had refused to sell agricultural implements to the Jurched that they had attacked Chinese settlements. The court accepted this defence and transferred and demoted Ch'en's accuser.[53]

In the 1480s the court finally recognized that aggression was too costly and that its troops were needed to repel the seemingly more dangerous Mongol invaders. It sought to regain the confidence of the Jurched by reopening the old border markets and by relaxing its regulations on tribute missions. Because it acted feebly and indecisively to prohibit smuggling, merchants and officials evaded the Ming commercial restrictions. The Ming, however, secured peace again on its north-eastern border.

During this period of relative peace, the Jurched made significant economic and cultural strides. The population of individual Jurched groups increased dramatically. Korean and Chinese sources cite groups composed of seven to nine thousand rather than the several hundreds of not many decades earlier. They indicate that the Jurched were developing an agrarian economy, since they requested agricultural tools and advice from China and Korea. Along with this economic change, there were transformations in Jurched culture.

Their contact with more peoples in East Asia led to intermarriages with Chinese, Koreans, Mongols, and other natives of Manchuria, and made them receptive to foreign cultures and institutions. This initiated the process that eventually transformed them from Jurched into Manchus.

In 1541 new Ming regulations shattered a half-century of peace and harmony between the Chinese and the Jurched. The arrival in 1536 of a mission composed of 2,140 Jurched undoubtedly persuaded the Ming court to revoke its previous policy. The court now limited the Jurched to one mission a year of less than five hundred men. It sharply curtailed the residence of foreign emissaries in the capital and presumably minimized the possibility of illicit trade. Its officials in the frontier markets and in Peking sought to reassert control over Chinese and Jurched merchants, so as to obtain a more advantageous position in trade.[54]

The economic hostility generated by these regulations resulted, not surprisingly, in wars between the Chinese and the various Jurched peoples. Economic grievances precipitated nearly all of these conflicts. It was only through the efforts of a general of Korean ancestry, named Li Ch'eng-liang, that the Ming weathered the first assaults by different Jurched leaders. Towards the end of the sixteenth century, however, Li 'is reported to have become gradually less energetic in suppressing the border tribes, and tried to appease them; he would make harmless raids into enemy territory, kill a few civilians on the way, and report victories'.[55] During one of his expeditions, Li's troops accidentally killed a friendly Jurched chief. Nurhaci, the latter's son and the grandfather of the first ruler of the Ch'ing or Manchu dynasty (1644–1911), demanded that Li recompense him for the death of his father. The Ming general rewarded him and confirmed him as a major noble among the Jurched. In this way, this minor lord from the Chienchou Jurched guard began to emerge as a powerful figure in Manchuria.

It is not necessary to repeat here in detail the accounts of scholars who have documented Nurhaci's rise to power and his military encounters with the Ming.[56] It is essential, however, to describe briefly Nurhaci's strategy and the source of his strength.

Nurhaci had learned an important lesson from the failures of the Jurched chiefs of the late sixteenth century. He realized that the peoples of Manchuria had to unify under a single leader before challenging China. He also recognized that he had a fine foundation for the creation of a unified Manchuria. During two centuries of contact with the Ming, various tribes in Manchuria had become developed agricultural communities capable of supporting large populations. They did not need to import grain from China. They had, in addition, founded a thriving iron industry and were no longer dependent on Korea or China for iron tools and weapons. Through their Chinese subjects and through personal observation, they were acquainted with the rudiments of Chinese civilization and recognized the decline of Chinese military and political power. Nurhaci made use of these advances and of this increased sophistication to unify Manchuria. By 1613, he had, through marital alliances and conquest, overwhelmed most of Manchuria, and in 1616, he proclaimed himself Emperor of the new Chin dynasty: a true Manchu, and not exclusively a Jurched, dynasty. This was composed not only of people of Jurched ancestry but also of many different and still unidentified inhabitants of Manchuria.

Until that time, Nurhaci had not challenged China. He behaved as a loyal vassal and on three occasions personally offered tribute to the court. It was perhaps during these trips that he noticed the steady deterioration of the Ming. The defence of the Chinese frontier had strained the resources of the government treasury. The resulting need for revenue induced the Ming to impose heavy taxes, especially on the peasantry, which in turn led to rebellions in the early seventeenth century.

Nurhaci meanwhile consolidated his economic and political power. He monopolized the trade in ginseng and reaped huge profits from selling that 'life-giving' root to the Chinese. His men reopened gold and silver mines, some of which had been closed since the years of the Mongol hegemony. Controlling the commerce in furs and pearls within Manchuria, he requested and obtained Chinese silver in return for his tribute offerings to the Ming court. Mongol and Chinese administrative and military practices attracted him, and he did not hesitate to adopt them for his own government. He used Chinese advisers extensively, and their proposals concerning political and military institutions proved invaluable in unifying and ruling the Manchus. But a description of these institutions is part of the story of the Manchu conquest of the Ming, which will be presented later.

During the early Ming period the Chinese initiated and fostered tribute and trade relations with the oases in Central Asia, the peoples of Mongolia, and the Jurched of Manchuria. They obtained highly coveted and useful goods, together with luxury items, and profited from their economic contact with the 'barbarians'. The Ming court carefully regulated and monopolized commercial and tributary relations so that Chinese merchants could not compete with it, and so that it could secure a mutually beneficial arrangement with the Inner Asians. Equally important, this relationship promised the court peace on its northern and western borders. From the middle of the fifteenth century onwards, when its army started to deteriorate and it could no longer enforce its regulations, it began to lose its previously advantageous position. Chinese officials sought to impose additional restrictions, which in turn led to attacks by the foreigners who had been denied Chinese products.

The Jurched went beyond sporadic raids to obtain Chinese goods. They attempted, with the assistance of Chinese defectors, to achieve a measure of self-sufficiency by growing their own food, producing their own metal tools and weapons, and devising a stable administrative apparatus for the growing population under their control. By the early seventeenth century, they were ready to challenge the Ming for control of China.

2 Chinese agents of foreign relations

The Ming court deliberately attempted to limit direct contact between the Chinese and Inner Asian envoys and merchants. This policy reflected, in part, a traditional fear that too frequent association with the 'barbarians' might corrupt the Confucian values and threaten the Chinese way of life. It had the further effect of reducing the opportunities for espionage and gathering of intelligence by foreign visitors. Perhaps the most significant consequence was that the Chinese government could more readily regulate the dealings of its own merchants with the peoples of Inner Asia.

This restrictive policy has given some westerners the mistaken impression that Ming China was abysmally ignorant of the institutions and customs of Inner Asia and sought to keep its people uninformed of developments in other states. It is true that China had few experts on foreign affairs. The court did not grant high status or generous rewards to those Chinese who dealt with foreigners. Interpreters and translators, for example, received poor pay and a low rank in the bureaucracy. The court, in theory, imposed strict limitations on the time foreign envoys could reside in China, thus reducing the opportunities not only for trade but also for fraternization and exchange of information between China and Inner Asia.

Despite these restrictions, some Chinese were well-informed about Inner Asia, and the court received fairly detailed and accurate reports on the peoples, customs, and institutions of the area. Ch'en Ch'eng's account of the seventeen principalities which he visited in Central Asia is an invaluable source of information about the products, clothing, religious practices, laws, and customs of the Timurid capitals of Herat and Samarkand as well as of the oases en route. Ch'en's report was copied into the official court chronicles, an indication that Chinese officials knew of it even though they may not have consulted it when making decisions. The court also had access to similar sources on the Mongols and the Jurched. Some border officials kept diaries of their dealings with the 'barbarians' and reported on their activities to the court. The leading officials carefully considered and evaluated these reports before determining their foreign policy. The court further gleaned information from envoys and spies from the Inner Asian states. It granted sizeable rewards for strategic intelligence concerning other lands. Since some foreign envoys stayed in China for a long time, the court had ample opportunities to question and examine them. The famous embassy dispatched by Shāhrukh in 1419 remained in the capital for five months, and several Central Asian missions of the sixteenth century lived in Peking for three to four years.

The early Ming court apparently sought to develop a group of experts on Inner Asia. The Yung-lo emperor frequently sent the same envoys to foreign states. He dispatched Ch'en Ch'eng three times to Central Asia and the eunuch Isiha five times to the Jurched. Some of the envoys were non-Chinese, and a large number knew the languages, customs, and laws of the lands in which they travelled. Most of the early Ming governors and military officials on the north-eastern and north-western borders were extremely well-informed about the 'barbarians'. Even officials in the central government had occasionally had previous experience on the frontier. The Minister of War, Ma Wen-sheng, the most prominent of these figures, had dealt with the Jurched in Manchuria and with the various peoples in Central Asia before his appointment as a minister in Peking.[1]

OFFICIAL CHINESE AGENCIES

The court assigned a number of individuals and agencies to deal with foreigners. Most had other duties as well. Those that did not, and instead dealt exclusively with non-Chinese envoys and merchants, were not extremely influential in the bureaucracy. Those Chinese who had the most intimate associations with foreigners frequently occupied the least prestigious positions in the government.

Emperors The emperors, in theory, provided the justification and sanction for all foreign relations. After all, foreign rulers paid tribute to them as representatives of the most powerful state in the world. A few emperors desired an expansion of China's economic dealings with Inner Asia. The Yung-lo emperor was the most enthusiastic promoter of wider contacts with the 'barbarians'. He recognized China's need for foreign goods in general and horses in particular. Later emperors approved of foreign tribute and trade because it offered them diverting luxury products. A few, however, reinstated stringent regulations on economic transactions with the 'barbarians'. It is difficult to determine the foreign policies of many of the later emperors, since they often permitted their underlings to devise and implement major decisions. A study of their expertise in foreign affairs is also a complicated matter. The first Ming ruler and the Yung-lo emperor, both of whom campaigned in Inner Asia, were clearly well-informed about their neighbours on the northern and western borders. Later emperors, who did not venture outside China and whose sole contact with foreigners was at court audiences, apparently knew little about Inner Asia.

Ministers   The ministries of Rites, Revenue, and War bore the main burden of foreign relations. The other three ministries, those of Personnel, Justice, and Works, dealt only indirectly with the Inner Asian peoples. The leading officials in the ministries of Rites, Revenue, and War wrote memorials to the emperor, debated questions of foreign policy, and implemented court decisions on foreign affairs.

The ministries occasionally disagreed on court policy towards Inner Asia. Research on this subject, however, has been limited, and the patterns of these conflicts within the government are not entirely discernible. My own studies suggest that there was a sharp cleavage between the Ministry of War and the ministries of Rites and Revenue. The latter, after the middle of the fifteenth century, sought to reduce the number of tribute and trade missions from Inner Asia. Earlier, they had not opposed the visits of emissaries to China and had perhaps even encouraged them. After the capture of the Chinese emperor in 1449, however, they complained that the embassies from the 'barbarians' strained the economic resources of the empire. They advised the emperor to reject tribute offerings of such useless luxury items as lions and jewellery. The Ministry of Revenue, which provided supplies for foreign emissaries, demanded a reduction in the size of tribute embassies. The Ministry of Rites, which furnished functionaries to train foreign envoys in proper rituals for court audiences, repeatedly urged the emperor to impose limitations on the missions from Inner Asia. These two ministries appeared oblivious of the dangers of such a policy. The Ministry of War, which was aware of the deterioration of China's military forces, recognized that this policy would provoke 'barbarian' attacks which China would be powerless to prevent. It pressed for policies which would not alienate the Inner Asians. On the other hand, it incurred ever-mounting expenses in providing escorts and lodging foreign envoys in postal stations and at the College of Interpreters in Peking, a circumstance which made it responsive to the demands for curtailment of the embassies. Yet its unwillingness to alienate China's northern and western neighbours on the whole outweighed its concern over the costs of the tribute embassies.

Two agencies within the Ministry of Rites had the principal responsibilities for dealing with foreign envoys. The Bureau of Receptions (Chu-k'o ch'ing-li ssu), the first of these, sent officials to meet the emissaries at the College of Interpreters and to inspect the tribute offerings. If the foreign goods met their standard, they permitted the envoys to reside at the College. They also presented the foreigners with rice, flour, meat, and tea, supplied servants, doctors, and drugs if necessary, and instructed the College of Translators (Ssu-i kuan) to translate the 'barbarian' documents into Chinese. The Court of Imperial Entertainments (Kuang-lu ssu), the second agency under the aegis of the Ministry of Rites, gave elaborate banquets for foreign guests. It provided liquor, meat, and delicacies, arranged decorations and flowers, and instructed the Office of Music to perform music and to offer entertainments. It held two or more banquets for ambassadors of powerful or strategically located states and tribes, but only one perfunctory feast for those from less important lands. Judging from this system of ranking, the agency was well-informed about the political, economic, and military standing of the different Inner Asian states.[2]

College of Interpreters The College of Interpreters, under the jurisdiction of the Ministry of War, was the official residence for all foreign envoys in Peking. The court fed, sheltered, and feasted the envoys in the College while they prepared for an audience with the emperor. The College also served as the location for officially sanctioned trade. Here, too, after the middle of the fifteenth century, the Ming court attempted, because of declining profits, to limit economic transactions with the Inner Asians. Approximately four hundred employees of the College cared for the needs of foreigners. Many held low ranks and performed menial tasks, and few ever achieved higher office. Organized under several Commissioners, also of low rank and poorly paid, they provided for the physical comfort of emissaries.[3]

The College, in addition, housed approximately sixty interpreters, at least half of whom specialized in the languages and cultures of Inner Asia. Poor salaries, low status, and few opportunities for advancement deprived the College of outstanding candidates. Few well-educated and ambitious young men aspired to serve in these positions. The quality of interpreters was inferior, particularly in the sixteenth century. Many were unqualified for their posts, and some sought pecuniary gain from their association with emissaries of the Inner Asian states. The Chinese sources repeatedly condemn them either for extorting illegal payments from foreign envoys or for encouraging the latter to make extravagant demands on the court.

The court was in a dilemma. It did not wish to provide high ranks and good pay for men whose sole responsibility was to deal with foreigners, but at the same time it needed people who were knowledgeable and qualified to communicate with the 'barbarians'. The dilemma was not resolved, and the College was often staffed by incompetent and corrupt interpreters. When the court sought to fill vacancies, it found few qualified applicants. As a result, it relied on a group of mediocre interpreters.

College of Translators The College of Translators, an agency of the Ministry of Rites, faced similar problems. It has received and, to a certain extent, deserved a bad press. The court organized it to train translators and to provide readable translations of foreign documents. As with the College of Interpreters, the court accorded it a lowly status in the administrative hierarchy. Its translators had scant opportunity for advancement, since the court rarely granted them official status. Numerous scholars have documented the inadequacies of the College. It lacked proper facilities and equipment, failed to attract capable and dedicated students, and was plagued by corruption. Because so few Chinese chose to serve as translators, the court, by the middle of the sixteenth century, made the positions hereditary. By forcing men to become translators and by according them little prestige, payment, or power, it recruited an incompetent, uninterested, and frequently corrupt group of translators.

Yet, despite their deficiencies, the colleges of Interpreters and Translators were, for their time, unique and remarkable. After all, how many of the European states in this period had government-sponsored offices to translate diplomatic documents from the Arab states or Mongol Russia? Nor did Europeans have such a system of receiving and providing for ambassadors as the Chinese. In addition, the fact that officials wrote accounts describing the inadequacies of the two agencies and demanding reforms and improvements indicates that there were those in the government who sought to develop a staff of competent interpreters and translators.

The interpreters and translators probably had more intimate daily contact with foreign envoys than any other Chinese. Their role in foreign relations was thus extremely important, and their knowledge of foreign customs and institutions was superior to that of most Chinese. It is difficult, nonetheless, to discover whether the court consulted them or used their expertise when forming foreign policy. The traditional Chinese histories ignore them and, as a matter of fact, tend to slight foreign relations, so that our knowledge of them is limited. The scholar-officials who wrote the histories ignored their useful contributions and primarily emphasized their illegal doings.

CHINESE CITIZENS

Certain officials and private citizens, without specific authorization from the court, played a crucial role in foreign relations. The Chinese histories mention only their outlandish and illegal actions. Their contributions to China's foreign policy and knowledge of foreigners are barely noticed, and it is solely through inference, rather than from specific references, that we may estimate their importance.

Local Officials Numerous local officials, particularly those assigned to the border, dealt directly with foreign envoys. Provincial governors, military men, village leaders, employees of the postal stations where the court lodged foreign ambassadors and merchants, and messengers and military escorts all associated with Inner Asians and other foreigners. Yet the Chinese sources reveal little about them except for a brief listing of their explicit legal responsibilities and accusations of corruption. The court frequently complained that these officials 'induced foreigners to demand forbidden articles, and if these were refused, to present false reports to higher officials; they took their share in whatever the Barbarians could lay hands on; they helped them steal, and collected fees at every opportunity and under various names'.[4] The court chronicles often fail to mention their beneficial

65

influence in foreign affairs. Yet their reports and memorials were frequently included in court records and no doubt influenced the making of foreign policy.

Merchants Chinese merchants undoubtedly associated with the peoples of Inner Asia both on the border and in Peking. The court permitted them to trade with foreigners at the College of Interpreters and at specially designated frontier markets. But it imposed innumerable restrictions on commercial transactions. The Ming histories, written by officials who in theory despised commerce, generally mention merchants only when the latter evaded the regulations concerning private trade and engaged in illicit commerce with the 'barbarians'. Despite this omission, it is clear that merchants, by necessity, understood foreign customs and economic and political conditions. Some had become extremely wealthy, and according to one recent student, 'had earned social recognition through their efforts'.[5] Whether the government used information supplied by these merchants in making foreign policy decisions is uncertain.

Eunuchs The original function of the eunuchs was to regulate the Imperial harem, but over the centuries they had come to staff a private bureaucracy, under the direct control of the emperor, with which he could circumvent the regular officials. In 1400, the court organized twenty-four eunuch-staffed offices to perform such tasks as caring for and supervising seals, gunpowder, temple construction, and the Imperial archives. The eunuchs extended their influence far beyond these functions. In 1420, the Yung-lo emperor created the Eastern Depot, staffed wholly by eunuchs, to act as an internal security force. What originated as a private surveillance system for the emperor had gained, by the middle of the dynasty, virtually unlimited powers to question, apprehend, torture, and imprison suspects. Partly through imperial action and partly through their own ingenuity, the eunuchs also played a key role in the economy. The emperors assigned corvée labourers to assist each of the twenty-four eunuch bureaux. In addition, eunuchs requested and often received craftsmen for state construction projects and manufacturing concerns, as well as for their own private needs. Other activities from which they profited included the supervision of the royal estates, management of the timber resources, involvement in the government salt monopoly, tax collection, and their own personal exemption from corvée labour and taxes.

It is not surprising then that eunuchs played a role in the foreign relations of the empire. Emperors introduced eunuchs to foreign affairs by sending them on diplomatic missions to nearby as well as distant countries. The eunuch envoys of the Yung-lo emperor reached eastward to Japan and as far west as Africa. The eunuch admiral Cheng Ho sailed the southern oceans; Li Ta accompanied Ch'en Ch'eng to Central Asia; Isiha on five occasions met Jurched leaders; and Hai-t'ung initiated relations with the Oirat Mongols. The emperors entrusted these ambassadors with varied tasks, the most common being to present gifts in return for tribute and to stimulate foreign states to send tribute missions. Eunuchs also brought the symbols of Chinese recognition to new 'barbarian' rulers, bestowing Chinese letters of enfeoffment, seals, robes, and other regalia. They offered condolences on behalf of the court for the death of important potentates and conveyed messages to foreign rulers. While on these missions, eunuchs made observations on economic, political, and military conditions which they no doubt reported to the court. Although few such reports have survived, gathering intelligence was one of the main aims of the eunuch emissaries.

Eunuchs had many other opportunities for contact with foreigners. According to the account of the tribute mission sent by the Timurid ruler Shāhrukh in 1419, eunuchs supervised the major activities of the emissaries. In 1375, the first Ming emperor sent a eunuch to the north-western frontier to initiate a tea and horse trade with border tribes.[6] Eunuchs managed the porcelain centre at Ching-te chen, and since much of the porcelain was produced for export, this also involved eunuchs in foreign relations. From the Yung-lo reign onwards, eunuchs took part in most of the major battles of the Ming dynasty as commanders or advisers. Not only did they occasionally determine tactics, but in several instances they also made the decisions that resulted in war. The advice of the eunuch Wang Chen, for example, was crucial in the disastrous decision to declare war on the Oirat Mongols in 1449, which led to the capture of the emperor by the 'barbarians'.[7]

In Ming times, eunuchs came from a variety of sources and backgrounds. Some were captured Mongols, Jurched, Annamese, and other foreigners. The court often sent these eunuchs as envoys to the states of Inner Asia. Chinese who castrated themselves or whose parents emasculated them comprised another group. Native lower-class Chinese, noticing that a few eunuchs attained great wealth and power, castrated themselves in hopes of social advancement. Chinese Muslims provided still another source of eunuchs. Ma, the most common surname among Chinese adherents of Islam, appears frequently as the name of eunuchs. The Muslim traveller 'Ali Akbar, who reached China in the sixteenth century, asserted that most eunuchs were Muslims.[8] This is no doubt an exaggeration; the court must have deliberately assigned Muslim eunuchs to deal with him.

The emperors probably believed that eunuchs, especially those of foreign origin, could easily communicate with 'barbarians'. Some eunuchs spoke foreign languages, and a few understood 'barbarian' customs and beliefs. Another reason for employing eunuchs was their lack of contempt for foreigners. Chinese officials generally regarded foreigners as uncivilized 'barbarians', but the eunuchs, who were themselves often aliens, appeared less disdainful. Similarly, eunuchs showed less scorn for foreign trade, not showing the distaste for and opposition to commerce professed, though not always practised, by officials. The court entrusted them with trading for horses, furs, jade, and other foreign goods which China needed. The Muslims, tradition-ally renowned as merchants, were the best businessmen among the eunuchs.

Western scholars have often accepted the traditional Confucian assessment of eunuchs. Robert Van Gulik in his book *Sexual Life in Ancient China* wrote that eunuchs 'were a source of evil and their influence must be defined as greatly detrimental to Chinese politics and economy'.[9] Some historians, both Chinese and Western, castigated eunuchs for failures in foreign relations, including the Oirat Mongols' capture of the emperor in 1449. Traditional Chinese writers con-demned the eunuch Wang Chen for persuading the emperor to lead the Chinese forces against the 'barbarian' chief Esen. But it should be noted that an emperor's active participation in wars was not unusual. Only three decades earlier, the Yung-lo emperor personally conducted his five campaigns against the Eastern and Oirat Mongols. And the founder of the dynasty was a great warrior.

The Chinese officials, as well as modern Western historians, minimized or ignored the contributions of the eunuchs to Chinese foreign policy. There is no doubt, however, that eunuchs widened China's contact with foreign states, secured, through trade, goods essential for China, and provided the Ming court with reliable, first-hand information about the various lands in Inner Asia.

In sum, there were numerous agencies and individuals, both official and unauthorized, who associated directly with the peoples of Inner Asia. Some were extremely knowledgeable, and a few individuals learned the languages of the 'barbarians'. Though the court rarely accorded them high honours or substantial rewards, they certainly had a major impact on the relations of China and Inner Asia. Curiously, it was perhaps those Chinese with unofficial status, merchants and eunuchs among them, who most clearly influenced these relations.

3 Trade and tribute

Economic relations between the Ming court and the peoples and states of Inner Asia were extremely complicated. A partial listing of these transactions would include tribute from Inner Asian rulers; unofficial tribute from Mongolian, Central Asian, and Jurched merchants; 'gifts in reply' (presents to the Inner Asian rulers and their families in return for tribute offerings); special gifts from the emperor to the Inner Asian chieftains; special gifts to the principal and assistant envoys of tribute missions; official trade at the College of Interpreters; illicit trade between Inner Asian envoys and merchants and Chinese merchants and officials; and border trade between the court and the Inner Asian merchants and states. It is often difficult to determine precisely the economic significance of these exchanges, for the Chinese sources yield pitifully little information on the subject. Nevertheless, it is possible to perceive whether trade and tribute relations generally favoured or harmed China over a span of time, and I shall select some examples from my own researches to indicate the patterns of Ming economic relations with the peoples of Inner Asia.

SPECIAL GIFTS AND 'GIFTS IN REPLY'

The court granted special gifts to the rulers and envoys of foreign states. A typical gift was that of the Yung-lo emperor to Togto, the prince of Hami. In 1406, the Ming ruler sent, by an envoy from Hami, sixty bolts of fine silk and 214 of coarse silk to Togto. He also gave six bolts of fine silk and six of coarse silk to Togto's paternal grand-mother and to each of the latter's consorts.[1] Since most of the special gifts to Inner Asian rulers recorded in the Ming sources were of this kind, it is inconceivable that they can have placed a burden on the

Chinese economy. The special gifts to envoys were, however, poten-
tially costlier. For example, the emperor awarded each Jurched envoy
with the rank of Regional Commissioner two lined garments of
coloured satin, the value in paper money of one bolt of coarse silk,
four bolts of coarse silk, and one robe of gold-brocaded fine silk, and
to each with the rank of Guard Commander, one lined garment of
coloured satin, the value in paper money of one bolt of coarse silk,
four bolts of coarse silk, and one robe of fine white silk. He also
presented one pair of boots and stockings to each man of either rank.[2]
Such gifts might not have been a burden if the number of Jurched or
other Inner Asian envoys remained limited. As the frequency and size
of tribute missions increased, however, the court's expenditure for the
special gifts grew. A mission composed of two thousand men, for
instance, could return to its native land with two thousand lined
garments of coloured satin, eight thousand bolts of coarse silk, and
two thousand pairs of boots and stockings, among other goods.

Similarly, gifts requested by the peoples of Inner Asia could prove
costly. The rulers and envoys of the 'barbarian' states frequently
sought special gifts from the court. The goods which they requested
most often were textiles, tea, and porcelain. The Central Asian states
repeatedly asked for dragon robes or other elaborate garments, an
appeal that the court usually rejected. The other peoples of Inner Asia
sought a variety of goods, including medicines, paper, musical
instruments, books, and weapons. The court had prohibited the export
of some of these products, but it occasionally ignored its own prohibitions. The oases of Central Asia and the Mongol tribes, plagued
by droughts or other natural catastrophes, at times besought the
court for grain, a request which the Chinese more often than not
granted. Though none of these requests was by itself exorbitant, their
total number increased alarmingly after 1449, and they constituted a
major burden on the Chinese economy.

The so-called 'gifts in reply' were simply a euphemism for trade.
In theory, the emperor, exhibiting his compassion and generosity,
provided presents in return for foreign tribute offerings. In practice,
however, the Chinese and the peoples of Inner Asia agreed upon an
exact rate of exchange, and though this rate fluctuated throughout the
dynasty, the two parties negotiated it before engaging in tribute and
'gifts in reply' transactions. Since both the Chinese and the Inner
Asians of necessity jointly approved of the terms, this was an arrangement based on equality and should properly be defined as commerce.

71

The exchange value of 'tribute' goods from Inner Asia indicates which products were especially prized by the Chinese. The court offered the most lavish presents in return for Inner Asian horses and camels. It established different rates for horses of different quality. In 1490, it laid down the following rates for horses: each Western horse – five lined garments of coloured satin; each average horse – one bolt of fine silk, eight bolts of coarse silk, and the value in paper money of two bolts of coarse silk; each new-born colt – three bolts of coarse silk.[3] The court even offered to pay three bolts of coarse silk for a horse or a camel that perished during the long trip to China. The emperors also valued metal and stone products. They rewarded the foreign envoys for tribute of jade, lapis lazuli, fine steel knives, and gold and silver vessels. They also proffered Chinese gifts for Jurched gerfalcons, ginseng, and walrus teeth, Mongol furs, and Central Asian sheep and sal ammoniac.

There are few complaints about the system of 'gifts in reply' in the early years of the dynasty, but numerous problems arise from the middle of the fifteenth century. The system apparently benefited both parties during the Yung-lo reign, as they each received goods of high quality that they wanted. This good relationship ended after the death of that emperor. The Chinese now accused the peoples of Inner Asia of offering inferior goods and of demanding higher rates of exchange for them. They condemned the 'barbarians' for seeking such contraband as weapons, iron implements, and history books. As one scholar has observed, 'it is difficult to admit that the [Inner Asian envoys] should have limited their trading activities to the premises of the Hui-t'ung-kuan [College of Interpreters] and the time allowed' and he added that it was clear that the envoys associated with the Chinese all the time.[4] A leading student of the Ming economy points to Chinese collaboration in this illicit commerce when he writes that 'international trade was officially outlawed, but in fact it was carried out with the connivance of local authorities'.[5] The peoples of Inner Asia, in turn, complained of inferior Chinese goods and of corrupt officials who demanded higher prices for Ming products.

Despite these difficulties, the Chinese carried on a vigorous import and export trade with Inner Asia, though the dearth of precise statistics frustrates any attempt to estimate its volume. Most of the many products which changed hands are, however, listed in the Chinese sources, and an examination of these lists indicates the value of this trade.

CHINESE IMPORTS

Animals Horses were the principal Chinese imports from Inner Asia. Almost all of the Central Asian, Mongol, and Jurched tribute missions presented horses to the throne. The elaborate 'gifts in reply' granted for horses reflect their importance to the Chinese. Horses were obtained principally through trade on the frontiers: Chinese tea was exchanged for Central Asian horses in the north-west, and Chinese textiles and grain for Mongol and Jurched horses in the north-east.

The Central Asians frequently and the Mongols on occasion sent camels to the Chinese. The Ming court recognized the value of camels, but depended on foreigners to supply them since it had neither the trained personnel nor the land necessary to breed and raise the animals. The Chinese knew that the camel could carry more weight than any other animal available to them. The average camel could transport a load of four to five hundred pounds, whereas the average mule carried approximately 250 pounds. Camels required less water and could satisfy their thirst for a long period with a drink of sesame oil. They also needed less pasture than horses or mules and were thus more suited to desert or high-altitude travel. Their hooves did not sink in the sand, and they reputedly gave warning of sandstorms and uncovered underground springs in sandy areas. Many Chinese used camel dung for fuel. Some ate its meat and prized its hump as a great delicacy, and a few employed parts of its body for medicinal purposes. The court imported the Bactrian or two-humped camel, for 'its massive physique' and 'its heavy winter coat'[6] were well suited to the hardships of climate and terrain on the caravan trails of Inner Asia.

Other tribute animals arrived at the court on occasion. The Central Asian states sent sheep, whose utility requires no explanation. An offering of several thousand sheep every few years was not unusual. The lions and leopards sent by Samarkand and Herat were less useful. A few wealthy court retainers and some of the more luxury-loving emperors coveted these beasts, but most government officials complained of the high cost of maintaining them. The Central Asian peoples offered lions and leopards so rarely, however, that the frequent court discussions concerning them convey a misleading impression of the seriousness of the problem.

Furs The Ming court cherished furs from Inner Asia. It recognized their value for the cold winters of North China. As a result, offerings

73

of furs were extremely popular with the Chinese. The Jurched commonly presented sable pelts, while the Central Asian states sent squirrel, sable, fox and ermine. The traffic in furs was apparently extensive. One tribute mission from Hami offered thirty thousand squirrel pelts in 1448.[7]

Gerfalcons The Mongols and the Jurched presented gerfalcons, which were of scant economic value. Falconry had, nonetheless, been popular since the fourth century, and the Ming emperors enjoyed this kind of hunting. They also used gerfalcons in diplomacy. The Yung-lo emperor, for example, gave some gerfalcons to the envoys of Shāhrukh, who were favourably impressed.[8]

Metals and stones The court received knives and swords from Central Asia. It rewarded the foreign envoys handsomely for such offerings. The Chinese apparently sought swords from a variety of sources. In the tribute missions from Japan, for example, 'swords were the staple commodities of export to China both in volume and value'.[9] The court also welcomed presents of mirrors, files, and axes. It acquired, though less frequently, gold and silver vessels from all of the principal peoples of Inner Asia. The sources fail to mention the quantities involved, so that it is difficult to estimate their economic value; the same applies to the agate, diamonds, and lapis lazuli imported from Central Asia.

Jade was undoubtedly a valuable import. The Chinese obtained much of their fine jade from Khotan in Central Asia. In summer, the inhabitants of that oasis searched along the nearby river beds for jade. They extracted white jade from what the Chinese called the 'White Jade River' (Po-yü ho) and dark or green jade from the 'Black Jade River' (Hei-yü ho).[10] The Chinese cherished this jade for ornaments, ritual objects, and such utilitarian products as axes and chisels. They recognized that jade fitted the requirements of long-distance overland trade: it was valuable for its weight and easily transported. Though they demanded fine jade, they often received jade of poor quality, particularly in the latter half of the Ming period. The court therefore reduced the remuneration of envoys offering inferior jade. Worthless and crude jade from Khotan, as well as from Hami, Samarkand, Herat, and other Central Asian sites, continued, nonetheless, to stream into China.

Jade was a luxury item, but its value to the Chinese economy cannot be denied. It was not one of the 'rare and strange items' of which

Chinese officials complained. It provided employment for numerous Chinese craftsmen who produced jade vases, cups, incense burners, and jewellery. The court used many jade utensils in trade and as gifts to foreign rulers. Ulugh-Beg, the ruler of Samarkand in the early fifteenth century, so admired a Chinese jade cup that he had his name inscribed on it.[11]

Medicines The Ming exported more medicines than it imported. There were, however, certain plants and drugs that the Chinese could only obtain from the territories of Inner Asia. The Jurched supplied the highly prized ginseng root. The Chinese believed that ginseng prolonged life, strengthened the stomach and cured weakness of the lungs, together with many other functions.[12] The Jurched also provided the 'glue from A-hsien', derived from oxen and asses. The Chinese employed this glue as a cure for paralysis, asthma, coughing, bloody dysentery during pregnancy, and other respiratory and circulatory ailments.[13] Various Central Asian oases offered sal ammoniac, which the Chinese used in the treatment of skin diseases and bronchial congestion and for incendiary weapons.[14] The oasis of Hami was a principal supplier of resin of the *Populus balsamifera* (*hu-t'ung*), a tree often mentioned in Chinese poetry. The Chinese used the resin in the treatment of poisonous fevers, abdominal swellings, and toothaches.[15]

This selective list of tribute and trade goods from Inner Asia challenges John K. Fairbank's assertion that 'there was little benefit to the imperial treasury in anything that a tribute mission might bring'.[16] Horses and camels were invaluable for the Chinese economy, and indeed it can be argued that horses were essential for the survival of the Ming state. Furs and jade, while not essential, certainly stimulated the economy, since they provided work for Chinese craftsmen. The value of gold, silver, knives, and swords needs no explanation. Even though one may question the efficacy of the various 'medicines' imported by the Ming, there is no doubt that the Chinese considered them important. Lions, leopards, and gerfalcons were exotic and truly useless goods, but the court received them only infrequently and along with other, more useful products.

CHINESE EXPORTS

The early Ming exports to Inner Asia did not impose a severe strain on the Chinese economy. As the dynasty declined and as more tribute embassies reached China, however, court expenditure increased and the quantity of exports grew. A listing and description of the export goods will show the general deterioration in China's position.

Paper money   The court presented paper money to nearly every Inner Asian tribute mission in the early Ming period. The foreign envoys used the gift to trade with Chinese merchants at the College of Interpreters and at the border markets. Since the foreigners spent the paper money in China, the court lost nothing. The inflation of the currency in the middle of the fifteenth century hurt the court, for it could no longer persuade foreign envoys and merchants to accept gifts of paper money.[17] Instead, it had to proffer more valuable goods to the 'barbarian' ambassadors.

Textiles   Since the Han dynasty (206 BC–AD 220), China had shipped silk to Inner Asia and thence to the Middle East and Western Europe. The term 'Silk Road' testifies to the significance of this trade. The Ming continued the practice of bestowing silks and satins on foreigners. These textiles were apparently the most popular Chinese gifts to Inner Asia. Foreign rulers repeatedly requested robes of these fabrics, requests which the court occasionally denied, for it reserved certain robes for its own officials and the emperor. These presents of silks and satins, like most Chinese gifts, scarcely affected the Chinese economy early in the Ming period, but they increasingly became a drain on the resources of the empire during the latter half of the dynasty.

Clothing   The court often gave boots and stockings to foreign envoys. It also satisfied their requests for hats, caps, and girdles. Some of these goods were extremely elaborate (for example 'a girdle adorned with plates of rhinoceros horn inlaid with gold'[18]), though such elegant and expensive apparel was seldom given to foreign ambassadors.

Drugs   The Ming used gifts of Chinese medicines to court the rulers of Inner Asia, who were delighted with the drugs and used them to treat a wide variety of illnesses. The Central Asians and the Mongols, in particular, even sought and received the services of Chinese doctors. Neither the Chinese nor the Inner Asian sources report on the effectiveness of the medical and medicinal treatments.

Silver The early Ming court rarely gave silver to the 'barbarians'. The rulers of Inner Asia could expect gifts of Chinese silver only on sending their first tribute mission to the capital; later embassies received other Chinese goods. In the latter half of the fifteenth century, as the Chinese need for Inner Asian horses became critical, the court wooed the Mongols and Central Asians with presents of silver, expending vast amounts in this effort. Several emperors were forced to prohibit the use of silver as gifts or in trade in order to prevent a disastrous outflow of the metal.[19]

Tea The Central Asians sought Chinese tea from the earliest days of the Ming dynasty, and the Mongols began to request tea in the late sixteenth century. The court, however, reserved tea for the north-western border commerce in horses with Hami and the nearby oases. The tea and horse trade is so important that I will deal with it separately at the end of this chapter.

Paper Paper was scarce in Central Asia and Mongolia. The court therefore permitted the envoys of Hami and the Mongols to buy a specified amount of paper. It occasionally offered paper as a gift to the foreigners. Yet this supply did not satisfy the Inner Asian demand, for numerous emissaries made special requests for paper.

Porcelain The Central Asians, the Persians, and the peoples of the Middle East prized Ming porcelains. Ulugh-Beg built a special pavilion for his large collection of porcelains. The Persian ruler Shāh 'Abbās (reigned 1587–1629) constructed a China house for his magnificent Chinese wares. The Topkapi museum in Istanbul houses over eight thousand Sung and Ming porcelains.[20] Some of the Central Asian tribes believed that Chinese porcelains possessed supernatural powers. In the Persian miniature paintings of the fifteenth century, 'there is hardly a manuscript in which [Chinese] blue and white vessels is not depicted'.[21] The Muslim traveller 'Ali Akbar was so entranced by Ming porcelains that he wrote a lengthy section in his travel account on the kilns of Ching-te chen, the porcelain centre of China.[22]

Despite this great interest and admiration, the Chinese and Persian sources barely mention economic transactions concerning porcelain. There are few records of the price and number of porcelains exchanged in the Ming period. Since eunuchs supervised the porcelain industry, Chinese officials and historians ignored it. The Arabic inscriptions on some of the porcelains indicate that the Chinese intended them for trade. Yet one can only concur with John Pope's lament that 'porcelain, much as it may have been admired, was not always the subject of such extensive comment as scholars today might hope for'.[23]

The general pattern of China's exports to Inner Asia now begins to emerge. In the early Ming period, the court offered paper money, textiles, and clothing to the foreigners. Its officials and merchants traded tea, paper, and porcelain for Inner Asian goods. The Chinese were giving away little of value, and there were few complaints of inordinate Chinese expenditure on trade and tribute. From the late fifteenth century onwards, the earlier and more favourable Chinese position was reversed. The foreigners now demanded silver, not paper money, and obtained many more silks, satins, boots, stockings, and porcelains. Though the court's position deteriorated, it never called for the total abolition of tribute and trade relations with Inner Asia. It merely sought to tighten its regulations so that it could secure additional benefits from economic transactions with Inner Asia. Though the court was unsuccessful in this effort, it appears that Chinese merchants profited from the loosening of regulations after the late fifteenth century.

THE TEA AND HORSE TRADE

If there are still doubts about the value of commerce to the Ming court, a study of the tea and horse trade removes them.[24] The Chinese bred horses, but they recognized that 'the horses of distant lands, usually to the West or North, and even of their nomadic enemies near at hand, were quite frankly superior'.[25] Being faster, larger, and hardier, the foreign steeds were ideally suited for warfare. Because the Ming was unable to raise its own war horses, the early emperors sent embassies to stimulate the Central Asians and the Mongols to offer horses as tribute. This effort was successful, for nearly every one of these foreign missions mentioned in the Ming histories and court annals presented horses to the court. Most of the Inner Asian states, however, gave tribute irregularly, and the number of horses that they offered was not fixed. As a result, they could not be relied upon to provide a continual flow of horses. The Chinese government, in addition, incurred enormous expenses in supplying tribute envoys, and it was in the best interests of the empire to find a cheaper way of obtaining horses.

One major and dependable source for horses was the tea and horse trade. The Northern Sung dynasty (AD 960–1127) had founded markets on the north-western border for the exchange of Chinese tea and Central Asian horses, but it was the Ming that developed and made great use of the trade. The Ming followed the example of the Sung in attempting to employ the government tea monopoly not only as a way of obtaining horses, but also as a potent means of pacifying unruly Central Asians. The 'barbarians' coveted tea for several reasons: it remained fresh longer than such other beverages as koumiss; it made water safer to drink; and it was a mild stimulant, particularly after prolonged exposure to the cold.[26] The Ming history relates that without tea the 'barbarians' would be 'afflicted and thereby ill' and that, should they trespass upon the borderlands of China, withholding tea would render them docile.[27] Theoretically, the court encouraged the tea-horse trade in times of peace and suspended it in times of war. In reality, the Chinese need for horses was so desperate that the trade was rarely cut off.

Government control of tea was, in Chinese eyes, essential to a rational and effective horse trade policy. The first Ming emperor imposed a monopoly on tea, and the government annually received approximately one million *chin* (one *chin* is a little over a pound) from the province of Szechwan and 26,000 *chin* from the province of Shensi, two of the largest tea-producing areas of the time. The court severely punished tea producers who sold tea illegally to merchants. It ordered its own soldiers to transport the tea, after it had been packed, to the Horse Trading Office (Ch'a-ma ssu) in Shensi. This transport system was precarious and unwise, for if the soldiers were needed for war, both the tea monopoly and the means of conveyance would be disrupted. The court, nonetheless, maintained the system for as long as it could and prescribed the death penalty for merchants who illegally transported or exported tea to the 'barbarians'.

In effect, the Horse Trading Office in Shensi was the only agency legally empowered to carry on the tea and horse trade. The court established four branches to trade with Hami and the tribes in the Lake Kokonor and Tun-huang (Sha-chou) regions. It assigned officials of the lowest (the ninth) rank of the established civil bureaucracy to the Horse Trading Office. Their position at the bottom of the government elite gives rise to speculation about the effectiveness and honesty of these bureaucrats. It is at least possible, if not probable, that these ill-paid and low-ranking officials might for a bribe have been willing to overlook the activities of smugglers. The court chose such humble clerks because of its contempt for commerce and its belief that high officials should not demean themselves in the market-place.

There is no doubt, however, that the government initiated and favoured the tea and horse trade. In 1375, the first emperor sent a eunuch with tea and other valuables to the north-western frontier to trade for horses. The 'barbarians' apparently enjoyed a good cup of tea, and they traded with the Chinese envoy. Commerce, once begun, was conducted on Chinese terms. The court gave the top half of gold tablets to the 'barbarian' chiefs and the bottom half to the Horse Trading Office. Every three years, a court official called on the 'barbarians', comparing their tablets with those stored in the Horse Trading Office. If the 'barbarian' tablets were genuine, he proceeded to trade Chinese tea for Central Asian horses.[28] The court also determined the prices of horses, but it could maintain these prices only by curbing the private export of tea. If the 'barbarians' had access to smuggled tea, they demanded more government tea in exchange for their horses. The elaborate court regulations presumably reduced smuggling by Chinese and 'barbarians' and maximized the government's control of trade.

The system was effective in the early years of the Ming dynasty. The Yung-lo emperor, in particular, vigorously pursued the tea and horse trade. Large numbers of war horses were needed for his campaigns against the Mongols and elsewhere. He therefore continued to send officials to trade with the 'barbarians' and to curb illegal outflows of tea. The number of horses in the empire expanded enormously during his reign. The rate of growth declined somewhat after his death, but the court did not suffer from a shortage of horses.

The invasions of the Oirat chief Esen in 1449 dealt a damaging blow to the tea and horse trade. Esen destroyed many of the settlements near China's north-western border, forcing some of the 'barbarians' involved in the horse trade to seek refuge in China while others drifted to remote areas of Inner Asia. The gold tablets were scattered or discarded. The Chinese army was unable simultaneously to repel Esen's forces and to transport tea for the north-western frontier trade. Esen's invasions increased the Chinese need for horses while making it harder to obtain them. His assaults on China and the influx of Chinese soldiers into Shensi increased the demand for grain. The transports of grain sent to relieve Shensi eventually disrupted the tea and horse trade.[29] The government, busily engaged in protecting itself from the

Oirats and other enemies, could not adequately patrol the borders, and tea smuggling consequently flourished.

In the late fifteenth century, the court attempted to resolve some of these problems. As a temporary measure it used silver to buy horses, but soon realized that it faced a disastrous outflow of silver if it continued this policy. It reimposed the prohibitions on the private export of tea, but could not enforce them on the border. It tried to use the Tea Exchange (k'ai-chung) system to deal with the deficiency of grain in Shensi and the government's inability to transport tea to the Horse Trading Office. Under this system, merchants delivering grain to the army stationed in Shensi received in return certificates entitling them to deal in government tea. None of these measures (the use of silver, the renewed curbs on smuggling, or the Tea Exchange system) ultimately stabilized the tea and horse trade. The court was still unable to find an effective method of transporting tea to the borders. It relied upon Chinese merchants to convey tea, and the latter used their leverage to ensure large profits for themselves. Unable to curb the merchants who met the 'barbarian' demand for tea, the court could not tempt the Central Asians with official tea.

Yang I-ch'ing, an early sixteenth-century official in Shensi, attempted to devise a comprehensive reform of the tea and horse trade as part of a general reconsideration of China's policy in the north-west. He had spent eight years as a functionary in Shensi before his appointment as director of the horse administration in the province. In 1505, he submitted to the court a long memorial on the tea and horse trade.[30] He asserted that China needed to reinstate the gold tablet system and to make effective the prohibitions on tea smuggling. He demanded that officials scrutinize the licences of tea merchants and the gold tablets of Central Asian merchants and envoys and sought an increase in the number of soldiers and functionaries patrolling the borders. Wishing to eradicate the 'evil grass' (his description of corrupt Chinese officials) which stifled the trade, he demanded harsher punishments for smugglers.

All of his proposals were conventional, for Yang envisaged a return to the system that existed under the first Ming emperors, a system supervised and controlled by the Chinese government. The only remaining problem lay in transporting tea to the Shensi border, and here Yang was compelled to seek an accommodation with the merchants. The merchants appeared to be the sole group capable of conveying tea, and Yang reluctantly turned to them. He ordered rich tea merchants to buy and transport tea to the Horse Trading Office in Shensi. That agency sold one-third of the tea for silver and paid the merchants with it. It could then use the remaining two-thirds in trade for Central Asian horses. The merchants, who garnered great profits from selling tea, objected to a government monopoly of tea sales. The government, which desperately needed the merchants to convey tea to the border, relented and permitted them to sell on their own account one-half of the tea that they transported. The court thereby sabotaged the last serious effort to deal with the problems of the tea and horse trade, perhaps because of its reluctance to antagonize the merchants or perhaps due to its inability to compel them to accept Yang's reforms. Even with this compromise, the court could not count on a supply of tea adequate for its needs in trade.

The rise of new and hostile powers in Central Asia further obstructed the tea and horse trade. In 1512, a Mongol chieftain conquered the tribes in the regions of Lake Kokonor and Tun-huang, tribes which had earlier supplied horses in exchange for Chinese tea. In the following year, the Muslim state of Turfan overwhelmed the oasis of Hami, another important participant in the commerce.[31] As a result, China was cut off from the major suppliers of horses for the tea trade. There were a few desperate attempts to revive the tea and horse trade in the sixteenth century, but all of them were futile.

In sum, the Ming court, though publicly scornful of commerce, initiated and nurtured the tea and horse trade with the Central Asian peoples through a series of official embassies in the early years of the dynasty. China needed horses and could not afford to remain aloof from commerce. The assertion of Ming officials that the trade was merely a convenient and inexpensive way of pacifying the 'barbarians' does not bear examination. So far from controlling recalcitrant tribes by withholding tea, the Chinese rarely denied the 'barbarians' tea because they needed horses and were reluctant to antagonize 'barbarian' horse traders.

After Esen's raids and the early sixteenth-century invasions by the Mongols and the Turfanese, the court abandoned the government monopoly of tea and compromised with the Chinese merchants, a class which it viewed with contempt. It allowed merchants to transport and sell tea privately on the border, initially imposing a sizeable tax in kind (about fifty per cent.). However, as the government's power waned and its demands became more modest, officials reduced the tea tax and merchants were unimpeded in trade, so that the warehouses of the Horse Trading Office were empty and the pasture lands and stables of China were without the prized 'barbarian' steeds. The Ming deficiency in horses certainly facilitated the Manchu conquest of China in 1644.

4 The Ch'ing
and the Russian advance

The Manchus who overthrew the Ming and founded the Ch'ing (1644–1911), the last dynasty to rule China, adopted many features of their predecessors' foreign policy. Their early attitudes and institutions are, in fact, almost indistinguishable from those of the Ming. As Fairbank and Teng explained over thirty years ago, 'since . . . the Manchus took over the Ming administration almost as it stood and altered it only by degrees, the Ch'ing system of government can really be understood only against its Ming background'.[1] The Manchus retained the tribute system and in theory treated foreigners as vassals of the Ch'ing empire. Foreigners wishing to trade with China endured the same humiliating restrictions that prevailed during the Ming period. They were forced to maintain the fiction that trade was the offering of tribute which the emperor rewarded with gifts from the Middle Kingdom.

The principal aims of the Ch'ing court in its relations with Inner Asia were similar to those of the native Ming dynasty. Defence against marauding neighbours was a major preoccupation. Throughout the first century of its rule, the court waged war against various peoples in Inner Asia, particularly the Western Mongols. It made strenuous efforts to sinicize friendly and peaceful foreigners and to prevent the unification of obstreperous and hostile ones. It further sought to dissipate the lure of the 'barbarian' style of life among its own people. Accordingly, it limited direct relations between Chinese and neighbouring foreigners and prohibited Chinese from migrating and settling in those regions of Mongolia and Manchuria which had submitted to Ch'ing overlordship. Unlike the Ming court, it allowed a few merchants to trade with the population of those areas, but it checked on their activities and forbad prolonged residence in the 'barbarian' lands or intermarriage with the Mongols.[2] Like the Ming, it recognized its need for foreign products and devised regulations enabling its officials to control foreign trade and to enjoy an advantageous position in commercial transactions.

THE EARLY CH'ING AND MANCHURIA

Before the Manchus conquered China, they were unified by Nurhaci. As he attracted adherents or conquered more territory, he initially organized his forces into four 'banners' (*gûsa*). These units, divided into white, yellow, blue, and red banners, were in turn composed of various *niru* (literally 'arrow', but in this context 'company'), each under the direction of a *niru-ejen* (literally 'master of arrows'). The rapid growth of the Manchu forces created a need for additional organizations. In 1615, Nurhaci added four more banners and established an intermediate unit, known as the *jalan*, between the banners and the *niru*. The number of banners remained constant at eight throughout the rest of Manchu history, but the number of *niru* and *jalan* expanded.[3]

Though the organization of the banners, *niru*, and *jalan* became increasingly complex and articulated, it was the abolition of the old tribal units that laid the foundation for Manchu unity. Nurhaci recognized that loyalty to the Manchu state must supersede the traditional tribal feelings.[4] On the other hand, he sought to preserve the cohesive family and clan structure which characterized the Manchu tribes. He wished the Manchus to transfer their loyalty from various petty chieftains to himself and his successors as rulers of a centralized state. This would minimize the threat of rebellions led by charismatic and popular leaders supported by their clansmen and tribesmen. Nurhaci refused to tolerate sub-groups of this kind, for they were not only dangerous but also ill-suited for the creation and administration of a great empire.

He decided instead to ignore tribal background in the composition of the banners. And, in fact, most members of individual banners did not come from the same territory.[5] Nurhaci feared rebellions by a group organized on the basis of territory and designed the banners to reduce that possibility. Some scholars have characterized Nurhaci's policy as an effort to eliminate 'feudalism', but a definition of that term is so elusive and leads to so many controversies that it may be easier to conceive of his system as an attempt to abolish the centrifugal, dis-unifying forces among his people.[6] He did not wish, however, to

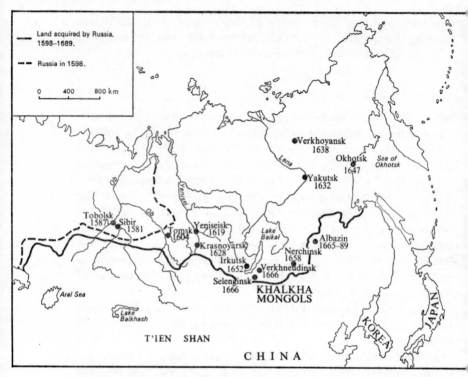

Russian expansion in Asia up to 1689

destroy all of the organizations that he had inherited from the tribal era of the Manchus. The banners strengthened the family by including not only the male soldier but also his immediate relatives. The *niru* retained the clan structure intact and occasionally comprised only one clan. It is clear, then, that Nurhaci attempted 'to obliterate tribal distinctions without destroying the clan structure'.[7]

Though the Eight Banners was primarily a military organization, its components, the *niru* and the *jalan*, fulfilled economic, social, and political functions. The head of the *niru* was a hereditary official who led his men in war and supervised their activities in peacetime. He conducted censuses once every three years and dispatched lists of all adult males eligible for military service to the central banner offices. By the time of the Manchu conquest of China, he was ordered to select only one out of every three males for the banner army and as guards for the major officials. The rest of the population farmed or worked as craftsmen, produced and maintained weapons, and provided food, clothing, and military supplies for its soldiers. The *niru* had numerous obligations to the government, including the digging of ginseng, the care and entertaining of Korean and Mongol envoys, the breeding and rearing of horses, the production of salt, the storage of tribute furs, the guarding of frontier areas, and the hunting of animals. Nurhaci held the heads of the *niru* responsible for the performance of these social and economic tasks.[8]

Nevertheless, he needed a group to oversee and control the *niru*. This task was too complicated for the *hošoi beile*, the traditional princely nobility, who might, in addition, seek to use their new power to retain their old prominence and consequently impede efforts to unify the Manchus. As more and more of the Manchus took up agriculture, the duties and needs of the government became more complex. Irrigation and flood control projects and the manufacture of agricultural tools were essential and the defence of the farm land required planning. Nurhaci and his successors recognized that they needed a regular bureaucracy to handle the manifold tasks of ruling a sedentary agricultural society, and they turned to Chinese defectors to assist them in forming the appropriate government agencies. By helping to oppose and abolish the old tribal councils, these Chinese advisers and bureaucrats were instrumental in the destruction of the Ming and in the rise of the new Manchu state.

The Manchus' relentless drive towards China consisted of an almost uninterrupted series of victories and economic gains. Nurhaci started to amass power discreetly in 1588 by marrying a granddaughter of the chief of the Hada, one of the four major tribes in southern Manchuria, and a daughter of the chief of the Yehe, another of the tribes. He accumulated a fortune through his monopoly of the commerce in ginseng, pearls, and furs, and through his tribute relations with the Ming court, which presented him with silk and silver for his offerings. Many lesser Manchu tribes joined him or came under his control in the late sixteenth century. Simultaneously, he attracted many Chinese and Mongols who either served in his administration or acted as advisers on technology, crafts, and mining. He deliberately maintained good relations with the Chinese in the early years of his rise to power, and in 1595 the Ming court even awarded him the rarely bestowed title of General of the Dragon and Tiger (*lung-hu chiang-chün*).[9]

Anticipating no opposition from China, Nurhaci, from his base among the Chien-chou Jurched, turned his attention to the conquest and unification of the rest of Manchuria. In 1593, he defeated a coalition of four Manchu tribes which sought to stem his seemingly irresistible growth in wealth, power, and territory. After this victory, he launched campaigns to subjugate his major opponents, one after another. In 1601, he suppressed the Hada tribes; in 1607, he overwhelmed the Hoifa peoples; and in 1613, he vanquished the Ula confederation. The only tribe that escaped early subjugation was the Yehe, a federation of four sub-tribes supported by the Ming government. Nurhaci did not neglect to ensure the administrative and cultural unity of the newly conquered territories. He incorporated the new groups into the banner system and established a bureaucracy and a system of laws for them. Some of his literate subordinates, following his orders, devised a written language for Manchu based upon the Mongolian script. He built a new capital city to which flocked craftsmen, bureaucrats, and merchants. By 17 February 1616, he clearly felt strong enough to challenge China, for on that date he proclaimed himself emperor (*han*) of a new Chin dynasty. His title, 'Emperor Genggiyen, whom Heaven has Designated to Nourish the Many Countries',[10] indicates that he intended to lay claim to universal rule. To ensure continuity, he named three of his sons and a nephew *hošoi beile* (the highest princely title) and placed each of them in command of a banner.

His next great task was to subdue the Yehe tribes. Since the Yehe had the support of the Ming court, Nurhaci forged an alliance with a federation of Inner Mongolian peoples known as the Five Tribes of Khalkha. He had cultivated relations with them as early as the 1590s by exchanging envoys, presents, and women. Nurhaci, in fact, became so close to and borrowed so much from this and other Mongol groups that the Mongols were the main 'transmitters of a great deal of higher culture, some of which was Chinese culture in foreign dress'.[11] The Manchus, with the invaluable assistance of the Mongols, routed a Chinese pacification force in 1618 and, taking advantage of this stunning victory, shortly thereafter overwhelmed the Yehe tribes. The lack of unity among the Yehe no doubt facilitated the Manchu conquest.

The Chinese reaction to Nurhaci's onslaught, though briefly offering some hopes of success, ultimately proved disastrous. Instead of seeking an accord with the Manchu ruler, the court, in another attempt to 'use barbarians to regulate barbarians', continued to incite friendly tribes to detach themselves from Nurhaci's federation and attack his forces.

It also closed the border markets where the Manchus had traded for Chinese products.[12] Infuriated by China's actions, Nurhaci pursued an aggressive policy. In 1621, he captured the major south Manchurian cities of Liao-yang and Shen-yang (later known as Mukden). In 1625, he moved his capital to Shen-yang, closer to the Chinese border, and in the same year, he brought the whole region of Liao-yang under his control. Perhaps growing over-confident, he made a strategic error and incurred his first severe setback. He crossed the Liao River in 1626 and headed for the guard of Ning-yüan. Here the Manchu troops met a well-supplied, superbly trained, and admirably commanded Chinese force which decisively defeated them. This disastrous encounter, followed a few months later by Nurhaci's death, temporarily halted the Manchus.

The Chinese, who for a short time had the upper hand, were now racked with internal discord and quickly lost their advantage. The court's lavish expenditure on luxuries, and its enormous expenses in the military campaigns against the Manchus and in the defence of Korea against Japanese attack in the 1590s, necessitated additional revenue. The court imposed most of this financial burden on the peasants. The land taxes on the peasants doubled between 1618 and 1636, while the gentry, through bribery and corruption, generally avoided payment. The dishonesty, incompetence, and demoralization of local officials dismayed many peasants and even some soldiers.[13] In northern Shensi, a relatively poor region, the financial strains on the peasants were even greater. Life had been a struggle for the peasants, in that impoverished and isolated area, throughout the Ming period, and the increased taxes weighed heavily on them. In 1628, a prolonged drought and the resulting famine provoked serious peasant unrest, which rapidly led to organized rebellions.

The efforts of the Ming government to control the rebels were hopeless. The men whom it assigned to crush the rebellions were generally unrealistic and undistinguished and lacked military experience. Its military forces were often corrupt and ill-led, and its leaders were unresponsive to the miseries of the peasantry. One scholar asserts that 'bungled campaigns, "official" atrocities, and inadequate institutions obviously occupy the dominant positions in the military record of the late Ming government'.[14]

The same inadequacies plagued Ming attempts to counteract the threats of Nurhaci's successors among the Manchus. Abahai, the eighth of Nurhaci's sons, emerged as the ruler of the Manchus after a brief period during which he shared power with his brothers. Nurhaci had envisaged a system whereby each of the heads of the eight banners would share power and the emperor would merely be *primus inter pares*, but Abahai quickly disabused his siblings of that notion. He first consolidated his position through executions and dismissals, then, in 1629, crossed the Great Wall and reached the outskirts of Peking before returning to his capital with a great deal of booty. Five years later, he overcame the Chahar Mongols, the most important single group in Inner Mongolia, and by 1638, he had pacified Korea, a tributary and a so-called 'vassal' of the Ming court. His troops made repeated incursions on Chinese soil throughout this time. The response of the Chinese court was feeble. It executed generals who failed to stem the Manchus, and it even replaced effective generals who alienated officials or eunuchs in the capital. The consequence of this policy was the defection of many important military figures.

Abahai, and later his half-brother and loyal retainer Dorgon, laid the framework for and then founded the Ch'ing dynasty in China. Abahai enlisted numerous Chinese in influential administrative and military positions. In 1636, he changed the name of the dynasty from Chin to Ch'ing and substituted 'Manchu' for 'Jurched' as the name of his people, prohibiting the very use of the term 'Jurched'. According to one authority, 'this change was made to obscure the fact that his ancestors had been under Chinese rule and that they are referred to in Chinese records as Ju-chen'.[15] When Abahai died in 1643, his son and designated successor Fu-lin was only five years old. Dorgon consequently acted as regent for the child. Within a year, Dorgon learned that peasant rebels had occupied Peking and that the Ming emperor had committed suicide. Taking advantage of the chaotic situation, the Manchus, with the aid of Chinese officials and troops opposed to the native peasant rebels, sent their armies into China, defeated the rebel forces, and seized the capital and most of northern China. The Mongols, who might have desired such a conquest for themselves, were too disunited to organize a large-scale assault, and the Manchus thus faced no external opposition. On 30 October 1644, Fu-lin was crowned the first Ch'ing, or Manchu, emperor of China. Though Fu-lin was nominally head of state, with the reign title of Shun-chih, Dorgon held the real power until his death in 1650; it was he who fashioned the early Ch'ing administration and devised its early policies towards Inner Asia.

THE FRONTIER MANCHUS

One of Dorgon's principal concerns in Inner Asia was with the ancestral homeland of the Manchus. He and the other early Ch'ing leaders wished to retain the purity of Manchu culture in order to prevent their people from being overwhelmed by the Chinese. Manchuria was thus extremely important in their calculations. The Ch'ing were willing to adopt Chinese institutions and culture within China but feared the sinicization of the Manchu frontier. The Manchus in the capital sought to keep Manchuria as a 'Manchu preserve, an emergency retreat if the need arose for the Manchus in China'.[16] They desired therefore to foster the use of the Manchu language and to promote Manchu customs and institutions. The early Ch'ing emperors were determined to maintain the martial spirit and frontier virtues of the old Manchu culture.

The main object of the Ch'ing in Manchuria was to preserve the status quo. Like the Ming emperors, the Manchus attempted to exclude Chinese from Manchu lands. They prohibited Chinese farmers from migrating to Manchuria and allowed Chinese merchants to remain there for only as long as was necessary to conduct their trade. The court attempted to limit contact between the Chinese and the frontier Manchus. It also made strenuous efforts to prevent frontier Manchus from intermingling with the Mongols or other nearby groups. The Ch'ing rulers apparently believed that isolating the Manchus would help to preserve their purity. In sum, they attempted to keep their frontier brothers away from the corrupting influence of Chinese civilization.

The Ch'ing, in pursuing these aims, developed two distinct policies. One was directed at the more reliable and perhaps more sedentary groups among the border peoples. The court incorporated them into the banner organization and gave them the responsibility of frontier defence. As bannermen, they not only served as soldiers but also earned their own livelihood in agriculture (the only occupation open to them, since the court prohibited them from engaging in commerce). Some entered the civil service bureaucracy and attained higher ranks than similarly qualified Chinese, but farming was the main pursuit of most of them. They formed small military colonies designed to be self-supporting. The court allotted them a specific area of land and restricted their movements, presumably in order to maintain and strengthen the border defences but also to limit their association with

91

the Chinese and with the hunting or fishing peoples of Manchuria or the descendants of the Wild Jurched. Later, when the Russians began to appear on the Manchurian frontier, the Ch'ing needed to expand its defence forces and was forced to rely on the Chinese for its banner troops. The Chinese started to form the majority of the frontier soldiers from that time onwards, and the earlier Ch'ing control of the banner troops weakened.[17]

The court dealt differently with the less sedentary tribes of northern Manchuria, particularly in the areas of Kirin and Heilungkiang. A few of them joined the banners, but the bulk remained in independent tribes. The Ch'ing sought to control this group by using the traditional Ming policies. It provided wives for the tribal chieftains in order to win their friendship. It insisted that they accept a status as vassals of the throne, though the court rarely if ever intervened in their internal affairs. The tribal leaders received honorary titles and ranks if the court approved of or benefited from their actions.

The most important device that the court used was the tribute system. It encouraged the tribes to bring sable pelts to the town of Ninguta up to the middle of the eighteenth century, then, after that, to Sanhsing. The tribute bearers received the same treatment that had been accorded to foreign envoys during the Ming period. The local officials fed and feasted them and cared for their horses for their entire stay in the border town. Elaborate ceremonies accompanied the actual presentation of tribute. The tribesmen offered their sable furs, which the frontier officials forwarded to the Imperial Household Office for examination and storage. In this way, the best pelts were reserved for the government. Court officials used some of the furs for themselves and sold the rest on the open market, making furs a source of government revenue. The court, in return, gave the tribute bearers silk, cotton, hats, stockings, garments, combs, needles, and other commodities.[18] Since there were few complaints about this system for most of the seventeenth century, it presumably benefited both sides.

The vital part of these transactions for the frontier peoples was the trade that followed the tribute presentations. The court permitted a carefully regulated trade between Chinese merchants and the tribesmen. The Chinese needed licences and passports to participate and could remain in Manchuria only while trade was being conducted. They received furs and livestock and provided silk, tea, tobacco, liquor, and iron vessels to the tribes. Even with official supervision, the trade was rather haphazard. Violence was not uncommon, and corrupt officials often derived enormous profits from illegal transactions. As government knowledge and control of Manchuria declined, the local officials garnered an ever higher percentage of the material gains from this commerce, leaving the court with only a small part of the true profit. In the early years of the dynasty, however, the government controlled its officials and thus assured itself of a reasonable income from the border trade.

The court divided Manchuria into the regions of Sheng-ching (later known as Feng-t'ien), Kirin, and Heilungkiang. It appointed a military governor in each of these regions to control the banner population and to deal with the independent but tributary tribes. At the beginning of the Ch'ing period most of the governors were sinicized Manchus from China, many of them related to the imperial clan. According to a recent study, their functions included the defence of the border, the establishment of government granaries, the control of the frontier tribes, the supervision of the tribute system, the creation and preservation of good communications and transport between China and Manchuria, the training of banner forces, and numerous other duties.[19] By the late seventeenth century, defence against the Russian thrust in the Amur River area had emerged as their principal duty.

The court, fearful of the development of rival centres of power, imposed severe limitations on military governors. It left some of the banner leaders in control of certain internal matters over which the governors had no influence. Since the court paid for most of the frontier administration, it could use economic measures to restrict the governors, whose powers were also checked by the shortness of their tenure of office. Their underlings, generally inhabitants of the area, were more knowledgeable about local conditions and on occasion wielded extraordinary powers. The governors could rarely count on much support from the people in their regions in personal disputes with the central government, and 'there was never recorded a case of a governor committing insubordinate acts against the court'.[20]

The appointment of five Boards in each region further restricted the governors. The five Boards paralleled the six Boards of the government in Peking. The only missing Board in the frontier government was that of Civil Appointment. The others (the Boards of Rites, Revenue, Works, Punishments, and War) all reported to the 'parent' Boards in Peking, thus limiting the authority of the military governors, particularly among the civilian population. As Manchuria's civilian population grew, the governors were further weakened. The lack of clearly drawn lines of authority no doubt prevented the rise of powerful governors, but it simultaneously prevented the effective working of frontier governments. Conflicts between the governors, their lieutenants, and the five Boards led to inaction and frustration and occasionally offered opportunities for graft and corruption.

Despite this major problem, the court appeared to have devised an effective relationship with the frontier Manchus. It drafted some into the banner forces and presumably encouraged them to shift their loyalties from tribal leaders to the central government. It established a tribute system as an effective means of political control and of securing Manchu goods. The bureaucratic and military administrations which it created, though flawed, still faced no serious threat from the frontier tribes, for these were not only dispersed into small units in the vast territory of Manchuria but were also content with their economic relations with the court. In fact, these tribes generally sided with the Ch'ing court in its early confrontations with the Russians along the Amur. The court prevented the large-scale migration of Chinese into Manchuria, thus preserving the purity of Manchu culture and reducing the possibility of its absorption or disappearance in Chinese civilization. The early Ch'ing rulers, in essence, enjoyed a workable relationship with the peoples of Manchuria, as long as they enforced the regulations on commerce, tribute, and bureaucracy. Any external force that appeared on the Manchurian border could disrupt the equilibrium in the relations between the Ch'ing and the frontier Manchus.

One new force that challenged the traditional Ming and early Ch'ing attitude and policy towards Inner Asia was Russia. Surprisingly enough, however, the Ch'ing managed to maintain its system of foreign relations until the nineteenth century. The Ming had preserved its system for almost a century, or at least until 1449, while the Ch'ing sustained its own policy for almost two centuries. Its success was truly remarkable, for it faced a great empire with immense political and economic resources, rather than nomadic tribes who could only engage in hit-and-run attacks on Chinese territory. Russia, nonetheless, accepted the restrictions that the Ch'ing demanded in treaties negotiated in the late seventeenth and early eighteenth centuries.

RUSSIA MOVES EAST

Since the Mongol conquest of the Russian city states in the thirteenth century, the Russians had been concerned with their eastern borders. As they threw off the Mongol yoke, they continued to move eastward and to occupy more and more territory. In the sixteenth century, the pace of Russian expansion quickened. Russian armies seized Kazan in 1552 and Astrakhan in 1556. In 1574, the Tsar gave the Stroganovs, a merchant family eager to explore the lands of the east, which were supposedly rich in minerals, a huge grant of land east of the Ural Mountains. Since warriors, led by a powerful chieftain named Kuchum Khan, occupied that area, the Tsar clearly intended that the Stroganovs should sieze control of the territory and dispossess that Inner Asian tribe. The Stroganovs were indeed fortunate to have within their ranks a certain Yermak Timofeevich, a Cossack bandit and adventurer whom government forces were pursuing and who thus wished to migrate to a more remote land. They persuaded him to move eastward to challenge the forces of Kuchum, and in 1579, he led a group of less than a thousand men, with supplies provided by the merchant family, on a campaign east of the Urals. By 1582, he had conquered Sibir, the capital of Kuchum's land and a town which later gave its name to the vast new domain of Siberia.[21] Though Kuchum's forces ambushed and killed Yermak and reoccupied Sibir in 1585, they never completely recovered from this defeat. Further Cossack groups continued to cross the Urals, and, in 1587, they made a capital, near Sibir, in the town of Tobolsk, at the junction of the Irtysh and Tobol rivers.

Once they had overwhelmed Kuchum in 1598, the Russians faced no further organized opposition in their march across Siberia. They could not move south because of such powerful groups as the Kazakhs, Kirghiz, and Western Mongols. Three expeditions in the south proved disastrous, and so the Russians followed the line of least resistance and advanced northward to Siberia. They easily vanquished the nomadic and hunting and fishing tribes in the area. In 1604, they founded the town of Tomsk, on the Tom River, and in 1619 built the fort of Yeniseisk on the Yenisei. Again attempting to expand to the south, they encountered difficulties in subduing the Buryat Mongols. In 1628, they forced the Buryats to send tribute, but it was only after some devastating clashes in the 1640s that they finally overcame that Mongol group. Shortly thereafter, in 1651, they constructed the town of Irkutsk and reached Lake Baikal. Their advance in the north was even more rapid. In 1632, Russian settlers founded a settlement, later named Yakutsk, on the Lena River: a base from which numerous expeditions attempted to colonize eastern Siberia. In the middle of the seventeenth century, an intrepid group reached Okhotsk, within sight of the Pacific.

The speed with which Russia colonized the vast domain of Siberia is almost unbelievable. Within half a century of the defeat of their major opponent in western Siberia, the Russians were on the shores of the Pacific. The colonists led brutal and dangerous lives. Since initial attempts to produce their own grain often failed, they were frequently short of food, and many starved to death. In some areas of eastern Siberia, agriculture was impossible. One settler wrote that the 'food is such, that in Russia even animals would not accept it'.[22] The colonists ate grass, roots, and other foul food, and occasionally resorted to cannibalism. The bitter cold for which Siberia is notorious caused numerous deaths, wiping out whole communities, and forcing many to abandon their settlements. The winter ice was treacherous, avalanches trapped some voyagers, and snowstorms took their toll. Supplies, which came from western Russia, were frequently lost en route, and the colonists thus lacked clothing, cooking utensils, and weapons. Hostile local inhabitants clashed with them. Deprived not only of many of the amenities but also of the necessities, the settlers were cruel to each other and to the local people who obstructed their path.

The Russian government and the settlers clearly had good reasons for enduring these hardships. They justified their imperialist expansion by citing the need for defence against another possible invasion by the nomadic tribes of Inner Asia. Certainly, this fear of a Mongol-like conquest of their land (as in the Mongol occupation from the thirteenth to the fifteenth centuries) cannot be dismissed, but material gain also prompted the Russians to make the required effort. The Russians had heard rumours of the vast mineral resources of Siberia, and in this mercantilist era great nations did not neglect territories possessing gold and silver. Seventeenth-century Russia required precious metals to pay for the wars with Sweden, Poland, and the Crimean Tartars, and for the efforts to Westernize the Russian state. The huge military campaigns and the incessant demand for Western products and advisers during the reign of Peter the Great (1689–1725) required revenue. Peter himself wrote that 'money is the artery of war'.[23] The Russian government was thus understandably interested in the reputed gold and silver resources of Siberia.

Furs were still another possible source of revenue for Russia. The demand for furs in a number of European states prodded the Russians into obtaining pelts for export. Some of the Western European states of the sixteenth and seventeenth centuries had become so prosperous that the wealthy desired and could pay handsome prices for furs. The Dutch, German, and English, in that order, were the principal importers of pelts.[24] The Russians, recognizing the profitability of the fur trade, supplied the Europeans with furs from their eastern frontiers. They also used pelts to reward officials, to provide gifts for nobles and clergymen, and to bribe hostile peoples on the borders. The demand for fur was consequently enormous, and hunters, reacting to the high prices offered for animal skins, sought to satisfy the need. As they depleted the supply in Russian-occupied lands in Siberia, they had to move further east and to colonize more land in that extensive region.

Another motive that may have impelled the Russians to pursue an eastward migration was the desire for direct relations with China. Like many European peoples, the Russians had read tales of the fantastic wealth of China. In their accounts, Jesuit visitors to the Ming and Ch'ing states emphasized the luxury of court life and the variety, beauty, and utility of Chinese goods. The Mongols, with whom the Russians were in contact again in the early seventeenth century, described China's great opulence and introduced the Russians to such Chinese products as tea and, perhaps, rhubarb. The Russian emissaries to China in the same period returned with reports that whetted the appetite of the Tsarist court.

The Russians, for a mixture of defence and economic motives, developed a unique method of colonizing Siberia. The government encouraged colonizers and adventurers to take advantage of the fine river system to proceed further into the Siberian heartland. The major rivers flowed from south to north, but many of the tributaries followed an easterly or westerly course. The Russians pressed forward along the rivers and used the excellent portages to move from one river to another. On the way, a group of settlers often built an *ostrog* (fort), in which future travellers could find supplies and from which hunters and settlers could fan out to occupy new territories. The forts, which consisted of residences, granaries, customs houses and other structures, were strategically situated at the intersections of rivers or at easily defended points along a river. Each successive *ostrog* was linked to the preceding ones, producing a very effective system of transport and communications and perhaps even an efficient means of calling for support in times of danger. By the middle of the seventeenth century, the towns and forts in Siberia served as channels for the speedy conveyance of merchandise and official mail. According to one account,

> Messengers sent on urgent government business from the Siberian towns – Tobolsk, Tiumen, or the ostrog of Turinsk – to the Sovereign at Moscow . . . go by the following route. From Verkhoturie they travel by way of the Chiusovaia River and the ostrogs of the Stroganovs. . . . One man . . . travelling lightly, is sent forth from Verkhoturie to hire carts, vessels, and oarsmen. . . . Going from Verkhoturie to the Chiusovaia, people with luggage travel three days by the land route to reach the end of the portage; from the end of the portage it takes three days' sailing down the Chiusovaia to reach the Kama. . . . Travelling posthaste . . . over the winter route from Verkhoturie to Moscow . . . takes three weeks.[25]

The ready availability of boats, carts, and other modes of transport indicates the remarkable success of the system. The colonizing effort met with little organized resistance, except for the lengthy opposition in the south by the Buryats.

The colonizers of Siberia consisted of a wide variety of peoples with differing interests and objectives. The Cossacks were part of the first wave and among the most colourful of the newcomers. This group, composed of adventurers and farmer-soldiers, originally resided in the Ukraine and gained attention in the fifteenth century when they refused to be transformed from free men into serfs by their Polish overlords. Instead they organized tightly knit, democratic communities which defended their freedom. They soon became extraordinary warriors and attracted many runaway peasants alienated by the oppressive conditions in Poland and Russia. Though often described as vagrants and freebooters, the Cossacks actually performed useful functions, one of which was acting as trail-blazers in Siberia. Some migrated to that at first isolated and seemingly desolate land to escape from the clutches of the government, while others received official encouragement to move.

Hunter-trappers who obtained furs for the Russian and Western European markets formed another wave of migrants. They trapped some of the animals, but they also received many from the local peoples through trade or by force. Shortly after their arrival, they formed armed bands, both for defence and for co-operation in hunting. When too many hunters were attracted to one area, some had to move eastward to secure additional furs. The incentive of greater profits from the fur trade in this way promoted the colonization of Siberia. As the Russian government became aware of the profits to be made, it sought to share in them. Customs houses were established in all of the major towns and forts. Hunters were required to bring their pelts to these government offices, and customs officials selected one out of every ten for the state. The government required all hunters to hold licences on penalty of severe punishments. It circumscribed the territory in which they could hunt and prohibited them from trapping certain species of animals.

The government imposed similar restrictions on the new class of fur merchants. It was a merchant family, the Stroganovs, that had initiated the first ventures in the exploration and conquest of Siberia. Soon many entrepreneurs arrived in the newly conquered areas to trade with the local peoples. To their chagrin, they found innumerable limitations on their commercial activities. The government issued passports to those fortunate merchants permitted to trade with the Siberian tribes. It demanded that merchants provide complete lists of their goods and precise indications of their destinations. Customs officials levied a ten per cent. tax on all of the products that merchants proposed to sell before merchants were given permission to trade. They were not allowed to sell weapons, metal tools, wine, or tobacco to the local peoples. Officials at the forts and towns en route searched merchants and inspected their goods to ensure compliance with government regulations. They confiscated contraband and meted out harsh punishments for infractions. The most important government edict was that merchants could not trade until the local peoples had presented tribute furs. The court would consequently receive the best pelts. Merchants were, in fact, 'forbidden to buy the most valuable furs from the natives'.[26]

The government imposed far fewer restrictions on settlers, the true conquerors of Siberia. Many Russian peasants migrated to Siberia of their own volition, hoping to avoid the onerous demands of the court. The government also lured and, in some cases, forced farmers to move to the new territory. Subsidies and exemption from taxes were two devices occasionally employed as bait by the court. The government even used criminals and prisoners of war as settlers. It was evidently anxious to populate Siberia and to make it self-sufficient in grain. The Tsar and his officials wished to discontinue the transport of food from the western part of the empire to the Asiatic part. If Siberia were to flourish and not be a drain on the Russian economy, it needed to be self-sufficient in the basic requirements of life. The government was prepared to send grain to areas afflicted by natural disasters, but not to subsidize the settlers in perpetuity.

The government expected the settlers to support not only themselves but also the non-farming population. It had encouraged craftsmen, clerics, and men involved in service occupations to settle in Siberia. Each group performed valuable tasks, but none had its own food supply. There was, in addition, a large and growing civilian and military bureaucracy that required grain. The government was reluctant to pay for the upkeep of all of these groups and instead relied on the Siberian peasants to provide the necessary grain. Farmers paid a tax in the form of grain, known as an *obrok*, which the court gave to its officials or stored in granaries for emergencies. Alternatively, it made payments in land to its officials, who presumably employed serfs or tenants to work on their properties. By the end of the seventeenth century, the government's policy of agricultural colonization appeared to have been successful in western Siberia, for that territory produced most of the grain that it needed. The elimination of the burden of grain transport meant even greater profits for the court from the fur trade.

To achieve its objectives and to ensure the smooth operation of its colonial scheme, the government established a well defined and stratified civil and military administration in Siberia.

The Siberian *prikaz* or, as one writer terms it, the 'Colonial Office for Siberia',[27] administered the new territory. Founded in 1637, its offices were in Moscow, and its chief was invariably a member of the boyar or noble class. The bureaucrats under him were clearly the most vital men in the *prikaz*, for they were the true experts, those Muscovite officials who were the most knowledgeable on Siberian affairs. Reports from local officials reached them and received careful attention and explicit replies. One source indicates that twenty thousand to thirty thousand reports and replies are still extant among the documents of the *prikaz*.[28] The *prikaz*, therefore, had access to an abundance of information about Siberia, although the accuracy and reliability of the reports are questionable.

Most of these accounts were dispatched to the *prikaz* by local governors, each of whom was known as a *voevoda*. These officials were appointed by the government, which favoured men with military backgrounds. Since each *voevoda* had ample opportunities for graft and could often amass a huge fortune through his position, there was much competition for such appointments and bribes were common, if not essential, in the selection process. Once appointed, the *voevoda* had tremendous power, for the central government, thousands of miles away, could not oversee his activities. He could act without fear of the government unless his abuse of power was so widespread and out-rageous that other officials submitted denunciatory reports to the Siberian *prikaz*. The Tsarist court sought to reduce corruption by limiting each *voevoda* to no more than two or three years in one post, by often appointing two to the same locality, and by auditing the accounts of the *voevoda* at the expiration of his term of office. But the *voevody*, recognizing that their appointments were temporary, took full advantage of their short tenure to accumulate wealth and felt no compulsion to maintain good relations with the local inhabitants. They frequently ignored the final auditing, leaving their posts before their successors arrived to peruse their accounts. The presence of two or more executive officers in one administrative area, far from limiting corruption, often disrupted local government, created jurisdictional disputes, and resulted in confusion. It is clear that under such con-ditions the reports submitted by a *voevoda* were frequently either deliberately falsified or self-serving.

The deficiencies of its colonial administration in Siberia made it harder for the government to achieve its objectives. Its principal aim was to acquire fur, which it planned to obtain as tribute (*iasak*) from the local peoples. In order to compel the tribesmen to offer tribute, the Russian authorities had to make a convincing demonstration of their military superiority. Once the tribes submitted, the *voevody*, the Cossacks, and the settlers adopted a policy of divide and rule, to reduce the likelihood of unified attacks on the forts, towns, and settlers.

As long as the tribes remained peaceful and presented tribute, the government did not interfere in their internal affairs. It scarcely attempted to introduce the local peoples to Russian institutions. Instead, the chieftains retained their own traditional powers, customs, and institutions. The government did not demand that they adopt the Russian language or accept the Christian religion. Local officials were instructed to gain the friendship of the tribes. They courted, in particular, the more powerful and affluent of the local people. Tribal chieftains received ranks and titles in the Russian military service, and obtained fine gifts from the court. A *voevoda* might invite them to elaborate feasts and introduce them to strong liquor. The court granted exemptions from tribute to a few of the more prominent and loyal chieftains. Through these efforts, the government hoped to win the allegiance of most of the principal tribes. Those which remained hostile were accorded no mercy. The court treated them harshly and even, we would now think, cruelly.

The government preferred to achieve its ends by peaceful means. This policy developed not from altruistic motives, but from self-interest. It seems clear that 'the government was interested in preserving the lives of the natives because the loss of a native's life meant the loss of furs which he could deliver, and extreme cruelty toward one native was likely to drive away several others'.[29]

The effectiveness of this policy relied almost exclusively on the honesty, capability, and humaneness of the Russian officials and settlers in Siberia. Faced with immense hardships and brutal conditions, however, these colonists became hardened to human suffering and some were callous in their treatment of the local people. Since a large minority of them were convicts, they were not the finest representatives of the Russian state. Many sought immediate gain and were not concerned with the long-term effects of their greed on future relations with the inhabitants of Siberia. The *voevody* and other local officials shared these attitudes of unprincipled contempt and strong distaste for the local peoples. There is no doubt that they victimized even the friendly tribesmen. They demanded excessive tribute, most of which never reached the court but instead served to enrich them. Raiding parties occasionally confiscated horses, food, and clothing from the natives and in several cases took hostages or tortured the inhabitants until their demands for furs, gold, or other valuables were met. Some Russian officials required local people to act as oarsmen, interpreters, and personal servants, or to provide wood, fish, metals, and other products for local officialdom. The tribes and tribal chieftains, who repeatedly complained of such abuses, responded either by refusing to offer tribute or by attacking Russian settlements in Siberia, thus provoking even more violent reactions from Russian officials and settlers.

Russian colonization of the new territory caused further discord. Like the Indians of North America, the local peoples of Siberia lost many of their hunting grounds to the newcomers. The Russian settlers forced them further to the east, expropriating land that they needed for their economy. Though the unique culture of these various groups, their languages, their customs, and their religions, were not threatened with extinction, their livelihood was imperilled. The Russian policy of colonization contrasted sharply with the prohibitions that the Ch'ing dynasty imposed on those Chinese who wished to settle in Manchuria or other parts of Inner Asia. By disrupting the economy of the local people and thus alienating many of them, the Russians obtained little support from the inhabitants of the Amur River area when they reached this region. These people preferred Ch'ing overlordship, for the reason that, though the Ch'ing dynasty demanded tribute, it did not encroach on their territory.

SIMILARITIES BETWEEN THE RUSSIAN AND CH'ING POLICIES

More striking than the differences between the Russian and Ch'ing attitudes and policies in Inner Asia were the remarkable similarities. Both governments considered themselves superior to the Inner Asian peoples on their borders. The Ch'ing Emperor and the Russian Tsar were revered as divine beings by their own peoples, and they expected foreigners to treat them as such. Before any diplomatic or economic exchanges, foreigners were required to give proof of their submission to the throne. The Ch'ing demanded tribute embassies to Peking, while the Russians requisitioned a tribute (*iasak*) of furs at the forts and towns in the territories which they occupied. Both governments placed similar restrictions on foreign emissaries to their respective states: the envoys needed passports or licences for admittance, followed prescribed routes to the capitals, and remained isolated throughout most of their stays in Russia or China.

The Ch'ing and the Russian courts had economic motives for their policies. Both believed that they could benefit from their transactions with the Inner Asians. In order to give themselves the best conditions for trade, they imposed monopolies on certain products. As the sole suppliers of these goods, they could set their own prices. Elaborate regulations were devised to prevent merchants from competing with the government and to restrain foreign merchants, envoys, and the local inhabitants from trading illegally with private entrepreneurs. When the Ch'ing and Russian courts were successful, they obtained furs and other valuable products cheaply. Russian and Chinese merchants, however, sought repeatedly to evade the commercial restrictions and thus threatened to reduce government profits. Since merchants usually had a wider variety of goods to offer and did not demand tribute, they enjoyed a definite advantage over their governments in trading with Inner Asia.

As long as the peoples of Inner Asia offered tribute and refrained from attacks on China and Russia, both courts generally resisted the temptation to interfere in the internal politics of the various tribes. They wished to establish cordial relations with the neighbours on their frontiers as a means of protecting their borders against incursions. Recognizing that military and political intervention might embroil them in full-scale wars, both governments deliberately avoided direct involvement. Their principal concern was to prevent the unification of the tribes under ambitious and aggressive leaders. The prospect of a confederation of this kind frightened those two states, both of which still had unpleasant memories of Mongol occupation. Both courts used a policy of divide and rule to counteract this threat, so whenever a strong and hostile chieftain appeared, they incited other tribes to overpower him.

The two courts relied on officials on the borders to implement their policies. Both were to be sorely disappointed by the performance of these officials, many of whom were grossly underpaid, and who accepted posts on the frontiers primarily to take advantage of the opportunities for lucrative though illegal transactions. They often acted in collusion with foreigners to evade the government's economic restrictions for their own profit. On the other hand, the court accounts also accuse them of enriching themselves through excessive demands for gifts from foreign envoys. The private citizens who dealt with the Inner Asian peoples were also often unscrupulous profiteers who victimized the local people.

Both governments attempted to curb the excesses of their officials, but most of their efforts were in vain. Not only did they pay the officials relatively poor salaries; they also accorded them low ranks and limited them to brief tenures in office. Frontier officials frequently received few or no government supplies and needed either to furnish their own or to force the local peoples to supply provisions. Faced with such difficulties and restrictions, even honest officials were tempted to indulge first in petty thievery and later in major corruption. Their reports on foreign relations or 'barbarian' affairs were often self-serving and designed to prevent detection of their own malpractices.

The principal foreign relations specialists in both capitals, Moscow and Peking, relied on these often inaccurate and biased accounts when devising their foreign policies. The Li-fan-yüan, the major Ch'ing agency that dealt with Inner Asia, and the Siberian *prikaz* had few other sources of information about Inner Asia or about each other's states and governments. They had no resident ambassadors, and they generally did not trust the reports of their own merchants who travelled to the 'barbarian' lands. During the seventeenth century and the early eighteenth, emissaries from China and Russia, whether visiting each other's courts or sent to Inner Asia, often met with cold, if not hostile, receptions and frequently impeded, rather than improved, relations with the states which they visited. The two courts obtained some intelligence from the envoys, but the Russian court, for example, had totally inadequate maps of Asia as late as the seventeenth century, forcing the Romanov Tsars to order their officials in Siberia to compile accurate and detailed maps. In this way, depending on deliberately distorted accounts from frontier officials and on sketchy maps and limited intelligence from envoys, merchants, and travellers, the two courts dealt with Inner Asia and finally came into contact with each other in the seventeenth century.

5 Sino-Russian conflict and compromise

Though one Russian mission had reached Peking in the last years of the Ming period, it was along the Amur River that the first confrontation between the two states occurred. The Russians were constantly seeking grain for their colonists in eastern Siberia, since without an adequate food supply they could not retain control of that territory. They were also always searching for further sources of precious metals. Later, as they faced competition in Europe from imported North American furs, they attempted to find new markets, the most promising of which, China, lay south of the Amur. When officials in eastern Siberia heard rumours of the fertility of the soil and the availability of gold and silver deposits along the Amur, it is not surprising that they wished to investigate such reports.

In 1643, the *voevoda* of Yakutsk, a town in the grain-starved section of Siberia, dispatched an expedition, led by Vasili Poyarkov, to explore the Amur River region. Poyarkov's instructions included orders to extract tribute from the local peoples and to obtain information about China. After enduring severe hardships while crossing mountains and in following the Zeya River, he and his band of about 130 men reached the Amur region, where they camped for two winters. Having transported few supplies, and unable either to raise their own food or buy provisions, they plundered nearby villages, killing and capturing the inhabitants and seizing their supplies. These raids naturally antagonized the local peoples and hindered the Tsarist court's efforts to gain the allegiance of potential tribute bearers. On the other hand, Poyarkov, by returning to Yakutsk in 1646 with glowing reports of the abundant natural resources of the Amur area, stimulated further attempts at exploration and colonization.[1]

Erofei P. Khabarov, the leader of the next expedition, gathered on his own a force of about 150 men to conduct an even more aggressive campaign to grab the wealth of the region. In 1649, he led a brief exploratory mission from which he returned the next year with glowing reports of the grain resources of the Amur basin. Within a few months, he set forth again for a longer and more serious effort to force the local peoples to submit. His troops quickly occupied the village of Albazin, strategically located at the junction of the Shilka and Argun rivers, and expelled the local prince, a certain Albazai. From their new position at Albazin, they made further forays into the Amur basin, encountering surprisingly little opposition, for the inhabitants, on learning of the Russian advance, fled and sought asylum in lands closer to Ch'ing China. Khabarov's forces massacred many of those who chose to remain and forced others to offer tribute. Though Khabarov's mission appeared to have been successful, his cruelty, barbarism, and unbridled desire for profit alienated the local peoples and in the end damaged Russian interests in Inner Asia.

The inhabitants of the region, in particular the Daur and Dyucher peoples, turned for assistance to the Ch'ing in China. Aroused by the reports of their vassals, the Ch'ing recognized the need for the defence of the Amur basin, but understandably failed to appreciate the threat posed by the Russians. As early as 1616, Nurhaci had crossed the Amur. In its first years, the new Ch'ing dynasty had extended its powers to the Amur, its principal objectives being to preserve the racial and tribal purity of Manchuria in isolation from other states and to collect tribute of furs from the various hunting tribes. The Russian presence was a serious threat to the effectiveness of the court's policies. It was essential to station more Ch'ing troops along the Amur and Sungari rivers and to control the local peoples within the line of these rivers.

Though the Ch'ing's initial response was inadequate, the court had succeeded in temporarily ousting the Russians from the Amur region by the late 1650s. They advised the local peoples to abandon their villages and move south, thus denying the Russians food and other supplies. In 1652, a Ch'ing force moved north to repulse Khabarov's troops. Under strict orders to capture rather than kill the Russians, they were quickly routed by the Tsarist forces. According to Khabarov's undoubtedly exaggerated account, the Ch'ing soldiers killed ten of his troops, while his forces killed 676 of the enemy.[2] The Ch'ing now admitted that they faced a dangerous and not easily intimidated foe and started to prepare a major expedition to oust the Russians. This new military force pursued the enemy detachment, harassing them all along the Amur and Sungari river areas. The Ch'ing policy of withholding grain from the Russians by encouraging the local peoples to leave their homes began to achieve results. The small Russian bands sent to forage for the main detachment returned with meagre supplies. Onufri Stepanov, who had replaced Khabarov as leader of the Russian forces in 1653, encountered greater difficulties than his predecessor and was apparently less capable of dealing with them, even though he 'roved the Amur like a pirate chief and exacted heavy tribute or pillaged the natives'.[3] The Ch'ing, after weakening the enemy in several skirmishes, finally in 1658 unleashed a frontal naval and land assault on Stepanov's forces. The Russian leader and over half of his troops died in the battle; the rest scattered throughout Inner Asia. After their victory, the Ch'ing destroyed the village of Albazin. It appeared that the Russians had been permanently expelled from the Amur region.

The Ch'ing then committed a strategic blunder by withdrawing their troops, instead of maintaining a force in the Amur basin to guard against further Russian incursions. Scholars have offered several explanations for this error. One is that the K'ang-hsi emperor, who ascended the throne in 1661, needed all the troops he could muster to quell disturbances and rebellions elsewhere in the first two decades of his reign. Another is that the court failed to grasp the seriousness of the Russian threat to Manchuria and to the rest of Inner Asia. It still did not realize that the various Russian bands in the Amur area were linked together and that they were connected with the Russian emissaries and officials who were then seeking an alliance with the Mongols west of Manchuria. As a result, it treated each of them as individual 'barbarian' raiders, rather than as representatives of an expanding and powerful empire. Like the Ming court, which remained blissfully ignorant of Tamerlane's power and of his intention to conquer China, the Ch'ing initially had only the haziest notions of the identity and true strength of the empire that confronted them in Inner Asia. Another explanation is that the court believed that the frontier Manchus, whom it had cultivated through the tribute and trade system, were perfectly capable of blocking other thrusts into the Amur region by themselves.

The Russians took advantage of the Ch'ing neglect of the frontier to re-enter the area from which they had so recently been expelled.

Russian adventurers and outlaws, not government-sponsored explorers or colonizers, initiated the renewed colonization. Late in the 1660s, Cossack bands, fleeing from Russian justice, settled in Albazin and established an outpost to which they could repair after periodic forays in Manchuria. They raided the local population and generated such hostility that, fearing reprisals from the Ch'ing, they sought and received pardons and official recognition from the Tsarist government. By cultivating the land outside the town and developing salt and iron industries they showed that they intended to stay. The construction in 1666 of the town of Selenginsk on the Selenga River, north of the area inhabited by the Eastern Mongols, was another striking indication that the Russians meant to remain in Inner Asia and to press for greater influence and control in the Amur region.[4] The Ch'ing now began to realize that the Russians were much more serious adversaries than they had earlier believed.

At the very same time, Gantimur, a local chieftain who in name was a vassal of the Ch'ing court, defected to the Russians in the town of Nerchinsk. From the Ch'ing standpoint, this defection set an appalling example to the frontier Manchus, who were supposed to protect the border and offer tribute. It also set a dangerous precedent, for it meant not only a loss of furs and other tribute articles but a threat to the entire system of Ch'ing relations with Inner Asia.

The Ch'ing could not devote resources to the Amur region until 1682. The court had to contend with a major rebellion in China. Wu San-kuei, one of the three principal rebels, had earlier been instrumental in paving the way for the Manchu conquest of China, but he now sought to found his own purely Chinese dynasty. This rebellion, known as the 'War of the Three Feudatories', lasted for almost a decade (1673–81) and, together with other minor uprisings and efforts to restore the Ming, prevented the court from dealing with the Russian intruders.

After the pacification of the rebels, the Ch'ing could finally act in the Amur region. In a letter dated 28 October 1683, the emperor explained to the Tsar his objections to the Russian presence in the Amur area and, by extension, in all Inner Asia: '[Russians] have, without a reason, invaded our . . . frontier, disturbed and injured our hunters, boldly engaged in robbery, and repeatedly harboured our fugitives, Ken-ti-mu-er [Gantimur] and others. . . . Although We had warned those reprobates repeatedly, they still had not shown the least scruple in violating the law.'[5] The court was also perturbed because the Russians offered asylum to Chinese criminals. Yet the Ch'ing provided sanctuary for dissident Russians and treated captured Cossacks extremely well. Even more surprisingly, China and Russia traded with each other throughout this time of tension and the succeeding period of armed conflict. Chinese silks, porcelains, rhubarb, and tea reached Russia while furs from Russia's domains arrived in China. It should be noted, however, that various middlemen, in particular merchants from the region of Bukhara, conducted the trade, the Chinese and the Russians rarely having direct contact, and that the caravans traversed the traditional Central Asian route. The Manchus may not initially have realized that their antagonists in the Amur area shared the same nationality and culture as the Russian and Bukharan merchants in Siberia and Central Asia.

By 1682, the court could concentrate its efforts on the Amur area. It sought first to remove the Russians. A secondary objective was to exclude Chinese colonization from Manchuria, an old policy on which the court was more firmly resolved than ever after such Chinese-led rebellions as the War of the Three Feudatories. The court started to make elaborate preparations for an attack on the Russian positions as soon as it had pacified the rebels within China. A reconnaissance mission undertook to explore how the Russians at Albazin could be overcome. After several months of travel through Manchuria, it returned with recommendations concerning the best route for an invading army, and the naval and land forces, weaponry and supplies that it would need. The court deliberated over these recommendations and, after numerous disagreements and disputes, finally settled on a policy. It recruited the bulk of its military forces from the frontier Manchus, leaving much of its army in China intact. It improved the transport and communications between China and the Amur region, constructed warships in Manchuria, created military colonies along the route to Albazin to furnish provisions for the expedition, and established bases and stockades for the support of its troops and for the speedy conveyance of official mail. Part of the strategy was to cut off supplies to Albazin and to prevent the settlers from growing their own food.[6]

The emperor appointed Sabsu, one of the members of the reconnaissance mission, to carry out this strategy. Yet even at this late stage he attempted to avoid outright war. He sent several letters to the Tsar, demanding the withdrawal of the Russians from the Amur and the end of Russian harassment of the frontier Manchus. Having received no reply, he ordered his troops to attack Albazin.

After some delay, the Ch'ing troops laid siege to Albazin in June 1685. They surrounded the town, placed their cannons, and were about to set fire to the wooden walls surrounding the fort when the Russian commander, recognizing the hopelessness of his position, surrendered. The Ch'ing troops permitted him, his soldiers, and his settlers to leave safely for the Russian town of Nerchinsk and granted the requests of some of the Russians to settle in China. Though the Ch'ing obliterated the town, the court did not maintain a force so far removed from the Chinese border. It expected that the frontier Manchus would prevent further incursions on its soil by the Russians. But Ch'ing expectations were ill-founded, for the local peoples on the frontiers could not cope with the invaders. Within a few months, the Russians returned from Nerchinsk and re-established their base at Albazin. Again, in 1686, the Ch'ing dispatched an army to besiege the town. The siege lasted for almost six months but was lifted when the Russians informed the Ch'ing emperor that an ambassador would arrive shortly to seek a negotiated settlement.

The conflict was peacefully resolved because both sides wanted to avoid war. Neither stood to gain from a prolonged conflict in the Amur region. The Russian court recognized that transport, supply, and personnel problems excluded the possibility of large-scale colonization in the area. It had faced little opposition in its expansion into Siberia but encountered a formidable foe along the Amur. The supply lines to Siberia were not well established. Even though the Russians coveted the grain resources and the mineral wealth of the Amur region, the hazards of an armed confrontation with the Ch'ing precluded such a risky venture.

The Tsarist court also feared an alliance of the Eastern confederation of Mongols, the Ch'ing, and the Western Mongols against them. The Eastern, or Khalkha, Mongols had demanded for some time that the Russians abandon the town of Selenginsk and were poised to attack the settlement. The Dzungars, occasionally in alliance with the Kirghiz, threatened some of Russia's Siberian possessions. So the Tsarist court was eager for a rapprochement with the Ch'ing if only to concentrate its efforts on the defence of the lands which it already occupied. Russian troops could not at this time defend both Siberia and the Amur region. Therefore the Russians were willing to renounce their claims in the latter territory in order to consolidate their strength in a land where they faced less opposition.

The Russians also sought to establish trade relations with China.

111

They coveted such Chinese products as silks, tea, porcelain, and rhubarb and were ready to relinquish their position in the Amur region in return for commercial privileges. As long as the Ch'ing permitted Russian caravans to enter China, the Tsarist court would not badger the frontier Manchus. Trade with China was much more profitable than defence of isolated Russian settlements along the Amur.

The Ch'ing, too, wished to avoid warfare with the Russians. Court officials recognized that they would be hard-pressed to maintain a large military force in the Amur area, which would be costly and might prove ineffective against a concerted effort by a powerful empire. Yet the Ch'ing court still feared that the Russians might contest its control of the local peoples along the Amur, particularly after the defection of Gantimur. One way of preventing the Russians from demanding tribute from the local peoples was to grant them tribute and trade privileges in return for a promise not to interfere in the affairs of the Ch'ing and to leave the local inhabitants of the Amur region alone. Since the Ch'ing coveted such Russian goods as furs, this concession did not necessarily damage China's economy. Indeed, trade with Russia could, if regulated, be extremely beneficial to the court.

THE MONGOLS, RUSSIA, AND CHINA

The Ch'ing fear of a Russian alliance with the Dzungar Mongols directed against China was the most pressing reason for a rapprochement with the Tsarist government. The Ch'ing court sought to prevent any movement among the various Mongol peoples towards unification. With Russian support the Dzungars would have a good chance of bringing together the other Mongols under their control. This prospect terrified the Ch'ing.

When Altan Khan and some of the Mongol nobility were converted to Buddhism in the late sixteenth century, it appeared that a shared religion would provide a spiritual basis for unity. But this proved to be an illusion, for no single leader with both the spiritual and temporal power to unify the Mongols arose. After the death of Altan Khan in 1582, no Mongol was capable of pursuing his attempt at unification. It is true that, early in the seventeenth century, the Dalai Lama had invested a leader of the Khalkha Mongols as the Tushetu Khan to reward him for his conversion to Buddhism, and to enable the newly established Khan to rally the Mongols around him. The first Tushetu Khan built the great Buddhist temple at Erdeni Juu, near the traditional Mongol capital of Karakorum, perhaps intending it to be a national temple. But the Mongols did not turn to him for leadership during the last years of the Ming dynasty.

The Manchus exploited the disunity of the Mongols to conquer some and to incorporate others as vassals. Ligdan Khan, a leader of the Chahar Mongols of Inner Mongolia who was the last direct descendant of the Mongol khans of the thirteenth century, was the first major chieftain to fall to the Manchus. Ligdan, an enthusiastic Buddhist who built many temples and monasteries, attempted to unify the Mongols, but his greed for the lands and wealth of others and his bullying of less powerful chieftains alienated the very groups whose support he sought. Many Mongols joined the Manchus in attacks on his territory, which resulted in his flight to the west and his death in 1634. His son readily submitted to the Manchus in the following year,[7] leaving them in control of most of the Mongols of Inner Mongolia. The death of the last descendant of the Mongol khans meant that later so-called khans would be self-chosen. Their lack of a recognized claim to the khanate may be another reason why none of them could unify the Mongols.

The Khalkha Mongols, who lived north of the Gobi desert in Outer Mongolia, were divided into at least five different territorial units at various times in the seventeenth and early eighteenth centuries. The Tushetu Khan, whose title was granted by the Dalai Lama, ruled much of northern Mongolia, including the developing town of Urga. His principal opponent among the Khalkha, the Zasagtu Khan, claimed the title of Khan for himself and controlled the area in western Mongolia along the Khangai Mountains. The Setsen Khan governed most of eastern Khalkha, and his people roamed around the Kerulen River basin. In 1725, the Sain Noyan Khanate was created out of part of the territory of the Tushetu Khan. The last of the major khanates did not survive after the seventeenth century. Its rulers, who adopted the title Altan Khan but had no connection with the Altan Khan who patronized Buddhism in the sixteenth century, controlled north-western Mongolia and were the first of the Mongol chieftains to have diplomatic relations with the Russians.

The Western Mongols were also divided into numerous groups. The Dzungars, who inhabited an area stretching from western Mongolia to the Dzungarian basin in Central Asia, began to accumulate power and territory early in the seventeenth century. Their chieftain Kharakhula received a royal title from the Dalai Lama for his help in defeating the latter's rivals in Tibet, and, using this title to help legitimize his actions, the Dzungar leader moved to overwhelm his rivals among the Western Mongols. One of these groups, the Torguts, fearing for their very survival, slowly migrated to the west until they reached the Volga River. In 1672, Ayuka, one of their princes, asserted his leadership over the Torguts. Unification of the tribes strengthened their defences against neighbouring Russian settlements. The Khoshuts, another tribe whom the Dzungars forced to leave their homeland, followed their leader Gushri Khan to Tibet, where they assisted the Dalai Lama against his opponents. They were so successful and dominant that Gushri became for a time the real ruler of Tibet.

Some of the Khalkha tribes attempted to use Buddhism to achieve hegemony over the rest of the Mongols. The Tushetu Khan of the mid-seventeenth century was the most ardent advocate of such a policy. He and the other chieftains sought to suppress shamanism and championed Buddhism. In 1639, he persuaded the khans of the Khalkha Mongols to accept his son as the 'Living Buddha', or the Jebtsundamba Khutukhtu.[8] Such acceptance by the major potentates of the Eastern Mongols assured the Khutukhtu of religious authority throughout eastern Mongolia. His success in winning and maintaining the support of the quarrelsome political elites of the Khalkha was due to their desire to escape the religious domination of a foreigner, the Dalai Lama. The khans feared that the spiritual mastery of the Dalai Lama might lead to Tibetan political control, and so they created their own religious authority. The Khutukhtu's residence, later known as the town of Urga, became the first big town and the religious and political capital of Outer Mongolia. Though the Khutukhtus secured the loyalty of the Mongols, the Tushetu Khans who had originally sponsored them could not exploit this opportunity to unify Mongolia.

In 1640, the Eastern and Western Mongols convened a meeting to discuss the possible unification of their lands. Their leaders, however, could not agree on any one chieftain around whom they could all rally. They devised a code of laws and pledged aid to any member attacked by outsiders, but the agreement was not taken seriously. Over the next half-century, succession crises and conflicts among the Khalkha Mongols wrecked further efforts towards an alliance. A succession dispute arose in 1661 after the death of the Zasagtu Khan. The Tushetu Khan became embroiled in the struggle and alienated many people in the neighbouring khanate. The conflict between the two khanates continued through the latter half of the seventeenth century and weakened both of them. Of the other two Khalkha khanates of the seventeenth century, the Altan Khanate declined from the 1630s onwards, and the Setsen Khanate faced grave succession problems in the 1680s. The Tushetu, Zasagtu, and Setsen Khans were thus relatively weak when faced with threats from the expanding Ch'ing, Russian, and Dzungar empires.

The Ch'ing court was naturally delighted with the disunity and the resulting weakness of the Khalkha Mongols. This was just what all rulers of China wanted in Mongolia. The Ch'ing court did not need to do anything to apply its policy of 'divide and rule', but simply took advantage of the divisions among the Mongols to enrol them as vassals. As early as 1637, before the Manchu conquest of China, the Mongols offered tribute to the Manchus.[9] Horses, camels, and furs were, as in the Ming period, the main tribute items, and the Manchus reciprocated with gifts of silk, grain, and tea. The Mongols' desire for trade certainly lessened their hostility to the Ch'ing. Yet the Setsen and Tushetu Khans joined together on several occasions in the 1640s to harass the new Ch'ing state, though the death of a particularly warlike Tushetu Khan in 1655 and the succession of his less aggressive son reduced the tension. A normal tributary and trade relationship developed which suited the Ch'ing, for it provided them with prized Mongol products while securing their borders against attacks from the Khalkha tribes.

The Ch'ing also sought to control the Khalkha by promoting the establishment of fixed territories for the Mongol tribes. A reduction in the range of Mongol nomadism might make it easier for the Ch'ing to stabilize the area. The creation of khanates with relatively stable boundaries meant that specific chieftains could be held responsible for incursions on Chinese soil launched from their territories. One of the main stimuli to a more sedentary life was the growth of Buddhist temples and monasteries. The Erdeni Juu monastery, built in the late sixteenth century, was the first of these. The Jetsundamba Khutukhtu's settlement at Urga, the second, promoted the slow but steady urbanization of Mongolia. A whole community clustered around his palace either to study with him or to care for his needs. Urga soon became a major religious and political centre, attracting many Mongols, Chinese, and, in the nineteenth century, Russians. Its population was not large; as late as 1820, this amounted to seven thousand people, fifteen hundred of whom were lamas.[10] Nonetheless, by Mongol standards, it was a large settlement. Its initial development was no doubt due to its association with the 'Living Buddha', but it was also blessed with an adequate water supply from the nearby Tula River and was shielded by the surrounding Bodgo Ula Mountains (now called Mount Choibalsang) from the bitterly cold winter winds of northern Mongolia. In the eighteenth century, it became an important halting place for caravans travelling from Russia to China and thus attained commercial significance.

The divisions among the Khalkha Mongols and their tendency to live in small villages appeared to reduce the problems that Ch'ing China faced in eastern Mongolia. Sedentary peoples would be less eager to leave their homes for raids on China. Though the Ch'ing did not occupy Khalkha territory and the Eastern Mongols remained independent, it seemed that China need not worry about frequent incursions by them. The Ch'ing and the Khalkha exchanged envoys, and their merchants and officials enjoyed a mutually profitable tribute and trade arrangement. But two other forces, the Russians and the Dzungars, upset this apparently balanced and peaceful relationship.

The Russians tried to reopen relations with the Mongols as early as 1616. In that year, a Russian embassy reached the land of the Altan Khan Sholoi Ubashi of the Khalkha.[11] The Tsarist court instructed the envoys to obtain information about the Mongols and the Chinese, to seek the Altan Khan's aid in repelling the attacks of the Kirghiz in Siberia, and to demand tribute from him. As the Russians began to face stiff competition in the European market from North American furs, they looked to the Chinese as consumers of their furs and sought as much commercial and political information as possible about the Middle Kingdom. The Altan Khan welcomed the Russian envoys and offered them some interesting though somewhat fantastic information about China. He also introduced them to such Chinese products as silk and, on later visits, tea.[12] One explanation for his solicitousness was his hope of securing Russian support against the Western Mongols, including the Dzungars. But the Russians rejected his requests for military aid, for they were simultaneously seeking a peaceful and mutually beneficial economic relationship with the other Mongols. Altan initially reacted to this rebuff by mounting a series of minor raids on Russian settlements and by joining the Kirghiz in harassing Russian colonists in Siberia. These unfriendly acts disrupted relations with the Russians for over a decade, but in 1633 the succeeding Altan Khan, fearing the threat posed by the neighbouring Chahar Mongols and the growing power of the Manchus, courted the Russians with a tributary mission and promised to submit to Russia. In the very

116

next year, he retracted his offer, when the Manchus suppressed the Chahar, reducing the threat to his territory. He permitted one of his subordinates to take an oath of allegiance to Russia but refused to do so himself.[13] Nonetheless, he and his successors maintained generally good relations with the Russians, and the Tsarist court continued to dispatch missions (a total of eleven from 1616 to 1678) to the land of the Altan Khan. Though there were intermittent periods of tension between the Russians and the various Altan Khans, the two sides enjoyed cordial relations until the disappearance of the Altan Khanate, conquered by the Dzungars.

The Russians also wanted friendly relations with the other Khalkha Mongols. They sent an envoy in 1647 to induce the Setsen Khan to accept their overlordship. The Setsen Khan showed some interest in a relationship with the Russians and dispatched his own mission to Moscow. Shortly thereafter, however, he died, and his successor had no intention of submitting to the Russians. Nor were the Tushetu Khans of the early seventeenth century interested in relations with Russia. Their principal concerns were their disputes with the other Khalkha Mongols and the Dzungars and their relations with the Ch'ing dynasty. The other Khalkha Mongols became concerned only when the Russians founded the town of Selenginsk in an area which they claimed for themselves. They dispatched emissaries in the 1660s to demand that the Russians abandon the outpost, but this was refused. The Khalkha sent several expeditions to attack the Russian settlements. Some Soviet scholars insist that the Ch'ing instigated these raids, but there is no evidence that the Ch'ing had that much influence on the Mongols at this time.[14] In any case, weakened by internal divisions, the Mongols could not oust the Russians. In 1685, for example, they laid siege to Selenginsk, but soon withdrew. By the end of the seventeenth century, therefore, the Russians and the Khalkha Mongols were at loggerheads.

The Ch'ing did not need to worry about assistance from the Khalkha to the Russians in the Amur area. In fact, a Khalkha alliance with the Ch'ing appeared likelier. Even if the Khalkha turned against the Ch'ing, they could not seriously threaten them, and it was not fear of the Khalkha that caused the Ch'ing to end their armed conflict with the Russians along the Amur.

One of the principal forces that prodded the Ch'ing and the Russians into reaching an agreement was, however, the Dzungars. They had played an important role in East and Inner Asian politics since the rise, in the early seventeenth century, of their chieftain Kharakhula, who had conquered the lands of the other tribes in western Mongolia, forcing the Khoshuts to flee to Tibet and the Torguts to flee to the Volga and subduing the Derbets. We have seen how he sought to suppress shamanism and promote Buddhism, hoping to use the new religion to foster unity among his own people and the other Mongols. His support of the Lama Jaya Pandita (1599–1662) was further evidence of his desire for the success of Buddhism. Jaya Pandita preached among the Dzungars, translated numerous Buddhist texts from Tibetan into Mongolian, developed an improved Mongol script for Oirat writings, and urged the eradication of shamanism. Kharakhula also nurtured Buddhism by constructing temples and monasteries and promoting the translation of texts and the training of lamas.

His most important objective, however, was the transformation of the Dzungars from a purely nomadic into a more sedentary society. He built a capital in western Mongolia, encouraged the development of agriculture, and imported Russian craftsmen to assist in construction projects and to train apprentices among his own people. By the time of his death in about 1635, his people were beginning to settle down.

Disputes over succession and conflicts with other Mongols hindered this process. In 1670, Kharakhula's grandson, by name Sengge, was murdered by a jealous older brother, an event that prompted a seven-year struggle for power. Galdan, another of Sengge's siblings, had been studying to become a lama in a Tibetan monastery. On learning of Sengge's death, he vowed to avenge his brother, returned to the land of the Dzungars, and set about gaining power. He rapidly defeated his older brother, but it was not until 1677 that he over-whelmed his last opponent. He continued his father's policy of promoting agriculture and manufacturing and craft industries. Contemporary Chinese and Russian sources indicate that Dzungar farmers raised wheat, millet, and barley and that Dzungar craftsmen produced articles of leather and cloth.[15]

Galdan was eager to lead a movement for Mongol unity which might also include other Inner Asian peoples. He received unexpected support from the fifth Dalai Lama of Tibet. In 1643, the Dalai Lama, with the support of Gushri Khan of the Khoshut Mongols, had crushed his religious rivals and achieved dominance for the Yellow Sect of Buddhism over all its rivals. Gushri was the real ruler of Tibet, but his successors were nomads and lacked interest in running the country. In the 1650s power reverted to the Dalai Lama who at first responded favourably to Ch'ing overtures. The Ch'ing wished to cultivate good relations with him, hoping that he might persuade the Buddhist Mongols to accept their sovereignty. They prevailed on him to visit Peking in 1652, but this trip did not persuade the Mongols, in particular the Western Mongols, to submit.[16] In fact, the Dalai Lama himself was not submissive. He supported Galdan, and his natural son, who succeeded him in 1682, bestowed the title of Boshugtu Khan (Khan of Divine Grace) on Galdan. This sixth Dalai Lama, and the regent who ruled in his name, remained anti-Ch'ing throughout his reign (from 1682 to 1705).

It was with the support of the sixth Dalai Lama that Galdan expanded into Central Asia. But Galdan did not reach the distant areas of Central Asia and only moved against the oases near the Chinese border. The more distant regions and towns (Samarkand, Bukhara, Herat, and others) had lost contact with China in the sixteenth century. As the Ming dynasty declined and turned its attention to the Mongols and Manchus, the rulers in these areas became disenchanted with China. As Joseph Fletcher has written, 'Central Asia . . . remained little concerned with China, and by the end of the Ming dynasty Central Asians saw China mostly as a distant empire, a market partly dependent on Central Asian commerce, and an enormous body of heathen whom Muslims would some day convert.'[17] Many of these towns and formerly powerful empires were themselves in a state of decline, and such new empires as Moghul India, Tsarist Russia, and Ottoman Turkey had as much to offer them as China, if not more. By early Ch'ing times, their relations with China were minimal.

Among the towns and oases near the Chinese border, the influence of Turfan had waned considerably. That oasis, under the leadership of the Moghul chief Mansur, had controlled many of the towns in eastern Turkestan in the sixteenth century and had forced the Ming dynasty to renounce its claims in some of these areas. Mansur's death, however, was followed by a struggle for the succession among his sons and incursions by Kazakh tribes seeking to profit from these dynastic conflicts. From the late sixteenth century onwards, the Moghul rulers lost influence and power. The White Mountain and Black Mountain Khojas, both of whom traced their descent to Muhammad and were considered holy men by the inhabitants of east Turkestan, replaced the Moghuls as the wielders of political power.

119

There was great hostility even between these two religious figures, who belonged to the Sufi order of Islam known as the Naqshbandiyya, and such conflicts immobilized and weakened the state. The White Mountain Khoja, forced to flee by the attacks of his rival, appealed for assistance to the Dalai Lama, who, in turn, urged Galdan to lead his troops into east Turkestan. The Dzungar chieftain, who probably required little prompting, invaded and, with the aid of the White Mountain Khoja, conquered Hami, Turfan, and other oases in 1679.

The Russians could not avoid noticing the expansion of the Dzungar empire. According to a recent study, they had been in touch with the Dzungars at least since 1607.[18] Most of the early contacts between the Russians and the Dzungars involved trade, and neither people knew much about the other until the middle of the seventeenth century. By that time, Russian settlers had reached areas into which the Dzungars were also beginning to expand. It appeared that a clash was imminent. Conflicts over boundaries, the collection of tribute from subject peoples in Siberia, commercial quarrels, and disputed rights of settlement in certain areas created tensions which occasionally erupted into minor battles. The Dzungars, together with the Kirghiz tribes, repeatedly attacked Russian settlements in Siberia in the 1670s and 1680s, even though trade between the two peoples continued to flourish. The Russians, who had already alienated the Ch'ing and the Khalkha Mongols, feared a Dzungar-Ch'ing-Khalkha alliance directed against their settlements in Siberia and among the Buryat Mongols.

Their fears were unfounded, however, for innumerable conflicts divided the Ch'ing and the Dzungars. Ch'ing diplomacy towards the Mongols aimed at preventing the rise of unified and aggressive tribes and ambitious rulers, and the Ch'ing court's economic policy was directed at controlling tribute and trade relations for its own profit. The rise of Galdan threatened the system which the Ch'ing wished to impose on their neighbours. The Ch'ing, of course, noticed Galdan's acceptance of a royal title from the Dalai Lama and realized that this gave him an aura of legitimacy among the adherents of Lamaist Buddhism. Still preoccupied with the War of the Three Feudatories in southern China, however, the Ch'ing were unable to prevent Galdan from soliciting and receiving the support of the Tibetan religious leader. They also appeared incapable of ending Galdan's increasing involvement in the affairs of the Khalkha Mongols, which ran counter to the Ch'ing policy of isolating the various peoples of Mongolia.

Economic relations between the Dzungars and China were the first

area of friction. Galdan and the K'ang-hsi emperor of China exchanged a few missions, and the Dzungar ruler, who traded with such
distant states as India and Russia without restrictions, wished to
expand his trade with China. He demanded that the Ch'ing permit
Dzungar embassies of several thousand people to enter China, but
the Ch'ing allowed only two hundred men from each mission to cross the
Chinese border.[19] Like the Ming court, which attempted to limit the
number and size of missions from the Oirat chieftain Esen, the Ch'ing
dynasty tried to restrict the embassies of Galdan. The court argued
that caring for such large missions would entail enormous expenses
and would nullify gains derived from tribute and trade relations. It
desired and needed the horses, camels and sable skins that Galdan's
merchants and envoys offered, but was unwilling to bear what it
believed to be unreasonable costs. Like his fifteenth-century predecessor Esen, Galdan was enraged by the court's restrictions and
sought an opportunity to take his revenge on China.

Tensions among the Khalkha Mongols gave him his chance. In the
early 1680s, the Tushetu and the Zasagtu Khanates were embroiled
in a dispute over fugitives. The Zasagtu Khan demanded the extradi-
tion of fugitives from his khanate who had sought asylum with the
Tushetu Khan, but his request was rejected. Some scholars have
suggested that disputes over grazing land and trading rights with
China and Central Asia exacerbated the hostility between the two
khans. The Jebtsundamba Khutukhtu, or Living Buddha, supported
his brother, the Tushetu Khan, in this conflict, while Galdan, whose
nephew was related by marriage to the Zasagtu Khan, favoured the
other side. Galdan, like Chinggis Khan and Esen, wished to unite
Mongolia under his rule, and his support for the Zasagtu Khan was
the first step towards this ambition and a definite threat to the Ch'ing.

The Ch'ing court now reversed its traditional policy of dividing and
ruling the Khalkha Mongols. It attempted instead to create a unified
state among the Eastern Mongols, which could serve as a buffer
against both Galdan and the Russians. The K'ang-hsi emperor
therefore sought to resolve the conflict between the Tushetu and
Zasagtu Khans. He urged the Dalai Lama to reconcile these two
devout adherents of the Yellow Sect. After some hesitation, the
Dalai Lama consented in 1684 to send an emissary to a conference
convened by the Ch'ing for the Mongols. His envoy died en route,
however, and the conference was delayed until October 1686, when
he dispatched another emissary. The Tibetan envoy joined a Ch'ing

official named Arani, the Jebtsundamba Khutukhtu, the Khans, and some Dzungar observers at the meeting, a convocation which to all outward appearances was a success. The Zasagtu and Tushetu Khans seemed to resolve their differences, and the only unpleasant aftermath was Galdan's charge that the Khutukhtu had not shown sufficient respect for the Dalai Lama's representative. He asserted that the Living Buddha sat on a throne similar to that provided for the Tibetan envoy and was rude to the latter.[20] This accusation was in fact a pretext for his own future involvement in Khalkha affairs.

Galdan complained to the Ch'ing court and to the Tushetu Khan, the Khutukhtu's brother, about the Living Buddha's behaviour. To underscore his displeasure, he sent his younger brother in the summer of 1687 to the Zasagtu Khan to prepare for an invasion of the territory of the other Khalkha chieftain. The Tushetu Khan appealed to the Ch'ing for permission to attack his two rival Khans. The Ch'ing, unwilling to drive the Dzungars into an alliance with the Russians against them, were not eager for a war with Galdan and turned down the Tushetu Khan's proposal. Nonetheless, the Tushetu Khan attacked the Zasagtu Khanate late in 1687 and killed its Khan. This gave Galdan of the Dzungars a pretext for reprisal. The K'ang-hsi emperor tried to prevent a conflict by bringing Galdan and the Tushetu Khan together for a conference. The Khalkha ruler attended, but Galdan refused the invitation.

Early in 1688, Galdan launched his invasion of the Khalkha territories. By early spring, he had captured the famous monastery of Erdeni Juu and driven the retreating Khalkha forces to the south-east towards Inner Mongolia. Galdan's victory forced the Tushetu Khanate to move its forces far to the south.

The Ch'ing had provided virtually no military assistance to the Khalkha during 1688, even though the Tushetu Khan had asked for aid several times. They were still not prepared to clash with Galdan, who took advantage of the weakness of the opposition to press further east and conquer the lands of the Setsen Khanate of the Khalkha, forcing the inhabitants to flee southward, towards the Chinese border.

The Ch'ing now found a large group of Khalkha Mongols on their frontiers. According to one source, the Tushetu Khan was accompanied by twenty thousand of his subjects, who were joined by a further twenty thousand stragglers soon afterwards. About a hundred thousand Mongols from the Setsen Khanate sought refuge in China, as did an undetermined number of Mongols from the Zasagtu Khanate who did not wish to co-operate with Galdan.[21] Some of the Mongols had at first hesitated to ask the Ch'ing for assistance and asylum. One group proposed moving into Russian, rather than Chinese, territory. The Jebtsundamba Khutukhtu, who opted for China, carried the day against them. He argued that his people shared the religion, Buddhism, and some of the customs of the Chinese, whereas the Mongols and the Russians had little in common. He might have added another significant consideration: the Mongols and the Tsar's subjects in Siberia had been engaged in a minor war for several decades, and it seemed unlikely that the Russians would succour their old enemies. The arguments that the Jebtsundamba Khutukhtu did use made a strong impression, nonetheless, for he was the only figure who commanded the respect of most of the Khalkha Mongols. This was why the Mongol refugees decided to appeal to the Ch'ing for help.

The positions of the four major parties in Inner Asia at the end of 1688 can be summarized as follows.

The Khalkha Mongols were a disunited and dispirited group who had been driven from their homeland by the Dzungar Mongols. Their inability to achieve a 'united front' among themselves or with the Dzungars had cost them dear. Having had serious conflicts with the Russians over Selenginsk and other areas in Siberia, they turned to the Ch'ing government for help in recovering their native lands.

The Dzungars, having failed to persuade the Khalkha to submit to Galdan's rule in the name of Mongol unity, and having innumerable disputes with them over pasture land and trading rights, had seized their land. They had the support of the Dalai Lama but needed an alliance with a major Eurasian empire if they expected to win in a war with China. Their relations with the Ch'ing court had soured because of Galdan's insistence on more favourable conditions of trade, his control of the Central Asian oases near the Chinese border, his conquest of the lands of the Khalkha Mongols, and the potential threat which he posed to Chinese frontier settlements. Even though his forces and the Russians had clashed repeatedly in the 1670s and early 1680s, he sought an alliance with the Tsarist court against the Ch'ing.

The Russians wished to protect their colonies in Siberia, establish formal trade relations with China, prevent the Dzungars and the Khalkha Mongols from interfering with their dominion over the Buryat Mongols and their outposts in Siberia, and perhaps retain some influence along the Amur River. The threat of a Ch'ing-

Khalkha-Dzungar entente against their isolated communities in Siberia alarmed them, though there was not the slightest prospect of such a union. Yet they made little effort to forge an alliance with the Dzungars and, even when offered an opportunity to destroy any possibility of a tripartite alliance against them, still rejected Galdan's entreaties for a joint offensive against China. This refusal probably stemmed from an unwillingness to alienate the Ch'ing, who could deny them trade and retaliate with attacks on their settlements in the Amur region.

The Ch'ing wished to safeguard their borders against Mongol and Dzungar raids, oust the Russians from the Amur region, replace them as collectors of tribute from the local peoples, and obtain at the lowest cost Inner Asian and Russian goods which they required. They too feared a conspiracy of their neighbours against China. The Khalkha Mongols were too weak and disunited to threaten China. The Ch'ing's greatest fear was of a Dzungar-Russian alliance, but it was not realized.

When we examine their interests, it is not surprising that the Russians and the Ch'ing finally concluded an agreement concerning Inner Asia. Each wanted to avoid war with the other. Both were apprehensive of the threat posed by the Dzungars, and neither wished to form an alliance with Galdan. The Russians sought trade with China, and the Ch'ing coveted certain Russian goods. The Ch'ing wanted to maintain their supremacy in the Amur region, while the Russians, recognizing that they could not at that time hold both Siberia and the Amur area, were willing to abandon their settlement in that territory in return for Ch'ing concessions on trade or other issues.

A SETTLEMENT: NERCHINSK AND ITS AFTERMATH

There had been several Russian missions to China since the early seventeenth century, and most have been exhaustively studied and written about. Most writers have maintained that the Ch'ing and Chinese treatment of the envoys and their attitude towards foreigners in general showed the rigidity of their foreign policy and their ignorance of the outside world. My view is that Ch'ing policy towards the Russians and the peoples of Inner Asia was often pragmatic and flexible. The successful outcome of their negotiations with the Russians in 1689, and again in several diplomatic exchanges in the eighteenth century, was due in large part to their ability to adapt their tactics to their objectives. After all, the Ch'ing rulers maintained their system of international relations and attained their goals in Inner Asia for almost two centuries, until the middle of the nineteenth century.

Ivan Petlin, who reached Peking in September 1618, was the first Russian to reach the capital of China. His instructions were to explore possible routes to China and to obtain commercial, political, and military information about the Middle Kingdom; he was not empowered to negotiate, nor was he sent as an official envoy. The Siberian governors, who furnished supplies for him and his men, gave him furs for his expenses, but did not provide him with gifts for the rulers of Inner Asia and China. The Inner Asian chieftains through whose lands he travelled, nonetheless, gave him a friendly reception, and the Altan Khan of the Khalkha even provided escorts for the mission.

The Chinese response to his arrival was neither surprising nor inflexible. Court officials allowed the group into China and met Petlin on several occasions. Their refusal to grant him an audience with the emperor was not unreasonable, since he had no diplomatic credentials nor had he brought gifts from the Tsar to the Chinese sovereign. As this was the Ming court's first contact with Russia, the Chinese needed more information before they could decide their policy towards it. The Chinese officials doubtless sought to find out about Russia from Petlin, and the Wan-li emperor entrusted the Russian envoy with a letter to the Tsar, inviting the Russian court to dispatch more emissaries and to engage in trade.[22] In sum, the Chinese court was cautious but friendly. It was not at all rigid, and it tried to remedy its ignorance of Russia.

Petlin returned to Russia with a report on his travels, the first serious account of China available to the Tsarist court. Unfortunately, since no one at the court possessed the knowledge of Chinese necessary to translate the emperor's letter, half a century elapsed before the Russians had a reliable translation of the invitation. Over thirty years passed before the Russians sent another mission to China, for they temporarily turned their attention to the colonization of Siberia while China underwent dynastic difficulties which led to the downfall of the Ming.

In 1653, the Russians, now feeling secure enough in Siberia, sent Fedor Baikov as their official ambassador to the new and vigorous Manchu dynasty in China, of which they had learned. Baikov's principal objectives were to establish trade relations with the Middle

Kingdom, study the China market, and report on Chinese goods of interest to Russia. He was also sent to find out about the military power and the ritual and religious ceremonies of China. He should, if possible, seek full diplomatic relations on the basis of equality.

Attempting to fulfil these tasks and to ensure the smoothest possible reception by the Ch'ing court, Baikov sent ahead a Bukharan merchant named Seitkul Ablin to inform the Ch'ing of his imminent arrival. Ablin, who was not an official representative of the Russian state and was unconcerned with upholding its dignity, apparently followed Ch'ing court protocol and raised no objection to the kowtow and to affirmation of the Tsar's status as a vassal of the Ch'ing empire. He received excellent treatment from the court, but his acquiescence in Ch'ing protocol created insurmountable difficulties for Baikov, who as an official envoy of the Russian government had been instructed to treat the Ch'ing emperor as another sovereign, not as the supreme ruler of the world.[23]

Ch'ing officials, who had approved of the behaviour of the Ablin mission, were bewildered and later offended by the attitude of Baikov's embassy. The Russian envoy refused to abide by the Ch'ing regulations. He did not kowtow on entering the city of Peking and rejected a customary demand to hand his gifts for the emperor to court officials before his audience in the imperial palace. His insistence on personally delivering the gifts to the Ch'ing ruler was regarded by the court as an intolerable act of disobedience. Some historians have viewed the Ch'ing's unwillingness to deal with Baikov as a perfect example of the rigidity and lack of adaptability which eventually, with the irruption of the European powers, led to their decline and downfall. But there was no need to compromise in the seventeenth century, and such conciliation might, in fact, have damaged China's economic interests. A concession to the Russian envoy might conceivably disrupt the court's control of foreign tribute and trade relations and lead to higher costs and fewer gains. It might also persuade the foreign envoys to refuse to abide by Chinese economic regulations. Nor was there any pressing military reason for a change in foreign policy. The Ch'ing had, by that time, pacified the Khalkha Mongols, imposed their own administration in Manchuria, still not faced the Dzungars' threats, and defeated the Russian forces along the Amur.

The contrast between the reception accorded the Baikov embassy and the receptions accorded the next three missions, those of Ablin (1660, 1669) and Milovanov (1670), is instructive. The Ch'ing court welcomed the envoys and permitted them to trade with Chinese officials and merchants. These missions, none of which was headed by ambassadors appointed by the Tsar, basically accepted the Ch'ing system of foreign relations. The Ablin mission of 1660 presented its gifts to the emperor's representatives and did not demand to offer them personally to the emperor. It also conveyed a letter from the Tsar suggesting the establishment of trade relations. The court obtained from Ablin the furs which it coveted and in return gave silk, tea, and other commodities to the Russians. The next Ablin mission, which reached China in 1669, was also extremely successful. The merchant from Bukhara abided by court procedures and restrictions and was rewarded with imperial gifts and permission to trade. He brought several thousand furs as gifts and as trade goods, receiving silk, precious stones, and textiles from the court. Both sides profited from this transaction and were consequently anxious to engage in further commerce.[24]

Even the incredibly tactless Milovanov mission failed to dampen the enthusiasm for trade. In a letter to the *voevoda* of Nerchinsk, the Ch'ing had requested the return of Gantimur, the Ch'ing vassal, referred to earlier, who had fled to the Russian outpost. The *voevoda*, acting without authorization from Moscow, replied by sending Ignati Milovanov with a letter demanding that the Ch'ing emperor proclaim himself a vassal of the Tsar. Fortunately for Russo-Ch'ing relations and for himself, Milovanov apparently did not translate this inflammatory message. Arriving in Peking in 1670, he was treated to an extraordinarily fine reception. The court repeatedly stressed the value of trade between the two empires. As the author of a recent study has noted, 'most striking was the persistence with which the Ch'ing officials impressed Milovanov with the commercial advantages of the Peking market'.[25] They requested furs in particular, and suggested that China would compensate the Russians with silks, precious metals, and other goods.

Diplomatic relations between the two states appeared to be cordial and about to be mutually beneficial, but this impression is misleading. Ablin and Milovanov were not official representatives of the Russian state, and neither objected to submitting as a private individual to the emperor's authority. A true ambassador, such as Baikov, might not be so amenable. More serious, the Ch'ing court had begun to realize that the Russians on the Amur were of the same nationality as the ambassadors from Moscow and Nerchinsk. In a letter to the Tsar sent at the conclusion of the Milovanov mission, the court asked the Russian government to restrain its subjects in the Amur area and to prevent them from terrorizing the frontier Manchus. The Russians, however, persisted in maintaining their positions in the Amur region.

The tensions that lay beneath the surface erupted during the mission of Nikolai G. Milescu in 1675. The Tsar sent Milescu, a sophisticated, well-educated, and widely travelled Moldavian diplomat, to negotiate a trade agreement with the Ch'ing and to find the shortest and most convenient route possible to Peking. He led the best prepared Russian embassy so far sent to China, for he was accompanied by interpreters of Mongol and Chinese, geographers, experts on Ch'ing affairs, falconers, and even a herbalist.[26] Together with these specialists, the embassy also carried furs, mirrors, watches, and other goods intended to appeal to the Ch'ing. The only apparent obstacle to the success of the mission was that Milescu would not accept a position of inferiority for the Tsar. Reports that a civil war in southern China had weakened the Ch'ing made him even less willing to contemplate any compromise of his principles.

The aims of the two states were incompatible. The Russians wanted proper conditions for trade, recognition of their equality with the Ch'ing government, and the dispatch of Chinese embassies to Moscow. The Ch'ing wanted the Russians to abandon the Amur area, to return Gantimur, and to renounce any claims to tribute from the inhabitants of the Amur region. The resulting impasse led to the disastrous failure of the Milescu mission.

Milescu's embassy encountered one difficulty after another. Rules of protocol and etiquette separated the envoy from Russia from his Ch'ing hosts. Milescu refused to hand over his gifts and letters to anyone other than to the emperor, objected to being treated as a representative of a vassal rather than a sovereign state, and persisted in referring to his gifts as 'presents' rather than 'tribute'. Secret reports from the Jesuits in Peking persuaded him to stand firm at least on the substantive issues. Ferdinand Verbiest, a Jesuit who apparently had informants within the inner circles of the court, kept him informed of the Ch'ing deliberations and plans and, in particular, of the progress of the war in southern China.[27] These reports made him even more determined to pursue his objectives, though he finally relented on court ceremonies. He presented his letters to the designated court officials and performed the kowtow in the presence of the emperor.

Neither side, however, compromised on the crucial issues of commercial relations, boundary disputes, control of the Amur region, and the return of defectors. Milescu and his Ch'ing counterparts resorted to innumerable devices to attain compliance with their demands. They each threatened to suspend trade, believing and asserting that the other side would suffer grievously if deprived of certain foreign imports. The Ch'ing hindered the merchants in Milescu's own mission from trading. With all these difficulties, the embassy never truly had much chance for success, and relations between the two parties deteriorated rapidly. Thus when Milescu presented a set of twelve articles which he hoped would govern future Russo-Ch'ing contacts, the court's reply was, predictably enough, in the negative. The articles covered freedom of travel for merchants, designation of preferred trade routes across both empires, elimination of restrictions on commerce, the proper ways of addressing the Tsar and the Ch'ing emperor, and other matters. Ch'ing officials did not provide a written reply to the document, and Milescu, in return, declined to kneel when receiving gifts from the emperor. This last unpleasant incident further marred relations and led to the dismissal of the embassy.

Some historians have castigated the court for its 'shabby' treatment of Milescu and his fellow envoys and for its rigidity when negotiating with them. Yet the Russians too were unaccommodating. Milescu categorically refused to relinquish Gantimur and gave only vague assurances of efforts to restrain Russians from attacking the local peoples of the Amur region. Since the Ch'ing gained no concessions from him, they had no interest in compromise. The court also faced no military threats from foreign powers which might induce it to adopt a more conciliatory policy. Instead, Ch'ing troops launched an offensive in 1685 and ousted the Russians from the outpost of Albazin. When the Russians returned in 1686, the Ch'ing again surrounded the fort and this time planned to destroy it.

The rise of Galdan and the Dzungar Mongols forced the Ch'ing to modify their policy towards Russia. The court feared an alliance of the Dzungars and the Russians which could prove detrimental and might, in fact, endanger China's security. Peking's realism is again discernible, for it now sought a reconciliation with Moscow. In 1686, when the Ch'ing court learned that a Russian envoy was heading towards China, charged with the task of opening treaty negotiations, it lifted its siege of Albazin. The situation in Inner Asia, in sum, shaped the course of the Sino-Russian rapprochement.

The Russians had selected Fedor A. Golovin to conduct negotiations with the Ch'ing. The two delegations scheduled a meeting in Selenginsk, where Golovin arrived late in 1687 with a force of fifteen hundred men. The outbreak of war between Galdan and the Khalkha Mongols, however, prevented the Ch'ing delegation from approaching the rendezvous. Golovin himself was besieged at Selenginsk by the Khalkha when the Russians refused to abandon their claims to that fort, to the region around Lake Baikal, and to other areas also claimed by the Mongols.[28] Galdan's offensive against the Khalkha Mongols diverted their attention from the Russian menace and permitted the Russian delegation to carry on with its efforts at negotiation. Meanwhile Galdan made overtures for an alliance with the Russians, but the latter, anticipating greater commercial gains from an entente with the Ch'ing, declined the offer.

The stage was finally set for the first serious negotiations between China and a major foreign power in modern Chinese history. The K'ang-hsi emperor dispatched a mission, accompanied by a large army and the Portuguese Jesuit Tomás Pereira and the French Jesuit Jean-François Gerbillon, to Nerchinsk, a Russian town not faced with the same military threats as Selenginsk. Both sides were anxious for an agreement, for reasons of security in the one case and for motives of trade in the other. The Jesuits were clearly helpful during the negotiations, though there is some controversy over their true influence on the two parties. They served as interpreters, for they could converse with the participants in Manchu, Chinese, or Latin. Since the Russian delegation knew neither Manchu nor Chinese and the Ch'ing delegation spoke no Russian, the Jesuits were indispensable.[29] Whether they actually affected the course of the negotiations is a matter of dispute. Pereira kept a diary which yields some fascinating insights into the discussions and shows the Jesuits as playing a big part in them.[30]

Late in the summer of 1689, the two parties concluded the Treaty of Nerchinsk, the first such treaty in the history of modern China. Interestingly enough, the Latin version of the document was the authoritative one, though there were also Manchu, Chinese, Mongol and Russian versions. The terms, by and large, favoured the Ch'ing. The Russians relinquished any claims to the Amur River valley, abandoned and destroyed the town of Albazin, agreed to return all future deserters and fugitives to the Ch'ing authorities (this clause was not retrospective and therefore did not apply to Gantimur, who continued to reside in Siberia), and promised, as did the Ch'ing, to punish any of their subjects who committed crimes of murder and theft and were captured and delivered to them by the other side. Even though the precise boundary throughout Manchuria was not defined and the Russians refused to delineate the Mongolian border, the Ch'ing achieved most of their principal objectives. They conceded that merchants with proper passports could enter China for trade (the clause for which the Russians renounced their territorial ambitions in the Amur region), but commerce had great potential economic value for them as well.[31]

The most significant Ch'ing concession, the actual signing of the treaty, is evidence of the flexibility of the Ch'ing court in its relations with Russia. By this act the court acknowledged the existence of another sovereign state. The tribute system, the cornerstone of traditional foreign relations, denied the equality of other states, precluding the negotiation of an agreement which even hinted that China and other states were on the same level. Yet the Ch'ing court was realistic enough, when faced with the threat of a Russian-Dzungar alliance, to modify its traditional conduct of relations with foreign powers.

The precise mechanism for commerce was ill-defined in the treaty. It remained for a Russian mission to China, led by a Danish merchant named Elizar Izbrandt Ides, to seek clarification of the conditions of trade. The Tsar's government coveted the presumed great profits of the China trade and sought the bulk of Chinese goods for itself rather than for its merchants. It instructed Ides to investigate economic conditions in China and to find out which were the foreign products especially desired by the Chinese and the Ch'ing and the principal Chinese goods available for trade. Ides was also to encourage the Ch'ing to permit Chinese merchants to travel to Russia. The Ch'ing would in this way share the burden of providing supplies and transport for caravans in the Sino-Russian trade. Ides' embassy arrived in Peking late in 1693, and the emperor, again manifesting his realism, granted him an audience and several banquets, even though the Tsar's letter to the court did not follow the prescribed pattern. Ides offered Siberian furs, mirrors, watches, dogs, and handkerchiefs to the emperor, and, in return, apparently received permission to circulate freely through much of the capital city.[32] On his return to Russia, he wrote a detailed account of Chinese music, furniture, customs, and products such as chopsticks, tea, porcelain, textiles, and fruits. This commercial information, which forms a large part of his report, shows that he fulfilled one of his principal objectives. Though he was unable

131

to persuade the Ch'ing court to send its own caravans to Russia, his mission was on the whole successful.

Ides prompted the Ch'ing court to define regulations for trade. In 1694, the Ch'ing decreed that one Russian caravan, consisting of no more than two hundred men (not including merchants), would be permitted to enter the capital once every three years. Initially, this regulation was enforced by border officials, but as the Russians increasingly used a trade route across Mongolia the court turned to the Tushetu Khan for aid in its implementation. The caravans could remain in Peking for up to eighty days to conduct trade under official supervision. Chinese merchants were forbidden to sell iron kettles, swords, knives, bows and arrows, and gunpowder to the Russians. Since the Russians were not official envoys, the court expected them to pay for their own expenses en route, but it provided lodging for them in Peking in the so-called 'Russian Hostel' (E-lo-ssu kuan), which had earlier housed the College of Interpreters, the Ming hostelry for foreigners. By housing the Russians in an official residence, the court could keep a close watch on them and could more readily enforce its regulations. Like the Ming, the Ch'ing court imposed stiff restrictions on trade in order to assure itself of gains from commerce.[33]

The Russian government also attempted to limit merchants for its own benefit. Merchants could accompany the state caravans only if they had a passport granted by the Siberian *prikaz*. They paid a ten per cent. tax on the goods which they transported to China and a ten per cent. tax on the Chinese products which they received in return. They had to follow a prescribed route through Siberia to China, and Siberian officials frequently inspected their commodities and belongings. Certain goods were reserved for government trade and use. The court prohibited private trade in rhubarb, gunpowder, firearms, gold, silver, tobacco, furs, and silk, and devised severe punishments for those seeking to evade such prohibitions. Needing income for its various wars and modernization programmes, Peter the Great's government sought to monopolize commerce in these goods for its own profit.

We are here concerned with Chinese relations with Inner Asia rather than with Sino-Russian trade as such, but a brief survey of the Russian trade will allow us to understand more clearly how the conflict between the Ch'ing and the Dzungars was resolved. Numerous studies of the Sino-Russian commerce have appeared, and the reader may refer to them for more details.[34]

From 1698 to 1718, ten official Russian caravans (one every other year, instead of the prescribed one every three years) reached China. One irritating incident after another plagued relations between the caravans and Ch'ing officials. The Russians clamoured for an increase in the number of the men permitted to enter China in each caravan and demanded higher prices for their goods. They also sought the right to permanent consular representation in Peking.

Perhaps the most important difficulty in Sino-Russian commercial relations was Moscow's inability to control its own merchants. Many of the merchants who accompanied the official caravans traded illegally with Chinese officials and merchants, depriving the Russian government of the income from the Chinese products and from taxes on the traders. Some merchants who coveted additional profits organized their own caravans and entered China with forged credentials. Approximately forty illegal caravans reached China during a period in which only ten official caravans arrived.[35] Probably as many, if not more, merchants brought goods to Urga, where Chinese or Mongol merchants transported them illegally across the border into China. Russian border officials either deliberately ignored these blatant violations of Tsarist court regulations or, in some cases, took part in such illicit commerce. All of these caravans provided stiff competition for the Russian government and flooded the Chinese market with furs, leather, and other previously coveted goods. Prices for most Russian products fell disastrously, and Peking had far too many Russian goods, especially furs. The prices for Chinese goods in Russia to Russian buyers, however, changed little throughout this time.

The Ch'ing government became increasingly dissatisfied with the caravan trade. Caravans were arriving too frequently, and Russian merchants and officials stayed much longer in Peking than the regulations of 1694 allowed. Since the Chinese government and merchants had a surplus of furs, there was no need to encourage further trade with Russia. In fact, some of the caravans caused the Chinese population so much trouble that it seemed wiser for the Chinese government to discourage and limit the flow of Russian merchants. As the author of a recent study notes, officials in China 'announced that trade with Russia was both unnecessary and unprofitable and was therefore to be prohibited'.[36] The Ch'ing court was also perturbed that the Russians still offered asylum to Mongol and Chinese fugitives and deserters in violation of the provisions of the

133

Treaty of Nerchinsk. Since this robbed the Ch'ing government of income from taxes and tribute and prompted other Chinese and Mongols to flee, its concern was understandable. The Ch'ing also resented the Russians' neutrality in the Ch'ing-Dzungar struggle and often accused the Russians of abetting the Dzungars. The Dzungars, first under Galdan and later under his nephew Tsewang Araptan, repeatedly challenged the Ch'ing in Mongolia, Central Asia, and Tibet.

The need for new negotiations between China and Russia was clear. In 1719, after the Ch'ing had refused to admit one embassy and caravan, the Tsar dispatched Lev V. Izmailov to resolve the differences between the two states. The Russians, fearing a total abolition of trade, instructed their envoy to compromise on several ceremonial matters and to elicit commercial concessions from the Ch'ing. They desired complete freedom of trade, with permission for Russian merchants to travel unhindered throughout China and without imposition of customs duties. They also wanted to have consuls in Peking, with jurisdiction over Russian subjects. Izmailov hoped that Lorentz Lange, the first secretary of the mission, would be accepted as the first such consul. The Russian court was willing to grant the same commercial privileges to Chinese merchants in Russia and Siberia.[37]

Fortunately for later historians, Izmailov was accompanied by a Scottish physician named John Bell. Bell kept a diary of the trip which is as invaluable for information about Inner Asia and China as the account of Ghiyāth al-Dīn Naqqāsh, written during the Ming period. He reports that the Izmailov mission left St Petersburg in July 1719 and reached Peking in November 1720. Travelling across Eurasia, the embassy encountered numerous Mongol and Central Asian peoples, including some Dzungars. Though Bell himself found that the Dzungars 'are not such savage people as they are generally represented',[38] the Russians assured the Ch'ing court that they had no intention of joining with the Mongol tribe in attacks on it. They insisted, in fact, that they were constructing forts in Central Asia to defend themselves against the Dzungars. Bell also noted the extensive commerce in the Mongol town of Urga, where Chinese gold, silk, porcelain, and tea were exchanged for Russian furs, leather, and woollen goods. Approaching the Ch'ing border, he was greeted by Tulishen, a Manchu official who had earlier led a Ch'ing embassy to Russian soil. This so-called 'barbarian expert', representative of the type of official whom the Ch'ing sorely needed and on occasion attempted to train, compiled lists of the Tsarist court's gifts and of the names of the men on the embassy and accompanied the envoys to Peking.[39]

Their reception at the court was cordial though their stay was relatively unproductive. The emperor gave several banquets for Izmailov, and Manchu and Chinese officials engaged in lengthy discussions with the Russian envoy. They failed to reach a settlement of the major issues, for the two sides were at cross-purposes. The Ch'ing court was preoccupied with the problems of the borderlands, the Dzungars, and deserters, while the Russians pressed for commercial concessions and an expanded Russian presence through the establishment of a Russian Orthodox church and a Chinese-language school for Russian students in Peking. The Ch'ing negotiators refused to consider other questions before a resolution of the Dzungar and territorial problems. The court did allow Lorentz Lange to remain in Peking, though it declined to refer to him as a 'consul'. Moreover, he encountered innumerable obstacles in attempting to carry out his duties. The court, blaming him for the growing friendship between Peter the Great and the Dzungar leader Tsewang Araptan, harassed him, using every means available to bureaucrats in China. He, in turn, reacted to these rebuffs with greater hostility and what appeared to his Ch'ing hosts to be rudeness. This led to his expulsion from China and to a Ch'ing decision to suspend relations with Russia until other issues had been resolved.

The solution was simple. 'If Russia were prepared to pay the price of noninterference in Central Asia for commerce with Peking, Peking was prepared to pay the price of commerce for Russian noninterference in Central Asia.'[40] The perfect opportunity for such a reconciliation arose after the deaths of the K'ang-hsi emperor in 1722 and Peter the Great in 1725. The new Ch'ing emperor recognized that China had to normalize her relations with Russia if she were to deal with the Dzungars. Peter the Great's successors recognized the folly of flirting with the Dzungars and thus alienating the Ch'ing court. It is not surprising then that the two sides came together.

In 1725, the Tsarist court sent Sava Vladislavich, a native of Herzegovina who had earlier emigrated to Russia, to reach an accord with the Ch'ing government. The Russians were prepared to be extremely conciliatory, and Sava's instructions stressed the importance of an accommodation, allowing him much leeway in attaining this goal. His embassy consisted of priests, geographers, and military men, many of whom had had some experience in China or Inner Asia. The

135

court provided him with lavish presents for the Ch'ing emperor, hoping to win the latter over with furs, clocks, telescopes, and mirrors. Sava prepared himself thoroughly by examining the reports of previous envoys and the records of previous negotiations with the Ch'ing. Having completed all these preliminaries, he set out with over fifteen hundred men for the Middle Kingdom.[41] The embassy reached Peking late in 1726 and started six months of intensive discussions with Ch'ing officials. In the spring of 1727, the negotiations were shifted to the banks of the Bura River close to the Russian town of Selenginsk, where delineation of the frontier could be more readily and speedily accomplished. At the border meetings, one of the Ch'ing negotiators proved intractable and stalled progress towards an agreement. The Ch'ing court finally recalled him, an unusual move for the rulers of China and an indication of how highly they valued a settlement. With both sides eager for a harmonious conclusion of their dispute, the negotiations proceeded smoothly.[42]

In August 1727, the two parties concluded the Treaty of the Bura, and in June 1728, the principal negotiators signed the Treaty of Kiakhta. The former, which was later incorporated in the more inclusive Kiakhta agreements, dealt primarily with the demarcation of the frontier along the Mongol border. Stone markers would mark the border from the Argun River to Kiakhta, a town under Russian control. This provision was a concession to the Ch'ing, for it removed the Russian presence in and threat to Mongolia. It further limited the opportunities for Russian aid to the Dzungars and permitted China a free hand in Mongolia and Dzungaria.

The Treaty of Kiakhta restated the provisions of the earlier treaty but also included articles that favoured the Russians. It granted a special hostel (the previously mentioned E-lo-ssu kuan) for Russian envoys in Peking and approved the construction of a Russian Orthodox church in the same area. A small number of priests would be permanent residents in the Russian compound, and four non-ecclesiastical students would reside in Peking long enough to learn spoken and written Chinese; they would then be replaced by other students. A language school, the first of its kind in Chinese history, was established for the students. The Russians, in addition, received the privilege of a form of extraterritoriality: that is, criminals would be returned to their native lands for punishment. Similarly, each government pledged to return deserters (whether soldiers, ordinary citizens, or criminals) to the other side, and specific methods of execution were prescribed for the subjects of the two states (strangulation for Ch'ing subjects and hanging for Tsarist citizens).[43]

The most important concessions for the Russians, however, were commercial. They retained the privilege of sending caravans once every three years to Peking, with no more than two hundred men who paid for their own expenses and provisions. The old 1693 regulations still applied to the caravan trade. But the Russians were much more interested in a new institution for commerce, the creation of markets on the Ch'ing frontier. The Ch'ing court founded trading marts in the towns of Kiakhta and Tsurukhaitu, the latter of which was situated on the banks of the Argun River and remained relatively insignificant. The Russian government preferred the Kiakhta to the Peking trade because it required less transport and relieved the Tsarist court of the burden of dispatching official state caravans. Russian merchants were not called upon to conduct the trade and to pay for transport and provisions, and the court benefited by collecting tithes and taxes. There was, in time, much evasion of Russian government regulations, but the Russian government still obtained a fairly sizeable profit from the Kiakhta commerce, which almost totally replaced the caravan trade to Peking.

The Ch'ing court too profited from the new commercial arrangements, which prevented large numbers of Russians from entering China or from crossing through Central Asia or Mongolia and saved the expense and difficulty of having embassies and caravans frequently arriving and residing in China for long periods. The border markets in Kiakhta provided China with valuable products at reasonable prices, unaccompanied by foreigners who needed to be looked after at China's expense.

It appears that the Manchus and the Chinese cherished and needed many of the Russian and Central Asian products available in Kiakhta. There were difficulties throughout the eighteenth century in the conduct of commerce at Kiakhta, and on several occasions the Ch'ing court suspended the trade. Merchants and officials evaded the regulations, Siberian officials sometimes harboured Mongol or Chinese deserters or fugitives, and Russian citizens occasionally maltreated or cheated subjects of the Ch'ing court – all of which led the Ch'ing to retaliate by closing the markets. But these interruptions were only temporary, and Russian and Chinese merchants soon gathered again for trade.[44]

In essence, the Ch'ing court gained its principal objectives within the framework of the tribute system. It is true that the government was pragmatic in its application of this system of foreign relations. It treated the Russians as equals by signing several treaties with the Tsarist court in the late seventeenth and early eighteenth centuries. But the Ch'ing obtained, in return, a pledge of non-interference in the affairs of the Inner Asian peoples bordering on China. This no doubt facilitated their efforts to protect their frontiers and to maintain and regulate commerce. Most important, it permitted the court to concentrate on its enemies in Inner Asia and to achieve its objectives there. For over a century after the Treaty of Kiakhta, the Ch'ing enjoyed a respite from Russian threats in Inner Asia and had the time to impose their own system in that territory.

6 The decline of Inner Asia

The agreement of 1728 and the end of hostilities between China and Russia coincided with the beginning of an era of decline in Inner Asia. The glorious days of great nomadic empires had passed. No leaders such as Chinggis Khan and Tamerlane appeared to unite the diverse peoples of the area into a mighty military force capable of engulfing much of Asia. China no longer needed to fear attacks from the neighbouring 'barbarian' tribes. It was now the European 'barbarians' that posed a far greater threat to China's security.

Scholars have offered numerous explanations for the decline of Inner Asia. One is the decreasing value and significance of the caravan trade between China and the West through Inner Asia. By the eighteenth century, the sea routes from Europe to China had superseded the overland routes. This change occurred partly because ocean-going vessels could carry heavy goods much more cheaply than the caravans. As Owen Lattimore has observed, 'caravan trade . . . did not alter the character of societies. With oceanic navigation there began the bulk transportation of raw materials, the processing of which transformed the economic activities and the social and political structure of whole nations'.[1] As naval technology improved, ocean travel became less hazardous than caravan journeys across bandit-infested deserts and mountains. China had to pay ever greater attention to the dangers and demands of the maritime European powers.

Another economic change that accompanied the decline and diminished the threat of Inner Asia to China was the slow but steady development of more sedentary societies there. One after another of the tribes of Mongolia, Manchuria, and Central Asia acquired a fixed territory and lost their willingness to undertake the large-scale migrations of earlier times. The move of the Torgut Mongols from the Volga River area to Dzungaria in 1771 was one of the last such journeys

139

of a major Inner Asian group. The growth of towns in the area further reduced the ability and desire of their settled inhabitants to raid Chinese territory. The Jebtsundamba Khutukhtu's residence in Urga attracted at first numerous lamas, and then, later, merchants seeking to cater for the material wants of the religious community, and the Russo-Chinese trade led to the creation of a major commercial emporium in Mukden in Manchuria. These two types of towns are examples of the trend towards Inner Asian urbanization in the eighteenth and nineteenth centuries, which led to fewer attacks by mobile bands on the traditionally sedentary civilizations.

Limitations on the mobility of the tribes in Inner Asia further reduced their potential threat to China. Before the seventeenth century, the groups along China's borders could raid frontier settlements and flee to remote areas in the vast steppes, deserts, and mountains of Inner Asia, where Chinese armies could not pursue them. With the Russian advance in Siberia and parts of Central Asia, the land to which they could flee and in which they could roam was reduced considerably. The Ch'ing and Russian empires squeezed the Inner Asian tribes into less and less territory, and neither wished to use the tribes against the other. Both had a vested interest in maintaining good relations with each other and in preventing the rise of a powerful state among the Mongols or the various Kazakh, Uighur, and other Central Asian peoples.

Thus, no great leader arose to unify Inner Asia. After the death in the seventeenth century of the last descendant of the house of Chinggis Khan, none of the leaders who vied for power had a true aura of legitimacy. The resulting disunity precluded the possibility of a potent Inner Asian threat to China or Russia. Each of the various peoples in the area grouped around one or more leaders, none of whom attracted a sizeable following, and they remained as separated and isolated units. The Jebtsundamba Khutukhtus, to whom most of the Mongols looked for spiritual leadership, came closest to being leaders of the Mongol people. But though they gained temporal power through the tremendous wealth in land, animals, and metals of the Buddhist church, they never became supreme political personalities capable of consolidating the numerous Mongol peoples and leading great armies.

Some writers have suggested that Buddhism was a principal factor in the decline of the Mongols. The conversion to Buddhism, it is claimed, diverted the Mongols from military pursuits by fostering attitudes of pacifism and quietude. Lamas formed a high percentage of the population and naturally lacked interest in military training. The rest of the population, forced to maintain this large clerical establishment as well as the Mongol princes and nobility, was impoverished and later incurred huge debts to Chinese merchants and usurers merely to supply themselves with the basic necessities. On the other hand, it should be noted that the introduction of Buddhism had not precipitated the decline of other states in East Asia. T'ang China (618–907) and Heian Japan (794 until about the twelfth century), cultures in which Buddhism flourished, were prosperous and powerful empires. So, Buddhism, by itself, was not the cause of the decay of Inner Asia, although, together with the factors already cited, it may have contributed to the decline.

THE PACIFICATION OF THE DZUNGARS

The Dzungars were the last real Inner Asian threat to Ch'ing China. Until the middle of the eighteenth century, they appeared to be cast in the same mould as the other great peoples of the steppes. They had a strong military force with a superior cavalry; they frequently had the spiritual support of the Dalai Lama; they had dynamic, resolute, and honest leaders; and the need for additional grazing land for their animals also gave them a pressing economic motive for their conquest of new territory. Their economic interests clashed with those of a sedentary civilization, Ch'ing China, as the latter sought to control and limit commercial and tributary contacts. The Dzungars bided their time, gradually overpowered neighbouring nomads and oasis states, and maintained correct relations with China almost up to the very time when they finally challenged the Ch'ing.

The principal weakness of the Dzungar empire, and the one that finally destroyed it, was the lack of unity not only among the Mongol people as a whole but also among the Dzungars themselves. As explained in fuller detail in the previous chapter, the Dzungar leader Galdan was the first to encounter this difficulty. By 1689, when he confronted the Ch'ing, he had already conquered eastern Turkestan, including Hami and Turfan, and had gained the support of the Dalai Lama. But he could not attract the Khalkha, the Eastern Mongols, to his cause. In 1688, he defeated them, but their leaders, instead of suing for peace and making common cause with their Mongol brother, fled to China. The Tushetu Khan and the Setsen Khan, as well as the important religious personage, the Jebtsundamba

141

Khutukhtu, sought the protection of the Ch'ing court, which refused to hand them over to Galdan.

The Ch'ing court had just signed the Treaty of Nerchinsk with the Tsarist court; this permitted it to concentrate on the pacification of the Dzungars without fear of Russian support for Galdan. Galdan's repeated attempts to secure an alliance with the Russians failed. The Ch'ing were thus well able to deal with the Dzungar leader and took full advantage of disunity in the Mongol camp. Galdan's nephew Tsewang Araptan broke ranks and withstood his uncle's efforts to bring him back into line, another striking indication of how badly the Mongols were divided. Some historians contend that Tsewang's defection, which led to several armed clashes between him and Galdan, was the most damaging single blow to Galdan's ambitions.[2] Whatever the explanation, Galdan's troops met determined opposition from the Ch'ing in their first military encounter at the Battle of Ulan Butung in 1690. The battle appears to have ended in a stalemate, though the Ch'ing historians claimed a victory. Even more critical, this inconclusive encounter prompted the Khans of the Eastern Mongols to convene a meeting at Dolonnor, where they reaffirmed their status as vassals of the Ch'ing court and paid homage to the Ch'ing emperor, whom they invited to the convention.[3]

These further defections sealed Galdan's fate. After 1690, he retreated to his native land at Kobdo in western Mongolia. Instead of accepting the reconciliation offered him by the Ch'ing court, he continued to prepare for a second offensive against eastern Mongolia and the Ch'ing. He rejected a pardon from the K'ang-hsi emperor and insisted, even from his relatively precarious position, that the Ch'ing deliver the Tushetu Khan and the Jebtsundamba Khutukhtu to him for punishment. The Ch'ing left him alone as long as he remained in his homeland without threatening other Mongol tribes or the Ch'ing borders. Peace reigned until a devastating famine in western Mongolia in 1694 prompted him to undertake an offensive against the Khalkha in the following year. He occupied their lands, and the K'ang-hsi emperor determined at this point to pursue a more vigorous course of action. He set forth at the head of an army of eighty thousand troops to deal once and for all with the Dzungar leader.

Having failed to anticipate such a move by the Ch'ing and having a much smaller army than his foes, Galdan retreated. His pursuers, however, caught up with him at Jao Modo, near the town of Urga, in June 1696. The better supplied and trained Ch'ing force overwhelmed the army of Galdan, who only escaped with a tiny band of about a thousand men. His empire started to crumble, as the inhabitants of eastern Turkestan rebelled against him and re-established their ties with the Ch'ing, while his nephew Tsewang Araptan occupied part of western Mongolia, including the area of Kobdo. Galdan continued to retreat, but he soon recognized that he could not outrun his pursuers. In May 1697, he died, apparently having poisoned himself. Thus ended the first major Dzungar threat to China.[4]

The Ch'ing, however, faced a formidable new foe in Tsewang Araptan, Galdan's successor among the Dzungars. Like his uncle, Tsewang did not immediately challenge the Ch'ing. He wanted to recover from the tremendous losses incurred in the wars with China and to expand in other directions before seeking further military encounters with the Ch'ing. His policy of encouraging agriculture and commerce resembled Galdan's efforts, and, according to Russian accounts, the Dzungars made notable strides in this direction. They might have continued to advance along this course if they had avoided wars with their neighbours.

Instead, Tsewang adopted an expansionist policy. In 1698, he launched his first westward campaigns against the Kazakhs, nomadic tribes of Turkic origin that wandered around Central Asia and along the Russian border. The rulers of the Kazakhs, divided into the Great Horde, the Middle Horde, and the Little Horde, appealed to the Russians for aid, but Peter the Great, distracted by problems in Western Europe and Turkey, rejected their request. This made it relatively easy for Tsewang to encroach on Kazakh lands. Russian passivity also encouraged Tsewang to follow his uncle in seeking an alliance with the Russians, but here he was to be disappointed. Though Peter the Great was willing to trade with the Dzungars, he never totally renounced his policy of preserving his hard-won accommodation with the Ch'ing.[5]

Frustrated in this direction, Tsewang turned to Tibet for an ally. The sixth Dalai Lama, or, more accurately, his regent, had, as I have mentioned, covertly supported Galdan in the Sino-Dzungar wars and still maintained close ties with the Dzungars. The Ch'ing court was eager to have him replaced and was not unhappy when he met an early death in 1705. Lha-bzan Khan, a Khoshut Mongol whose tribe had played a major role in Tibetan politics since the middle of the seventeenth century, lured the Dalai Lama to his home base around Lake Kokonor and had the holy man assassinated.[6] It appears that

Lha-bzan Khan had the support of the K'ang-hsi emperor for this act and for the subsequent enthronement of his own nominee as Dalai Lama in 1707. But this new Dalai Lama was merely a puppet, useful primarily for the Khoshut ruler's political machinations. Lha-bzan Khan thus incurred the wrath of many Tibetan lamas and nobles who had attempted to install their own candidate as the new religious authority and who feared that the Khoshuts favoured the rival Buddhists of the Yellow Sect. Recognizing that they could not dislodge Lha-bzan Khan without outside assistance, they sought the support of Tsewang.

The Dzungars welcomed this opportunity and planned to occupy Tibet. Tsewang's principal objectives were to depose Lha-bzan Khan and to capture a young boy, held by the Ch'ing in an outpost on the Tibetan border, who was considered in Tibet to be the actual re-incarnation of the Dalai Lama. In 1717, he achieved his first objective when his armies overran the Khoshut forces and killed Lha-bzan Khan. He could not, however, expel the Khoshuts from their strong-hold in the Kokonor region. Nor was he able to seize the claimant to the position of Dalai Lama, and his troops damaged their own cause by looting and destroying temples and private residences in Lhasa.[7] Having suffered under both the Khoshuts and the Dzungars, the Tibetan lamas and nobility were now not hostile to Ch'ing intervention in Tibetan affairs.

The Ch'ing unquestionably sought to oust the Dzungars from Tibet. They feared that a new Dalai Lama, under the influence of Tsewang, might incite the various Mongol peoples to unite against China. Almost as soon as the Ch'ing court learned of the Dzungars' conquest of Tibet, it dispatched a preliminary expedition, which suffered a disastrous defeat in 1718. Two years later, two better supplied forces routed the Dzungar armies, recovered the city of Lhasa, and installed their own Dalai Lama on the throne. Shortly thereafter, the Ch'ing court recalled its troops, partly to allay Tibetan fears of a permanent occupation, partly to avoid the expense of maintaining a large garrison in a foreign land, and partly to soothe the Khoshuts, who felt threatened by Chinese troops so close to the Kokonor region. None-theless, a war with the Khoshuts in 1723–24 and intervention in a Tibetan civil war in 1727–28 forced the Ch'ing to place a permanent garrison in Lhasa and to appoint an Imperial resident (*amban*) there. From 1728 until the late nineteenth century, Tibet remained under Ch'ing sovereignty, and the Dzungars lost all influence in the area.[8]

Tsewang still proved troublesome in other regions. In 1713, he had attacked and briefly occupied Hami until a sizeable Ch'ing army expelled his forces. He retreated northward to Dzungaria, thus eluding the Ch'ing troops who were not well enough supplied to pursue him to his home base. Taking this defeat in his stride, he again resorted to a western campaign against the Kazakhs, and this time was so successful that the Little and Middle Hordes accepted Russian overlordship in return for protection from Dzungar attacks. By 1731, the Little Horde were Russian vassals, and in 1740, the Middle Horde also submitted.[9] Tsewang still sought an alliance with the Russians, but, after a brief flirtation and an abortive attempt to make the Dzungars acknowledge Russian domination, the Russians rejected his proposal and in the very year of his death concluded the Treaty of the Bura with the Ch'ing.

Meanwhile the Ch'ing court did not remain idle. It too wished to find allies in its struggle against the Dzungars (yet another example of the old policy of 'using barbarians to regulate barbarians'). The K'ang-hsi emperor attempted, in particular, to persuade the Torguts, a branch of the Western Mongols who had been forced to migrate to the Volga River region by Dzungar encroachments on their lands, to join him in pacifying the Dzungars. He knew that the Torgut Khan Ayuka had married his daughter to the Dzungar ruler, but relations between the two Mongol peoples remained strained. He had a convenient pretext for sending an embassy to Ayuka, since Ayuka's nephew, while on a pilgrimage to Tibet, had been forced to seek asylum within China because of the tense situation in Central Asia. Ayuka asked the Ch'ing to release his nephew, and the emperor, in return, sent an embassy led by Tulishen (mentioned on page 134) to the Torgut ruler. Tulishen left China in 1712 and, after interminable delays during which he waited for permission from Russian officials to proceed, reached the town of Saratov on the Volga River. Here he remained for seven months before Ayuka granted him entry into Torgut territory. The delay was caused by the Russians, who wished to maintain their neutrality in the Ch'ing-Dzungar struggle and feared that an alliance of their nominal vassals, the Torguts, with the Ch'ing might lead them into an unwanted and unrewarding war. They knew that Tsewang was annoyed that their officials in Siberia had permitted Tulishen to negotiate with Ayuka. They therefore told Ayuka to decline any overtures from the Ch'ing envoy.

Tulishen thus failed to conclude an agreement with the Torguts, but he returned with valuable information and observations.[10] His meeting with Ayuka was unproductive. The Torgut ruler explained that the Russians prevented him from effecting an alliance with the Ch'ing, and Tulishen maintained that the journey across Mongolia and Central Asia was at present too hazardous to permit Ayuka's nephew to return. Their conversations were friendly, but Tulishen recognized that nothing could be gained from a protracted stay in the land of the Torguts. He returned to Peking in 1715 and presented a report, the *I-yü lu*, on his experiences and a map of his journey.[11] Both were useful to the throne and indicate that the Ch'ing rulers sought information about foreign lands.

The Ch'ing court was not discouraged by this failure. It encouraged the Khalkha Mongols to resist the Dzungars and occasionally rewarded them for their efforts. Tsereng, a Mongol prince of the Tushetu Khanate, was so helpful that the court awarded him his own Khanate. In 1725, it created the Sain Noyan Khanate out of part of the Tushetu Khanate and made Tsereng the first ruler of the new Khanate. On the other hand, the Ch'ing demanded taxes and labour service from the Khalkha in order to finance their wars against the Dzungars. This policy alienated many Mongol nobles and eventually led to a rebellion in the middle of the eighteenth century.

By 1727, the year of Tsewang's death, the Ch'ing court had, none-theless, isolated the Dzungars, though it did not immediately take advantage of its success. The Dzungars could not rely on aid from the Tibetans, the Russians, or the Khalkha Mongols. In 1730, seeking to profit from the weakened position of the Dzungars, the Ch'ing dispatched one mission to the Russians and another to the Torguts. The envoys hoped to obtain support against the Dzungars, and as a result complied with the regulations of their hosts. They offered valuable gifts and kowtowed to the Tsarist ruler, an indication of Ch'ing treatment of the Russian court as an equal and of its eagerness to gain allies. As Reischauer and Fairbank have noted, 'The Manchu court . . . seems to have been quite prepared to have its representatives perform the ceremonial kowtow (which the Russian court expected of Oriental envoys), just as it expected Russian envoys to perform the kowtow in Peking. This was tantamount to admitting that the supremacy of the Son of Heaven was not world-wide, but was confined to the empire of East Asia.'[12] Within two years, the Ch'ing court sent a second embassy to urge the Russians to provide assistance. These efforts proved fruitless, for neither the Russians nor the Torguts pledged direct military aid. At about the same time the Ch'ing suffered a disastrous defeat in their offensive against the Dzungars. In 1731 a force of ten thousand Manchu and Chinese troops, sent to overwhelm Galdan Tsereng, Tsewang's successor, was routed.[13] Without any allies, however, the Dzungars could not exploit their victory, and in 1738, they negotiated a temporary truce with the Ch'ing by which they pledged to reside west of the Altai Mountains and not to intervene in affairs along the Chinese border.

The Ch'ing court was fortunate indeed that the Dzungars were still hampered by disunity. The old problems of succession crises and internecine warfare reappeared to plague the Western Mongols. Their difficulties were exacerbated by the limited opportunities for expansion. The Russians were now masters of a large part of Kazakh territory, and the Ch'ing controlled Khalkha Mongolia, Tibet, and some of the oases in the Tarim River basin of Central Asia. Squeezed into less and less land by the Ch'ing and Tsarist empires, the Dzungars weakened and were plunged into internal strife. Galdan Tsereng's reign ended uneventfully with his death in 1745, but one of his sons was deposed in 1750 and another in 1752. These *coups d'état* led many Dzungars to flee westward, and some even defected to China.

The Ch'ien-lung emperor, who now ruled China, recognized a good opportunity to eliminate forever the Dzungar threat to China. Weary of the internecine struggles and civil wars, many Dzungar tribesmen fled to Eastern Mongolia or China and accepted Ch'ing overlordship. Among those who defected were the Khoits, a Western Mongol tribe earlier subjugated by the Dzungars. Amursana, one of their leaders, led five thousand of his soldiers, together with their families, into China.[14] These defections further weakened the Dzungars and persuaded the Ch'ien-lung emperor to organize a punitive expedition to the enemy's home base. Promised the title of Khan of the Khoits by the Ch'ing emperor, Amursana joined the Ch'ing force in 1754. Within a few months, the Ch'ing had occupied Dzungaria, encountering little opposition, since many of the enemy troops surrendered peacefully. At this point, Amursana desired greater rewards than those pledged by the Ch'ing emperor. He revolted against him and organized the Khoits and Dzungars under his command for a campaign against the Ch'ing.

The disunity that had plagued the Mongols since early Ming times led to Amursana's downfall. He had counted on an alliance with the Khalkha Mongols, who were also rebelling against the Ch'ing, but the two sides failed to unite. Some of the Western Mongols even deserted Amursana, as the Ch'ing lured them with rewards of military titles and material goods. Deprived of such necessary support, Amursana had no chance of success. Yet he continued to fight and persistently evaded capture. Early in 1756, a large Ch'ing force defeated his troops but could not capture him. Within a few months, he organized yet another rebellion. This time, the Ch'ing emperor sent a capable and evidently ruthless general named Chao-hui to deal with the rebels.[15] Though Chao-hui twice found himself in difficult circumstances, he finally annihilated the opposition by the summer of 1757. Even then, Amursana eluded his pursuers, fleeing first to Kazakh territory and then to Siberia, where he contracted smallpox and died shortly thereafter. The Ch'ing troops demanded his body, but the Russians would only permit them to view the corpse. The Russian refusal provoked a short-lived crisis in Sino-Russian relations which was finally resolved in the 1760s when the Tsarist court returned Amursana's bones.

Many of Amursana's troops met a more horrible end. Chao-hui was under no restrictions and thus butchered any Dzungar captives. One source estimates that he killed half a million Western Mongols during his campaign, though this figure may be too high.[16] The remaining Dzungars either fled to Russia, where they constituted the Kalmyk Mongol community of the nineteenth and twentieth centuries, or to Mongolia, where they blended with the Khalkha.

The Ch'ing emperor was delighted with the final destruction of the Dzungars. He erected two sizeable monuments in Ili, with inscriptions in Chinese, Manchu, Oirat, and Tibetan, to commemorate his victory. One passage of self-congratulation reads: 'Oh, ye people of Dzungaria! . . . For generations in turn you have turned out to be thieves. The mighty ones have robbed the indigent ones, and those many assembled have oppressed those who were few. . . . Now the Daiching [Ch'ing] nation was supported by Heaven. It was not at all the might of men.'[17]

The Muslim communities south of Dzungaria and of the T'ien Shan took advantage of the Dzungars' troubles to seek their own independence. They had been subjects of the Dzungars for most of the time since the White Mountain Khoja had assisted Galdan in occupying their land in 1679. When the Ch'ing first defeated the Dzungars in 1754, the two principal Khojas regained confidence in their power and sought to assert their independence. They took a disastrous step in that direction by killing several Ch'ing envoys who requested tribute from them. The emperor responded by sending Chao-hui to impose Ch'ing rule on these Central Asian oases. The Ch'ing general occupied the towns of Kashgar, Yarkand and Aksu among others and truly conquered the area referred to in the nineteenth century as Sinkiang, or 'New Dominion'. The White Mountain line of Khojas survived only by moving west to Kokand, outside the boundary of their homeland in Kashgaria. Even the Khan of Kokand, recognizing the military might of the Ch'ing, offered tribute to the Ch'ing throne in 1759.[18]

By 1760, the Ch'ing dynasty seemed to be at the height of its power in Dzungaria and Central Asia. It was difficult to conceive of any challenge to China's domination of that area in the foreseeable future. The Ch'ing troops had totally and irrevocably destroyed the Dzungar empire and occupied Dzungaria (or Ili, as it now began to be called). The Ch'ing had also acquired a vast domain in Central Asia, including the nearby oases of Hami and Turfan as well as the distant commercial centres of Aksu and Kashgar. Ch'ing supremacy in most of Inner Asia appeared to be beyond challenge.

But China's strength in the area was illusory. The Ch'ing court had expended enormous financial and military resources in the conquest of Dzungaria. Throughout the first half of the eighteenth century, it mounted several costly expeditions to deal with the Dzungars. These imposed a heavy burden on the Chinese government finances. Perhaps even more critical, the Ch'ing now reversed the Inner Asian policy which had been followed since early Ming times. The first Ming emperor had advised against an expansionist course in Central Asia. Instead, he and his successors adopted the tribute system, frontier markets, and the 'use of barbarians to regulate barbarians' as the means of conducting relations with such oases and towns as Hami, Kashgar, and Samarkand. The annexation of Sinkiang, however, placed tremendous strains on the Ch'ing economy. It required a civil administration and an occupation force and involved a commitment to the defence of the region, whose mixed population of Uighurs, Kazakhs, Kirghiz, Mongols, and many other groups included some who were hostile to China. Paradoxically, the acquisition of more Central Asian territory may have harmed her short-term interests.

CH'ING DOMINATION OF MONGOLIA

The Ch'ing control of Khalkha Mongolia was also a mixed blessing. Ch'ing domination certainly enriched a few Chinese merchants, but it impoverished much of the Mongol population. Seeking to prevent foreign influence and to preserve the existing political and economic system in Mongolia, the court hindered the economic development of its northern territory. It delayed the modernization of Mongolia and bred anti-Chinese feelings among the Mongols.

One of the principal Ch'ing goals was to isolate Mongolia. The Ch'ing emperors attempted to keep the Russians out of the land of the Khalkhas as a defence measure. Though the emperors themselves had little economic motive for this exclusionist policy, it seems clear that Chinese merchants viewed it as a means of limiting competition and of ensuring a monopoly of the Mongol trade. Like the Ch'ing policy towards Manchuria, this course was influenced by military and commercial considerations. The Ch'ing government ordered the creation of Mongol garrisons along the borders to prevent the entrance of Russian officials and merchants. Simultaneously, Ch'ing negotiators attempted to elicit a Russian pledge of non-interference in Mongol affairs. By the Treaty of Kiakhta of 1728, the Russians agreed, in return for commercial concessions, to abandon contacts with the Mongols. And the Russians kept this promise for much of the eighteenth and nineteenth centuries.

The Ch'ing court was also determined to prevent Chinese colonization or intrusion in Mongolia. It required Chinese merchants to obtain licences before they were allowed into Mongolia. The licences expired within a year, by when the merchants had presumably left the country. Restricted to the sale of the items specified in the licences, the merchants were also forbidden to trade in products of any military value. Their other activities within Mongolia were also circumscribed. They were not allowed to own land, construct permanent houses or other buildings (except in Urga), or marry the Mongols. Economic relations with the Mongols were to be brief and closely supervised by Ch'ing and Mongol officials. The Ch'ing court made a valiant effort to stop wily Chinese merchants from taking economic advantage of the less sophisticated Mongols. It sought, in sum, to prevent the disruption of the traditional Mongol economy.[19]

Similarly, Ch'ing officials tried to preserve, within limits, the old Mongol system of administration. They deliberately kept their presence in Mongolia inconspicuous. In 1691, at the Convention of Dolonnor, the Mongol khans had submitted to the Ch'ing throne in return for protection from the Dzungars. The Ch'ing court accepted its new vassals but did not impose an entirely new administrative system on them. It permitted the Mongols to retain most of their own institutions and to maintain their own people in official posts. The Ch'ing court, nonetheless, confirmed the accession of tribal chieftains and insisted that the primary allegiance of Mongol leaders was to the Ch'ing emperor, not to the various khans of earlier days.

The Ch'ing, in fact, attempted to reduce the role and functions of the khans. It ennobled almost seventy other Mongols and awarded them powers equivalent to those of the khans. Ch'ing officials courted the new nobles with gifts, military titles, and princesses. By gaining the allegiance of these nobles, the Ch'ing hoped to curb Mongol raids on China and to obtain assistance in dealing with the Dzungars. The Ch'ing court created a bureaucracy as another means of control. It divided the Khalkha Mongols into a series of Leagues, further reducing the influence of the traditional khanates. The chieftains of the Leagues were Mongols, but they were ultimately responsible to a Ch'ing military official initially based in Uliassutai. From the middle of the eighteenth century, that official administered the affairs of Western Khalkha, while an official in Urga took charge of Eastern Khalkha.[20]

Ch'ing policy was, as one historian of Mongolia has written, 'essentially a conservative and reactionary one'.[21] But the Ch'ing simultaneously developed policies that undermined these main goals. While attempting to retain and encourage the nomadic style of life, it was bringing about major changes in Khalkha. It sought to limit the seasonal migrations of the Mongols in order to facilitate control over them and to recruit troops and collect taxes. By allotting the various Mongol tribes fixed territories and by not permitting them to move across these artificially imposed boundaries, the Ch'ing undermined the traditional economy. The establishment of a stable administration, with an expanding bureaucracy supplying information and revenue to the Ch'ing court, further fostered the breakdown of the old communities and resulted in the growth of towns. Lamaism too was conducive to a more sedentary society. Buddhist monasteries and temples required a nearby supply of food, craftsmen, schools, translators of Tibetan and Chinese texts, and bureaucrats to manage the estates and other property donated to the church by believers or by the government. The Jebtsundamba Khutukhtu himself rapidly became one of the wealthiest individuals in Khalkha, and he and the Lamaist hierarchy were supporters of increased centralization and urbanization.

Though the Ch'ing court was unsuccessful in creating a closed, static society, it appeared to have achieved its other goals in Mongolia. It prevented direct Russian involvement, devised regulations for Sino-Mongol trade and imposed restrictions on Chinese merchants, and lessened the power of such older wielders of authority as the Khans. One would have expected that, by the middle of the eighteenth century, the Ch'ing would have created a stable administration and faced no effective rivals or opposition in Mongolia. Yet this was not the case, and the explanation lies partly in the economic exactions imposed by the Ch'ing on Mongol nobles and commoners.

The Ch'ing court did not actually impose onerous monetary taxes on the Mongols, but it did demand other services that burdened the Khalkha Mongols. Annual tribute missions presenting horses, camels, animal products, and various gold and silver vessels were expected by the Ch'ing. Occasional embassies announcing the death of a major chieftain or the enthronement of a new ruler, or offering congratulations on an emperor's birthday or marriage, were also mandatory. These demands, however, entailed relatively few expenses. It was the demands for corvée labour and military service that made life unpleasant for the Mongols. The Ch'ing ordered the Mongols to maintain a series of guards or watch posts along the border which they shared with the Russians. After the conclusion of the Treaty of Kiakhta in 1728, the court required the Mongols to supply troops and materials for these stations. Though the watch posts were generally successful in keeping Russians out of Mongolia, they were a heavy financial burden. Each watch post consisted of thirty to forty soldiers, whose food, horses, clothing, and armaments were supplied by the various Mongol Leagues. Furnishing provisions for several thousand men was no easy task for a country with a population of well under a million people. Similarly, the maintenance of postal stations, which the Ch'ing demanded, was an expensive and difficult duty. The Mongols had to provide men, horses and supplies for a courier system that primarily benefited the Ch'ing and facilitated their control of the land of the Khalkha Mongols. Even more galling, Chinese merchants, without any official functions, often lodged at the postal stations on their travels through Mongolia. Moreover, the watch posts and the postal stations not only entailed vast expenditures for supplies, but also meant a loss of herders and animals and diverted the use of some border territories from grazing land to the needs of the two institutions.[22]

The Ch'ing-Dzungar wars imposed additional strains on the Mongol economy. On various occasions in the eighteenth century, major battles were fought in Khalkha, as the Dzungars attempted to unite all of the Mongol peoples under their rule. Even more important, the Ch'ing demands for assistance aggravated the financial problems of the Mongols. Ch'ing officials bought sheep, horses, and other animals at artificially low prices, or else confiscated them. They requisitioned so many herds that some Mongols were left without sufficient animals for breeding. The Mongol corvée and tribute obligations increased steadily throughout the Dzungar wars. And the Mongols themselves were often recruited to serve in the Ch'ing army, again diverting essential manpower from the Mongol economy.

Despite the restrictive Ch'ing regulations, Chinese merchants also victimized the Mongols. The Ming had forbidden their people from crossing into Mongolia except on official business. Sino-Mongol trade had been conducted either in Peking or at specially designated border markets. Smuggling of Chinese goods into Mongolia was not unusual, but it was only in the middle of the sixteenth century that Chinese merchants began to evade the regulations on a large scale. By the time that the Mongols submitted to the Ch'ing in 1691, Chinese traders had made inroads in Mongolia. Men from the province of Shansi travelled among the Mongols offering Chinese goods essential for the local economy.[23] Fewer Mongol missions with sheep and horses travelled to the frontier markets or organized trading expeditions in the guise of tribute embassies to Peking. Chinese traders now arrived in Mongolia to purchase these animals. This change in patterns of trade benefited the Ch'ing, for their expenses in caring for Mongol tribute missions were reduced. Yet the Ch'ing court recognized that Chinese merchants might, through their sharp trading, antagonize the Mongols, which was why it had devised the regulations to control the traders that have been mentioned above.

Some of the court's own policies, however, impeded its efforts to curb the Chinese merchants. The Treaty of Kiakhta had eliminated the only serious competition, the Russians, that faced Chinese traders. The Chinese were thus given a virtual monopoly in Mongolia, a tremendous advantage in the conduct of trade. They also encountered few difficulties in evading the Ch'ing restrictions on commerce. A few judicious payments to Ch'ing officials who issued trading licences, or to frontier officials, assured the merchants of total freedom in trade. And they used this freedom to acquire a dominant position in the Mongol economy. They trafficked in contraband, stayed in Mongolia for longer periods than specified in their licences, founded permanent shops in the leading towns, entered the land of the Khalkha Mongols without licences, and intermarried with the Mongols. Even the Ch'ing-appointed supervisors of trade in Urga and Kiakhta failed to control Chinese merchants and, in fact, were often bribed by them. As the eighteenth century wore on, there were fewer and fewer checks on the activities of the Chinese in Mongolia.[24]

The Mongols were caught in a dilemma in their commercial relations with the Chinese. They brought their goods, principally animals and animal products, to market in the spring and summer, but they needed Chinese commodities throughout the year. Mongol herdsmen often contracted debts during the winter at high rates of interest in order to obtain such Chinese products as cloth, grain, tea, pots, nails, and saddles. When spring finally arrived, the Mongols were frequently unable to pay back the amount borrowed and the accumulated interest and thus incurred even greater debts. In times of great natural disasters – droughts, diseases among the herds, and so on – their economic situation was truly dire. The Chinese made them more dependent through unfair and deceitful trade practices. Unscrupulous merchants took advantage of the Mongols' credulity and lack of sophistication to swindle them and occasionally to offer inferior products. Their commercial astuteness and their evasion of trade regulations created a favourable balance of trade for them and caused many Mongols to fall into debt.[25]

Some of the Chinese accumulated vast fortunes through their dealings with the Mongols. Several became wealthy mainly by lending money at exorbitant rates of interest: in some cases, five per cent. a month. Others enticed prosperous Mongol nobles and princes to purchase luxury products at absurdly high prices, again siphoning off the resources of the Mongols. Yet others joined together to form large firms for the conduct of trade, and a few of these firms eventually became associated with specific Leagues or tribal units among the Khalkha. They established trade monopolies and were often the sole bankers (*tüngshi*, from the Chinese *t'ung-shih*, or 'interpreter') for their particular Mongol trading partners. And this offered them many opportunities for profit from usury.

The Ch'ing court was thus unable to prevent the Mongols from incurring enormous debts. As their debts mounted, many Mongols lost their herds and reluctantly migrated to the newly-developing towns, where they worked at odd jobs to support themselves. Most barely made a living, and in the urban areas they formed a discontented class that was generally hostile to China. The Ch'ing court itself was partly responsible for the gradual impoverishment of the Mongols. Its demands for taxes and particularly for corvée forced the Mongols to seek loans from Chinese moneylenders.

The Ch'ing court was also partly responsible for the growing economic power of the Lamaist Church. It did not deliberately attempt to enrich the Buddhist hierarchy, but its policies did lead to the development of large land-holding monasteries and temples. It had no intention of creating rival centres of power, and sought to prevent the centralization of the Lamaist Church. It opposed the concentration of Mongol financial resources in the hands of the Jebtsundamba Khutukhtu and supported the creation of local monasteries not under the sole jurisdiction of the Living Buddha. In general, the court did not subsidize the building of religious establishments or the printing of texts. Its policies nevertheless contributed to the consolidation of the Lamaist Church. The Ch'ing demands for corvée drove some Mongols to become *shabi*, or serfs, of the monasteries and temples, as dependants of which they were not obliged to pay taxes or provide labour to the government.[26] This enhanced the power and prestige of the Buddhist hierarchy, which was not always sympathetic to China. It further resulted in the development of larger and larger towns around the major religious centres, a process of urbanization that weakened the traditional nomadic economy.

The combined effect of all these factors was to generate bitter anti-Ch'ing feelings by the middle of the eighteenth century. Only one incident was needed to spark off a rebellion. This occurred in 1756, when the Ch'ing executed the Jebtsundamba Khutukhtu's half-brother for allegedly warning the Khoit rebel Amursana of an impending Ch'ing plot to arrest him. Rumours spread throughout Mongolia that the Ch'ing court had forced the Khutukhtu to watch the execution of his half-brother and that it had detained the Living Buddha himself.[27] A general named Chingunjav organized the resulting unrest into open rebellion.

Chingunjav could not succeed without outside assistance. He turned first to the Russian court for support. Though the Russians were sympathetic to his cause, they did not immediately grant him economic or military assistance. St Petersburg authorized its officials to maintain relations with him, but by the time it took a more active interest in his rebellion this had been crushed by the Ch'ing. Denied

Russian aid, Chingunjav had attempted to form an alliance with Amursana. As so often happened in the long history of relations between the Dzungars and the Eastern Mongols, however, efforts at unity were doomed. Though Chingunjav and Amursana kept in touch with each other in 1755 and 1756, they never concluded an alliance. Unity was essential to their success, but the leading nobles on both sides rejected any compromise that would reduce their own power. Internal squabbles within the two camps further hampered plans for concerted action against the Ch'ing.

Chingunjav's last hope of assistance rested with the Khutukhtu. The Living Buddha could sway the Khalkha nobility into assisting the rebels, and his role turned out to be crucial. Chingunjav sent several emissaries to persuade the Khutukhtu to declare his support for the uprising. The Khutukhtu delayed a final decision and as a result faced tremendous pressure from the Ch'ing court to side with it. He ultimately succumbed and proclaimed his allegiance to the Ch'ien-lung emperor, disavowing any support or sympathy for the 'traitorous' Chingunjav.[28] In 1757, the Khutukhtu had a second chance to dissociate himself from the Ch'ing by requesting Russian aid in a movement for the national independence of the Mongols, but he refused to take the decisive step, a decision that in the end cost him his life.

Chingunjav's own personality made his cause hopeless. He had initiated his revolt impetuously, without any assurance of support except from the troops directly under his command. The bulk of the Khalkha nobility, following the lead of the Khutukhtu, allied themselves with the Ch'ing, depriving Chingunjav of their valuable expertise and financial resources. He failed to arouse feelings of nationalism among the Mongols, and the *esprit de corps* of his own troops was virtually non-existent. When he was in precarious straits, his forces, without much hesitation, deserted to the Ch'ing side. Chingunjav did not formulate long-term plans, and most of his campaigns showed little concern for co-ordination and purpose. His sole concerns were, apparently, with power and plunder. His troops indiscriminately attacked and destroyed many Chinese shops and killed Chinese merchants. This sporadic violence attracted a few followers, but perhaps alienated many nobles, dismayed by the lack of overall planning and organization of his rebellion. As C. R. Bawden has observed of Chingunjav's forces, 'there was never a hint of an intent to change the social order . . . a negative xenophobia rather than a positive will towards national independence seems to be what inspired the rebels'.[29] The disunity and absence of major objectives that so often afflicted the Mongols again disrupted their campaigns against the Ch'ing.

The Ch'ing easily suppressed the rebellion. After depriving Chingunjav of support from the Dzungars, the Khutukhtu, and the majority of the Mongol nobility, they moved their own troops, as well as loyal forces from Inner Mongolia, into Khalkha. The Ch'ing forces readily occupied the strategic positions, including the watch posts along the borders, and started to deal with the rebels. Their tactics were brutal: they executed numerous captives and enslaved many women and children. In contrast to the Ch'ing suppression of the Dzungars, however, there was no effort to wipe out the peoples of Mongolia completely. Though their land was devastated and many of them were impoverished, the Mongols survived. The principal innovation introduced by the Ch'ing was the regulation that future reincarnations of the Jebtsundamba Khutukhtu would be found in Tibet.[30] This would presumably minimize the threat of a union of the spiritual authority with a Mongol national independence movement. And it ensured that the Khutukhtu would not have close relatives, such as the Tushetu Khan, with great political power.

The Mongols remained part of the Ch'ing empire until 1911. There were no large-scale uprisings directed against the Ch'ing. Nor did the idea of national independence appear very frequently in the late eighteenth and nineteenth centuries. It took time for the Mongols to recover from the devastation of the rebellion, and even then, the abuses (by both the Ch'ing government and the Chinese merchants) that had provoked the uprising were not remedied and were perhaps aggravated. Chinese merchants continued to dominate the Mongol economy, the Ch'ing demand for corvée went on impoverishing the Mongols, the rising number of lamas limited the growth of the population, and various Ch'ing policies damaged the nomadic economy, inducing many Mongols to flock, without employment opportunities, to the towns. The Ch'ing court prevented the Russians from entering Mongolia until the middle of the nineteenth century, preserving its trade monopoly in Urga and other towns. Chinese merchants still often offered inferior goods and received valuable animals and animal products in exchange.

The Ch'ing's pacification of the Dzungars and the Khalkha Mongols, and their conquest of some of Central Asia, set the stage for the eastward migration of the Torguts, another Western Mongol tribe. The rise of the Dzungars in the seventeenth century had forced the Torguts to move into Russian territory. For almost a century, the Torguts had been relatively autonomous, but, from the 1720s, their Khans became less powerful and came under the influence of the Russian court. The Russians, in fact, nominated some of the Khans and sought to conscript Torguts for their army. They also appeared eager to christianize the Torguts, a prospect which the lamas of the Mongol tribe viewed with dismay.[31]

Faced with these threats and unwilling to accept Russian over-lordship, the Torguts were pleased to learn that the Ch'ing court, which had for long been trying to win them over, had crushed their traditional foes, the Dzungars, by 1758. Their leaders decided to avert Russian domination and perhaps regain their independence by moving into the area formerly occupied by the Dzungars. Most of the commoners began to migrate to the east in 1770; those who remained, together with the Dzungars who fled westward after their defeat by the Ch'ing, were the ancestors of the Kalmyks of Russia. A body of approximately 170,000 Torguts started on the journey towards the Chinese border; they were attacked by the Kazakhs and other nomadic peoples and suffered heavy losses. Less than one-half reached their destination in Dzungaria (Ili).[32] On learning of the Torgut exodus, the Russians demanded that the Ch'ing force the Torguts to return. But the Ch'ing court welcomed the long-lost Mongol tribe and permitted it to settle in Ili. It provided the indigent migrants with 185,000 animals, as well as large quantities of tea, cloth, grain, cloth garments, tents, and silver. The emperor invited the Torgut leaders to his summer palaces in Jehol and rewarded them with luxury gifts and with royal titles. To commemorate the return of the Torguts, he erected a stone monument with inscriptions in Chinese, Manchu, Tibetan, and Mongol near the Potala Buddhist temple in Jehol.[33]

AGENCIES OF FOREIGN RELATIONS AND ECONOMIC DEALINGS

The early Ch'ing court pursued some of the same policies as the Ming and adopted similar institutions. It attempted to limit relations between its own people and the officials and merchants of Russia and Inner Asia. Once it controlled Mongolia, Manchuria, and parts of Central Asia, it sought to isolate those areas from outsiders. Yet it recognized their need for Chinese goods and the desire of Chinese merchants for the products of Inner Asia. Thus a regulated system of trade continued in the Ch'ing period.

The Ch'ing had access to reliable and valuable information about Inner Asia. Such envoys as Tulishen returned to China with records of the countries and peoples that they visited. The two Ch'ing missions that travelled to Russia in the 1730s certainly brought back reports on their travels and observations. As in the Ming period, Russian and Inner Asian envoys remained in Peking for a long time (the Russian envoy Lorentz Lange, for example, stayed in the Ch'ing capital for several years), allowing the Ch'ing court to accumulate data on and impressions of the foreigners. The court-sponsored publication in 1800 of the *Wu-t'i Ch'ing-wen-chien* (a dictionary, or actually a series of word lists, in Chinese, Manchu, Mongol, Tibetan, and Eastern Turki) indicates a remarkable knowledge of foreign languages and an interest in information about Inner Asia.[34] The innumerable multilingual inscriptions celebrating Ch'ing successes are further evidence of the international awareness of the Ch'ing.

Experts in foreign affairs were readily available to the government. The Ch'ing delegation at Nerchinsk in 1689 consisted of the president of the principal agency of foreign relations, the Li-fan yüan, another specialist in 'barbarian' affairs, and three other men. Tulishen, the Ch'ing envoy to the Torguts in 1712, and Tsereng, the Mongol ennobled as the Sain Noyan Khan by the Ch'ing, concluded the Treaty of Kiakhta for the Ch'ing. Certain men were repeatedly appointed to deal with foreigners. The diplomat Tulishen was typical of the experts employed in Ch'ing times. He started his career in foreign relations as an ambassador to the Torguts. During his journey to the Torguts, he was in touch with many Russian officials and became knowledgeable about Russian customs and attitudes. After his return, he was often sent to meet Russian envoys at the Chinese border and to accompany them to the capital. For example, he greeted the Russian envoy Izmailov in 1719. His last important assignment was that of Ch'ing negotiator with the Russians at Kiakhta in 1727 and 1728.

Like the Ming emperors, the Ch'ing rulers, in theory, governed the conduct of foreign relations. Yet some did not exercise their full powers. It was the early emperors who took an active role in the formulation of foreign policy. The K'ang-hsi emperor, for example, personally led several campaigns against the Dzungars and frequently met the representatives of other states to discuss major issues. His grandson, the Ch'ien-lung emperor, who ruled from 1736 to 1796, also played a significant role in shaping foreign policy and by deciding to conquer and occupy such new land as the oases of Central Asia. The emperors of the nineteenth century were more isolated and less involved in foreign policy, permitting ministers and local officials to conduct relations with the Inner Asian states and dependencies of China.

The Li-fan yüan, founded in 1638, was the single most important agency in the Ch'ing court's relations with Inner Asia. It had been preceded by the Mongolian Office (Meng-ku ya-men), but, as the Ch'ing initiated relations with areas other than Mongolia, they created the Li-fan yüan to deal with all the lands north and west of China.[35] The Board of Rites, the other major agency concerned with foreign relations, concentrated on the states to the east and south. The Li-fan yüan was directly responsible for all China's relations with Inner Asia, though each of the Ch'ing's dependencies in the region also had a separate military administration.

Thus the Li-fan yüan dealt with foreign envoys and tributaries. As in the Ming period, the court met the expenses of official diplomats. The Russian envoy Lorentz Lange, for example, daily received one fish, one sheep, one fowl, one bowl of milk, two ounces of tea, two ounces of butter, two ounces of lamp oil, two small measures of rice, some salted cabbage, and wood, and those who accompanied him were supplied with lesser amounts of each commodity.[36] In dealing with the peoples of Inner Asia, the Li-fan yüan offered supplies according to rank, with the major princes receiving more luxurious and costly goods than lowly envoys. It provided transport from the borders to Peking and arranged banquets for the tribute bearers en route and in the capital. Its principal function concerning tribute was to prepare the foreign envoys for their audience with the emperor. This could take a long time, particularly with recalcitrant envoys who refused to abide by the tributary scheme. The audiences themselves resembled those of the Ming in their elaboration and were clearly designed to impress the tribute bearers. Nikolai Milescu, the Russian envoy of the late seventeenth century, offers a description of the spectacular ceremonies and surroundings, including the use of fifty large elephants, innumerable horse-drawn chariots, and countless musicians and entertainers – all of which display certainly impressed him.[37]

As the Ch'ing expanded into Inner Asia in the eighteenth century, the main function of the Li-fan yüan shifted from the care of tribute envoys to the actual administration of new territory. In fact, the number of tribute embassies from Inner Asia probably declined, for trade between Chinese merchants and officials and the peoples of Inner Asia was conducted on the Chinese border or in Mongolia, Manchuria, and Central Asia. From the eighteenth century onwards, there were fewer Ch'ing complaints of excessive expenditure on tribute embassies. The Ming problem of costly foreign missions, which had imposed a financial burden on the Chinese court, was now relatively insignificant.

To administer the various regions of Inner Asia, the Li-fan yüan was organized into several departments. One bureau supervised the reception of the princes of Outer Mongolia and another welcomed the princes of Inner Mongolia. Other departments dealt with the affairs of Inner Mongolia, Outer Mongolia, and Eastern Turkestan (those portions of Central Asia under Chinese control), and several offices dealt with judicial matters, the translation of documents from Inner Asian rulers, and the training of students in the languages of Inner Asia. A number of subsidiary departments (Secretaries, Treasury, and so on) supplemented and supported these principal bureaux.[38] The Li-fan yüan also had some jurisdiction over postal stations, watch towers, the ranking of the Mongol nobility, the registration of adult males, and the assemblies of Mongol chieftains which were convened every three years to deal with legal and territorial problems. It implemented the Ch'ing policies of providing specific domains for the Mongol princes and of frustrating their efforts to achieve Mongol unity. One method that it used to reduce disaffection among the leading Mongols and Inner Asians was the granting of annual salaries or subsidies to the leading princes, the generosity of the grant depending on the nobleman's rank.

Language schools Also under the purview of the Li-fan yüan and the Grand Secretariat (Nei-ko), the agency ultimately responsible for the translation of foreign documents, was the E-lo-ssu wen kuan (the Russian Language School), whose regulations resembled those of the schools established for the Inner Asian languages. The court appointed two administrators, two instructors, and several assistant instructors to the school, which was probably founded between 1689 and 1693, to train twenty-four students at a time in Russian. Some of the early instructors were Russians, and the students were Manchu bannermen. The government provided supplies for the students but accorded them a low official rank on completion of their studies, a policy which it

161

inherited from the Ming treatment of students at the College of Interpreters and the College of Translators. Like the preceding dynasty, therefore, the Ch'ing was unable to recruit highly motivated and dedicated students. The E-lo-ssu wen kuan was thus doomed to failure, and the repeated complaints of government officials attest to the inadequacies of the translators and interpreters.[39]

Nonetheless, the government's efforts were not totally unproductive. The Li-fan yüan sponsored the extremely successful E-lo-ssu hsüeh (Language School for Russians). Founded in 1728, the school offered training in Chinese and Manchu for six carefully chosen Russian students at a time. The Ch'ing court provided the instructors and bore part of the students' expenses, an indication that the Ch'ing recognized the value of effective communication with foreigners, though they did not cherish it enough to improve conditions for their own students of Russian. Apart from the Russian students of Chinese and Manchu in Peking, there were undoubtedly Chinese merchants and officials on the Chinese borders who knew the Inner Asian languages and also Russian. So the Ch'ing had some access to frontier people conversant with the languages of the 'barbarians'. How often it consulted them in matters of policy is still not clear.[40]

Local officials The enormous distances separating Peking and the administrative districts of Inner Asia allowed local officials great leeway in decision-making. Urga, the centre for the administration of eastern Mongolia, was about a thousand miles from Peking, and couriers coming on foot from the capital took an average of forty-eight days to reach Ch'ing officials there. The comparable figures for Uliassutai, the seat of the government for western Mongolia, were about 1,600 miles and 83 days on foot, for Ili about 3,300 miles and 193 days on foot and 43 days by horse, and for Mukden in Manchuria about 500 miles and 15 days on foot and 8 days by horse.[41] Such difficulties in communication necessarily weakened the central government's control over local officials, who had virtual autonomy in deciding how to deal with urgent problems. The Ch'ing sources often accuse them of using their power for their own gain. Central government officials and investigators complained that they engaged in profiteering and victimized the 'barbarians', impoverishing them and driving them into rebellion. According to some reports, they even assisted Chinese merchants to evade government regulations on trade, in exchange for large payments.

Merchants Like the Ming, the Ch'ing attempted to restrict the commercial dealings of merchants. It differed from the preceding dynasty, however, in its recognition that it could no longer maintain a monopoly on commerce and limit private trade. One scholar has even gone so far as to write that 'the officials' basic attitude towards commerce was not that it was a necessary evil but that it was a necessary good likely to turn evil unless properly controlled'.[42] There is abundant testimony from travellers that merchants, despite these restrictions, played an important role in trade with Inner Asia. John Bell, who accompanied a Russian mission to China in 1719, noted that 'the merchants are immensely rich by their inland and foreign trade, which they carry on, to great extent, with the Russians and Tartars'.[43] Merchants not only traded in Peking and the borderlands, but actually travelled, often without authorization, deep into Mongolia, Manchuria, and the new territories in Central Asia. Some resided permanently in Inner Asia, intermarried with the local inhabitants and became well-informed about the customs and languages of the peoples among whom they lived. How often the court consulted them concerning foreign relations is uncertain.

Eunuchs Eunuchs were politically much less important in Ch'ing than in Ming times. Court annals scarcely refer to their involvement in foreign relations. But a number of foreign envoys repeatedly mention eunuchs as guides and official welcomers.[44] It seems likely that such continual contacts offered them opportunities to influence Ch'ing relations with the peoples of Inner Asia. A few of them doubt-less learned a great deal about foreigners, but the Li-fan yüan and the court apparently made little use of their expertise.

Ch'ing economic relations with Inner Asia differed considerably from those of the Ming. After the agreements at Kiakhta in 1728, few Russian tribute embassies reached the Ch'ing capital in the eighteenth century. Most exchanges of goods were conducted on their common borderlands at Kiakhta. Similarly, after the incorporation of much of Inner Asia into the Ch'ing empire, the number of tribute embassies from that region declined. The special gifts and 'gifts in reply' to rulers and envoys, which had imposed such burdens on the Ming economy, were no longer major irritants in relations between the Ch'ing and Inner Asia. Trade began to replace tribute as the primary vehicle for economic dealings between China and the neighbouring peoples. There were still complaints from both sides of defective goods and of collusion between officials and merchants to evade government regulations and to victimize both the 'barbarians' and the Chinese on the border. Since the bulk of trade was now conducted in Inner Asia, the number of such complaints, however, decreased. Chinese merchants were profiting from their economic arrangements in Mongolia and Manchuria, and the Ch'ing were unable to prevent them from taking advantage of the poorer herdsmen and farmers in these areas.

The goods that the Ch'ing imported from Inner Asia were remarkably similar to those brought to China during the Ming period. Animals and animal products headed the list, horses for warfare, camels for transport, and sheep for food and clothing. Chinese merchants prized the animals and travelled deep into the heart of Inner Asia to obtain them. Not only did furs from Mongolia and Manchuria attract the Chinese and arrive in Peking, but Siberian furs had begun to reach China by the early Ch'ing period. Central Asian jade was still another common import. In sum, the Ch'ing generally acquired both useful and luxury products through their trade with Inner Asia.

Like the Ming, the Ch'ing relinquished goods it possessed in abundance. Chinese merchants offered cotton, silk, and clothing to the peoples of Inner Asia. They also sent such popular goods as tea, porcelain, and drugs. In times of crisis, China's neighbours requested and often received grain in return for their products. One of the new exports was wild rhubarb, a plant that grew in north-west China. Chinese and Europeans used its root as a purgative. A sixteenth-century Chinese medical encyclopedia encouraged its use as a remedy for malarial fevers, for the fevers of children, and for women's diseases, particularly those involving congestion of the pelvic organs.[45] European herbalists of the same period recommended it for diseases of the liver, kidney, and spleen, swellings about the heart, spitting of blood, shortness of breath, ringworm, pleurisy, madness, and frenzy. In short, rhubarb was 'good at all times, and for all ages, and likewise for children and women with childe'.[46]

Noting the great European demand for the plant, the Russian government realized that the rhubarb trade could be extremely profitable. Peter the Great founded a Chief Apothecary Office to inspect rhubarb and declared a monopoly of the trade. Central Asian merchants, many from the region of Bukhara, travelled to north-western China to buy rhubarb, which they then transported and sold to Russian officials. The Russians, in turn, served as middlemen, selling the rhubarb to the Western European states at high prices. In seeking to preserve its monopoly of the rhubarb trade, the state prohibited its own merchants from participating in the commerce and imposed stiff penalties on private trade. Nonetheless, many Russian merchants, often with the aid of corrupt officials, obtained rhubarb illegally from China and sold it to their own countrymen or to Western Europeans. Admitting the futility of state control of the trade, Catherine the Great finally abandoned the monopoly of rhubarb in the 1790s.[47] With the arrival of Western European vessels at the ports of southern China, the Russian monopoly of rhubarb was terminated, and rhubarb ceased to play an important role in relations between the Ch'ing and Inner Asia.

PART THREE:
INNER ASIA AND THE FALL
OF THE CH'ING

7 Cracks in the Ch'ing empire: Muslim revolts

By 1760, China appeared to be at the height of its power in Inner Asia. It had achieved most of its principal objectives in the region. Russia had been virtually excluded, and Mongolia, Manchuria, and much of Central Asia were isolated and dependent on China. The Ch'ing court had prevented the unification of the various peoples of Inner Asia and thus faced no true military threat from them. Its troops occupied the newly conquered towns and oases of Central Asia, and an administration, which often granted authority and self-governing privileges to local princes and chieftains, was established. The Dzungars, the last major opponents of Ch'ing hegemony in the region, had been destroyed, and their former territory was now rapidly becoming colonized by Chinese Muslims from north-west China. Chinese merchants travelled to the neighbouring border regions to trade for goods coveted by the Ch'ing. Trade continued to replace tribute as the commonest form of economic interchange between China and Inner Asia, thus reducing some of the tensions generated earlier by the arrival of tribute missions. The Inner Asian peoples, who needed products from a more settled civilization, relied exclusively on Chinese merchants, who in turn took advantage of their monopoly to enrich themselves and, in the process, impoverished the local inhabitants.

By 1860, exactly a century later, the Ch'ing system in Inner Asia had crumbled. Russian influence had spread in Central Asia and in the Amur and Ussuri regions, and Russian merchants had won trading privileges in Ili and Urga. Chinese merchants faced a renewed challenge, and their success was not assured, for some of the Inner Asian tribes resented what was, in their view, economic exploitation by the Chinese. Discontent with Ch'ing rule increased. First riots, and then full-scale rebellions, were evidence of resentment at Ch'ing supremacy in Central Asia and Inner Mongolia, while attacks on Chinese merchants and raids on Chinese-owned shops were common in Outer Mongolia.

The Ch'ing court may have over-extended itself by attempting to administer vast territories in Inner Asia. It abandoned the cautious Ming policy and tried to govern areas with predominantly non-Chinese peoples. There is strong evidence to suggest that the Ch'ing court wished to grant limited autonomy to local rulers and to devise equitable tax and military obligations. It also attempted to prevent unscrupulous Chinese merchants from deceiving and exploiting the Inner Asians. But its own merchants and officials undermined efforts to sustain a fair and reasonable colonial regime in Inner Asia. They violated Ch'ing agreements and regulations, thus alienating the local peoples and provoking rebellions.

The growing European pressure on China exacerbated Ch'ing difficulties in Inner Asia. It is well known that the European states, coveting Chinese raw materials and dreaming of the tremendous potential Chinese market for foreign goods, repeatedly demanded an expansion of trade with China. Ch'ing officials rejected their requests until the Opium War of 1839–42 forced the Ch'ing court to accede to the European demands. Its defeat in that war with Great Britain, as well as its initial failure to suppress the Taiping rebellion of 1850–64, exposed the inadequacies and corruption of the Ch'ing forces, and particularly of the banner armies. The obvious incompetence, demoralization, and ineffectiveness of the banner troops encouraged the peoples of Inner Asia to challenge the Ch'ing armies, whom they had earlier feared.

MUSLIM THREATS TO CENTRAL ASIA

The first cracks in the Ch'ing Inner Asian system appeared in the recently incorporated areas of Central Asia. This is surprising in view of the moderate policy of the Ch'ing court, which was primarily interested in the defence of its north-western border and in the use of Sinkiang and the other newly acquired territory in Central Asia as buffers against foreign intrusion. In the view of one prominent nineteenth-century Ch'ing official, 'Sinkiang was the first line of defence in the Northwest. It protected Mongolia, which in turn protected Peking. If Sinkiang were lost, Mongolia would be indefensible and Peking itself threatened.'[1] The concern for defence was directed both at the Uighurs, Kazakhs, and other tribes of Central Asia and at the Russians who continued their relentless drive to the east. Isolating the region from foreign influence was still a cardinal aim of the Ch'ing court, but it was now faced not only with Russia but also with Great Britain, which was moving into Central Asia to prevent any incursions on its colonial possessions in India. Like the Ming, the Ch'ing sought to prevent the unification of the various Inner Asian tribes and perhaps to exacerbate already existing conflicts. Undoubtedly, the economic differences between the pastoral nomadic Kazakhs and the sedentary Uighur farmers and town-dwellers in its new Central Asian domain facilitated its task. Additional minorities, including Manchus, Mongols, non-Muslim Chinese, and others, provided even more obstacles to unification. To promote the recovery of the land which it had devastated during the Dzungar wars, the Ch'ing court attempted to foster the economic revival of the region. It encouraged colonists from the Chinese Muslims of Shensi and Kansu, commonly known as Dungans, and from the Uighurs who lived south of the T'ien Shan (Heavenly Mountains) to migrate westward to the new dominions in Ili. The immigrants received grants of land in the fertile Ili valley on which they could raise grain, fruit, and cotton. Irrigation projects were essential, and the government promoted and occasionally sponsored them. Colonists also had access to extensive natural and mineral resources, including iron, gold, and copper. Though the court imposed regulations on commerce, it permitted trade between its own merchants and those of Sinkiang and of the nearby khanate of Kokand. Taxes on land, the products of the mines, and commercial exchanges constituted the main Ch'ing demands in return.

In sum, the aims of Ch'ing colonial administration in Central Asia need not have aroused opposition. There were a few government-supported instances of repression of the Muslim religion, but the court did not sanction any other ways of tampering with the customs and institutions of the local peoples. The Ch'ing promotion of the economy of Sinkiang is reflected in Professor Fletcher's assertion that 'by and large the sixty-year period of Ch'ing control from 1759 until 1820 was marked by order and greater material prosperity than the region had known for at least a century'.[2]

To pursue their objectives, the Ch'ing established an administration with a maximum of local self-rule. A viceroy or military governor was in charge of the oases north and south of the T'ien Shan. His principal subordinates included two assistant military governors, one stationed north of the T'ien Shan and the other south. The court assigned agents or intendants in the main towns, in particular Hami, Urumchi, Kashgar, Khotan, and a few others. To facilitate the defence and administration of the new dominions, the Ch'ing built twenty-five separate fortresses around Urumchi and Ili and eighteen small ones south of the T'ien Shan. Each was manned by a specified number of soldiers, the total number of troops being about thirty thousand by the late eighteenth century. Military colonies were often attached to the fortresses to make them more self-sufficient and to reduce government expenditure. Nearly all the officials were Manchus, which was to prove damaging as the Ch'ing court declined in the nineteenth century.[3]

This Ch'ing force governed through local chieftains. Muslim leaders handled day-to-day affairs, while the occupation forces were confined

China in 1760

to ensuring that taxes were collected and that order was maintained. The Muslim chiefs, known as *begs*, actually collected the taxes and maintained order; they also administered justice, and supervised trade. Their interests more and more frequently coincided with those of the Ch'ing officials in the area, as both sought domestic security, and commercial and economic prosperity. They often co-operated to maintain control over the population of Sinkiang.

Ch'ing administration of the region depended largely on the Ch'ing officials who accepted appointments in the 'barbarian' lands. Even with the best of intentions, the Ch'ing court could not create an effective system of government without honest and dedicated officials. Its efforts to maintain an equitable tax structure and to revitalize the economy of the region could readily be sabotaged by its own appointees. At first officials were carefully selected but by the early nineteenth century their only apparent qualification was often their 'connexions with the inner court'.[4] Since few Chinese officials were allowed to serve in Sinkiang, the court relied exclusively on a small group of Manchus who often sought to grow rich from their service in the new territories. They exploited the local people, demanding exorbitant taxes and excessive labour services. Corrupt *begs* joined them in victimizing the local populace and in impoverishing the region.

The decline in quality of the Manchu troops stationed in Sinkiang further hindered effective rule. The banner troops, once the most powerful military force in East Asia, began to deteriorate in the late eighteenth century. One common explanation for this is that China engaged in no major land wars from 1759 until the middle of the nineteenth century, and there was no need for the banners to maintain their military readiness. Whatever the explanation, the bannermen started to adopt other occupations, including farming and trading, and their military skills became dulled. They assimilated with the Chinese and lost both interest and expertise in warfare. Relatively low pay and miserable conditions in frontier service led first to demoralization and then to efforts, legal or illegal, to improve their situation. The corruption that prevailed among the leading Manchu military and civil officials in Sinkiang encouraged the soldiers to imitate their superiors in victimizing the local people.

The troubles besetting China in the nineteenth century aggravated the difficulties of Ch'ing rule of Sinkiang. Needing additional revenue to cope with the Taiping rebellion and other uprisings of the 1850s, the court raised the taxes on the non-Chinese peoples of that region.

This policy brought the predominantly Muslim population to the verge of rebellion. And the Ch'ing court's transfer of many of its troops from Sinkiang eastward to counter the military threat of the Taiping in the Chinese heartland provided the Muslims with an opportunity to regain their independence.[5]

The exploitation of the region by Manchu officials paved the way for rebellion, particularly after 1820. Earlier, the excesses of the bureaucracy and military officials had been held in check, but from that date onwards the restraints were less effective and the quality of officials declined. The latter neither respected nor learned much about the languages and customs of the peoples whom they ruled.

Quite clearly, the Ch'ing policy of occupation reversed the Ming plan for dealing with Central Asia. And some court officials no doubt questioned the new policy. One reply to their objections has been framed in the following way by a leading nineteenth-century official: 'People often complain that the defence of Sinkiang is too expensive. Is that true? . . . To compare with the earlier days under K'ang-hsi (1662–1722) and Yung-cheng (1723–1735), when the battle fires were threatening Peking, when the people on the frontier were exposed to constant danger, when the government had to transport all supplies across the distant desert . . . to continue a desperate struggle which consumed up to more than seventy million taels [of silver] . . . which period has been more wasteful?'[6] The same official argued that the occupation forces made a large frontier army unnecessary, in the long run reducing government expenditure, that the institution of military colonies not only served to supply the Ch'ing forces but also created an additional source of revenue, and that the new territories offered opportunities for colonization for the growing population of China.

On the other hand, the Ch'ing court's claims to Sinkiang committed it to the defence and control of the region. In the 1860s, the court was forced to divert resources badly needed elsewhere to suppress a rebellion in Sinkiang. Some scholars even assert that this shift in resources limited China's ability to cope with the Western powers and Japan in the late nineteenth century. So the occupation of Sinkiang and parts of Central Asia was, in many ways, a mixed blessing for the Ch'ing.

Given the Manchu corruption and exploitation, it is only natural that dissatisfaction with Ch'ing rule grew. The adherents of the so-called New Teaching (*Hsin-chiao*) of Islam became the chief fomenters of the rebellion that eventually engulfed north-western China and

Central Asia. This Muslim sect was influenced by the mystical Sufi order, which strove to reform and purify the entrenched *ṭarīqa*, or 'way'. A few scholars have suggested that the New Teaching arose partly as a reaction to the fear of Buddhist and Taoist influence on Muslims, but the latest research indicates that the sect was part of a broad conservative movement that played a role in the political life of India, Southeast Asia, the Caucasus, Afghanistan, and Western Central Asia at the time. It opposed the modernizing European currents in these lands, insisting on purity of doctrine and ritual. The most recent student of this relatively little-studied movement believes that it was basically a branch of the Old Teaching (*Lao-chiao*), or Naqshbandiyya school. It shared the Naqshbandiyya's mysticism and belief in political involvement.[7]

The unique features of the New Teaching were primarily a series of rituals. Loud chanting (*dhikr-i jahrī*), as opposed to the silent remembrance of God (*dhikr-i khafī*) of the Old Teaching, was the most notable characteristic of the sect. It also emphasized vigorous movement of the body during prayers and the worship of saints. A Muslim named Ma Ming-hsin is credited with the introduction of the New Teaching into China. Ma reached China in 1761 after a lengthy residence in the Middle East and Central Asia. He quickly attracted a large following in the north-western province of Kansu, and by 1781 he and his associate Su Ssu-shih-san felt strong enough to challenge the adherents of the Old Teaching and the Ch'ing government. A civil war erupted, and the New Teaching forces were defeated only with the arrival of Ch'ing forces from other Chinese provinces, just as Ch'ing troops had been needed to crush an earlier non-religious revolt in Ush-Turfan in 1765. The orthodox Muslim sect apparently recovered rather rapidly, for in 1784 it launched a second rebellion that required even greater Ch'ing effort for its suppression. After the suppression of the revolt, the government decided to eliminate the threat posed by the sect and proscribed the New Teaching. Together with the prohibition of the sect, the court also introduced regulations that impinged upon all the Muslims, a policy that eventually caused trouble. But meanwhile the Ch'ing secured peace for thirty-five years.[8]

Resentment over Ch'ing repression of Islam, however, grew and finally flared out into open rebellion. The first manifestation of this dissatisfaction was the revolt in 1815 in Sinkiang of Ḍiyā 'al-Dīn, a Muslim chieftain who led a short-lived rebellion with the aid of Kirghiz tribesmen and was soon crushed. The next challenge to

Ch'ing authority was more serious. A descendant of the White Mountain Khojas, a certain Jahāngīr Khoja, took advantage of the turmoil in Sinkiang to return from his place of exile in Kokand in an attempt to reclaim his ancestors' lands. Like Ḍiyā 'al-Dīn, he received the support of the Kirghiz, and in 1820 started to harass China's new dominions in Central Asia. The Ch'ing armies forced him to withdraw but could not annihilate his forces. He apparently had the support of much of the local population, which had been victimized by the *begs* and the Manchu officials. Even so, if the Ch'ing had been more vigorous, there should have been little difficulty in overwhelming the dissidents. Instead, some court and local officials favoured a compromise with Jahāngīr, particularly after they had to endure his raids for several years. And it was only through deception that the Ch'ing captured him in 1828, another indication of their weakness.

Jahāngīr's capture did not end China's difficulties in the region. His relative success encouraged other Muslims to challenge Ch'ing rule. Two years after his capture, his brother Khoja Muḥammad Yūsuf made several incursions from Kokand into China's Central Asian domain to plunder it before returning to the safety of that western khanate. The next major rebellion was that of the Seven White Mountain Khojas in 1847, a revolt that again originated in Kokand. From their base in Kokand, the Khojas attacked China's north-western frontier and caused havoc there until the Ch'ing troops finally forced them to withdraw. One of them, a certain Walī Khan Turä, reappeared in 1857 to plague Sinkiang and occupied parts of the region for some months. Continual raids from Kokand on Ch'ing troops in Sinkiang occurred right up to the eve of the great Muslim rebellions of the 1860s.

Since the majority of these raids and rebellions stemmed from Kokand, one might assume that Kokand and China were constantly at war. But that was not the case for at least part of the late eighteenth and early nineteenth centuries. Kokand had freed itself from the domination of Bukhara in the 1750s, and its ruler, Erdeni Beg, attempted to ensure its continued survival through judicious diplomacy. In 1760, he sent a tribute embassy to Peking to initiate relations with the Ch'ing court. For the next fifty years, contacts between the two states were generally cordial, the Ch'ing apparently treating Kokand respectfully and not as a subjugated, inferior vassal. Approximately twenty-three official missions from Kokand reached China in the period 1760–1810, most offering their tribute in the town of Kashgar and about one out of every three continuing the journey to Peking.[9] The Ch'ing government provided the envoys with food, lodging, and transport and offered gifts in return for their tributary articles. Both sides, as we shall see, appeared to profit from this arrangement.

Meanwhile Kokand was afforded the opportunity to consolidate its own position and to seize territory from its less powerful neighbours. It first overwhelmed some Kirghiz tribes to the north and east. The Ch'ing, which considered these tribes as vassals, objected but did not act to prevent the Kokand conquest. Kokand, too, offered sanctuary to the various khojas fleeing from the Ch'ing forces that subjugated Sinkiang in 1759. The Ch'ing started to react to this unfriendly act only during Jahāngīr Khoja's revolt in the 1820s. Another seemingly hostile policy was the Kokand encouragement of dissidents in Kashgar and other Ch'ing-controlled areas in Central Asia. The peoples of Kokand and Sinkiang shared a common religion, Islam, and a common annoyance with and perhaps hatred of the Ch'ing. Yet almost a century passed before Kokand was able to detach Sinkiang from China for a brief period.

Kokand was more successful in its campaigns in the west and against the Kirghiz and the Kazakhs. By the late eighteenth century, it had conquered the town of Khojend and most of Ferghana, and by 1809, its influence reached as far west as Tashkent. In the east, the Kokand khans encroached on the Kirghiz and Kazakh lands. Claiming that these two nomadic tribes harassed the trading caravans of Kokandian merchants, the khans asserted their right to pacify the pastoral peoples, particularly the Kirghiz. Their unstated objectives were to conscript the Kirghiz for their army and to use the economic resources of the Kirghiz for their own needs.[10]

By 1810, Kokand was a major power in the region, and its khans felt ready to adopt a more militant policy towards China. Some of the principal advocates of such a strategy were the Kokandian merchants who wanted fewer Ch'ing restrictions on their trade with Sinkiang and the interior of China. Kokand was renowned for its commercial expertise, the merchants of the town of Andijan, in particular, being recognized for this throughout Central Asia. As one Chinese of the nineteenth century noted, 'if Khoqand [Kokand] merchants quit Kashgharia, distribution of goods in this region will cease, causing a tremendous inconvenience to Uyghur [Uighur] natives'.[11] Kokandian merchants had often accompanied official tribute missions to China and had returned to their land laden with Chinese goods. The Ch'ing court raised no objections, for until 1810 the merchants generally abided by the regulations, engaged only infrequently in illicit trade, and did not make exorbitant demands for additional supplies and gifts. There are few complaints in the Ch'ing sources about these merchants.

The principal area of activity for the Kokandian merchants was, however, not the interior of China, but Sinkiang. Ch'ing regulations required them to have valid passports or licences, issued by Manchu officials, if they wished to trade in Sinkiang. The court also imposed a tariff on commerce, varying from about three to five per cent. on Kokandian merchants to five to ten per cent. on Sinkiang merchants who crossed the border to trade. Trade was, nonetheless, brisk and beneficial to all parties. Kokand obtained porcelains, tea, silk, silver, and rhubarb, while the Ch'ing received horses, leather, furs, knives, and other goods. Kokandian merchants started to serve as middlemen between China and Russia, particularly in providing Chinese rhubarb to Russia. Towards the end of the eighteenth century, Kokandian merchants began to evade the prescribed taxes, to smuggle a large volume of goods, and to bribe Ch'ing officials to ignore such illegal acts. The rulers of Kokand attempted to legalize these activities by persuading the Ch'ing to reduce taxes and to eliminate restrictions on commerce. The Ch'ing court remained implacable, prompting even greater tensions and more blatant evasions of its regulations. With the upsurge in the number of official and unofficial trading missions after 1810, tensions between the Ch'ing and Kokand grew. Disputes over commercial transactions, excessive demands for supplies by the Kokandians, and other causes of economic contention repeatedly arose.[12]

The settlement of Kokandians in Sinkiang also provoked tensions. Some merchants decided to live near their source of Chinese goods in order to facilitate trade and perhaps to heighten the opportunities for smuggling. They often bought land in Sinkiang and used this as a base for expanding their commercial enterprises. Acquiring illegally obtained rhubarb and tea, they broke the Ch'ing monopoly of these products and amassed vast fortunes. The rulers of Kokand, noticing the wealth of their Sinkiang-based merchants, requested permission from the Ch'ing court to appoint a tax collector or consul (*aksakal*) to supervise and benefit from the activities of their traders in China's north-western dominions. Meeting the adamant refusal of the Ch'ing, they became increasingly hostile to the Ch'ing court and retaliated by supporting the khojas in their early nineteenth-century revolts against Ch'ing rule. Their vital position along the Russian and Central Asian trade routes had enriched them through taxation, trade, and customs duties, and they used their wealth to subsidize the New Teaching forces that plagued the Chinese border.

In the 1820s, the Ch'ing reacted by denying Kokand trade with Sinkiang and by arresting several of its merchants. These acts had unfortunate repercussions for the Ch'ing, for in 1830 troops from Kokand poured across the border and seized enormous quantities of goods from Sinkiang. In 1832, the Ch'ing court reluctantly relented, permitting Kokandian merchants to trade and allowing Kokand to station a tax collector and agent in Kashgar. This Ch'ing concession encouraged Kokand to make additional demands, which its agent and merchants supported. Its merchants, fearing competition for the trade of Sinkiang from Chinese merchants, also became embroiled in hostilities with the Ch'ing court. Kokand was thus an influential patron of the Muslim revolts of the middle of the nineteenth century. And it might have provided even more aid for the Muslims of north-west China had the Russians not begun to move into Central Asia and to threaten the very existence of Kokand. An adventurer from Kokand, nonetheless, eventually assumed the leadership of the principal Muslim rebellion against the Ch'ing.

This rebellion erupted in the Chinese province of Shensi, not in Sinkiang. Its precise cause is still uncertain, but it appears that a dispute between some Muslims and Chinese over the sale of bamboo poles ignited the spark for the devastating rebellion which followed.[13] The Ch'ing had already accused Muslims of helping the Taiping rebels who briefly occupied the north-western provinces. The incident of the bamboo poles led to violent fighting between the two communities, building up to a Muslim rebellion by the end of 1862. Though the New Teaching hierarchy was not involved in the initial outbreak, Ma Hua-lung, the recognized leader of the sect, quickly became a prominent figure among the rebels. From his base in north-eastern Kansu, he promoted anti-Ch'ing sentiment and fought for independence from China. The rebel forces were extremely successful, and within a short time most of Shensi and Kansu were no longer under Ch'ing rule.

The rebellions soon spread to Sinkiang. Muslims in that region sympathized with the efforts of their co-religionists to the east and in the town of Kucha initiated their own revolt in 1864. They rapidly ousted the Ch'ing troops from Kucha and from much of Sinkiang as well. Ili, the old homeland of the Dzungar Mongols, held out for almost two years before falling to the Muslim rebels. By 1865, Ch'ing troops had been effectively excluded from China's possessions in Central Asia. The rebels seemed to be in a good position to resist a Ch'ing counter-attack. But they remained divided into isolated and self-contained groups, with no unified leadership. At least five different rebel organizations controlled regions and towns in Sinkiang. Most of the leaders were adherents of the New Teaching, but they did not accept the political supremacy of any single religious figure.

A rebel ruler in Kashgar, a Kirghiz chieftain, finally appealed to Kokand to send a descendant of the khojas to Sinkiang, hoping that a khoja might succeed in unifying the Muslims throughout the region. The Khan of Kokand responded by dispatching Buzurg Khan, the last of the khojas of Kashgar, along with his military subordinate Ya'qūb Beg, to Sinkiang. Ya'qūb Beg, an ambitious, aggressive soldier, eventually took charge of the anti-Ch'ing forces and became the principal opponent of the court. Previously, he had been only a minor military figure in Kokand, and his record had been marred by a defeat in a battle with the Russians in 1864. Nonetheless, the Khan of Kokand selected him to accompany the khoja eastward, and he rapidly took advantage of his good fortune to seize power in Sinkiang. He first deposed the Kirghiz chieftain who had invited him and the khoja. By adroit diplomacy and grand promises of rewards, he then gained the allegiance of the Kirghiz and Uighurs of southern Sinkiang. In 1868, he induced the khoja Buzurg Khan to go into exile. He was totally ruthless in dealing with recalcitrant peoples. 'For example, after he was welcomed into Khotan, he invited the local chiefs to a feast. When he gave the signal, his guests were seized and immediately executed.'[14] Using these and similar tactics, Ya'qūb Beg consolidated his power in Kashgar and occupied one town after another in Sinkiang. His troops moved into Kucha in 1867, Korla in 1869, and Turfan in 1871. It appeared that the obvious next direction for expansion was into Ili, but Ya'qūb was not destined to move into this region.

Ya'qūb imposed his own rule on the newly conquered territories of Sinkiang. He assumed the title *Athalik Ghazi*, or 'Champion Father', and took this appellation seriously. His first step was to nationalize the land under his control; part was sold to provide income for the government and part was granted to his retainers to ensure their loyalty. To identify and then eliminate dissent, he organized a highly

177

effective secret police which kept close watch on those suspected of disloyalty and placed numerous restrictions on the populace. To raise revenue for his state, he imposed stiff taxes on peasants and, what was perhaps more lucrative, demanded contributions from merchants for 'police protection'. He failed to achieve his other main goal, the conscription and maintenance of a powerful military force, partly as a result of his own policies. He relied principally upon Kokandians because his efforts to recruit the local peoples of Sinkiang were clumsy and yielded few enthusiastic soldiers. Prospective recruits were distressed by the harsh discipline in Ya'qūb's army and, after the initial conquests had been made, by the 'news of the meagreness of spoils'.[15]

In short, Ya'qūb's policies alienated many inhabitants of Sinkiang who might otherwise have supported him. They resented the spying of Ya'qūb's police force upon their activities. Merchants resented the taxes on their transactions which, together with the disruption of their trade with China, placed enormous financial burdens on them. The peasants, too, loathed the onerous taxes demanded of them, particularly when they observed that much of their money was squandered on court luxuries. Since Ya'qūb's army consisted primarily of Kokandians and other outsiders, the peoples of the region may have considered it an occupation force.

The Ch'ing initially missed this opportunity to profit from the discontent of the Uighurs and Kazakhs of Sinkiang. At first, they were preoccupied with the Taiping rebels. Yet even after the final defeat of the Taiping forces, the Ch'ing court was ineffective in its efforts to crush Ya'qūb. It was hampered by the inefficiency and complacency of its military leaders, the poor and ineffective appeals made to the local peoples, and the inadequacy of supplies for its soldiers. Late in 1865, the governor-general of Shensi and Kansu reported that he 'recently checked the treasury and there were only a little more than one thousand taels of silver left. . . . The essential supplies for the army, such as iron, gunpowder, cloth, bamboo, and wood, all have to be imported from outside.'[16] The unpaid, demoralized, and ill-supplied Ch'ing soldiers began to mutiny. Meanwhile some of the generals in the region dispatched false reports of victories to the court, which was lulled into an illusory sense of security. Even more damaging, the Peking government and the commanders in the field constantly wavered in their policies towards the insurgents, sometimes seeking to annihilate them and sometimes attempting to achieve a peaceful resolution of the conflict. Such conditions and policies precluded the possibility of recovering the rebellious areas.

RUSSIAN THREATS AND CH'ING RESPONSES IN CENTRAL ASIA

Unlike the Ch'ing, Russia was able to profit from the disturbances in Central Asia. It had attempted to acquire territory, or at least to gain influence, in the region since the seventeenth century. Trade had been its first objective, and here it encountered difficulties. Central Asian merchants, in particular those from the region around Bukhara, wished to preserve their highly profitable monopoly of East–West commerce and acted to prevent Russian merchants from trading directly with East Asia. They therefore harassed Russian merchants who strayed too far to the east, sometimes capturing and even enslaving them. The nomadic Kazakhs had also been a source of trouble for the Russians, for they preyed upon Russian caravans, confiscating goods and killing or enslaving merchants.

The Russians decided on a more aggressive policy to promote their commercial interests. In 1717, their troops had suffered a disastrous defeat at the hands of the Khivans, so they began to concentrate on the northern areas of Central Asia. By the middle of the eighteenth century, they had secured the 'submission' of the Little and Middle Hordes of the Kazakhs, but it took longer to bring these two nomadic groups under effective control. Kazakh resentment at Russian incursions into their pasture land and at the influx of Russian settlers into their territory was manifested in revolts and raids in the latter half of the eighteenth century. Before the Russian conquest, they had been free to move to grazing lands near water in summer and lands relatively free of snow in winter, but Russian regulations limited their mobility, jeopardizing their whole way of life. The Russian state exacted taxes in money, which often forced the Kazakhs into debt. On top of this, the Russian tax collectors and other officials assigned to the newly incorporated Kazakh territories made matters worse by maltreating the local people and by making excessive financial demands on them.

It is no wonder then that the Russians made little progress in pacifying Central Asia in the century after their conquest of the Little and Middle Hordes. They had alienated the Kazakhs, and needed to have time and to make efforts to win control over the other local peoples. Affairs in Europe diverted their attention, and it was only

179

after the 1830s that they could concentrate on Central Asia. Another inhibition on their expansion in Central Asia was the Russians' unwillingness to alienate the Ch'ing and risk loss of their trade with China, which itself wished to gain influence over the Kazakhs. It was only when China showed obvious signs of decay after the Opium War that the Russians again started to press forward in Central Asia.

The Russian government first overwhelmed the Kazakhs and then turned to the three principal khanates of the region. The details of Russia's expansion in Central Asia need not be recounted here. It will be sufficient to summarize the Russians' progress. By 1847, their lines of fortresses reached to the Syr-Darya River. They had defeated the Great Horde of the Kazakhs and the khanate of Kokand several times and were on the verge of conquering them when the outbreak of the Crimean War in 1853 shifted their attention to the west and delayed their plans for eastern expansion. Yet they soon recovered after their defeat in the Crimean War and renewed their offensive in Central Asia. By the end of the 1850s, the Great Horde of the Kazakhs, the last formidable independent nomadic group in the region, succumbed to the superior Russian forces. The Russians, using their forts along the Syr-Darya as bases, then moved against Kokand, reducing it a town at a time. They occupied Chimkent in 1864 and, in the following year, they took Tashkent, which they made the capital of their newly created province of Turkestan. In January 1868, they signed a peace treaty with Kokand, by which the latter virtually became a vassal of the Tsarist court.[17]

The Russians had carefully avoided warfare with the khanates of Bukhara and Khiva until they had achieved their objectives in Kokand. Bukhara, which comprised the fertile Zarafshan River valley and the traditionally prosperous commercial and craft centre in Samarkand, was Russia's next antagonist. The Khan of Bukhara reacted to Tsarist advances in Central Asia by declaring a holy war against the Russians, a decision that led to his downfall. There were tentative but fruitless attempts to conclude an agreement. In May 1868, Russian troops attacked and quickly suppressed the Muslim forces guarding Samarkand. Within a few months, the Khan of Bukhara signed a treaty by which he relinquished much of the Zarafshan valley to Russia, permitted Russian merchants to trade without hindrances in Bukhara and the surrounding regions, and accepted some direction from Moscow. The Russians were now free to move against Khiva, a khanate directly south of the Aral Sea and including the Amu-Darya River. In 1873 General K. P. von Kaufman, the principal Russian military official in Central Asia, forced Khiva to submit to a Russian protectorate.

The Russian offensive, which had initially been prompted by commercial considerations, now appeared to have broader objectives. Protection for its merchants, the desire for free unrestricted trade, and the determination to abolish slavery influenced Russia's policy. But in the 1860s, a new economic motive prompted Russian interest in the area. Russian expansion in Central Asia coincided with the outbreak of the American Civil War, which halted the flow of cotton from the southern United States to Europe and Russia. In seeking new sources of cotton, the Russians turned to their vassals in Central Asia. They sought to expand the area allotted to cotton-growing in the region, a policy that gave rise to at least two problems. One was that the reduction in the amount of land used for grain production or for pasturage led to a shortage of grain. Another was that the influx of Russian settlers and cotton-growers reduced the amount of land available to the local people and generated great hostility towards the Tsarist state. Some of the settlers forcibly and illegally seized land without compensating its owners. Though the government did not wish to alienate the local inhabitants, its appetite for cotton was so great that it often ignored legal niceties and legitimate complaints from dispossessed Kazakhs, Uzbeks, and others.[18]

Several other motives caused the Russians to intervene in Central Asia. Russian manufacturers needed an outlet for their products and saw the khanates along Russia's traditional borders as lucrative markets for their wares. There was, however, another, probably more powerful stimulus. The British, partly to protect India, the jewel of their empire, had crossed into Central Asia and were determined to halt Tsarist expansion. The Russians feared British designs on the region and were concerned about the defence of their borderlands. This threat made them even more anxious to acquire territory and to establish a buffer against possible British incursions.

From this brief survey of Russian involvement in Central Asia we begin to understand the Tsarist court's interest in and delight at Ya'qūb Beg's conquest of Sinkiang and the Muslim revolts in northwestern China. Even before the upheaval in that region, they had gained a foothold in the Chinese border areas. Indeed the Ch'ing government had needed little prompting to grant them commercial privileges: it was turning to the old policy of 'using barbarians to regulate barbarians' in an attempt to resist European pressures. By making extraordinary concessions to the Russians, it hoped to drive a wedge between the various foreign states making demands on China and to gain the support of the Tsarist court against Britain and France in particular. In 1851, the Ch'ing initiated this policy by permitting the Russians to trade and to establish consulates in the towns of Ili and Tarbagatai. Russian merchants made good use of this privilege to expand trade, and in 1860 Tsarist officials in China extracted yet more privileges from the Ch'ing court. Britain and France had defeated China in a short war in that very year and had obtained valuable economic concessions as a result. The Ch'ing, infuriated by the tactics and demands of the British and the French, attempted to employ Russia as a counterweight to the two Western European states. By the Treaty of Peking of 1860, it let Russia into Sinkiang, allowing Russian merchants to trade and Russian consuls to be stationed in the commercial emporium of Kashgar. Four years later, the Russians received, by the Treaty of Tarbagatai, a sizeable territory north of Lake Issyk-kul previously under at least nominal Ch'ing control.[19]

The Russians seized these opportunities. Merchants arrived in Sinkiang, promptly started to trade with the local people, and just as promptly urged the Russian court to obtain even more commercial concessions from the Ch'ing. Simultaneously, the court dispatched, under the aegis of the Imperial Geographical Society, several expeditions to explore its new frontier lands. Nikolai M. Przhevalski (1839–88) led one of the first of such missions and was eventually to guide five separate expeditions to Mongolia, Sinkiang, Tibet, and the Ussuri region. He returned with valuable reports on the vegetation, climate, birds, and animals of the area through which he travelled, and some of these accounts were translated into English, German, and other European languages, arousing even greater interest in Inner Asia.[20] These and similar expeditions yielded vast stores of information for the Russian court. In 1873, a certain Viktor Uspenski had published a remarkably accurate article on the history and geography of Hami, an indication of the preciseness and comprehensiveness of Russia's knowledge of the area.[21]

It is not surprising, then, that the Russian government was concerned about Ya'qūb Beg's activities in Sinkiang. The Muslim ruler, while still a subject of the Kokand khanate, had fought against Russian troops in the early 1860s and since his rise to power in Sinkiang had shown his hostility towards Russia by his generally unpleasant treatment of Russian travellers and explorers in the region. St Petersburg was also worried by his seemingly close connections with the British and feared that the British might support his efforts to establish a Muslim empire and harass Russian settlers and traders in Central Asia. Some Russian merchants were, in fact, attacked and their goods confiscated; commerce in the region was disrupted; and Muslim bandits continually endangered Russian trading caravans. In 1871, the Russians finally moved both to protect themselves and to take advantage of China's weakness in order to enlarge their own territory. Their troops occupied the fertile and strategically located Ili region, to which the Russian border was by this time adjacent. Russian officials disguised this expropriation of Chinese lands by maintaining that they intended merely to safeguard commerce and to prevent Muslim incursions in the area. They insisted that their forces would withdraw as soon as the Ch'ing armies proved themselves capable of defending Ili.[22]

The Ch'ing response to the Muslim rebellions in Shensi and Kansu, Ya'qūb Beg's conquest of Sinkiang, and the Russian occupation of Ili was delayed until after the final pacification of the Taiping rebellion in 1864. In 1866, after the failure of several feeble efforts, led by Ch'ing generals, to recover China's north-western provinces, the court appointed Tso Tsung-t'ang, the brilliant Chinese military strategist and leader who had been remarkably successful against the Taipings, to conduct the military campaigns against the Muslim rebels. Tso assumed the title of governor-general of Shensi and Kansu and reached his new base in the north-west in 1868. His preparations for his campaign were thorough, but the delays caused by his meticulousness attracted much criticism from other officials, who, either from jealousy of his power or vexation at his seeming procrastination, repeatedly accused him of inefficiency and cowardice.

Tso, however, recognized that victory would not be achieved by military means alone. He concentrated on the economic reconstruction of Shensi and Kansu rather than on vengeful devastation of the rebellious provinces. He knew of the poverty, in particular the lack of grain, in the north-west and devised a plan meant both to provide sufficient food for his troops and to gain the allegiance of the local peoples. He ordered his troops to found military colonies to produce their own food, thus assuring an adequate supply of grain before engaging the enemy. He also hoped to attract the local peoples back to the land. To this end, and to foster economic recovery, he organized

183

irrigation projects, dug wells, planted approximately half a million trees, built roads and bridges, and promoted silk and cotton production in the region. Another of his plans was to recruit at least some of his troops from the local population, perhaps another example of the policy of 'using barbarians to regulate barbarians'. Though he was only partially successful in this effort, he was more successful in another objective, that of increasing military and industrial production in Shensi and Kansu. Because of his support, Shensi and the town of Lanchou in Kansu soon possessed a woollen mill, arsenals, and foundries for the production of cannons and guns. Many of these establishments had European advisers.[23]

All Tso's policies and activities required vast sums of money. Again, he was determined to have an adequate reserve of funds before initiating an offensive. Shensi and Kansu could provide neither the necessary revenue nor the proper supplies. External sources of income would have to furnish the expenses for the campaign. The Ch'ing court ordered several prosperous provinces to supply the needed revenue, but their contributions were irregular, and Tso could not depend on funds from them. Instead, he turned to loans from Chinese merchants and later from foreign bankers and the Imperial Customs in Shanghai. Though Tso's policy eventually permitted foreigners to gain great influence over the Ch'ing economy, it provided him, in the short run, with the income essential to sustain his forces and to pay his European advisers.

With adequate supplies and revenues, Tso now deliberately launched his military campaign. Slowly, too slowly from the point of view of some court officials, he moved against the rebels. By the end of 1869, he had recovered the province of Shensi. But, as he acknowledged, his most formidable foe was Ma Hua-lung, the leader of the New Teaching sect, whose power was centred in Kansu. After his long preparations Tso's campaign culminated in 1871 in a decisive victory over Ma's troops. All that remained was a series of 'mopping-up' operations which ended in 1873 with the capture of the rebel town of Su-chou.

Tso knew that his task was not completed with the military conquest of Shensi and Kansu. He needed to revive the economy of two provinces that had been devastated in a decade of banditry and warfare. He dealt first with the people of the region, and most scholars concur that his treatment of friends and enemies alike was firm and judicious. Most of the Chinese were allowed to remain in the newly pacified territories or to return to their native villages. Some of the Muslims were also permitted to return to their original homelands, but most were resettled elsewhere. Tso noted the animosity between the Chinese and the Muslims and wished to separate the two groups in order to avoid a resumption of hostilities. To overcome the natural Muslim reluctance to abandon the homeland, Tso offered free land, houses, animals, and tools to the resettled Muslims. Though he proscribed the violently anti-Chinese New Teaching, he did not prohibit the practice of Islam. He disapproved of a direct assault on the Muslim religion, believing instead in gradually exposing Muslims to Confucian civilization and offering them opportunities for education and social advancement.[24]

Tso's conquest of the north-west was facilitated by the disunity of the opposition. The rebels in Shensi and Kansu damaged their cause by remaining in isolated and separate units. It was relatively easy for Tso to concentrate on one small band of rebels after another. He rarely faced a massive force that could rival his own. Probably more crucial, however, was Ya'qūb Beg's unwillingness or inability to assist the Muslim rebels. This was a fatal blunder, for the defeat of the rebels reduced the chances of a successful Pan-Islam movement in Central Asia. And it allowed the Ch'ing court to build up its strength for an eventual encounter with Ya'qūb.

Tso wished to initiate such a campaign, but faced great opposition at the court. Li Hung-chang, probably the most renowned Chinese statesman of the nineteenth century, advocated a policy that emphasized defence of the east coast of China. He pointed out that a strong navy was essential to repel Japan and the aggressive European powers. China, he maintained, needed to construct modern ships and to train officers and men in the new techniques of naval warfare if it wanted to retain its independence, and this effort would require vast expenditure; no money could be spared for a reckless enterprise to recover the remote territory of Sinkiang. Tso replied with the argument that areas conquered by the Ch'ien-lung emperor, one of the great rulers of the dynasty, should not be abandoned. His most telling argument was that the fall of Sinkiang would endanger first Mongolia and then Peking. To clinch his plea for funds for the attack on Sinkiang, he asserted that China stood to lose land in the north-west whereas the European powers on the east coast merely sought commercial concessions, not territory. Thus there was no military danger along the coast.[25] The court agreed with his assessment and diverted its limited financial resources from maritime defence to a north-west offensive. Tso again requested and received permission to contract foreign loans, using the customs revenue of Shanghai, Canton, and other ports as security. Food was a major concern to Tso, for Sinkiang's traditional deficiency in grain would be made even more serious by the arrival of his troops. So he ordered some of his soldiers to plant crops and to raise sufficient food for the rest of the army. In the later stages of the campaign, he received unexpected support from Russia, which supplied him with food.

The stage was finally set for a confrontation between the Ch'ing forces and Ya'qūb Beg, whose harsh rule, heavy taxes, and oppressive secret police had alienated many of his subjects. Moreover, he could not rely on assistance from the Russians, though a treaty bound their governments together. In 1872, a certain Baron Kaulbars negotiated on behalf of the Russian government a commercial agreement with Ya'qūb which provided the Russians with valuable trading privileges. Yet the Kokandian adventurer did not intend to abide by the terms. He apparently expected assistance from Turkey and Great Britain and believed that he could afford to ignore and perhaps antagonize Russia. The Muslim Ottoman Empire had enough problems of its own and was therefore in no position to aid Ya'qūb, and the British too eventually abandoned him. Britain had initially been attracted to Central Asia because of its interest in protecting India from possible Russian incursions and in promoting trade between India and Kashgar. Several English travellers, the most prominent of whom was Robert B. Shaw, returned from Ya'qūb's territories with glowing reports of the possibilities for lucrative trade with the region.[26] Like the Russians, the British, through their emissary Thomas D. Forsyth, had, early in 1874, signed a treaty with Ya'qūb by which they obtained vital commercial concessions. But their hopes for a growth in trade with the region were never fulfilled.[27] This no doubt reinforced their unwillingness to supply tangible military aid to Ya'qūb. Further, they did not wish to alienate the Ch'ing court and thereby risk losing influence in all China merely for the sake of an advantage in Sinkiang.

Bereft of allies, Ya'qūb was relatively easy prey for the Ch'ing armies. Tso Tsung-t'ang finally unleashed his forces late in 1876 and quickly took the strategically located town of Urumchi. Ya'qūb, in a panic, dispatched an emissary to persuade the British to mediate in the dispute. The British, unwilling to commit their own resources to a defence of Ya'qūb's state but eager to prevent his downfall, arranged a meeting between the Chinese ambassador in England and Ya'qūb's envoy.[28] Tso's advances in Central Asia were so rapid, however, that this mediation proved pointless. In the spring of 1877, his troops occupied Turfan. A few weeks later Ya'qūb died, probably from a dose of poison; it is not clear whether he committed suicide or was murdered. In any case, his people could not agree on a successor, and the Chinese forces profited from this disunity to annihilate the Muslim state, taking the towns of Aksu in October and Kashgar in December 1877. By 1878, Tso's troops had recovered nearly all of Sinkiang.

The Ch'ing court now turned its attention to Ili. In 1871, when the Russians occupied Ili, they had promised to return the region to Ch'ing rule once China proved capable of governing it. Now that Tso's successes showed China's ability and willingness to do so, the Russians began to hedge and demanded trade concessions before a settlement of the Ili question. The Tsungli Yamen, the new government body created in 1861 to handle China's foreign relations, despaired of dealing with Russia's representatives in China and decided to send its own mission to the Russian capital. It selected a Manchu official named Ch'ung-hou, a man accustomed to foreign diplomatic practice but totally ignorant of the geography and history of Central Asia, to lead the embassy. His instructions were vague, and he evidently had no conception of the nature of the powers delegated to him by the court. He also faced a determined and experienced group of Russian diplomats unwilling to abandon Ili without some major concessions. All these factors led to a diplomatic disaster for China: the Treaty of Livadia of 1879. Though this agreement provided for the return of the town of Ili to the Ch'ing, it also contained clauses that were extremely damaging to China's interests. One ceded the rich and strategically vital Tekes valley and the T'ien Shan passes controlling access to Kashgar and Khotan, a provision which allowed Russia to dominate the roads leading to Ili and western Sinkiang. Another granted an indemnity of four million roubles to compensate the Russians for the expenses incurred in their occupation of Ili. Yet another gave them permission to trade and to establish consulates in Hami, Turfan, Urumchi, Chia-yü-kuan, Ku-ch'eng, Kobdo, and Uliassutai.[29]

Peking was appalled to learn of what its emissary had signed away. Tso Tsung-t'ang adopted the most extreme position, requesting permission to threaten Russia with war if it refused to withdraw its troops from the whole Ili region. Tso's supporters demanded severe punishment for Ch'ung-hou, accusing him of overstepping his authority in granting such unprecedented concessions to the Russians. Li Hung-chang, who wished to concentrate the government's meagre financial resources on maritime defence, adopted a much milder tone. Indeed, at the beginning of the court deliberations, he argued for a ratification of the treaty without modifications. Sensing the opposition to this suggestion, however, he adopted the opposite view within a short time and urged some changes in the commercial provisions of the treaty. He still refused to align himself with those advocating a hard-line policy towards Russia. Court officials, nonetheless, overruled him and initiated their attempts to revise the treaty by arresting the hapless Ch'ung-hou and sentencing him to death. The foreign community in China was shocked by what appeared to them a barbaric and unjustified punishment, and they protested vehemently. Even Queen Victoria joined them in appealing for the diplomat's life. In response to the pressure from the foreigners, the court finally pardoned Ch'ung-hou, a defeat for the more militant among the Ch'ing officials.[30]

This incident, together with the advice of sympathetic foreigners, prompted the court to restrain its own war party. Tso persisted in his demand for an expedition against the Russians. Li's more moderate views, however, prevailed, particularly when the British and French representatives in China advised the Ch'ing to seek a peaceful resolution of the crisis. Perhaps as important in the court's change of attitude was the counsel of Colonel Charles Gordon. 'Chinese' Gordon, who had gained the respect of the Ch'ing for the support which his 'Ever Victorious Army' (a Chinese force commanded by Western officers) had provided in the suppression of the Taiping rebels, returned to China in 1880 at the invitation of English officials in China, the Ch'ing government, and Li Hung-chang. During his brief stay, he wrote a memorandum in which he proposed among other things that those officials who advocated war with Russia should be executed. Recognizing that any military encounter with the Russians would spell disaster for the Ch'ing, he stated his views forcefully and with great effect. The Ch'ing court did not take his suggestions literally, but it did dispatch another embassy to Russia to mediate in the dispute.[31]

Tseng Chi-tse, the son of the renowned statesman and military leader Tseng Kuo-fan, was selected to lead this delicate mission. He accepted only with great reluctance but, unlike Ch'ung-hou, he assiduously studied the issues separating the Ch'ing and Russian courts. His careful investigation of the geography, economy, and history of Central Asia strengthened his resolve to recover Ili at almost any cost. His task was facilitated by Russia's difficulties during this time. The government at St Petersburg was already embroiled in disputes with most of the European powers and, in particular, with Great Britain. Since the British appeared to support the Ch'ing demands for a reconsideration and revision of the Treaty of Livadia, the Russians could not totally ignore the Ch'ing court and its envoy. They feared possible British reprisals if they adamantly refused to make any concession. Their gains in the negotiations with Ch'ung-hou did not justify the risk of war with Britain.

Russia's internal problems further served to deter its officials from adopting a hard line in their meetings with Tseng. The court faced severe financial problems, due partly to a recently concluded war with Turkey and partly to lavish expenditures on luxuries; its army was rife with corruption and was, in any case, too small to take on China in an all-out war ranging from Central Asia all the way to the Amur River valley; and its political power and legitimacy were challenged by dissident students and intellectuals who resented the autocratic power and the economic inequality fostered by the government.

Tseng and China were the beneficiaries of the domestic and international problems that plagued the Russians. Tsarist officials differed on the tactics to be employed in the negotiations with the Ch'ing envoy, and Tseng took advantage of their indecisiveness to attain his objectives. After many delays and disputes, the two parties finally reached a compromise and signed the Treaty of St Petersburg on 24 February 1881. The Ch'ing agreed to provide an indemnity of nine million roubles, to relinquish land west of the town of Ili, to permit the establishment of Russian consulates in Su-chou and Turfan, and to allow Russian merchants to trade permanently in Mongolia and for a limited period in Sinkiang, without having to pay Chinese taxes. The Russians abandoned the Tekes valley and the passes leading to Khotan and Kashgar, accepted a reduction in the number of consulates in Sinkiang, and retracted their demands for additional trade routes through the region. Both sides had recognized the futility of an expensive and debilitating war and restrained their more militant and aggressive officials. Some Ch'ing officials, nonetheless, believed that by their forcefulness they had induced the Tsarist court to accept many of their demands.[32]

The culmination of Chi'ng policy was the inclusion of Sinkiang in the regular administrative structure of China. That vast region had formerly been governed by the Ch'ing military, and court officials had considered it a colony useful for its strategic and commercial possibilities. They had appointed military commissioners to co-operate with the local rulers in order to prevent attacks by the non-Chinese population against the neighbouring Chinese provinces, to collect taxes and administer justice among these peoples, and to repel Russian and British intruders from the region. Tso Tsung-t'ang and others of like mind now proposed that Sinkiang should be organized as a Ch'ing province. They argued that the region was too important to be left under solely military rule. The court concurred, and in 1884 made Sinkiang a province, abolishing the old military administration. It appointed a civil bureaucracy under the direction of a provincial governor to replace the military commissioners. Despite this change, Ch'ing control of the region was not strengthened. Rebellions against Ch'ing rule continued throughout the closing years of the nineteenth century. In 1895, a particularly violent revolt erupted in Kansu and soon spread into parts of Sinkiang. Like so many of the earlier outbreaks in the region, it originated as a struggle between the Old and New Teaching sects and then expanded into an anti-Ch'ing rebellion. The government quelled the revolt within a year, but it had to contend with numerous other uprisings in the period before the dynasty fell in 1911.

The controversy over the wisdom of the Ch'ing decision to recover Sinkiang and Ili still rages. On the one hand, there are those who primarily emphasize the benefits: 'Psychologically, it [the conquest of Sinkiang] restored pride to the crumbling Ch'ing dynasty. . . . Diplomatically, it put the Chinese into a position to demand the return of the Ili Valley from Russia, and gave the court a new confidence in foreign relations. An active and assertive policy was now substituted for the passive and defensive approach to foreign affairs.'[33] On the other hand, some argue that the damaging consequences far outweighed the temporary gains. They point out that the Ch'ing, like the Ming, concentrated on defence against the 'barbarians' from the north and north-west and tended to ignore the threat posed by 'barbarians' from the south. Unlike the Ming, however, the Ch'ing dynasty attempted to govern the neighbouring territories in the north-west, rather than simply maintain peaceful relations with their rulers. In attempting to control these regions, the Ch'ing invested vast financial and human resources. Though Tso Tsung-t'ang's military feats were truly remarkable, it is at least questionable whether this enormous investment really strengthened the state.

The Ch'ing court certainly preserved its control, however tenuously, over the non-Han populations in the north-west, but it encountered difficulties in other regions. Tso's campaigns diverted funds from maritime defence and from efforts to industrialize, making China even more vulnerable to threats and attacks by the European powers and the Japanese. This shortage of funds was one of the reasons why the Ch'ing government failed to put up an effective and successful defence against the Japanese in the Sino-Japanese War of 1894–95 and against the European dismemberment of China in the last years of the nineteenth century.

8 Cracks in the Ch'ing empire: Manchuria and Mongolia

Ch'ing policy in Manchuria was challenged even though that frontier region appeared tranquil in the early 1800s. It seemed that the Ch'ing had succeeded in keeping Manchuria isolated and free from foreign interference. Until the early nineteenth century, the court had been fairly successful in excluding Chinese immigration to the region. It had also negotiated agreements with the Tsarist court in 1689 and 1728 that limited Russian expansion in the Amur valley. The Kiakhta trade largely satisfied the Russians for most of the eighteenth century. Though the Russians and the Ch'ing accused each other of bad faith and the markets were occasionally closed, trade continued and in fact expanded throughout this period. Border raids, thefts of livestock and other goods, harbouring of fugitives and deserters by Russian officials, poor quality of products offered in trade, the lawless behaviour of merchants, and intimidation of the local inhabitants by travelling envoys and merchants all provoked unpleasant incidents and bitter feelings. Yet commerce was profitable, and the Russians sought to expand and improve conditions for trade. In 1805, the Tsarist court dispatched Count Golovkin to negotiate for changes in economic relations.

Golovkin was instructed to persuade the Ch'ing to permit Russian navigation of the Amur, an increase in the number of markets along the Russian-Chinese borders, and the opening of the port of Canton to Russian trade. Like nearly all the other Russian envoys to China, he was also expected to gather information. His government wanted him to bring back reports on China's relations with its Inner Asian neighbours, the possibility of Russian trade with Tibet and India through China, and the military strength and potential of the Ch'ing

192

empire. But Golovkin did not reach Peking. The chief Ch'ing official in Urga demanded that the envoy practise the kowtow before a figure whom he described as a representation of the emperor. When Golovkin refused, he was denied entry into China. The Russians were clearly annoyed by this insult, but were too embroiled in domestic and European affairs for the next thirty or forty years to pursue their objectives in Manchuria.

Manchuria, with its seemingly unlimited territory, its fertile soil, its abundant natural resources, and its relatively small population was, however, extremely alluring to the Chinese. As late as the 1850s, the total population of the region was only three million, or just over eight to the square mile. The Chinese were eager to emigrate into the region and the Ch'ing court itself had been partly responsible for the first influx of Chinese colonists into Manchuria. From the early years of the dynasty in the seventeenth century, in order to buttress their defences against the Russians and other possible foreign intruders, the Ch'ing had brought in Chinese farmers to establish agricultural colonies for the maintenance of the Manchu banner troops. Ch'ing officials also employed Chinese conscripts in postal stations, and as sailors and craftsmen. The original recruits had been dissident scholars and officials who had opposed Ch'ing rule; by the eighteenth century, many of the settlers were ordinary criminals. A large number were forced labourers or slaves, but a few managed to pursue their own occupations. They were in great demand as artisans, merchants, doctors, and, indeed, in almost any occupation that required literacy and a knowledge of Chinese.[1]

Even more important and numerous were the illegal immigrants into Manchuria. The tremendous growth in the population of China in the eighteenth and nineteenth centuries necessitated a search for new, underpopulated land. Agricultural failures in several of the north-eastern provinces of China made this even more urgent. Chinese merchants started to move into the frontier land of Manchuria. Though the Ch'ing court had attempted to limit their activities and to monopolize certain of Manchuria's natural resources, the merchants by the early nineteenth century were easily evading government regulations and engaging in a highly profitable trade with the local peoples. At first they obtained furs, ginseng, liquor, sheep, and leather; by the late nineteenth century they added soybeans, beef, and opium to their acquisitions. The frontier tribes, having been exposed to Chinese culture and Chinese goods, developed a desire for such products as tea, silk, cotton, and various luxuries. To satisfy the demands of both the Chinese and the frontier tribes, merchants needed great resources of capital, and as trade developed in the middle of the nineteenth century, a few large enterprises, supported by vast wealth, dominated the commerce. The merchants from the province of Shansi, in particular, were among the principal agents of trade and were responsible for the creation of banks in the 1880s and 1890s to facilitate commerce and to exploit the resources of Manchuria. As well as the merchants, who often engaged in illicit transactions, other Chinese also sought to profit from the riches of the land northeast of China. Individual Chinese slipped across the border to find ginseng, furs, gold, and other products to meet the Chinese demand. By its inability to prevent such illegal immigration, the Ch'ing inadvertently paved the way for a more permanent group of settlers.

Chinese peasants, forced off their own land by high taxes, natural disasters, and population pressures, were attracted by the virgin lands across the frontier. Hearing reports from itinerant traders and fortune hunters of the fertility of the soil, peasants started to migrate to Manchuria in the early nineteenth century. The Ch'ing government at first attempted to restrict the flow of Chinese, but its weak and demoralized banner troops in Manchuria failed to halt the colonizers from the south and, in fact, often assisted them to elude detection in return for bribes. This clearly demonstrated the decline of the Ch'ing. A further manifestation of the erosion of their power was a policy which they initiated during the Taiping rebellion. To obtain desperately needed funds for its armies, the court sold so-called 'waste' land in southern Manchuria to Chinese settlers. These settlers not only cultivated their own legally purchased land but also impinged upon the territory inhabited by the indigenous herdsmen, hunters, and fishermen.[2]

This influx of Chinese colonists totally disrupted the Ch'ing system in Manchuria. The banner troops were increasingly ineffective, and as the Russians began to threaten the Amur region in the 1850s, the Ch'ing relied more and more on Chinese forces. Many of the bannermen, whose livelihood depended on their cultivation of their own land, could not compete with the Chinese immigrants and often, simply for survival, sold their land to the newcomers. The frontier tribesmen, at whom much of Ch'ing policy was directed, found that Chinese settlers were acquiring their land – in some cases merely by asserting squatters' rights, but in others by outright purchase from the tribal peoples themselves. The tribesmen, too, could not compete with the Chinese in farming the land. Their exposure to Chinese culture stimulated a yearning for Chinese goods and a desire to imitate Chinese dress, values, and patterns of life. Many of them sold their land in order to buy the Chinese products which they coveted. They temporarily enjoyed their luxuries and led dissipated lives, but soon found themselves paupers. With the gradual impoverishment of both the bannermen and the tribesmen, Ch'ing administrative institutions no longer operated properly. The tribute system and the official trade that accompanied it, for example, were now of scant economic significance. Direct private trade with Chinese merchants replaced the officially sanctioned commerce.

Russian penetration of the Amur subverted the Ch'ing administration and eventually forced the Ch'ing to reverse their policy in Manchuria. In the 1840s, Russia could finally turn its attention to East Asia, partly as a result of a brief period of peace in its relations with the other European powers and the Ottoman Empire and an accompanying short span of internal tranquillity. Perhaps an even greater stimulus for Russian action was the change in the East Asian balance of power precipitated by the Opium War. The Treaty of Nanking of 1842, which had concluded the war, granted major economic privileges to Great Britain, and within a few years, France, the United States, and other Western states received similar concessions. Realizing that these agreements threatened Russia's trade position with China, the Russian government attempted to protect its profitable relationship with the Ch'ing. The Kiakhta trade had been extremely valuable in the early nineteenth century, the Russians principally providing textiles and some furs and receiving chiefly tea and some silk from the Ch'ing. China's new arrangements with the maritime powers, which could transport bulkier goods more cheaply than those states dependent on the land routes through Eurasia, undermined Russia's favourable economic relations with the Ch'ing.

Russia's appointment of Nikolai Muraviev as governor-general of Eastern Siberia was the first response to the new situation. Muraviev recognized the extent of China's deterioration, as evidenced in the Opium War, and determined on a forceful policy to take advantage of its weakness. Totally disregarding Russia's treaty obligations with China, he ordered his troops to conduct exploratory missions along the lower Amur. On one of these explorations in 1850, the Russian contingent founded a base on the shores of the river and dubbed it

Nikolaevsk in honour of Tsar Nicholas I.[3] Some government officials in St Petersburg opposed this aggressive policy, objecting that such forcefulness might alienate the other Western powers, particularly Britain, and damage Russian interests in Europe.

The outbreak of the Crimean War in 1853 silenced most of the opposition to Muraviev. As Britain and France were Russia's enemies in this struggle over Turkey and Russian navigation in the Black Sea, Muraviev now had greater freedom of action. He no longer needed to worry about their reactions to his policies and faced less opposition from St Petersburg. In fact, one of his subordinates routed a combined Anglo-French naval force along the Amur. In 1854 and again in 1855, Muraviev deliberately broke Russia's earlier treaties with China by sailing down the Amur. He was accompanied not only by a detachment of his own troops but also by colonists who wished to settle along the banks of the Amur. His territorial claims, which included the then astounding notion that Russia had exclusive rights over the left bank of the river, went far beyond any previous statement issued in the name of the Russian government.[4] Even Russia's defeat in the Crimean War in 1856 did not deter him in his effort to expand Russia's frontiers. He continued to navigate the Amur and to establish settlements along its course.

The Ch'ing response to Russian expansion was ineffective. Court officials were more concerned about quelling the devastating Taiping rebellion, which threatened the very existence of the Ch'ing empire. They also faced severe pressure in the south-east from the British and the French, who sought further commercial concessions as well as diplomatic representation in Peking. With these other problems preoccupying them, they persisted in delaying confrontations or negotiations with the Russians. When in 1857 and 1858 the Russian envoy Count Efim Putiatin attempted merely to discuss the boundaries along the Amur, the court refused him entry into Peking, requesting instead that he deal with I-shan, the Ch'ing military governor of the Manchurian region of Heilungkiang. Putiatin, in turn, refused to negotiate with anyone other than the authorities in the capital.[5]

Realizing that Putiatin could not be coaxed into meeting him on the Manchurian frontier, I-shan, on his own initiative, resumed negotiations with the belligerent Muraviev. Their meetings resulted in the Treaty of Aigun of 1858, by which, according to one estimate, China lost 185,000 square miles. The treaty defined the boundary between Russia and China as the Amur, the left bank going to Russia, while the Ussuri River to the sea was temporarily to be in the joint possession of the two states. It denied access to the Amur, Ussuri, and Sungari rivers to all states other than China and Russia, but permitted Russian and Chinese merchants to trade on the three rivers.[6] I-shan had made some major concessions to the Russians, thus causing Peking to revive an old Ch'ing tactic.

The court now reverted, though not consistently, to the policy of 'using barbarians to regulate barbarians' in its dealings with the foreigners. It was less apprehensive of the Russians, with whom it had maintained relations for over 150 years, than of the British, with whom it had only recently concluded a war, and of the French. The two Western European powers, which also desired commercial privileges and official representation in Peking, in addition had armies and navies poised to attack the Chinese heartland. In May 1858 a combined Anglo-French expedition bombarded a Chinese position in the northeast and entered the city of Tientsin. Though the Russians had taken no part in the fighting, the Ch'ing court invited them to act as advisers during the negotiations which followed the cessation of hostilities. The Ch'ing may have been motivated by the hope that their invitation to the Russians might accentuate the discord between the Russians and the two European powers, and might also obtain for them Russian support in placating the seemingly more dangerous and aggressive Westerners. For their contribution to the peace talks, which was minimal, the Russians certainly received concessions from the Ch'ing court. In June, a month after the Anglo-French attack, Putiatin and a Ch'ing delegation concluded the Treaty of Tientsin, by which the Ch'ing waived many of the former restrictions on Russian trade with China, opened several ports to Russian merchants, offered most-favoured-nation treatment to Russia, and promised a speedy study and delineation of the Sino-Russian borders. Putiatin, in return for these favourable terms, attempted, if occasionally half-heartedly, to temper some of the harsher British and French demands on China, and the resulting Ch'ing treaties with the two Western states were perhaps less onerous than they might otherwise have been.[7]

The Ch'ing court now discontinued its policy of favouring the Russians. After considerable delays, a new Tsarist envoy named Perovski finally elicited a ratification of the Treaty of Tientsin from the Ch'ing. But the court refused to ratify the Treaty of Aigun, particularly after a fortuitous victory over a small British force which sought to obtain ratification of its own treaty with the Ch'ing. Even the arrival in 1859 of a higher-ranking Russian envoy, Nikolai Ignatiev, failed to stir the Ch'ing court and to shake its confidence. Ignatiev could gain no satisfaction and waited for the British and the French to act. The two European states moved a large force into position to 'punish' the Ch'ing for its deception and for its overweening self-confidence, and in the late summer of 1860 they unleashed an assault on Tientsin. They quickly took the city and advanced towards Peking. In a panic at the success of the 'barbarian' invaders, the emperor ignominiously fled the capital, hoping to find sanctuary in his palace at Jehol (in modern Inner Mongolia). The Ch'ing troops, demoralized by the emperor's flight, scarcely resisted the invaders, and the Western troops had occupied Peking by the end of the year.[8]

The Ch'ing court, perhaps regretting its earlier treatment of Ignatiev, called upon the Russian envoy to intercede on its behalf with the two hostile European states. Ignatiev, in turn, used his advantageous position to obtain more concessions from the court, occasionally profiting from China's ignorance of Russia's limited naval and military strength in East Asia to intimidate the Ch'ing into accepting his terms. It appears that he barely intervened in the negotiations between the Europeans and the Ch'ing, but he claimed credit for having reduced the British and French demands on the court, and the Ch'ing officials apparently accepted that he had. In November 1860, he received his reward, the Sino-Russian Treaty of Peking. This new agreement confirmed the territorial arrangements of the Treaty of Aigun and eventually added over one hundred thousand square miles to the Russian gains in the Amur region. It also defined the boundary between the empires in Central Asia, expanded opportunities for trade in newly opened border markets, and permitted the establishment of consulates in China and Russia.[9] Similarly, the British and French concluded treaties with the Ch'ing which granted them extensive economic and diplomatic privileges.

The initial results of this favourable treaty disappointed the Russians. Though they founded the port of Vladivostok, they could not compete with the British for the China coast trade, particularly after the opening in 1869 of the Suez Canal, which further reduced the distance from Europe to East Asia. Their overland commerce with China did not substantially increase over the next three decades. While the population of Siberia almost tripled in the last half of the nineteenth century, the total number of people by 1900 (slightly over seven million) was still paltry for that part of the world. The government, in addition, was unable to attract large numbers of settlers to the newly acquired lands north of the Amur. Shortages of food and of most other supplies, poor transport and communications, unfriendly local people, and a seemingly hazardous and untamed environment deterred colonists and impeded Tsarist efforts in the region.

The Russians therefore turned to the control and colonization of their more accessible, recently conquered territories in Central Asia. Although our main concern here is with *China's* relations with Inner Asia, it is necessary to summarize Russia's efforts in Central Asia in order to understand its policy along the Amur River and in Manchuria.

As soon as the Russians occupied the khanates of Bukhara, Khiva, and Kokand, they began to foster a particular kind of economic transformation. They viewed these lands as colonies for their own enrichment. Yet they recognized that their exploitation of the area should also benefit the local inhabitants. They therefore aimed to improve irrigation facilities, introduce new agricultural tools and methods, and build roads. Their overriding concern, however, was with profit for the Tsarist government in European Russia. And they frequently tolerated harsh exploitation of the Kazakhs, Uzbeks, and other subjugated peoples as long as they received the goods which they coveted. Cotton was the most valuable import from the region, and the Tsarist government allowed Russian peasants to use questionable tactics in expropriating the pasture lands of the local inhabitants in order to plant cotton, as long as it obtained its share of the produce.[10] It did not really care that the emphasis on cotton production deprived Central Asia of self-sufficiency in food, and forced the local people to rely on grain imports. Many non-Russians, compelled to abandon their nomadic pastoral life-styles due to the influx of Russian settlers, moved to such cities as Tashkent, accelerating the urbanization of the region. It is true that the government sought, if somewhat ineffectively, to prevent forcible seizure of land, and, if it failed, it found employment for the local inhabitants in mining, timber, and related industries. It also reformed the archaic administrative and legal apparatus in the region, promoted education, expanded trade, founded newspapers and libraries, and abolished slavery and inhumane punishments. But to secure cotton and other raw materials for its industries, the Russian government was tolerant of abuses. It strenuously encouraged peasants to migrate eastward to Central Asia. The most significant stimulus to colonization was the improvement of transport, and in particular the building of railways. Rail lines stretching from European Russia to all three of the khanates were laid in the 1870s and 1880s, paving the way for the flood of Russian settlers in the late nineteenth century.[11]

Hoping similarly to spur the economic development of their Far Eastern lands north of the Amur, the Russians now conceived the plan of a railway across Siberia to Vladivostok. This Trans-Siberian Railway would not only facilitate the movement of settlers to that sparsely colonized region, but would also speed up the flow of goods across Russia and enable the Tsarist government to compete with Britain and the other naval powers for trade with China. In 1891, the Tsar approved the plans for the railway, and construction began shortly afterwards. It appeared that the Russians were on the verge of a major breakthrough in their economic relations with East Asia.

The most serious obstacle to Russian ambitions in north-east Asia was now posed by the Japanese. Since the Meiji restoration of 1868, Japan had embarked on a policy of rapid industrialization and had capitalized on its newly established military strength to challenge Ch'ing hegemony in Formosa, Korea, and the Ryūkyū Islands. This clash of interests led to the Sino-Japanese War of 1894–95, in which the Japanese decisively defeated the Ch'ing forces. By the resulting treaty, the Japanese acquired, among other possessions, control of the Liaotung peninsula, assuring them of a base in southern Manchuria.

The Russian government's response was immediate and dramatic. It realized that such a cession of Chinese territory to the Japanese endangered its own designs in Manchuria. Under the leadership of its Minister of Finance, Count Sergei Witte, who had also been instrumental in the decision to build the Trans-Siberian Railway, it organized a consortium, with Germany and France, to exert pressure on Japan to abandon claims to the Liaotung peninsula. Japan did, in fact, bow to these pressures, and that vital coastal region reverted to China.[12] The Russians quickly claimed credit for preserving Chinese territory intact and joined with the French in providing a loan so that the Ch'ing could pay the indemnity that the Japanese demanded. In return, the Tsarist court was eager to gain Ch'ing approval for a project of great importance to Russia. The Russians had formulated a plan for building the Trans-Siberian Railway along a less circuitous route than was originally conceived. They wished to save about 350 miles by taking the railway south-east from the Siberian town of Chita across Chinese territory in northern Manchuria to Vladivostok, instead of keeping it on Russian soil around the great northern loop of the Argun and Amur rivers.

When Russia pressed for acceptance of its demands, the Ch'ing recognized the hopelessness of resisting one of its few potential allies among foreign states. The Sino-Japanese War had exposed China's military weakness, so that the Ch'ing needed to cultivate good relations with one or more of the great powers to avert further losses. In 1896, the leading Chinese statesman, Li Hung-chang, travelled to St Petersburg, ostensibly to attend the coronation of Nicholas II, but with the real purpose of negotiating a treaty with Russia. With the payment of three million roubles to Li, the Russians gained their principal objectives within a few months. A secret treaty signed by Li and the Foreign Minister, Lobanov-Rostovski, called for mutual defence against aggressors. To facilitate the common defence, a joint Russian-Chinese stock company received permission to build the Chinese Eastern Railway across Manchuria. Shares in the company were sold on the open market, but the Russian government managed to purchase the bulk of them. The agreement provided that China could buy the railway after thirty-six years, but the Russians deliberately inflated the costs of constructing the line, thus preventing the Chinese from repurchasing it within that time. China would regain ownership of the railway after eighty years without payment, but by then the Russians expected to have a virtual monopoly of the Manchurian economy. Russian citizens administered the railway, and the line had its own police force, with a large Russian component. The Tsar's government had attained its principal objectives and within a few years had even more opportunities to improve its position in Manchuria.

China's disastrous defeat in the Sino-Japanese War prompted the foreign powers, including Russia, to take advantage of the Ch'ing court's weakness in the last five years of the nineteenth century. Germany, using the pretext of the murder of two of its missionaries, occupied Tsingtao on the Shantung peninsula in 1897 and soon demanded special rights throughout Shantung province. The other European states followed suit, France claiming a special interest in southern China and Britain advancing a claim to the Yangtze valley region. Some of the more adventurous Russian officials also wanted a share of the spoils. Count Witte, who had earlier negotiated successfully for the construction of the railway lines across Manchuria, now objected to further incursions on Chinese territory and sovereignty, fearing that such additional burdens might lead to the collapse of the Chinese empire. The court overrode Witte's opposition and demanded and received a twenty-five-year lease of the Liaotung peninsula as well as an option to build a railway from Harbin, a town in Manchuria along the path of the Chinese Eastern Railway, south to Ta-lien (which the Japanese later named Dairen), a vital ice-free port in Liaotung. Control of the ports of Ta-lien (renamed 'Dalny' by the Russians) and Lu-shun (renamed Port Arthur by the British) was the principal Russian gain in 1898; it provided them with vital advantages in their competition with other states for the China trade and with ample opportunities and facilities to encourage the colonization of Manchuria.[13]

The Boxer Rebellion of 1900 provided even greater opportunities for Russian infiltration in Manchuria. This outbreak, which started in Shantung and spread to Manchuria, was a response to the political and economic failures of the late Ch'ing dynasty. It grew into a fervent anti-foreign movement and eventually obtained the half-hearted support of the Ch'ing court. The rebels attacked and destroyed Christian churches, ripped up telegraph and railway lines, and laid siege to the foreign legations in Peking. From the Russian standpoint, the most pernicious activities of the Boxers were their deliberate attacks on labourers building a branch line of the Chinese Eastern Railway from Harbin to Ta-lien. These hostile acts offered the Russians a convenient pretext for dispatching troops into Manchuria. Witte again attempted to prevent such an intrusion, but his opponents, making capital of the Boxers' destruction of expensive railway equipment and their maltreatment of captured Russian labourers, persuaded the court to send an occupation force. After several pitched battles, one column of Russian troops took Harbin while another occupied Hailar and Tsitsihar, all of which were towns along the Chinese Eastern Railway. One notorious incident occurred during this short-lived war: 'The [Russian] Governor of Blagoveshchensk forced the Chinese merchants in the city to cross the Amur River; those who resisted were killed on the spot. The merchants proceeded to the river *en masse*, but there were no ferries to carry them across, while behind them were Russian Cossacks . . . who forced these three thousand men and women, old and young, to plunge into the river where they were all drowned.'[14] The Russians then launched an offensive into southern Manchuria, and captured Kirin and Mukden in the autumn of 1900. The fall of Mukden signalled the end of the fighting, and by that time the Russians had approximately 173,000 soldiers in Manchuria.

The Russians immediately sought to profit from their spectacular and easy military successes. One of their commanders negotiated a secret treaty with a military governor in Manchuria, which granted Russia great influence not only in Manchuria but also in Mongolia and Sinkiang and which permitted it to station troops as far south as the Mukden region.[15] It even appeared that the Russians would shortly detach Manchuria from Ch'ing control.

The Ch'ing court reacted to all these Russian advances by completely reversing some of its earlier policies. It abandoned its attempt to preserve Manchuria as a refuge for the Manchus and permitted and even encouraged Chinese colonization. The reason for the change was simple: the court wished to prevent Manchuria from falling to the Russians. One region after another was opened to Chinese settlers in the last half of the nineteenth century. With the construction of railways, the flood of immigrants could not be stopped. The population of Manchuria in the years 1895–1900 has been estimated at nine million, in 1906 at thirteen million, and in 1916 at twenty million.[16] Many of the immigrants were farmers from Shantung and Chihli (modern Hopei) who had earlier obtained seasonal employment in Manchuria but had now decided to settle there. The court sold them land and in 1908 even established a Frontier Agricultural Settlement Bureau to assist them in resettling. Most of them remained in agriculture, and the total area under cultivation in Manchuria grew tremendously; the average annual rate of growth from 1908 to 1931 was 2.8 per cent., and the rate from 1895 to 1908 was probably comparable.[17] Some of the newcomers found employment in the gold-mining and coal-mining enterprises that the Ch'ing authorized in the latter half of the century, and a few became trappers in order to satisfy the European demand for furs.

The influx of Chinese settlers undermined the culture and the economy of the frontier Manchus. Local peoples in the area found that the Chinese were constantly encroaching on their lands. Many of them, whose pasture land or whose hunting and fishing habitat was lost to Chinese settlers, became impoverished and relied on loans from Chinese merchants in order to survive. Some coveted Chinese goods, and they too incurred enormous debts to satisfy their desires. Their economic decline was accompanied by a general cultural deterioration which led to the virtual disappearance of some tribes and to the assimilation with the Chinese of some others. By the early 1900s, in some parts of Manchuria Manchu culture ceased to exist and the Manchu language died out. The Ch'ing government was doubtless aware of this trend but was obliged to tolerate it. If it wished to prevent a Russian takeover, it needed to open Manchuria to Chinese colonization.

Similarly, it needed to adapt its government in Manchuria to these changes. The Chinese naturally wanted and deserved greater political power, and this required the shifting of authority from the frontier Manchus to the Chinese. There was also no doubt that a new civilian government was needed to replace the military structure established in the seventeenth century. After some hesitation, and after the disastrous Boxer Rebellion, the court bowed to the inevitable. In 1906, the Ch'ing authorities in Peking offered a concession to those who sought reform by forming provincial assemblies in Manchuria, like those in other Chinese provinces, with powers to deliberate and to advise local officials and the central government. They also introduced reforms in the military which reduced the role of the Manchu banner troops and provided for the sinicization of the army, particularly among the officers.[18] In 1907, the court took the decisive step of reorganizing Manchuria under a governor-general, with local civilian governors for the three provinces of Fengtien, Kirin, and Heilungkiang. Under this plan, the civilian authorities dominated the military and were, in fact, responsible for the training of an adequate defence force. Though the governor-general was supreme, the local governors, together with various executive bureaux, intendants for education and finance, and judges, had jurisdiction over day-to-day affairs.

Yet these changes in the political structure were deceptive. It is true that some of the new Chinese residents gained political power commensurate with their numbers and with their economic and social influence. It also appears that the court successfully introduced some reforms in education and the economy and established a relatively independent and modern judiciary. But the provincial assemblies were corrupt and represented the monied élite. Neither they nor the judiciary were able to check the growing power of the governor-general, who was thus free to override any legal restraints. The governor-general was often an autocrat, and the lack of curbs on his power paved the way for the warlordism that prevailed in Manchuria after 1911. This unstable situation in Manchuria in the early years of the twentieth century furnished excellent opportunities for the Russians to claim a sphere of influence in the area, and it was only through Japanese intervention that the Russians were frustrated.

The Japanese government was perturbed by Russian expansion in

Manchuria. It too considered China's north-eastern provinces as rich areas for investment, invaluable sources of raw materials, fertile land for Japanese settlers, and strategic bases on the Asian mainland. When the Ch'ing court allowed to leak out the news of the secret treaty forced upon its representative by the Russians in the aftermath of the Boxer Rebellion, the Japanese were appalled, for the document virtually ensured Russian military and economic control over Manchuria. Japan and some of the European powers viewed with dismay the possibility of a Russian sphere of influence in Manchuria and advised the Ch'ing court to refrain from ratifying treaties with individual states until a general settlement of the Boxer dispute had been arranged. The Russians, concerned in their turn about the attitudes of the other European countries, now offered more lenient terms to the Ch'ing court, including a promise to remove their troops from the north-eastern provinces in return for the neutralization and demilitarization of those regions and an indemnity for the losses incurred by the Chinese Eastern Railway. Japan was still not satisfied, fearing future Russian moves in Manchuria. Recognizing the likelihood of war with Russia, it attempted to deprive Russia of the support of the European states in the event of such a clash. Its efforts culminated in the creation of an alliance with Britain in 1902, which obliged Britain to prevent Germany and France from supporting Russia in a war with Japan. The British consented to the alliance, for they were still apprehensive of Russian territorial designs in Central Asia, Tibet, and Northern India.[19]

Meanwhile a strong clique at the Tsarist court, led by Alexander Bezobrazov, persisted in expounding expansionist views and thus in challenging Japanese interests in East Asia. They gained the support of the Tsar, despite the opposition of such experienced advisers as Count Witte, whose advice for moderation in relations with China and Japan went unheeded. It appears that Bezobrazov and his associates wished to provoke a conflict with Japan. For example, though Russia had agreed in 1902 to evacuate its troops from Manchuria, it delayed the withdrawal. Bezobrazov now demanded additional concessions from China in return for the removal of the Russian forces. He also pursued an aggressive course in Korea and demanded economic privileges from that backward state, a policy that once again caused him to collide with the Japanese. Though he and the Tsar continued to negotiate with Japan throughout 1903, they had no intention of reducing their demands and effecting a compromise.

The stage was now set for the Russo-Japanese War, which erupted in February 1904. The over-confident Russian government, weakened by lack of planning, a demoralized army and navy, political corruption, and finally the 1905 Revolution, was no match for the Japanese. Japanese battleships quickly overwhelmed the Russian Pacific fleet and captured Port Arthur; the Japanese army inflicted heavy casualties on Russian forces at the Battle of Mukden; and the Japanese navy sank most of the Russian Baltic fleet at Tsushima in May 1905.

The decisive struggle at Tsushima, Russia's internal difficulties, and the financial burden of the war borne by Japan compelled both sides to seek a settlement, which within a short time led to an alliance. The President of the United States, Theodore Roosevelt, brought the two parties together at Portsmouth, New Hampshire, to resolve the conflict. By September 1905, the negotiators had concluded a treaty which provided the Japanese with jurisdiction in the Liaotung peninsula, including Port Arthur and Ta-lien (now renamed Dairen), and ownership of the southern portion of the Chinese Eastern Railway from Changchun to Dairen (now renamed the South Manchurian Railway). The agreement further prohibited the stationing of Russian and Japanese troops in Manchuria.[20]

After the conclusion of the treaty, the two former adversaries drew closer together in order to face the United States, their common rival. The country which had earlier facilitated the peace negotiations between the Russians and the Japanese now became their enemy. Russia resented the strong and barely repressed American sentiment favouring Japan in the recent war. Japan began to realize that it was the United States which would pose the strongest challenge to its efforts to achieve military and economic pre-eminence in East Asia. American discriminatory policies against Japanese immigrants, symbolized by the so-called 'Gentlemen's Agreement' of 1907 limiting Japanese immigration into the United States, impeded cordial relations between the two nations. Both Russia and Japan thus had a vested interest in joining together to preserve their hard-won gains against possible American intervention, and in 1907 they signed a secret treaty recognizing each other's special prerogatives. Japan conceded that Russia was pre-eminent in north Manchuria and Outer Mongolia, while Russia acknowledged Japan's special interests in south Manchuria and Korea. Each state would naturally have a monopoly of the railway, telegraph, and other industrial concessions in its particular spheres of influence.[21]

When the American railway entrepreneur Edward H. Harriman attempted to undermine their monopoly in the succeeding years, they acted in collusion to frustrate him. He wished to purchase the South Manchurian Railway and the Chinese Eastern Railway as part of a scheme to own a railway encircling the globe. Both the Russians and the Japanese, however, rejected his overtures. Though the Ch'ing government finally granted him a railway concession in Manchuria in 1909, his proposed route cut across the Japanese and Russian areas of influence. Lacking co-operation from those two states, his project was doomed. And the Japanese and Russians extinguished any American hopes for the proposal by signing a second secret treaty in 1910, pledging to maintain a united front against further attempts to interfere with their self-defined special prerogatives in Manchuria.[22]

By 1911, the year of its final collapse, the Ch'ing court no longer held sway in Manchuria, the land of its ancestors. Its objective of keeping Manchuria as a preserve for the Manchus had been subverted. Its formerly lucrative commerce with its north-eastern domain was virtually nonexistent, as the Russians and the Japanese exploited the wealth of the region. Its prohibition on Chinese colonization of Manchuria had long been evaded, and its later reversal of this policy and encouragement of Chinese immigration had failed to achieve the objective of preventing Russian and Japanese incursions. And it found itself in the embarrassing position of granting concessions amounting to virtual control of Manchuria to the Russian and Japanese courts.

THE OPENING OF MONGOLIA

Ch'ing policies in Inner and Outer Mongolia also met with failure. The court had planned to isolate Mongolia from Russian influence and from Chinese colonists. Another of its stated aims was the fragmentation of the Mongol leadership, preventing the rise of a charismatic figure who could unify the Mongols and challenge Ch'ing rule. In order to pursue this objective, the Ch'ing had assigned fixed territories to the Mongol tribes, and as overlords of the Mongols, the Ch'ing emperors demanded taxes and labour service from their subjects. They tolerated and probably approved of the Lamaist church as long as it raised no objections to Ch'ing policies.

By the early nineteenth century, it was clear that the Ch'ing government was unable to implement these policies. Chinese merchants flooded into Mongolia with impunity and dominated the Mongol economy, forcing many of the local people into debt. Usurers preyed upon the Mongols, creating a poor impression of China. Unlike the Mongols of old, however, the inhabitants of Mongolia in the nine- teenth century no longer avenged themselves against Chinese economic exploitation by raiding Chinese border settlements. They were too dependent on Chinese merchants to afford the risk of antagonizing those who supplied them with vital goods. The Ch'ing tax burden, which under ordinary circumstances might have been tolerable, now became onerous and heightened the poverty among the Mongols.

Social and economic conditions in Mongolia deteriorated through- out the nineteenth century. The Mongol people suffered not only from Ch'ing taxation and Chinese trade and usury, but also from the heavy and unjust taxes and other exactions imposed by their own nobility. Most contemporary accounts are filled with stories of the appalling financial and personal exploitation of the free Mongol herders and townsmen by their rulers; the condition of slaves was even worse. Oppressed by the Ch'ing court, Chinese merchants, and their own princes, many Mongols became destitute and were forced to sell or abandon their flocks.

Many of the dispossessed herders fled to the towns.[23] It should be noted that their arrival did not precipitate an urban revolution either in Outer or in Inner Mongolia. They remained on the periphery, while Chinese and other foreigners performed most of the commercial and industrial functions. The new Mongol refugees often lived in poverty, with little chance of earning much income. Some starved to death, some survived by begging or pilfering, and some women became prostitutes or concubines of Chinese merchants. Moreover, the towns to which they moved were relatively small. As late as 1876, for example, the total population of Urga amounted to less than thirty thousand.[24] Some of the towns were created for reasons which had little bearing on economic conditions in Mongolia. Uliassutai developed as an administrative and military base, Urga as a religious centre focused on the residence of the Jebtsundamba Khutukhtu, and Kobdo as a town for the China trade. Few, if any, originated to meet the real economic needs of the local people. Yet they were eventually to begin to transform the Mongol economy, certainly an indication of the failure of a Ch'ing policy that sought to prevent economic or political changes.

Even more striking evidence of the difficulties encountered by the Ch'ing was the growing power of the Lamaist church. The Ch'ing inadvertently contributed to its prosperity by forcing many overtaxed herders to seek the tax-free status enjoyed by the church and its dependants. The Lamaist hierarchy employed many of them as *shabi*, or serfs, to care for the church's animals, and imposed taxes and labour service on them. By the late nineteenth century, the *shabi* were in the same deplorable economic state as the herders who were still liable for government taxation. Their tax burden to the church was heavy, and their responsibilities for the maintenance of temples and monasteries grew. The church itself expanded into various economic enterprises. It owned large herds of animals and vast expanses of territory, lent money at high rates of interest, made enormous profits by co-operating in the trading ventures of Chinese merchants, and leased or sold land to Chinese farmers. A contemporary estimate that it controlled half of the wealth of Outer Mongolia is not thought unreasonable by most scholars.[25]

Few of the ordinary lamas shared in the prosperity. As many as forty per cent. of Mongol males were lamas, and the great majority of them received little, if any, income from the church, maintaining themselves by their own exertions as farmers, herders, or merchants. Most shared the harsh conditions of life of the ordinary Mongol laity. Their celibacy kept the Mongol population small and was a factor in delaying economic growth. Only a few enjoyed the benefits of belonging to the hierarchy. Even they were often of humble birth and achieved their high positions through their own efforts. Since hereditary succession in the church was, of course, impossible, the lamaseries offered a chance of social advancement, which was one reason why the poor attempted to enrol their sons as monks. Once lamas had attained high rank, however, they tended to ignore their origins. Several of the Jebtsundamba Khutukhtus led dissolute and debauched lives, often expending vast sums of church funds for their own private pleasures. The last two incarnations were notorious for their sexual and alcoholic excesses.

The Ch'ing court was successful in preventing the unification of the ecclesiastical with the secular authorities but was unable to curb the legal, social, and economic abuses of the church. After the Mongol rebellion of 1756–57, it decreed that future incarnations of the Jebtsundamba Khutukhtu could only be discovered in Tibet, reducing the possibility of a Mongol nationalist alliance between him and the native princes. This policy prevailed throughout the dynasty and worked effectively until the final years of the last Jebtsundamba

Khutukhtu. But the Ch'ing court could not alter the attitudes and practices of the Lamaist church. The church leaders were capricious and repeatedly imposed severe punishments on innocent people. They perpetuated damaging superstitions and often impeded the adoption of modern techniques or developments, including veterinary medicine.

It may be that I have painted an unduly harsh portrait of the church and have minimized its real contributions. The lamas preserved the traditional manuscripts, translated and reproduced important texts, managed almost all of the schools, provided medical care based on Tibetan medicine, and maintained useful arts and crafts, including tailoring, the making of musical instruments, and the production of yurts.[26] Yet in terms of Ch'ing policy the church's excesses outweighed its contributions, for they created the kind of social unrest that the Ch'ing dreaded.

Despite the illegal immigration of Chinese colonists, the increasing impoverishment of lower-class Mongols, the oppressive rule of the Mongol nobility, the frequently corrupt administration of the Ch'ing officials stationed in Mongolia, the rise of towns, and the growing economic and social power of the Lamaist church, the Ch'ing government had managed to maintain its precarious hold on Mongolia until its first military encounters with the Europeans. It kept foreigners out of Mongolia, thus ensuring that the Mongols would remain economically dependent on China. But the Opium War of 1839–42 and the subsequent joint Anglo-French expeditions of 1858 and 1860 had demonstrated China's military weakness and limited its ability to isolate Mongolia from the rest of the world.

The Russians had received permission to trade in Urga in Outer Mongolia and in Kalgan in Inner Mongolia as a result of the Treaty of Peking of 1860. In 1861, the Russians founded a consulate in Urga, and Russian merchants started to live in the town. The new residents often brought their families with them; they built their own quarter in Urga, erected an Orthodox church, and even managed the post office.[27] Russian travellers, explorers, geographers, and scientists journeyed through Mongolia, conducted experiments, and returned with accounts of their experiences. N. M. Przhevalski and A. M. Pozdneev were two of the most renowned of these; their accounts were published in book form during the last quarter of the nineteenth century. Their reports, as well as the lobbying of merchants and some officials, prompted the Russian government to seek even more concessions.[28] In 1881, Russian merchants were granted the right to trade in Kobdo and Uliassutai, and the Russian government established one consulate in Uliassutai in 1905 and another in Kobdo in 1911.[29]

The Mongols were unduly optimistic about the arrival of Russian merchants. They hoped that Russian competition with the Chinese might offer them more favourable commercial terms, but they were to be sorely disappointed. The total number of Russians in Outer Mongolia was small compared to the number of Chinese traders. As late as 1910, for example, there were fewer than three thousand Russians in Urga, compared to more than twenty thousand Chinese. Most of the Russians remained in that town and rarely ventured into the steppe, thus allowing Chinese merchants to monopolize the trade with Mongol herders. The Russians were generally permanent residents, while the Chinese traders travelled throughout Mongolia and crossed in and out of China, thereby enjoying opportunities to carry goods from China to Mongolia without much difficulty. Probably the most significant advantage enjoyed by Chinese merchants was that they often represented large firms; their Russian competitors acted as individuals and thus had less capital and fewer goods available.[30]

After the Sino-Japanese War of 1894–95 and the start of construction of the Chinese Eastern Railway in about 1896 the Russian challenge to Chinese traders intensified. The Russian government hoped to extend railways through Mongolia in order to stimulate its own merchants to go there and to facilitate the flow of goods between Russia and Mongolia. Ironically, the building of the railways, including lines from Peking through Kalgan to Urga (completed in 1909), actually resulted in a flood of Chinese immigrants into Mongolia. There was, nonetheless, an increase in the number of Russian travellers to Urga and the steppe regions. In 1901, the Russians went further by creating the Mongolor, or Joint Stock Company for Mining Enterprise in the Tushetu and Setsen Khan Aimaks of Mongolia, under the financial auspices of the Russo-Asiatic Bank, to develop the mineral resources of Mongolia. Shortly thereafter, Mongolor started mining gold in several places in Mongolia.[31]

The Ch'ing government attempted to counter the growing Russian presence in Mongolia. As in Manchuria, it reversed its policy on Chinese colonization in Mongolia, removing restrictions on such immigration. This policy was effective, for, as one writer notes, 'the number of Chinese shops in Urga had increased tenfold from 1875 to 1890, and more opened every year until the revolution of 1911–1912'.[32]

Even more significant, the court actively promoted migration by founding a government-sponsored colonization bureau in 1906. The court also introduced reforms in education and in the government structure and adopted an active campaign of sinicization. It strengthened its military forces in order to meet what it saw as a Russian threat. All these efforts were costly and led to additional taxation of the Mongols. Realizing that this might lead to unrest, the court attempted to gain the support of the Jebtsundamba Khutukhtu by offering him lavish gifts. Unfortunately, it was not as considerate in its treatment of the rest of the population, and it erred in its selection of officials to administer these new policies. Unnecessarily harsh and oppressive tactics were employed – certainly no way to gain the favour of the Mongols. Sando, the last high-ranking Ch'ing official in the area before the revolution of 1911–12, even alienated the Jebtsundamba Khutukhtu with his actions.

The Mongols were perturbed by the stream of Chinese settlers arriving on the newly constructed railways, the increase in taxes and corvée, the purchase of pasture land by Chinese farmers, and their own growing indebtedness to Chinese moneylenders and firms. Some of the Mongol nobles had only themselves to blame for their insolvency. They squandered vast sums on obtaining Chinese luxury goods. Whatever the causes, unrest in Outer Mongolia often erupted into riots and revolts. From the evidence currently available, it appears that these were local uprisings and not well-organized national revolts. Most of them resulted from local conditions, and the great majority of these incidents consisted of sporadic outbursts against Chinese residents and property. Chinese shops were attacked and pillaged, and some Chinese were manhandled and even killed. After 1881, when a particularly notable outbreak against Chinese firms occurred, the number of such incidents increased. By the first decade of the twentieth century, it was not unusual for there to be several violent demonstrations within a year. At the same time, revolts against the local Ch'ing officials in Mongolia were continually breaking out.

Similarly, in Inner Mongolia uprisings directed against the Ch'ing and against Chinese merchants were relatively frequent. Recently released primary sources indicate that insurrections certainly occurred in 1861, 1864, 1870, 1890, 1899, and 1901. As with the uprisings in Outer Mongolia, however, 'there was no common idea behind these happenings, nor central planning'.[33]

In short, Ch'ing rule of Inner Mongolia and Outer Mongolia was now being challenged seriously for the first time since 1635 and 1691 respectively. By 1900, the Ch'ing government faced Mongol revolts and insurrections and Russian military and economic threats in Mongolia. Its policy had clearly failed, and the stage was set for the Mongol independence movement of 1911. Similarly, as mentioned earlier, it encountered difficulties in Sinkiang, for the Muslims in the area were restive. It had lost control over Manchuria to the Russians and Japanese. At the same time, its hold over Tibet had been shaken. In 1903, a British force under the leadership of Colonel Francis Younghusband invaded Tibet, forcing the Dalai Lama to seek refuge in Urga. Within a year, the two states signed a convention which clearly detached Tibet from Ch'ing control and virtually ensured British jurisdiction in that remote land. In 1906, Britain recognized Ch'ing suzerainty over Tibet, but *de facto* control remained in British hands.[34] Still another region had been lost to China.

AGENCIES OF FOREIGN RELATIONS AND ECONOMIC DEALINGS

Unlike the K'ang-hsi and Ch'ien-lung emperors of the early Ch'ing dynasty, most of the rulers of the nineteenth century appeared unconcerned with developments in Inner Asia, allowing their officials to play a vital role in policy. In the last quarter of the century, the Empress Dowager Tz'u-hsi held the reigns of power in the name of her son and other relatives who were enthroned as emperors. She had little expertise in foreign affairs and often relied on her officials to deal with Inner Asia.[35] Such men as Li Hung-chang repeatedly negotiated with the Russians about China's dependencies in Sinkiang, Mongolia, and Manchuria and apparently had an almost free hand in these negotiations. The rigidity and inflexibility frequently ascribed to traditional officials appear to be stereotypes. At least a few influential officials recognized the need for changes and proposed a reversal of outmoded policies. It was doubtless due to their efforts that the Ch'ing started to promote Chinese colonization of Inner Asia in the last years of the nineteenth century. Their suggestions probably also led to modifications in those features of court ceremonial that demeaned foreign emissaries (chiefly the kowtow).

The 1860s also saw the establishment of a new organization to deal with foreigners. In 1861, the court founded the Tsungli Yamen to supplement and perhaps impose unity on the Li-fan yüan and various other agencies concerned with foreign relations. This organization differed from the Li-fan yüan in that it was to become a true Foreign Office rather than an institution intended to govern and set standards for unruly 'barbarians'. It faced a situation drastically different from that hitherto faced by the existing agencies, for the Treaty of Peking permitted foreign envoys to reside in the capital. The court needed officials to look after these new resident envoys, and the Tsungli Yamen, in particular, fulfilled this task. One consolation for the court was that it no longer paid for the expenses incurred by the foreign ambassadors.

Influential officials opposed the creation of the Tsungli Yamen and sought to limit its powers. Having failed to prevent the founding of this body, they succeeded in persuading the court to establish it on a temporary basis, on the understanding that as soon as the foreigners no longer posed a threat, it would be abolished. The powers and jurisdiction of the Tsungli Yamen were ill-defined. It 'neither had monopolistic executive powers nor extensive policy-making powers over China's foreign affairs'.[36] The Grand Council, the highest-ranking government agency, still formulated foreign policy and examined all the vital documents relating to foreigners. Local officials often made important decisions on foreign policy on their own initiative. Specifically designated border officials, including the Imperial Commissioner at Urga, were not under the jurisdiction of the Tsungli Yamen. In emergencies, specially appointed military commissioners, such as Tso Tsung-t'ang, conducted relations with the states of Inner Asia without consulting the Tsungli Yamen. In short, no single agency controlled Ch'ing foreign relations. The Tsungli Yamen bore the additional burden of the traditional Chinese scorn reserved for those who dealt exclusively with foreigners. One such indication of this disrespect was the ramshackle building provided for the Tsungli Yamen. Another was the previously cited limits on its authority. Yet another was that it was occasionally denied access to documents concerning foreign relations by the Grand Council or other high-ranking bodies.

Despite these difficulties, the Tsungli Yamen was well-organized and well-led and contributed significantly to easing Ch'ing relations with foreigners. Imperial princes often provided the leaders of the agency; they frequently held positions as Ministers or Grand Councillors concurrently, and their tenure in the Tsungli Yamen was unspecified. In the early years, some of them were among the most capable and distinguished officials in the Ch'ing bureaucracy, bringing the agency some sorely needed prestige. It was divided into five secretariats, only one of which, the Russian Bureau, dealt with border relations and the peoples of Inner Asia; the rest concerned themselves with the European states, for the Tsungli Yamen appeared to emphasize relations with the Western powers. Several interpreters and translators, most of them for European languages, were assigned to the Tsungli Yamen; those who knew Russian were the ones principally useful in affairs concerning Inner Asia. The contributions of the agency lay not only in foreign relations but also in the creation of conditions conducive to domestic reform. It was instrumental in promoting the building of telegraphs, railways, shipyards, and the other accoutrements of industrial society. It is also credited with having fostered the translation of Western books, the introduction of innovations in school curricula, and the dispatch of students to foreign universities.[37]

The Tsungli Yamen was effective for about twenty years, after which it declined for another twenty until its final demise in 1901. For the first two decades of its existence, it attracted highly regarded officials who also held more important positions in the government. But as foreign encroachments continued, and the Tsungli Yamen was unable to prevent such incursions, it became the object of much criticism by traditional Chinese officials and started to lose the services of the more talented and higher-ranking bureaucrats. The foreigners too were perturbed by the inefficiency and the stalling tactics employed by the Tsungli Yamen, and they required its abolition as part of the settlement after the Boxer Rebellion. In 1901, the court replaced it with the Wai-wu-pu (Foreign Office). Since the officials of the Wai-wu-pu served solely in this new agency, their tasks were more manageable.[38]

Prompted by the suggestions of the Tsungli Yamen, in 1862 the court established a language school, known as the T'ung-wen-kuan, to train translators and interpreters. The school incorporated the old Russian-language school and shared the same building as the Tsungli Yamen. Like the Ming, the government of the late Ch'ing period was unable to attract capable men to the school. Personal involvement with foreigners was still barely tolerated, and a career in foreign relations was not a prestigious occupation. It was only with the appointment of the American missionary W. A. P. Martin as director of the T'ung-wen-kuan that more highly motivated and effective candidates appeared at the school. During its short existence, the school trained many later renowned interpreters, translators and diplomats who dealt with the European states.[39] For its supply of translators and interpreters of the Inner Asian languages, however, the court apparently relied on the border peoples.

As in earlier periods, unauthorized people frequently intervened in Sino-Inner Asian relations. Ch'ing officials in Sinkiang, Mongolia, and Manchuria were so far away from the central government authorities that they often made major decisions concerning Inner Asia on their own initiative. They were certainly more knowledgeable about the geography, customs, and languages of Inner Asia than the authorities in Peking and were probably more capable of making accurate assessments of the political and economic situation in neighbouring areas. The central government often consulted them, but just as frequently accused them of illegally side-stepping court regulations and of taking advantage of their position for their own personal profit.

It also accused merchants of evading government taxes when trading with the peoples of Inner Asia. Chinese merchants now travelled to the neighbouring 'barbarian' lands; they did not wait for tribute embassies from Inner Asia. In all these regions they were extremely successful, and many Ch'ing officials accused them of shoddy and illegal exploitation of the local peoples. The Muslims of Central Asia and the Mongols expressed their resentment of these merchants in a series of violent uprisings in the late nineteenth century.

As we have already noted, during the late Ch'ing period there were drastic changes in the economic relations of China and Inner Asia. Tribute embassies no longer played an important part in commercial dealings. Chinese merchants conducted the bulk of the trade, though they now faced competition from merchants representing other states, including the Russians. The court no longer bore the expenses of supplying and maintaining foreign tribute embassies in a lavish style. Yet another difference from pre-nineteenth-century days lay in the types of goods exchanged between China and Inner Asia. The Ch'ing government continued to seek animals and animal products from the nomadic tribes, but it also coveted raw materials for industry from Mongolia, Sinkiang, and, in particular, Manchuria. China competed with Russia, and later with Britain and Japan, for these products, and all four nations sought to develop the rich mineral and timber resources of these regions. To facilitate the development of Inner Asia, all the foreign states concerned, especially Russia, attempted to build railways with the object of improving communications with Europe. The construction of railways was essential for the transport of bulky raw materials from Inner Asia to Russia, Japan, and Europe, and each of the powers sought rail concessions from China in these regions.

The peoples of Inner Asia still generally wished to obtain the same products from China that their ancestors had sought from the Ming. They needed grain, simple craft articles, tea, and drugs, and their other imports included silk, linens, and various luxuries for the dissipated ruling classes. As had the Ming, the Ch'ing apparently fared reasonably well in its economic dealings with Inner Asia. They secured the goods which they required and in return offered products of which they had a plentiful supply. The Inner Asians did not fare so well and resented exploitation by Chinese merchants, a situation that bred discontent and rebellion.

PART FOUR:
CHINA AND INNER ASIA
IN THE TWENTIETH CENTURY

9 China's loss of Inner Asia

The year 1911 found China's position in Inner Asia deteriorating. Its power had shrunk considerably since it had reached its height in the middle of the eighteenth century. Even as late as 1860, China preserved a satisfactory, if tenuous, hold over Mongolia, Manchuria, and Sinkiang, and still retained a virtual monopoly in trade with these regions, ensuring sizeable profits for itself. By 1910, however, its relations with Inner Asia had been drastically altered. Chinese merchants challenged the Ch'ing court's economic dominance, engaged in illicit trade with the local population of these regions, alienated the various peoples by unethical and illegal transactions, and caused many Manchus, Mongols, and Muslims to transfer their allegiance from China to other states. Russia and Japan had separated Manchuria from China, and were preparing to exploit its economic resources and to use it as a base for further incursions in Inner Asia and China. Both Inner and Outer Mongolia were in turmoil, and anti-Chinese and anti-Ch'ing sentiments were expressed in the sporadic looting of Chinese shops and in riots against the local Ch'ing government. By the early twentieth century, some Mongol nobles began to organize these unplanned outbursts into systematic efforts to achieve independence. Similarly, Sinkiang was seething with unrest, since the Kazakhs, Uighurs, and other Muslims resented Chinese and Ch'ing dominance. The rebellions of the 1860s and 1870s had devastated the province and had caused the deaths of a high percentage of the population both through actual military engagements and through the resulting famines and diseases. According to some sources over half the population died, though this may be an exaggeration, for many of the people may have crossed into Russia or have eluded Ch'ing census-takers.

The nationalist currents that had swept over Europe in the nineteenth century now began to reach Inner Asia. The Russians and the British were among the first to introduce the idea of nationalism into the Chinese domains in Inner Asia, and the indigenous non-Chinese leaders responded immediately to the new ideology. The Mongols of Inner and Outer Mongolia and the Uighurs and Kazakhs of Sinkiang sought to establish their own national states, and this bolstered efforts to overthrow Chinese rule.

The Ch'ing could not devote its entire attention to these urgent problems in Inner Asia, since it faced challenges to its very existence. The sorry history of its encounters with the European powers and Japan in the late nineteenth century is well known. One after another of these states took advantage of China's military weakness and economic backwardness to extort economic concessions and to acquire Ch'ing territory. Domestic unrest spread. The Ch'ing were unable to cope with the internal pressures and the foreign incursions and failed to introduce the changes needed to satisfy their own reformers and to sustain a viable state in the world of the late nineteenth and early twentieth centuries. A few attempts at reform in the educational system, in the promotion of industrialization, and in the creation of provincial assemblies, all of which the Empress Dowager reluctantly and with little enthusiasm approved in the first decade of the twentieth century, amounted to too little and were introduced too late. They did not win over the reformers and revolutionaries, who persisted in their efforts to depose the dynasty.

Ironically, even the fall of the Ch'ing in 1911 (and the resulting shift to Chinese, as opposed to Ch'ing, leadership) failed to stem the decline of China's military and political strength and to bring the reformers to power. Instead, the man who eventually emerged as the President of the newly proclaimed Republic, a prominent military official named Yüan Shih-k'ai, lacked interest in reform, was repeatedly forced to accede to the demands of the foreigners, and ultimately attempted to establish his own dynasty. Despite these defects, he was able to maintain a national government over all China. He died in 1916, just before proclaiming himself the new emperor of China, and with his death the national government of China collapsed. From 1916 to 1928, no single individual, party, or movement was able to unify China. A number of warlords ruled in the various provinces, and some claimed jurisdiction over the entire country. But they proved unable to fulfil their aim, leaving a power vacuum which the peoples of Inner Asia, not to mention foreign states, exploited.

It is instructive to note the similarities between the policies and objectives of Ming China and those of twentieth-century China. During both periods, China has been concerned with the defence of its border areas from foreign raids and incursions and has realized, similarly, that military measures alone would not suffice. In Ming times, nomadic tribes constituted the main menace; by the present century, great powers, including Russia and Japan, posed the principal threats. In both cases, the Chinese governments attempted to prevent the unification of the various foreign peoples in the frontier regions. The Ming sought to keep these groups at odds with each other by dispensing lavish material rewards to one or several of them and by calling on them for military support against more obstreperous foreigners. The Chinese regimes of the early twentieth century made significant economic and territorial concessions to one or several of the major Western powers in the hope that these would serve as a shield against more onerous demands by other states. Like the Ming, the governments of the post-1911 period were concerned with the forces which might attract their own people across the border. To cite one example, 'the population of Sinkiang was composed of various racial groups, such as Mongols, Kasakhs, Moslems, and Uighurs. These racial groups were also the elements composing the population of neighbouring Russia. Should these peoples join hands and make trouble, Sinkiang would face a grave situation.'[1] To prevent such a danger, the Chinese regimes attempted to restrict the movements of their subjects.

The Chinese governments of this century have been more aware than the Ming of their need for economic contacts with Inner Asia. They have recognized that Manchuria, Mongolia, and Sinkiang offer vast, sparsely settled and fertile land for the burgeoning Chinese population. In the late nineteenth century, the Ch'ing had established colonization bureaux to promote Chinese settlement in these border regions. The Yüan Shih-k'ai regime, and later the Nationalist and Communist governments, all recognized the significance of Inner Asia as a source of coal, oil, and timber, as well as of animals, animal products and certain crops. They certainly required access to these products if they wished to modernize their economy, and Inner Asia could become a major supplier of such goods.

SEMI-INDEPENDENT SINKIANG

Sinkiang did not succumb to a foreign power after the fall of the

Ch'ing dynasty and the consequent confusion. Nor did it sever its ties with China, though many of the local Muslims, Uighurs, and Kazakhs bitterly resented the repressive policies of the late Ch'ing. From 1911 to 1949 it was not effectively ruled by a Chinese national government. Yet it remained within the Chinese orbit. One of the principal reasons for this lay in the policy of its first governor, Yang Tseng-hsin.

Yang assumed power in 1912 after a brief period of confusion. It is surprising that he managed to survive in the face of the dissatisfaction of the non-Chinese peoples and of the external pressure of the Russians. His success was based partly on the military capabilities of the Muslim detachment under his command, but mostly on his recognition of the desirability of gaining the allegiance of the local peoples. He thus permitted some autonomy to the chieftains. His main preoccupation, however, was to enforce restrictions on his bureaucracy so as to limit corruption and to prevent exploitation of the non-Chinese. He maintained an effective system of controls over his government, imposing harsh sanctions on those who illegally alienated the local peoples. His economic policies were also designed to reduce the tax burden on the Uighurs, Kazakhs, and others and to win their support. He abolished some of the more onerous corvée services, reduced the outrageous interest rates demanded by Chinese usurers, and attempted to improve the economic conditions of the inhabitants.[2]

This is not to say that he was a democrat or harboured great feelings of affection for the local peoples. On the contrary, he remained aloof from the reformers and revolutionaries of China and was often ruthless in dealing with opposition. He also used the traditional tactic of seeking to accentuate the differences between the various peoples in the region in order to reduce threats to his rule. Separating the oasis-dwelling Uighurs and the nomadic pastoral Kazakhs was one of his principal objectives. By employing these policies and tactics, he mastered a difficult situation in Sinkiang.

When he took power, his first task was to bring the varied population under his control, and here he even had difficulty in gaining the support of some of the Chinese in the province. A number of Chinese soldiers and merchants residing in Sinkiang were members of a revolutionary party which in 1911 and 1912 had organized revolts in Ili (the region north of the T'ien Shan) and Ti-hua (Urumchi, the capital of Sinkiang). Both uprisings had failed, but the movement that they represented remained potent. Many of the revolutionaries belonged to secret societies which in the nineteenth century had attempted to depose the Ch'ing government. After the fall of the Ch'ing, the Republican movement became strongly committed to more revolutionary aims than those espoused by Yang. A secret society known as the Brothers and Elders Society, or the Association of Elder Brothers (Ko-lao-hui), which sought converts primarily among the military, provided the leadership for the militants in Sinkiang.[3]

Having little success in Ili and Ti-hua, the leaders of the Brothers and Elders Society moved their base of operations to the oases of southern Sinkiang. They engaged in banditry and fostered a wave of assassinations throughout the region. Their violent tactics terrorized the local population, and their assassinations of important officials reinforced these fears. They murdered the magistrates of Yen-ch'i and Kucha, the Commissioner of Kashgar, and many other minor bureaucrats. Yang clearly needed to quell these disturbances if he expected to maintain a stable regime. His main tactic in achieving this goal was the elimination of the leaders of the secret societies. Without them, he believed, the societies would fade away. He embarked upon a policy of dealing with their leaders one by one in their strongholds, occasionally offering pardons to the prominent military men among the dissidents, and transferring them to remote military outposts. On other occasions, he duped rebel leaders into attending banquets or meetings and then had them captured and executed. With the main instigators of revolt effectively neutralized, the secret societies posed no further serious problems.

Yang faced other threats in Ili. Ili had been the centre of the revolutionary forces and was hostile to Yang's regime. A few months after his accession, therefore, he made several conciliatory gestures which resulted in the signing of an agreement in June 1912. This provided for the unification of Ili and Sinkiang under the leadership of Yang, who in turn pledged allegiance to the Republican government of Yüan Shih-k'ai. In return, Yang granted important civilian government posts to the revolutionary leaders in Ili. He retained the high military posts for his own loyal and carefully selected men. Again, Yang weakened the leaders of those who opposed him before attempting to gain influence over the rest of the population. Within the next few years, he either replaced these leaders or moved them into purely ceremonial positions in which they wielded no authority. In the process, he encountered little opposition in the region.

He handled the Muslim revolts in Sinkiang with the same ease.

Almost as soon as he took power, he faced a serious uprising in Hami. The previous Chinese governor had been partly responsible for the outbreak, for he had executed eight Muslim rebels without investigating their grievances. Yang sought to achieve a compromise with the rebels, which entailed a reduction in the labour service imposed on the Muslims. An army revolt in 1918 in the autonomous region of Altai was much more serious. Exasperated by the corruption of local officials and by the government's withholding of their own salaries, the soldiers rebelled and deposed the existing rulers. For some time Yang had wished to incorporate the Altai region into his domain, and he immediately requested permission from the warlord clique that controlled the government in Peking to dispatch troops to quell the rebellion. The Peking authorities, who could barely govern the heartland of China, approved his request. He quickly instructed his subordinates to seize and execute the rebel leaders, which they did with little difficulty. Many of the corrupt officials were replaced, Yang's own administrative machinery was installed, and peace reigned in the region.

Having resolved most of the internal problems of his province, he was, in 1916, confronted with an irritating and possibly dangerous situation stemming from across the border in Russia.[4] In the late nineteenth and early twentieth centuries, corrupt officials and land-hungry peasants had exploited the inhabitants of Russia's new Central Asian domains. By their greed they had provoked riots, rebellions, and other disturbances. Russia's involvement in the First World War aggravated the tensions already present in the region. The peoples of Russian Central Asia still served as sources of cotton and horses, invaluable products for the war effort, but relied on imports of grain from western Russia. As the war dragged on, less grain was available from outside sources. So the Uzbeks and other local peoples asked permission to plant grain instead of cotton, a request which the Russian government frequently ignored or refused.[5] Tensions exploded, however, with the attempt to conscript Central Asians into the Russian army. The Russians had not previously sought recruits from the minority nationalities of the eastern part of the empire to fight on the Western Front, but in 1916 they reversed this policy and started to conscript Kazakhs, Uzbeks, and other minorities. Many of these groups, predictably enough, responded with a series of uprisings against the Russians. Some fled and sought sanctuary across the Chinese border.

223

CHINA AND INNER ASIA IN THE TWENTIETH CENTURY

The great majority of these refugees were Kazakhs. Yang Tseng-hsin estimated that 300,000 of them had poured into Sinkiang by the end of 1916. The governor of Sinkiang was not pleased with the sudden influx of Kazakhs and was reluctant to settle them in his province. He believed that the food supply in his domain could not be stretched to feed the newcomers. He also feared that they might subvert his regime. With these objections in mind, he repeatedly urged the Russian government to repatriate the Kazakhs without reprisals and prompted the Peking authorities to make similar demands. The Russians, however, would only readmit the Kazakhs on their own conditions, one of which was the surrender for punishment of the Kazakh leaders. Many of the Kazakhs rejected these terms, and Yang and the Peking government had to make strenuous efforts before St Petersburg relented. Their task was no doubt facilitated by the 'disturbances' in Russia during that period. Whatever the reason, most of the 300,000 Kazakhs returned to Russia by late 1917, though some probably did so with reluctance. There are indications that the Russians did not keep their promise, for 'reports received by Governor Yang mentioned that a number of these refugees had either been killed or were dead of mistreatment by the Russian officials'.[6] Yang was, in any case, relieved of the burden. The Kazakh refugees were no longer his problem.

No sooner had he resolved the Kazakh imbroglio than his Russian neighbours posed more difficulties. The February Revolution of 1917 had deposed the Romanov dynasty, Russia's rulers for about three centuries. The ineffectiveness of the Provisional Government that replaced the dynasty and ruled from February to October was clearly apparent in Central Asia. Concerned with maintaining its power in the heartland of Russia and unable to extricate itself from the European war, it could devote little time to the problems of the Kazakhs in the steppes and the Uzbeks and others in the towns. The grain shortage in Central Asia became more serious, and the Provisional Government purchased little cotton. Some of the conservative Muslim leaders in Bukhara and Khiva were appalled by the seemingly liberal policies of the new government. On the other hand, the liberal Muslims attempted to take advantage of the confusion in Russia to establish an autonomous state. There was thus much ill-will towards the Russians.[7]

The Bolshevik *coup* late in 1917 aroused even more suspicions among the Muslims. Judging from their ideology, the Bolsheviks were committed to a policy of self-determination for the minorities in

Russia, but in practice they were unwilling to abandon Tsarist territory, particularly land with such valuable resources. Moreover, they had persuaded themselves that control of Central Asia was essential for defence. But they encountered the determined opposition of many local peoples who noticed this excellent opportunity to regain their independence. If the Bolsheviks wished to preserve the empire carved out by their Tsarist forebears, they would have to reconquer it. They took the first step early in 1918 with the devastating and bloody conquest of Kokand. This violence generated even greater fear of Bolshevik domination, or perhaps of Russian domination generally. Thus, when, a few months later, a Communist force attempted to subdue Bukhara, it faced stiff resistance and was defeated. The Soviet government was forced to recognize the independence of that town, and, in the next year, of Khiva. These regions remained autonomous for a year or two. In 1920, however, a strong Bolshevik force under the command of Mikhail Frunze crushed the organized resistance in both towns and imposed Communist rule on the Muslims.[8]

The hostility of the Central Asians towards the Bolshevik regime in Russia provided a suitable environment for the White Russian forces which, in the Civil War of 1918–21, strove to overthrow the Bolshevik government in European Russia. For the White Russians, Central Asia was a convenient base from which to attack the Bolshevik forces (the Red Army). The Muslim rebels, on the other hand, were perhaps more anti-Russian than anti-Bolshevik. Their insurrections could be classified as movements of national independence concerned with Central Asia rather than with European Russia.

Though the Central Asian Muslims and the Whites had different objectives, they shared a common enemy and occasionally worked together. The main White forces in Asiatic Russia were under the command of Admiral A. V. Kolchak and were based in the Siberian town of Omsk. Kolchak was in touch with Dmitri Horvath, who controlled the Chinese Eastern Railway, Anton Denikin, whose base was in the Caucasus, Nikolai Yudenich, centred in north-western Russia, and Grigori Semenov, supported by the Japanese in eastern Siberia. But these various groups never settled on one leader, thus allowing the Bolshevik forces to concentrate on eliminating one White detachment at a time, without having to worry about a unified response to their military offensives.[9] The British, French, Americans, and Japanese had sent troops into Russian territory, and Kolchak

225

was in touch with them. But although he received supplies and financial aid from these foreign powers, he never formed a proper alliance with any one of them, and this doubtless damaged his chances of success. Throughout 1918 and the first half of 1919, he was, nonetheless, on the offensive against the Bolsheviks. Once the Bolsheviks had decided, however, to concentrate their forces against him, he suffered several severe setbacks, and by late 1919 he no longer posed a threat to them. Early in 1920 he was given up by some of his own allies to the Bolsheviks for trial and execution.[10]

Meanwhile, battered remnants of Kolchak's forces, under the leadership of General Boris V. Annenkov, desperately sought refuge in Sinkiang. Yang Tseng-hsin was wary of granting them asylum, for he feared involvement in the Russian Civil War. He was also concerned about the additional strains that these refugees would impose on the economy of Sinkiang. Having difficulty in securing an adequate supply of food for his own people, he was not at all happy at the prospect of caring for an additional force of about seven thousand Russians. To ensure the stability of his government and to prove his neutrality to the Bolsheviks, he instructed his border guards to disarm the White soldiers as soon as they entered Sinkiang. Though he provided the foreigners with food and supplies, he started negotiating with the Bolsheviks, with the eventual repatriation of the refugees in mind.[11] To show his good faith to the Bolsheviks, he quelled efforts by a former Tsarist consul in Sinkiang to recruit an anti-Bolshevik brigade and to engage in raids across the border into Russia. He was willing to offer sanctuary to a few Russians, but would not tolerate the use of his province as a base for provocative raids against Bolshevik-controlled regions. Nor was he willing to allow the Japanese, who were eager to detach parts of eastern Siberia and northern Manchuria from Russian control, to cross into his province to assist the White forces in Sinkiang to continue the war against the Bolsheviks.

Besides actively discouraging the resumption of hostilities by White troops based in his province, Yang also promoted harmonious relations with the Bolsheviks. In May 1920, he negotiated an agreement with Lenin's envoys covering the repatriation of the White Russian refugees in Sinkiang, regulations for trade, and the future exchange of envoys and diplomats. Early in the following year, most of the White Russians, having received assurances of amnesty from the Bolsheviks, returned to their homeland; Annenkov remained in captivity in Sinkiang for a time, escaped, and was then recaptured and shot.[12] A few months later, Yang allowed a Bolshevik Russian force to enter his province and joined with it to overwhelm the last White detachments, troops who had occupied the Altai region. Their leader, a man named Bakich, fled to Outer Mongolia, where he was captured and executed.

Yang further ingratiated himself with the Communists by not interfering in their attempts to pacify the Basmachi of Central Asia. The Basmachi were composed of Muslims who had reacted adversely to the Soviet conquest of Bukhara, Khiva, and the Kazakh steppes. From 1921 to 1924, they fought ferociously against the waves of Communist troops dispatched to destroy them. The Communists at one point called on Enver Pasha, who had earlier played a role in the Young Turk movement and had been a Minister of War in post-war Turkey, to assist in ending the rebellion. Instead, he joined the rebels and became a leader of the Basmachi. Since the White forces were defeated in 1921, however, the Basmachi were isolated and a relatively easy prey for the Communist troops. Without British, Japanese, or Chinese support, the Basmachi were doomed, and by 1924 their last serious uprising was crushed by the Communists.[13] The government in Moscow now divided its Central Asian domains into five separate republics in order to prevent a unified opposition, and for a time in the 1920s it moderated its policies in the region. It temporarily allowed the local peoples a measure of autonomy and fostered the economic development of the area. It was, of course, pleased that Yang had not assisted the Basmachi, and relations with him became even friendlier.

The culmination of the increasing closeness between Yang and the Soviet Union was the treaty of 1924. By this agreement, the Soviet Union was granted five consulates in Sinkiang, including ones in Urumchi and Kashgar, while Yang's government could establish the same number in Soviet Central Asia, including ones in Tashkent and Alma-Ata. As a result, trade between the Soviet Union and Sinkiang expanded at a much faster rate than commerce between Sinkiang and the rest of China. The Soviet Union coveted the mineral resources as well as the cotton and hides of Sinkiang. They were no doubt impressed with the potential of the province, which had a relatively small population and parts of which were highly fertile. Attracted by the abundant resources of the region, Moscow encouraged Sinkiang to shift its economic and political orientation from China to the Soviet Union. The Soviet Union had the advantage of geographic proximity, for its territory bordered on Sinkiang, while that province

227

was fairly distant from the rest of China, and travel eastward was hampered by deserts and other natural barriers and by poor transport facilities. Soviet officials pursued this advantage by extending railways into the region. Eager to gain the support of the local population, they portrayed the Chinese as exploiters and themselves as protectors of the non-Chinese minorities. The peoples of Sinkiang and their governor Yang Tseng-hsin could now choose between China and the Soviet Union. And it became clear by the late 1920s that they had selected the Russians and had forced many Chinese merchants to leave the province.[14]

The Chinese themselves were at least partly responsible for this chain of events. They had, in fact, taken advantage of the inhabitants of Sinkiang in commercial transactions. Many officials on China's north-western border were corrupt and knew little about the non-Chinese minorities whom they were supposed to govern. Finally, the instability of the Chinese government in the period from 1911 to 1928 permitted Yang great freedom to develop and implement his own policies. Though he frequently notified the Peking authorities of important decisions, he was the true ruler of Sinkiang and his power was unchallenged.

The re-establishment of a stable central government in 1928 under the Kuomintang, or Nationalist Party, promised to change relations between Sinkiang and the Chinese authorities. The Kuomintang was the creation of Sun Yat-sen, the so-called 'Father of the Chinese Republic'. Sun and his allies and followers had been instrumental in deposing the last Ch'ing emperor, but had not won political power. Until the early 1920s, the Nationalist Party floundered and witnessed the gradual loss of influence of the central government in Peking, which was controlled by Sun's warlord enemies. In 1923, Sun, realizing that he needed foreign assistance, negotiated an agreement with Soviet agents from his base in Canton which provided him with military and economic support. The agreement also called for the Chinese Communist Party, which had been founded in 1921, to unite and co-operate with the Nationalists. Within a short time, the Nationalists, assisted by Soviet advisers and supplies, had a centralized political party, backed by a strong military force.[15] Sun did not have time to use these newly created institutions to reunify China, for he died in 1925. His eventual successor, Chiang Kai-shek, was the ultimate beneficiary of the efforts of Sun and the Soviets. In 1926, with the support of the Chinese Communists and the Russian advisers, he organized the Northern Expedition, a military expedition launched from Canton to the north, which soon made him master of the eastern coastal provinces of China. With the success of the Expedition assured, early in 1927 Chiang turned against his Soviet and Chinese Communist allies, claiming that they intended to subvert his regime and to assassinate him. By the summer of 1927, therefore, the alliance between the Communists and the Nationalists was severed, and Chiang had arrested or executed most of the Communist leaders or forced them to flee to remote areas. In 1928, he established an anti-Communist national government with its capital in Nanking.

It seemed a propitious time for China to assert its sovereignty over Sinkiang. Yang Tseng-hsin appeared willing to deal with Chiang, but at this critical juncture in the year 1928 he was assassinated. Chin Shu-jen, his successor, had been an official in the provincial administration. Unfortunately, Chin did not continue his predecessor's policies. His government, in contrast to Yang's, was characterized by corruption and nepotism. He sought to enrich himself and his associates by unscrupulous transactions, increased taxation, and the imposition of government monopolies on the more lucrative commodities and resources of the province. His policies bred great dissatisfaction among the people of Sinkiang and simultaneously prevented a rapprochement with the Nationalists.[16]

Unlike Yang Tseng-hsin, Chin interfered in the internal affairs of the non-Chinese population of Sinkiang. Like the Yung-lo emperor of the Ming dynasty five centuries earlier, Chin became embroiled in the succession to the throne of Hami. And he failed just as miserably as the fifteenth-century monarch had done. Indeed, his efforts in Hami led inevitably to his downfall.

He resented the independence enjoyed by Hami. Therefore, when the prince of Hami died in 1930, Chin attempted to abolish the rank of prince and to limit the autonomy of the town. He also encouraged Chinese farmers from Kansu to move into Hami. The Uighurs of Hami rebelled against this blatant interference with their political system. Chin immediately raised an army, composed primarily of White Russians who had remained in Sinkiang after the bulk of their fellow refugees had been repatriated in the early 1920s, and defeated the insurgents in Hami. In 1931, the latter, in turn, appealed for help to the Muslims in the neighbouring province of Kansu. Ma Chung-ying, a twenty-year-old Muslim soldier, responded to this call, but after some heavy fighting was forced to retreat from Sinkiang.[17]

Meanwhile Chin's policies alienated more and more of his supporters and offered Ma a second chance to depose him. By calling on the White Russians, Chin had lost the support of the Soviet Union. By his niggardly rewards and by his oppressive rule, he soon alienated the White Russians too. Discontent with Chin's regime increased, and Ma sought to profit from this unrest by launching a second offensive. In 1933, his troops reached the outskirts of Chin's capital at Urumchi before being turned back. Even with this victory, Chin had not gained any popularity among his own people. Another offensive by Ma in the spring of 1933 forced Chin to flee to China. At this juncture, a soldier from Manchuria named Sheng Shih-ts'ai came to the fore in Sinkiang in order to fill the vacuum created by Chin's departure. Late in 1933, he too faced an assault by Ma (or 'Big Horse', as he was often called). Ma definitely held the upper hand in this campaign; in January 1934 he besieged Urumchi and seemed to be on the verge of crushing Sheng. At this point, the Soviet Union covertly intervened by sending troops and aeroplanes to aid Sheng. With this substantial assistance, Sheng drove Ma out of the heartland of the province. Ma sought sanctuary in the western Sinkiang town of Kashgar. Realizing, however, that he could not withstand the combined forces of Sheng and the Soviet Union, Ma made an extraordinary and still inexplicable move. He handed over the command of his troops to his brother-in-law and crossed into the Soviet Union. Whether he was promised assistance for a future attempt to establish his own Eastern Turkestan republic or whether he received assurances of lavish rewards is uncertain. His fate after he had reached the Soviet Union, and the use which Soviet leaders intended to make of him, also remain unknown.[18]

The relationship between Sheng Shih-ts'ai and the Soviet Union is probably the strangest of all the peculiar aspects of the history of Sinkiang in the 1930s. It is commonly assumed that the Soviet Union supported Sheng in order to counteract Japanese influence in this region. In 1931, the Japanese had invaded Manchuria, and in 1933 they added Jehol to their empire. The leaders of the Soviet Union believed that the Japanese were Ma Chung-ying's principal supporters. They feared that Japan, using a base in Sinkiang, planned to detach a large part of Siberia from the Soviet Union. Such a plot seemed plausible enough to Soviet leaders, whose early rule of their land had been challenged by the Japanese occupation of eastern Siberia. From their point of view, they had no choice but to back Sheng Shih-ts'ai, a soldier whose earlier career gave no indication of any particular political allegiance. They were concerned with their own security and with the possible extension of their economic and political influence over Sinkiang, while Sheng was primarily interested in his own power and not in ideology.

A strange marriage of convenience between Sheng and the Soviet Union thus came about. Sheng played upon Soviet fears of Japan and repeatedly claimed that Japanese agents were furnishing military supplies and other kinds of assistance to Muslim bandits and rebels. As a result, the Soviet Union readily offered help. In May 1935, the Soviet Union and Sheng signed a secret agreement which provided that Soviet advisers and technicians would help in modernizing Sinkiang's agriculture, in exploring for mineral resources, in arranging for loans, in improving health and education facilities, and in renovating Sheng's government and army.[19] The Soviet Union was consequently able to exert tremendous influence in nearly all aspects of the economic and political life of Sinkiang. Furthermore it received commercial privileges, accompanied by only moderate customs duties, and thus had access to the animal products and mineral resources of the province. Probably as significant was the fact that the Soviet government served as a partner with the government of Sinkiang in the development of its industry. Jointly owned companies for the extraction of minerals and petroleum, for the creation of an airline from Alma-Ata to Hami, and for the building of roads and the construction of a railway from Sergiopol to Urumchi were established, and flourished from 1935 until the Soviet Union's involvement in the Second World War in 1941. Sheng cemented his relations with his Soviet benefactors by adopting a policy of anti-imperialism and of alliance and friendship with the Soviet Union. He established relations with the Chinese Communist Party and welcomed several of its prominent leaders, including Mao Tse-tung's brother Mao Tse-min, as residents in his province. In 1938, he travelled to Moscow, where, in exchange for additional Soviet economic aid, he joined the Communist Party of the Soviet Union.[20]

In return, the Soviet Union not only helped him to crush the opposition in Sinkiang, but also tolerated his excesses. In 1935 and again in 1937, it sent troops and supplies to assist its ally in crushing Muslim rebellions. After its intervention in 1937, the Soviet Union stationed a garrison in the town of Hami to protect Sheng and its own interests in Sinkiang from the Japanese. It also acquiesced in Sheng's ruthless treatment of actual or presumed opponents. As early as 1935, Sheng accused the Soviet consul-general and some inhabitants of the province of a 'Trotskyite' plot to assassinate him and to impose a German- and Japanese-supported puppet regime on Sinkiang. The Soviet leadership, which was itself preparing for the Moscow purge trials of 1936–39, did not object to the terror that Sheng unleashed against the so-called 'Trotskyites'. He executed several hundred men in this first incident. Using this plot as a pretext, he created a brutal secret police force which was indiscriminate in its arrests and executions, often punishing innocent people and, in particular, oppressing Muslim nationalists. There is no evidence that the Soviet leaders attempted to restrain the secret police. There are also reports that they acceded to Sheng's wish by executing his arch-enemy Ma Chung-ying, then residing in the Soviet Union.[21]

The closeness of Sheng's association with the Soviet Union in the late 1930s precluded proper relations with other states. The British sought to disrupt the Soviet monopoly of trade, and their other contacts, with Sinkiang. In 1935, one of their representatives, Eric Teichman, attempted to improve the British economic and diplomatic position in Sinkiang, but his appeals fell on deaf ears.[22] Nevertheless, the British persisted in seeking economic influence, particularly in the town of Kashgar, until 1939, when Sheng, accusing them of subversive activities, banned them from his province. Sheng also deliberately limited relations with the Nationalist Party in China. Relations between Sinkiang and China were in any case hampered by poor roads, banditry, and wars between various warlords, and trade, both between merchants and governments, was relatively insignificant.

Only with a change in the relations between the Soviet Union and China did Sheng move closer to Chiang Kai-shek. After Chiang's purge of the Chinese Communists in 1927 and the total rupture of the Nationalist-Communist alliance, formal relations between the Soviet Union and the Nationalist regime were severed. And in 1929 their relations were further impaired by a short war in Manchuria. Only after the Japanese invasion of Manchuria in 1931 did the two parties come together. Both feared further Japanese incursions on their territories, and in December 1932, recognizing their common interests, they established formal relations. Their contacts remained correct, though somewhat distant, until the start of the Sino-Japanese War in July 1937. About a month later, Chiang Kai-shek, looking for outside assistance, turned to the Soviet Union and signed a non-aggression pact by which the Soviet government guaranteed to provide military supplies and technical aid. Accordingly the Soviet Union was soon sending engineers, military advisers, soldiers, and pilots to Chiang to help him to counter the Japanese threat.[23] This renewed alliance with Chiang fitted in with the Soviet Union's United Front, anti-Fascist policy enunciated in 1935, a policy reflecting fear of the Germans and the Japanese. And the Soviet Union's assistance to the Nationalists was invaluable. As the former American Foreign Service official O. Edmund Clubb has noted, 'at a time when Britain and the United States were continuing their profitable trade with the Japanese, the Soviet aid to China was substantial and critical'.[24]

Most of the supplies which the Soviet Union sent were shipped through Sinkiang to the wartime Nationalist capital in Chungking. The Nationalists thus needed to cultivate proper relations with Sheng Shih-ts'ai. By slow degrees, Sheng and the Chinese government began to associate ever more closely, and circumstances eventually prodded them into an alliance.

The Soviet entry into the Second World War pushed Sheng into an alliance with Chiang Kai-shek. The German invasion in June 1941 forced the Soviet Union to concentrate its resources on its own very survival. Its influence in Asia diminished considerably, and Sheng could no longer count on it for economic and military assistance. Reacting very quickly to these changing circumstances, Sheng looked elsewhere for the support that he claimed to need in staving off Japanese and other potential aggressors. He exchanged envoys with the Chinese Nationalists, the only group close enough to help him, and by mid-June 1942 cast his lot with them. It may appear that Sheng had not really changed sides, since the non-aggression pact which Chiang and the Soviet Union had signed in 1937 had not been rescinded. But relations between the two parties had cooled considerably after June 1941, when the Soviet Union could no longer provide Chiang with loans, military supplies, and other assistance. Chiang now turned to another 'barbarian' state for support: the United States. After 1941, the bulk of his foreign supplies came from the United States, and Chiang turned his back on the Soviet Union, which appeared unable to withstand the German attack. He detached himself further from the Soviet Union by using much of his military equipment against the Chinese Communist Party, rather than against the Japanese. Sheng had thus forged an alliance with a Chinese regime that was virulently anti-Communist and not on friendly terms with the Soviet Union.

233

Sheng now moved against both the Soviet Union and the Chinese Communists. In 1942, after allying himself with the Chinese Nationalists, he demanded that the Soviet Union recall several of its officials, whom he accused of subversive activities. He apparently ordered the execution of his own brother, who had Communist leanings. Asserting that he had uncovered yet another 'plot' to overthrow him, he arrested the representatives of the Chinese Communist Party residing in his province and had many of them executed. Mao Tse-tung's brother was one of the many who perished during this purge.[25] Sheng probably did not realize that his actions would result in Soviet reprisals. Within a year of his 'unfriendly acts', the Soviet Union began to recall all its trained personnel and equipment from Sinkiang. The most telling blow was the withdrawal of the Soviet garrison from Hami, the only major military force in the region. Sheng was thus virtually defenceless. He was now dependent on a provincial force, mainly recruited from non-Chinese peoples who despised him and had been subjected to his brutal purges and executions. Some of these people, who had been affected by nationalist ideology, wished to be free of any Chinese domination and to establish their own nation state.

The Nationalists attempted to profit from the precarious position in which Sheng now found himself. Chiang Kai-shek wished to reassert rule by a Chinese national government over Sinkiang for the first time since 1911. Regarding Sheng as an obstacle to the attainment of this goal, he immediately but quietly began to place men loyal to him in the Sinkiang hierarchy. He also moved troops either into the province or into areas adjacent to it. Aware of this challenge to his power, Sheng early in 1944 humbly appealed for Soviet aid in return for economic concessions. The Soviet Union, which no longer trusted him, did not respond.[26] Sheng's last major action in Sinkiang was an effort to prevent Nationalist control by the usual claim of a 'plot' by Nationalist officials in Sinkiang against him. He managed to arrest some of them before the Nationalist government ordered his transfer from Sinkiang to a post in Chungking. Having no true base of power and supported by only a small and inadequate military force, he acquiesced in this demand. Sinkiang was finally rid of a brutal and corrupt despot, and China appeared to have regained control of a province lost for over thirty years.

But Chiang Kai-shek's hopes proved to be illusory. Even in the waning years of Sheng's regime, there had been local uprisings which were finally organized as full-scale rebellions by the Kazakh leader

Osman, or Usman Bator. By 1944, he came to dominate much of the region south of the T'ien Shan. Shortly thereafter, the Uighurs, Mongols, and other peoples north of the T'ien Shan in Ili joined the rebellion, and by January 1945 the two rebel groups combined to form the Eastern Turkestan Republic, an independent state free of Chinese influence.[27] Chiang Kai-shek assumed that the Soviet Union had instigated the revolt and was supplying the rebels. It may be that the rebels received some support from the Soviet Union and the Communist Mongolian People's Republic, but there is no doubt that they really represented great discontent and feared a renewal of Chinese rule. Chiang, nonetheless, believing that Soviet support prolonged the rebellion, demanded that the Soviet Union desist from assisting the insurgents.

The Soviet Union, though denying any involvement, was instrumental in bringing the two parties together. At this juncture in late 1945, Stalin and his government were eager to preserve the gains which they had secured as a result of secret negotiations with the United States at Yalta and a treaty signed with the Nationalist regime in August. They therefore hoped for a speedy settlement of the dispute in Sinkiang. With the Soviet Union acting as a mediator, the Nationalist Party and the various non-Chinese rebel leaders negotiated an agreement by January 1946. The Eastern Turkestan Republic was abolished, and Sinkiang was described as a province of China. In return, the Nationalist government granted the local peoples a large measure of autonomy.[28] Chiang Kai-shek's party now had a golden opportunity to gain favour with the non-Chinese inhabitants of Sinkiang. It was only necessary for them to carry out the provisions of the agreement. Nevertheless, due to corruption, inefficiency, and a callous disregard for the wishes and customs of the largely Muslim peoples, the Nationalists repeatedly ignored the assurances which they had given in this agreement. They appointed Chinese officials or local inhabitants with strong pro-Chinese feelings to rule the province, they engaged in illicit and corrupt activities, and they imprisoned local leaders on trumped-up charges. In particular, the Uighur Masud Sabri, who ruled the province for a time in 1947, aroused tremendous hostility by his Chinese-oriented policies.[29]

Masud Sabri's actions provoked nationalist rebellions and independence movements which ultimately failed because of internal problems. The lack of unity that had prevailed since the fifteenth century still confronted and bedevilled the various non-Chinese peoples of Sinkiang.

The Uighurs and Mongols of Ili rebelled and adopted a strong anti-Chinese stance. On the other hand, the Kazakh Osman, who had earlier led the Kazakh opposition to Chiang Kai-shek, now became fearful of Soviet influence in Sinkiang and joined with the Nationalists in an anti-Communist coalition. He apparently moved into Peitashan (an area adjacent to Sinkiang and the Mongolian People's Republic, which was blessed with an adequate water supply and with a strategic location threatening Hami, Turfan, and other towns in the vicinity). There he and his Nationalist supporters became embroiled in armed clashes with troops from the Mongolian People's Republic, each side accusing the other of aggression.[30] Whatever the truth of these allegations, it is certain that the differing responses of the local peoples weakened them considerably. Without any unified political leadership, they were not strong enough to resist the Chinese forces. The Chinese Nationalists, however, were themselves in a state of disarray. They could not profit from the disunity of the peoples of Sinkiang. When it was clearly too late, they made a major concession. In December 1948, they replaced the hated provincial administrator Masud Sabri with a Muslim named Burhan. What they did not know was that Burhan was in close touch with, and ready to aid, the Chinese Communist Party.[31]

With the help of Burhan and through their own policies, the Chinese Communists were soon to bring Sinkiang within the orbit of a Chinese national government for the first time in four decades. In August 1949, many of the Muslim leaders of Ili and Sinkiang died in a still unexplained aeroplane crash, a fortunate 'coincidence' for the Communists, since it eliminated potential indigenous opposition. At about the same time, Burhan proclaimed his allegiance to the Communist cause. His action persuaded many of the Nationalist troops in the province to go over to Mao Tse-tung's side. The Communists, recognizing his contribution, appointed him governor of the province and accepted him as a member of the Communist Party.[32] The Nationalist forces were by now crumbling throughout China, and the surrender of most of their troops in Sinkiang certainly facilitated the Communists' task of rooting out the remaining opposition. Some of the Kazakhs, acknowledging the futility of their efforts, fled through Afghanistan and India on their way to Taiwan or other more congenial lands. Osman, one of the few who chose to continue the struggle, resisted the Communist forces until his capture in February 1951; he was executed in the spring.

The peoples of Sinkiang had certainly missed a good opportunity to obtain their independence during the Civil War between the Nationalists and the Communists that raged in China from 1945 to 1949. Their internal squabbles and lack of unity, however, prevented them from taking advantage of this chance. Similarly, in late 1945 the Nationalists ruined their chances of exerting real influence in Sinkiang. They had formed an agreement with the non-Chinese inhabitants which offered these a measure of autonomy. But they actually reneged on this agreement and thus lost any goodwill and support which they might have expected from the local people. It remained for the Communists to conclude an alliance with the Muslim leader Burhan which permitted him to retain the rank of provincial governor of Sinkiang for six years and quickly brought them the support of many of the non-Chinese peoples.

INDEPENDENT MONGOLIA

Mongol discontent with Chinese rule, and particularly with Chinese domination of commerce and with the influx of Chinese refugees, grew throughout the late nineteenth and early twentieth centuries. Some of the Mongol nobles who had become indebted to Chinese moneylenders wanted to escape from Chinese control. The Sain Noyan Khan, in particular, who was in great debt to the Chinese, spearheaded this movement. He and other dissident Mongol nobles noticed the growing Russian involvement in Outer Mongolia and attempted to use the Tsarist court for their purposes. Early in 1911, they knew that the Ch'ing court wished in the forthcoming renegotiation of the Treaty of St Petersburg of 1881 to reduce the number of Russian consulates in Outer Mongolia and to limit Russian influence in the area. They were thus confident of obtaining Russian support. Similarly, they tried to use the hatred of the ordinary Mongols for the Chinese in the movement for independence. The ordinary Mongols, who were looting Chinese shops and occasionally attacking and injuring Chinese merchants, were responsive to such appeals. In order to succeed within the traditional scheme of things, the Mongol nobility needed to persuade the Jebtsundamba Khutukhtu to provide wholehearted support for their efforts.

In July 1911, they received the Khutukhtu's blessing and immediately sent a delegation to Russia to secure the assistance of the Russian government. The Russians procrastinated, fearful of the reactions of the other European powers and of Japan, and offered only vague assurances of supporting Mongol autonomy against the encroachments of the Ch'ing.[33] The disappointed Mongols returned to their homeland with little to show for their efforts. They had hoped not only for Russian aid in achieving independence for Outer Mongolia but also for support for, or at least lack of opposition to, the establishment of a Pan-Mongol state incorporating the Mongols of Inner Mongolia, Manchuria, and the Buryat region. But it was only with the outbreak of the Chinese Revolution in late October that year that some of their expectations were finally achieved. The Russians, now aware of the collapse of the Ch'ing government, sent rifles, cartridges, and sabres to the Mongols in December, and within a few days the Mongol insurgents in Outer Mongolia founded a new independent state, with the Khutukhtu as the 'Great Khan'.[34] They also set up five ministries to assist the 'Living Buddha' in governing their land. There is no doubt that they sought national *independence* rather than a true social revolution which might curtail their powers.

Believing that they could not survive without foreign protection and aid, the Mongol leaders turned to the Russians. And the latter did conclude an agreement with the Mongols, though they rejected some of the more extravagant Mongol claims and demands. This agreement, dated 3 November 1912, proclaimed Outer Mongolia's autonomous status and its right to its own army. It also clarified trade relations between the two parties and pledged Russian assistance in Mongol efforts to exclude Chinese troops and colonizers from Outer Mongolia. In addition to this agreement, the two sides signed a protocol which affirmed the commercial and political rights of Russian citizens and traders in Outer Mongolia and which prevented the Mongols from signing a treaty with any other power (presumably China and Japan were the powers borne in mind) that might cancel or curtail such privileges without Russian consent.[35] Certain issues which were deliberately not mentioned in the agreement and protocol were probably equally significant. The Mongols had hoped for Russian acquiescence in the creation of a state encompassing the Mongol groups living in other regions. There had already been Mongol insurrections against Chinese rule in the Barga area of Manchuria and in Inner Mongolia, but the Russians did not favour a union of all the Mongols. Earlier in 1912 they had signed a secret treaty with Japan by which they recognized Japan's special interests in eastern Inner Mongolia among other areas. This agreement precluded Russian support for Pan-Mongol aspirations and clearly damaged the chances of the independent Mongols achieving this goal. Only in a curious treaty with Tibet, signed on 11 January 1913, did the Mongols receive the recognition which they coveted, and this was due primarily to Tibet's own need to obtain external affirmation of its independence from China.[36]

The response of the new Chinese government was largely ineffective. Yüan Shih-k'ai threatened the rebellious Mongols with an armed invasion, but his threat was meaningless, for his armies were engaged elsewhere. They were needed, for example, to deal with the rebels in Inner Mongolia.

The Chinese government forces also had to contend with a Kalmyk Mongol adventurer named Ja Lama, or Dambijantsan, from the Russian town of Astrakhan. In 1912, that mysterious figure, who claimed descent from the great eighteenth-century warrior Amursana, defeated Chinese troops in Kobdo in western Mongolia and brought that region within the influence of 'independent' Mongolia. He may, though this seems uncertain, have had benevolent intentions, but his ruthlessness and violent tactics (at one time, 'the living hearts were torn out of the chests of Chinese prisoners of war, and the [war] banners were daubed with their blood'[37]) earned him the wrath of the conquered population as well as that of some of his own previous supporters. Yet it was Russian troops, not Chinese, who overthrew him in 1914 and temporarily excluded him from Mongolian politics. In 1919, he returned and reassumed control of Kobdo.

Just as the Chinese could not suppress Ja Lama, they could not induce the Khutukhtu's regime in Outer Mongolia to rescind new regulations that revoked the privileges previously enjoyed by Chinese merchants. The Mongols eliminated earlier provisions that had made an entire clan liable for the debts incurred by any one of its members, and Yüan Shih-k'ai was unable to obtain a reversal of this policy. Though Chinese merchants continued to collect old debts, their trade with the Mongols was reduced and Russian merchants slowly began to replace them.

In effect, the weak Chinese government had no alternative but to accept a compromise over the status of Outer Mongolia. In November 1913, it consented to an agreement with Russia which confirmed the autonomy of the Mongol state. In return, it had its nominal suzerainty over Outer Mongolia recognized, but this provision had little value, for China relinquished any right to send troops or colonists into the region or to interfere in the internal affairs of the Khutukhtu's land.[38]

China in 1970

241

Yüan Shih-k'ai was forced to renounce official control of territory that had recognized the authority of China since 1691. The Russians were delighted with this agreement, and the Chinese had reconciled themselves to it. The Mongols, however, were not pleased to be under even limited Chinese jurisdiction. The Sain Noyan Khan therefore visited Russia and sought support for total Mongol independence. His efforts were fruitless, and in his frustration he initiated contacts with the Japanese aimed at soliciting their assistance. But the Japanese, abiding by their secret understanding with Russia in the matter of spheres of influence, refused to intervene. The result was the tripartite treaty of 1915, signed by China, Russia, and Outer Mongolia, which confirmed Outer Mongolia's autonomy and China's suzerainty. Though it permitted the Chinese to station officials in Urga and several other towns (and, in theory, to approve the rulers of Outer Mongolia), it is clear that the treaty favoured Russian interests and was detrimental to China. Russian commercial privileges were confirmed, and Russian advisers, equipment, and loans began to arrive in Outer Mongolia.[39]

The Chinese lost influence in Inner Mongolia as well. Since the late nineteenth century, the Ch'ing dynasty had promoted Chinese colonization of the region to prevent its conquest by another power. This, in turn, had precipitated uprisings. The Japanese profited from this hostility to China to gain influence in Inner Mongolia and through their secret agreement with Russia in 1912 received recognition of their primacy in eastern Inner Mongolia. They wished to secure similar Chinese recognition. In 1915, they presented Yüan Shih-k'ai with their Twenty-one Demands, some of which insisted on Chinese concessions in Inner Mongolia. Knowing that the war in Europe riveted the attention of most of the powers which might have blocked Japanese attempts at expansion, and concerned with maintaining his own power in China, Yüan conceded and accepted the Demands. Chinese influence was thus slowly being replaced in Inner Mongolia by Japanese power, and in Outer Mongolia by Russian.

But the Russian Revolution of 1917 and the accompanying chaos offered China a magnificent opportunity to reassert its control over Outer Mongolia. In the short time since 1911 that it had played a crucial role in Outer Mongolia, Tsarist Russia had stimulated valuable reforms in health, the economy, and education. Its growing influence inevitably resulted in a reduction of Chinese control. With the onset of the Revolution in Russia, the Russian presence in Outer Mongolia diminished, and many of the Mongol princes and nobles were distressed by the radical groups now coming to power in Russia. The Chinese commissioner in Urga, Ch'en I, took advantage of this new situation and initiated a campaign to gain favour with the Mongol nobility. By early 1919 he had succeeded in persuading them of the necessity of attracting Chinese support and protection. The princes would renounce the autonomy of Outer Mongolia provided for in the treaties of 1913 and 1915 signed by Russia, Mongolia, and China, in return for guarantees of their wealth, status, and privileges.[40]

Unaware of Ch'en I's brilliant diplomatic successes and disconcerted by the slow pace of his negotiations, the military clique that controlled Peking and considered itself the Chinese national government dispatched an officer named Hsü Shu-cheng (or 'Little Hsü', as he was often called) to impose Chinese authority over Outer Mongolia. Ignoring his instructions to concentrate on military matters and to leave political and diplomatic issues to Ch'en I, Hsü Shu-cheng recklessly undid Ch'en's painstaking work. Without consulting Ch'en, he met the leading Mongol princes late in 1919 and demanded their submission to China. His crude threats forced the Khutukhtu and the Mongol princes to renounce their autonomy, but also earned him their enmity. He continued to alienate them by imposing stiff taxes and ruthless autocratic rule. His forces appeared ready to occupy the entire region, and the Mongols seemed unable to prevent their advance.

It was by the intercession of another Chinese soldier, not by their own actions nor by the assistance of other powers, that the Mongols were saved from further exploitation by Hsü. Chang Tso-lin, a warlord in southern Manchuria, was perturbed by the threat which Hsü's growing power in Outer Mongolia posed to his own territory in Manchuria. He therefore helped to engineer a *coup* in Peking that deposed Hsü's allies and forced Hsü himself to withdraw from Outer Mongolia in June 1920. The Chinese in this way lost their last chance in the twentieth century to bring Outer Mongolia back into the Chinese sphere. Their own internal divisions and their lack of a truly centralized government dashed hopes for a reconstruction of the Ch'ing empire.[41]

Outer Mongolia itself, however, received only a brief respite from foreign intrusion. Japan and Russia were the main foreign protagonists involved in Mongol politics from this time onwards. The Japanese, as noted previously, had attempted to profit from the troubles in Russia during the Revolution and the subsequent Civil War, sending their own troops to occupy eastern Siberia and helping anti-Communist leaders to detach Russian or Russian-influenced regions from the Communist government. Grigori Semenov, a Cossack leader from the Ussuri River region, was the first of the anti-Communists to receive Japanese support. In February 1919, with the consent and advice of several Japanese in his entourage, he proclaimed his intention of founding a Pan-Mongol state composed of Outer Mongolia, Inner Mongolia, the Mongols of Manchuria, and Buryat Mongolia, with a capital in Hailar. An Inner Mongolian religious figure named Neisse-Gegen was selected as the leader of the movement, but it was Semenov who actually held the reins of power. For a time, Semenov was extremely successful, but as the Soviet Union began to recapture its 'lost' territory in Siberia his position deteriorated and Japanese aid was reduced. His threat to Outer Mongolia had disappeared by about the time that Hsü Shu-cheng fled from Mongolia in 1920.

Towards the end of the year, another fanatical anti-Communist, Baron Ungern-Sternberg, who also had some connections with the Japanese, challenged Chinese and Soviet interests in the region. With a force consisting partly of his own troops and partly of troops who had fought for Semenov, he first attacked Urga in October 1920 and was repulsed by Chinese troops commanded by Ch'en I, who had been reinstated as the leading Chinese representative in Outer Mongolia after Hsü's abrupt departure. But although Ch'en's forces withstood Ungern-Sternberg's first offensive, their subsequent actions damaged their chances of repelling a second attack. They looted Russian shops in Urga, injured some Mongols and maltreated the Jebtsundamba Khutukhtu, thereby alienating the local people. Thus, when Ungern-Sternberg launched a second offensive in February 1921, his task was facilitated by a groundswell of Mongol support. His defeat of the Chinese troops and his arrival in Urga were greeted with great enthusiasm at first, but his fanaticism, his prejudices (he was, among other things, anti-Semitic, anti-black, and anti-Communist), his repressiveness, and his insulting treatment of the Khutukhtu soon alienated the Mongols. He was more interested in organizing an army for incursions on Soviet territory than in ruling Outer Mongolia. He therefore sought to use Outer Mongolia as a base for his more important objectives and exploited the Mongols to provide men and money for his military enterprises. Even the Khutukhtu, who had hitherto been eager to cultivate relations with this strange newcomer, now turned against him.[42]

While support for Ungern-Sternberg was evaporating among most conservative Mongols, a few of the more radical groups took the step of appealing to the Soviet Union for assistance in expelling this anti-Communist foreigner and in preserving Mongol autonomy, if not independence. A Mongol delegation led by Sukhe Bator and Choibalsang, later to be the two most important Communist rulers of the Mongolian People's Republic, visited the Soviet Union and was warmly welcomed by Lenin and by the other Soviet leaders. The Soviet leaders pursued some of the same policies and objectives in Outer Mongolia as their Tsarist predecessors. They wished the Soviet Union to have access to the natural resources and the animal products of Outer Mongolia, to keep it from falling into the hands of a hostile power, and to replace Chinese merchants as the dominant foreign economic influence. Ungern-Sternberg provided the Soviet Union with the perfect justification for involvement by attacking Soviet territory in the Far East. Soviet troops therefore joined with a Mongol army to resist him. By July 1921, the joint Soviet-Mongol force had occupied Urga and forced him to flee. Within a few months, Soviet troops captured and executed him.[43]

The Mongols were now free to establish their own state. With Soviet help, their radical leaders created the Communist Mongolian People's Republic. The Jebtsundamba Khutukhtu was the nominal head of the government, but it was Sukhe Bator, the Minister of War, who really wielded power. One of the first tasks that confronted the new government was a definition of its relations with China. In 1921, this was temporarily resolved by the signing of a secret agreement with the Soviet Union which implied that the Mongolian People's Republic was no longer part of China. But the Soviet leaders soon retreated on this point, for they were eager to establish formal relations with China. They feared that a hostile Chinese government might allow its territory to be used by more aggressive powers for assaults on Soviet soil. After several fruitless meetings, therefore, they finally negotiated an agreement with the Peking government in 1924 and laid the basis for a nominal redefinition of Sino-Mongol relations. Among other things, the Russians conceded on paper that China was sovereign in the Mongolian People's Republic and pledged to withdraw their troops shortly. They established relations with China at little cost, for even after 1924 they retained a dominant influence in the Mongolian People's Republic. They enjoyed a favoured position in trade with the republic, sent numerous technical and economic advisers to their

245

so-called 'satellite', and co-operated with the Mongols to exploit the country's natural resources, to improve communication and transport facilities, and to guide the largely nomadic Mongol society to a more sedentary way of life. Though some Chinese merchants and shops survived until the late 1920s, the Mongol government deliberately discriminated against them and favoured commerce with the Soviet Union.

Despite the Sino-Soviet agreements of 1924, the Mongolian People's Republic was effectively detached from Chinese control and came increasingly under Soviet influence. I cannot here deal at length with domestic developments in the Mongolian People's Republic since 1924, for my concern is China's relations with Inner Asia, and the Soviet Union now replaced China as the foreign country which had the greatest influence on the republic. Nonetheless, several major changes in the political life of the Mongolian People's Republic should be mentioned. In 1923, Mongol forces captured and killed Ja Lama and brought his region, Kobdo, under their control. In 1924, the eighth and last Jebtsundamba Khutukhtu died, and the Mongol regime predictably enough did not seek a successor. Instead it abolished the rank. Along with this change came other critical developments. In 1923, Sukhe Bator had died (poisoned by the Khutukhtu, according to some present-day Mongol historians), and his death initiated the impetus towards greater imitation of Soviet political and economic developments. Many scholars have noted the striking parallels between the history of the Mongolian People's Republic and that of the Soviet Union from that time to the present (especially in the patterns of collectivization and industrialization in both countries). Whether this be sufficient proof of Russian control or not, it certainly indicates great Russian influence. In any case, in 1924 a new constitution was written, the name of the capital was changed from Urga to Ulan Bator ('Red Hero'), and the present form of government was clearly formulated.[44] Chinese merchants could no longer exploit Mongol herdsmen, for foreign trade became a monopoly of the Mongol state. With this new economic regulation, China was definitely divorced from developments in the Mongolian People's Republic.

China also faced obstacles in its attempt to maintain control in Inner Mongolia, but here the gravest threat stemmed from Japan, not from the Soviet Union. Seeking to prevent the loss of Inner Mongolia to either of these foreign powers, the warlord governments which ruled northern China from 1911 to 1927 vigorously promoted Chinese colonization of the region. Their main purpose was presumably to assimilate the Mongols of Inner Mongolia, as the Chinese of the late Ch'ing period and the early twentieth century had sought to assimilate the Manchus of Manchuria. The Nationalist government of Chiang Kai-shek pursued the same policies and thereby alienated the local people. A strong Inner Mongolian nationalist movement developed in response. In order to control this movement and to facilitate their administration of the region, the Nationalists divided Inner Mongolia into four provinces: Suiyüan, Jehol, Chahar, and Ninghsia. They sought to use a traditional tactic of preventing the unification of the various Mongol groups which might pose a threat to Chinese rule. But by the late 1920s, they faced opposition from both the Inner Mongolian nationalists and the Japanese.

From 1931, the Japanese pressure on Inner Mongolia intensified. When the Japanese occupied Manchuria in 1931, it seemed clear that their advance would not stop there. And this assumption was borne out by their takeover of Jehol in 1933 and their creation of the autonomous Mongol province of Hsingan in western Manchuria. They hoped no doubt that their creation of a seemingly independent region for Mongols would help them to gain favour among the Mongols under Chinese control. The Chinese response was to bring additional pressure to bear upon the Mongols of Inner Mongolia. Chinese merchants and bankers from the province of Shansi, who had profited enormously from economic transactions with Jehol, had incurred major losses with the fall of Jehol to the Japanese and certainly favoured the Nationalist policy of inducing the Mongols, by force if necessary, to accept Chinese ways and maintain their allegiance to China. In response, an Inner Mongolian nationalist movement led by Prince Te (known in Mongol as Demchukdonggrub) was founded to combat the forced sinicization of the Mongols. Prince Te co-operated with the Japanese and hoped for their support for a Pan-Mongol movement. But the Japanese did not cultivate relations with the Pan-Mongols to help in the establishment of an independent Mongol state embracing the Mongols of East and Inner Asia.[45] Their principal objective was to replace Chinese domination with their own. They wished to expel the Chinese merchants and obtain control over the economy of Inner Mongolia. There were basic weaknesses in Japanese policy, however, and these included their greediness in exploiting the resources of the Mongol regions under their control and their inability to gain the confidence of the vast majority of the Mongol population, and not merely of the nobility.

The Japanese continued to take the initiative in Inner Mongolia in the early 1930s. They covertly assisted anti-Chinese forces in Chahar in 1934. In the following year their puppet forces in Manchukuo (as they called their puppet state in Manchuria) engaged in pitched battles with troops from the Mongolian People's Republic for the control of the Buir Nor region. They supplied Prince Te, who had by this time founded the Pailingmiao Inner Mongolian Autonomous Political Council, with military equipment for a projected attack on Suiyüan, and here they experienced one of their few failures. In 1936, Prince Te initiated his offensive, but he met determined opposition from Fu Tso-i, the governor of the province, and from Yen Hsi-shan, the warlord of the neighbouring province of Shansi. The Chinese troops from the two provinces decisively defeated Prince Te's forces and administered a severe setback to his plans as well as to those of the Japanese. Inner Mongolia remained a bone of contention between the Chinese and the Japanese-supported Mongols, instead of being detached from China.[46]

Taking this rebuff in their stride, the Japanese meanwhile continued to threaten the Mongolian People's Republic. The Soviet Union, which had a vested interest in the Mongolian People's Republic, feared a Japanese invasion of the region and let it be known that it would defend its ally (or, as some might say, its 'satellite'). In March 1936 in an interview with the American publisher Roy Howard, Joseph Stalin emphasized his strong support for the Mongolian People's Republic. Within a few days, the officials of the two countries signed an agreement by which they pledged to assist each other in case of foreign attack, a provision clearly directed at the Japanese.[47] The Japanese attempted to gain favour with the Mongols by appealing to their common religion of Buddhism, as opposed to the Christianity or atheism of the Russians. But the Mongols distrusted them, fearing their aggressive intentions, and the Japanese thus made no headway.

The Japanese did become embroiled in conflicts with the Soviet Union concerning territory in the Mongolian People's Republic. These disputes became more acute after the start of the Sino-Japanese War in 1937, for the Japanese resented the economic aid given by the Soviet Union to Chiang Kai-shek's government. In 1938, the first Soviet-Japanese clash erupted over Changkufeng, a high point overlooking the border between the Soviet Union and Manchukuo. Both sides laid claim to it, and several battles ensued during the summer. The Japanese, who were also contending with China and had been urged by sympathizers in Germany to compromise, finally relented, allowing the Soviet Union to fortify its position in Changkufeng.[48] Within a year, however, a much more serious conflict broke out between Japan and the Soviet Union over the area of Nomonhan (known as Khalkinbol to the Soviet leaders), a rich pastureland on the frontier between the Mongolian People's Republic and Manchukuo. The Soviet government apparently believed that the Japanese attack on the region in 1939 presaged an effort to conquer the Mongolian People's Republic and then threaten the Soviet Far East. And it dispatched its most powerful weapons and one of its most brilliant military technicians, General Grigori Zhukov, for this test of strength. Joining with the Mongol army and depending on large armoured forces, Zhukov surrounded and annihilated the Japanese in August that year. According to one source, the Japanese lost about 55,000 men, of whom 25,000 were killed.[49] In that very month, the Japanese were chagrined and embarrassed to learn of the non-aggression pact negotiated by their ally Germany and the Soviet Union.[50] They were thus isolated and had no choice but to seek an end of hostilities with the Soviet Union. By the end of the year, they had abandoned their efforts to pursue their offensive in Nomonhan. There were no further disputes with the Soviet Union, and finally in April 1941 the two former adversaries signed a non-aggression pact. The Japanese recognized the independence of the Mongolian People's Republic, and the Soviet Union, in turn, recognized the Japanese puppet state of Manchukuo. It was presumed that the Soviet leaders would reduce their supplies to the Chinese and would not object strenuously to the Japanese occupation of China. Relatively free from Japanese pressure, the Mongolian People's Republic was able to furnish horses, animal products, and other goods to the Soviet Union throughout the Second World War, thus giving assistance to the Soviet war effort. Frustrated by this failure, 'Japan's attention turned southward to the Asian empires of France and Great Britain' and 'the last possible support for Mongol union – the Japanese – had been destroyed'.[51]

As the war turned to the advantage of the Allies, both Chiang Kai-shek and Stalin manœuvred for an advantageous position in the post-war period. The Chinese, whose suzerainty over the Mongolian People's Republic had been recognized in the 1924 accord with the

Soviet Union, still wanted to control all of Mongolia. The Soviet leaders, on the other hand, wished to preserve the status quo: that is, the maintenance of the Mongolian People's Republic as an independent state under Soviet influence. Stalin was in the stronger position, since the Soviet contribution to the Allied war effort was more effective than that of Chiang's government (which had accomplished little in resisting the Japanese), and his armies were stronger than Chiang's. The United States, the other major power in the Pacific war, needed Soviet support against Japan and was eager to persuade Stalin to revoke his 1941 agreement with Japan, declare war against that country, and send men and material for the invasion of the Japanese islands. President Roosevelt knew that he needed to make concessions to attain this objective and these concessions could only be at the expense of Chinese designs in East Asia. In February 1945, therefore, unaccompanied and perhaps unencumbered by any Chinese representatives, he met Stalin in Yalta to discuss the future of the Pacific region. The secret agreement which resulted from the meeting provided, among other things, that the status quo in the Mongolian People's Republic would be maintained. The American President also made concessions in Manchuria, which will be discussed in the last section of this chapter. In return, Stalin pledged Soviet participation in the final offensive against Japan.[52] Though Japanese envoys throughout 1945 repeatedly attempted to entice him to renew his non-aggression pact with offers of territorial concessions in Manchukuo and the Far East, Stalin abided by the Yalta agreements, which in any case embodied a more profitable arrangement for him. Lacking support from the United States on this issue, Chiang Kai-shek was forced to accept the agreement reached by Stalin and Roosevelt. In a treaty and a series of accords negotiated after the use of atomic bombs on Japan in August 1945, he agreed to a plebiscite to be held in the Mongolian People's Republic, offering independence or incorporation as part of China. As everyone expected, the Mongols opted for independence, and in January 1946, Chiang recognized the Mongolian People's Republic as an independent state.[53]

In 1946, the Soviet Union had attained its objectives in the Mongolian People's Republic. Both it and China had sought to profit from trade with the Mongols and had attempted to use the republic as a buffer against the intrusions of foreign powers. Stalin was particularly concerned about a foreign threat through the republic to the Trans-Siberian Railway. By the post-war settlement, the Soviet Union succeeded in maintaining its influence over the Mongolian People's Republic. Yet China still bore a grudge, and in 1947 it had a chance to revenge itself on both the Soviet leaders and the Mongols. Claiming that the Mongols had deliberately invaded Sinkiang during the Peitashan incident, the Chinese representative at the United Nations vetoed the application by the Mongolian People's Republic for admission to that body. The Chinese were successful here, but at the cost of losing all influence over the Mongolian People's Republic.

One Chinese group was more successful in preserving Chinese rule over Inner Mongolia. This group was not Chiang Kai-shek's government, but the Chinese Communists, who were bringing more and more territory under their control. In the mid-1930s, the Japanese had founded the state of 'Mengchiang', or the Autonomous Government of Inner Mongolia, with Prince Te as the leader of one of the territorial units under that government. But Japan's involvement in the military conquest of China from 1937 onwards diverted its attention from Inner Mongolia. Its efforts in the region diminished during the rest of the war, but the government of Chiang Kai-shek was unable to profit from the reduced scale of Japanese involvement. At the conclusion of the war, it was the Chinese Communists who quickly moved to fill the vacuum created by the departure of the Japanese. There was already a large group of Chinese colonists in Inner Mongolia, but the Communists sought allies among the Mongols in the region. By 1 May 1947, they had established the Inner Mongolian Autonomous Region, with a large number of Mongols in key positions in its government. A sinicized Mongol named Ulanfu was selected as the head of the new government. Ulanfu had earlier studied in the Soviet Union and in the 1930s had joined the Chinese in resisting Japanese incursions on Suiyüan. In the 1940s, he joined the Chinese Communist Party and served it well by emphasizing revolution rather than Mongol nationalism.[54] The Mongol nationalists under Prince Te attempted to set up an independent Inner Mongolian government in 1949, but this attempt was abortive, and Prince Te was forced to flee to the Mongolian People's Republic, which returned him to China for imprisonment in 1952.

MANCHURIA UNDER FOREIGN CONTROL

By the early twentieth century, Manchuria was the object of the attention of numerous states. The Japanese, whose principal interest was in the grains, beans, and mineral resources of Manchuria, established Dairen as their main centre and had a sphere of influence in southern Manchuria. The Japanese government promoted emigration to Manchuria, but its efforts met with little success. Relatively primitive conditions, and the competition of Chinese labourers and refugees flooding into Manchuria, deterred many Japanese from seeking their fortunes there. The Russians too were interested in the resources of Manchuria, but their principal goals were to preserve their control over the Chinese Eastern Railway and to expand opportunities for investment and trade.

From their centres in Harbin and northern Manchuria, they seemed to have accomplished their objectives. By 1913, the railway was guarded by a force of 21,000 Russian troops, and the manager and many of the employees were Russian. The Manchus, on the other hand, were in a deplorable state. One contemporary observer, who studied their social and economic conditions, concluded that 'the Manchus are a very poor people'.[55] Chinese colonization in the area swamped the Manchus, whose traditional culture and language could not survive this pressure. Many became assimilated with the Chinese, their former subjects. The Ch'ing government, and its republican successor after 1911, encouraged Chinese colonization in Manchuria. But Yüan Shih-k'ai, the President of the Chinese Republic, did not actually control Manchuria. An indigenous warlord of bandit origin named Chang Tso-lin, based in Mukden in southern Manchuria, was the principal Chinese official in Manchuria, and he rarely acted in conjunction with the Peking authorities. Lacking unity, the Chinese response to Japanese and Russian influence was impotent.

Chinese policy remained, as in earlier times, to create disunity among the foreigners. Before 1917, the Chinese failed dismally. The Russians and the Japanese had come to an understanding after their war in 1904–05 which ensured a peaceful and mutually profitable relationship. Both feared British and particularly American economic competition in Manchuria and banded together to prevent such intrusions. They carved out spheres of influence, Russia in the north and Japan in the south, and agreed not to interfere with each other's zones. For example, when in 1915 the Japanese submitted their Twenty-one Demands, which included a ninety-nine-year lease of Port Arthur and Dairen and mining and commercial concessions, the Russians did not assist the Chinese in resisting the Japanese. Similarly, both Russia and Japan attempted to take advantage of a plague in

Manchuria to extract further concessions from China. Seeking to satisfy the enormous European demand for furs, Chinese trappers had hunted the marmot, a plague-infested animal. An epidemic of pneumonic plague occurred in 1910–11 as a result, and the Chinese government at first had difficulty in coping with it. Citing Chinese incompetence and inefficiency, the Russians and the Japanese wished to import their own doctors and medical staff to protect their citizens in Manchuria, which of course amounted to yet another intrusion on Chinese sovereignty. The Chinese finally founded their own North Manchurian Plague Prevention Service, an agency which ultimately handled the epidemic with distinction.[56] Neither the Japanese nor the Russians would help the Chinese to contend with the other.

The Russian Revolution totally disrupted the Russo-Japanese entente. The Japanese were concerned by the rise of the Bolsheviks and quickly attempted to profit from the chaos of the Russian Revolution and the Civil War, to protect their position in Manchuria and perhaps to acquire additional territory in the Far East. In May 1918, they concluded a secret treaty with the Peking government to work together against the Bolsheviks – the type of agreement that the Chinese had sought for some time. They also subsidized the White Russian troops, including the forces of Grigori Semenov. But their most effective assault on the Bolshevik position in Manchuria was their support of Dmitri Horvath, the Tsarist manager of the Chinese Eastern Railway. Early in 1918, Horvath dissociated himself from the new Bolshevik government and received Japanese financial aid for his continued operation of the railway to transport White Russian troops and supplies. The Chinese supplied him with guards for the railway to replace the Bolshevik guards who had been recalled.

The Bolsheviks responded by seeking to detach China from Japan and the other powers involved in assisting the White Russian cause. In 1918, Georgi Chicherin, the commissar for foreign affairs, wrote to Sun Yat-sen as well as to the military authorities in Peking, making known the Bolshevik intention of renouncing the special privileges extracted from China by the Tsarist court. In July 1919, his deputy, Lev Karakhan, issued a declaration in which he stated the Bolsheviks' willingness to abandon their claim to extraterritoriality and made other unprecedented concessions. His remarks about the Chinese Eastern Railway are shrouded in controversy. In some versions, he is quoted as having renounced all rights to the railway. The Soviet leaders later claimed, however, that this section of his statement was garbled in the telegraphic transmission to China. What he really offered, according to these Soviet accounts, was joint Sino-Soviet operation of the railway.[57] Whatever the offer, the Chinese government in Peking did not respond, though public opinion was favourably impressed at a time when hostility to imperialism was running very high in China.

The later offers by the Soviet Union were less generous. As the Red Army overwhelmed the White Russian opposition, the Soviet leaders became more confident and perhaps regretted the earlier terms which they had granted. Their confidence was bolstered even further by the sudden fall of Horvath. In March 1920, Russian citizens in Manchuria, encouraged by the Soviet contingent there and aware of the growing stability of the Soviet government, deposed Horvath, leaving the political future of the Chinese Eastern Railway ambiguous. The downfall of one of its chief enemies prompted the Soviet Union later in the year to renounce, or perhaps clarify, portions of the Karakhan Declaration, making it less attractive to the Chinese. Since they were, nonetheless, eager to establish relations with Peking, the Soviet leaders continued to negotiate with the warlords in the capital. As the power of the Peking military officials was challenged by Chang Tso-lin and other rival warlords, they too showed a willingness to compromise with the Soviet Union. Though under great pressure from the Western powers to reject any agreement with the Soviet Union, they finally came to terms with the Soviet representatives. The Sino-Soviet treaty of May 1924 initiated equal diplomatic relations between the two parties, ended the Soviet Union's special privileges in China, confirmed the Soviet Union in its ownership of the Chinese Eastern Railway and China in its political and military control of the railway, and dealt with other diplomatic matters.[58] A separate conference was to be convened to work out the details of the future operation of the railway. However, Chang Tso-lin's refusal to abide by an agreement in which his own point of view was not represented delayed the convening of this conference. And it was only after a separate treaty, which differed only slightly from that approved by the Peking and Moscow regimes, had been signed by the Soviet Union and himself, that he withdrew his objections.

The stability promised by the negotiation of these treaties was short-lived. And the disruptions which followed were precipitated by developments in China, not in the Soviet Union. The lack of stability in the Chinese government provoked a serious crisis within two years of the presumed settlement on paper of the Chinese Eastern Railway question. In 1925, a struggle for power had erupted between Chang Tso-lin and Feng Yü-hsiang, the so-called 'Christian General' who controlled Peking at that time. Chang wished to use the Chinese Eastern Railway to transport his troops. Late in 1925, however, the Soviet railway manager, A. V. Ivanov, insisted on payment in cash before accepting Chinese forces on the railway. Infuriated by this demand, one of Chang's subordinates arrested Ivanov and seized some railway property.[59] The Soviet Union reacted strongly to this illegal act, threatening military action. Eager for a military confrontation with the Soviet government, Chang apparently sought assistance from the Japanese, who refused to help him. As a result, he was forced to retreat, and, in 1926, he released Ivanov and pledged himself to abide by the railway regulations concerning payment in cash. Chang resented this humiliating defeat, and clearly the tensions between him and the Soviet Union did not end here. By 1927, he had succeeded in gaining influence in Peking and took advantage of his position to harass the Soviet officials there. On 6 April of that year, the Soviet embassy and the headquarters of the Chinese Eastern Railway in Peking were raided on his orders, and he confiscated records indicating Soviet assistance to Feng Yü-hsiang and to Chiang Kai-shek's Nationalist Party, and therefore involvement in Chinese domestic politics. The embarrassed Soviet officials protested, but to no avail, for Chang shortly thereafter published the incriminating documents.[60] It was with relief, therefore, that the Soviet leaders greeted the news of Chiang Kai-shek's Northern Expedition and of his capture of Peking in June 1928.

But their feelings of delight were only temporary. Chiang had already severed his alliance with the Chinese Communist Party and no longer needed the Soviet economic and military assistance that had been provided during the honeymoon period between the Soviet Union and the Nationalists from 1923 to 1927. He also valued Manchuria very highly and for the next two decades that region, perhaps to his detriment, played an important role in his policies. The assassination of Chang Tso-lin, planned and carried out by officers of the Japanese army in June 1928, offered Chiang Kai-shek a marvellous opportunity to influence events in Manchuria, for Chang's son and successor, Chang Hsüeh-liang, quickly allied himself with the Nationalists. With Chang on his side, Chiang could play a more active role in Manchuria. Chiang was clearly perturbed by the

Soviet Union's influence in Manchuria and particularly by its operation of the Chinese Eastern Railway. It should be noted that the Soviet officials dominated the railway: only twenty-five per cent. of the employees were Chinese, and less than one-third of the administrative posts were occupied by Chinese. Chiang was prepared to use any pretext to dislodge Soviet officials from the region. Like Chang Tso-lin, he decided to raid an official Soviet agency in the area. On 27 May 1929, his forces attacked the Soviet Consulate in Harbin, arrested several officials and private citizens, and seized official documents.[61] Chiang's subordinates justified and explained the raid as a means of uncovering Soviet efforts at subversion and collaboration with enemies of the Nationalist government. Within a few months, Chiang took control of the Chinese Eastern Railway. There was no doubt that he had violated the Sino-Soviet agreements of 1924 concerning the railway. He did not perhaps realize that he could now no longer count on assistance from other powers, which did not look kindly upon a unilateral abrogation of a treaty, should the Soviet Union choose to challenge his actions.

And the Soviet Union did indeed choose to force a return to the status quo. After a series of fruitless negotiations and several attempts by Chiang to persuade the United States and other powers to restrain the Soviet government, an undeclared war broke out in Manchuria. During these six months of hostilities, Soviet land and naval forces inflicted severe losses on Chinese troops. By December, the Chinese had suffered enough, and their negotiators joined with the Soviet representatives in signing the Khabarovsk Protocol, by which the Soviet leaders received all that they wished. They resumed their role as part-operators of the Chinese Eastern Railway; Soviet subjects arrested in the Harbin raid were released; Soviet consulates and commercial establishments in Manchuria were reopened; and Chiang's government pledged itself to prevent White Russian opponents of the Soviet Union who were found in the region from making incursions on Soviet territory and from attacking Soviet citizens and property.[62] The protocol also called for a Soviet-Chinese conference to discuss and settle minor problems in Manchuria. But the Chinese repeatedly attempted to postpone the conference, and they procrastinated once it was convened. On the one hand, they feared additional demands for concessions by the Soviet Union, and on the other hand, they still hoped for foreign support in resisting their dreaded enemy.

Sino-Soviet hostility over Manchuria became irrelevant, however, as

CHINA'S LOSS OF INNER ASIA

a result of Japan's actions in the region from September 1931. The Japanese had for some time coveted the mineral resources, the agricultural fertility, and the tremendous potential for investment and development in Manchuria and became dissatisfied with control merely of the South Manchurian Railway and of Port Arthur and Dairen. They hoped that their control of the whole territory might stimulate more Japanese citizens to migrate to Manchuria and ensure their future domination there. There appears to be no doubt also that they intended to use Manchuria as a base for additional inroads into Inner Asia, and, in particular, into regions controlled and influenced by the Soviet Union. In September 1931, therefore, the Japanese Kwantung Army took control of most of Manchuria. The Chinese warlord Chang Hsüeh-liang moved from southern Manchuria to the area within the Great Wall, seeking to avoid clashes with Japanese troops which might offer Japan a further pretext for incursions in the south. Despite Chinese appeals, neither the European powers nor the United States used military or economic sanctions in an attempt to stop the Japanese. They applied diplomatic pressure, supported by the findings of the report prepared by the Lytton Commission (appointed by the League of Nations to restrain Japan), but all to no avail. The Japanese rapidly occupied Manchuria, founded the state of Manchukuo early in 1932, spirited P'u-yi (the last Ch'ing emperor) out of Tientsin, and after a while persuaded him to ascend the throne of the new state. P'u-yi's enthronement was an attempt to give an aura of legitimacy to what was in fact direct Japanese colonial rule.

The Chinese response was a reversion to the traditional tactic of 'using barbarians to regulate barbarians', a policy which on this occasion proved disastrous. Chiang Kai-shek turned to the Soviet Union, hoping that a resumption of relations with that state and an alliance with it might serve as a balance against Japan and might conceivably lead to hostilities between Japan and the Soviet Union, a conflict which would divert Japanese attention from China. He was successful in establishing relations with the Soviet Union but was unable to foment a war between it and Japan. In December 1932, Sino-Soviet relations were restored, but the Soviet leaders refused to sign a treaty of mutual defence.[63] Thus, when the Japanese occupied Jehol in 1933, the Soviet Union was not obliged to resist this incursion and did not do so. Noticing the passivity of the Soviet government, the Japanese pressed it for additional concessions. They wished to gain control of the Chinese Eastern Railway, and, with their troops already

257

occupying Manchuria, their bargaining power was strong. The Soviet Union had no alternative but to abandon the railway. Its relatively weak military position in the region precluded an armed confrontation with the Japanese. Constant raids, bombings, and sabotage of the railway by White Russians and Chinese bandits covertly encouraged by the Japanese hastened the Soviet decision to renounce ownership. In March 1935, the Soviet Union finally consented to the sale of the Chinese Eastern Railway to the Japanese for 140 million *yen* (or, according to one estimate, one-eighth of the cost of its construction), a great bargain for the Japanese.[64] When, shortly afterwards, Soviet railways employees were replaced by Japanese, the Japanese takeover was complete.

Having succeeded in their military objectives in Manchuria, the Japanese now sought the economic profits offered by this rich land. Their efforts at colonization, as we have noted, failed; some of their other projects met with better results, but were not as spectacularly profitable as they had anticipated. The world-wide depression of the 1930s, the military conflicts of the same period, the start of the Sino-Japanese War, and later the outbreak of the Second World War, disrupted Japanese plans for the Manchurian economy. For example, the level of agricultural production in 1930 was not achieved again throughout the period of Japanese occupation. As it turned out, the Japanese attempt to make the Manchurian economy more self-sufficient (though still dependent on Japan) entailed difficulties and necessarily led to a reduction in total output. The Japanese sought to limit Manchuria's dependence on other states for grain and linen and emphasized the production of such goods as opposed to soybeans and sugar beet, previously the standard crops. Such a transformation, nonetheless, resulted in a decline in agricultural production. The rate of industrial growth in Manchuria was more rapid. The Japanese built additional railway lines, and fostered a shipbuilding industry in Dairen and a machine tool industry in Harbin. The electric power, chemical, and non-ferrous metal industries also made striking advances. This industrial development was accompanied by the growth of large urban centres. The population of Mukden, which was 177,000 in 1906, stood at almost two million during the Japanese occupation.[65] The only impediment to further industrial expansion was the lack of capital, since Japan needed most of its monetary resources for the war with China, and later for the war with the United States.

From 1936 to 1941, armed clashes, as we have noted, marred relations between Japan and the Soviet Union along the Manchurian frontier. In 1937, however, the start of the Sino-Japanese War indicated that Japan had chosen to subdue China and had temporarily abandoned plans for further incursions in the Inner Asian borderlands of the Soviet Union. The Soviet Union, moreover, was preoccupied with its western frontiers as Europe moved towards war. Though there were serious conflicts between the two powers along the Manchurian and Mongolian borders, neither wanted or could afford an all-out war with the other. In the same way, the Japanese resented the Soviet aid granted to China but did not do much in reprisal. And the hostility was somewhat mitigated by the Soviet-Japanese non-aggression pact of 1941. And so Japanese control of Manchuria remained relatively unchallenged by the Soviet Union from 1935 to 1945. There was some resistance by the Chinese in Manchuria, but it was not strong enough to threaten Japanese control.

As the Japanese defeat in the Second World War became clearly imminent, both China and the Soviet Union attempted to secure the most advantageous position for the post-war scramble over Manchuria. The victorious Soviet army held a definite advantage over the demoralized and largely ineffective Nationalist troops. The United States wanted Soviet participation in the final assault on the Japanese islands, which was expected to be a long and bloody operation. At Yalta in February 1945, the United States offered Stalin favourable terms in Manchuria in return for his entry into the war against Japan. Agreement was secretly reached that the Soviet Union and China would jointly operate the Chinese Eastern Railway and the South Manchurian Railway, that Dairen would be internationalized (though the special interests of the Soviet Union would be recognized), and that Port Arthur would be leased to the Soviet Union as a naval base. The Soviet Union would be responsible for the reconquest of Manchuria, but it would acknowledge Chinese suzerainty in the province.[66]

Though Chiang Kai-shek wanted to control all of Manchuria, he was in no position to contest the arrangements devised at Yalta. After much hesitation, manœuvring, and posturing, he signed a series of agreements and protocols in August 1945 which confirmed the Yalta agreements. He consented to the internationalization of Dairen (with a Soviet citizen as chief official in the port and a Chinese as his assistant), and to the use of Port Arthur as a base for China and the Soviet Union (with the latter assuming responsibility for its defence, and the former in charge of its civilian government). He also agreed to the joint administration and ownership of the Chinese Eastern Railway and the South Manchurian Railway, now brought together and referred to as the Chinese Changchun Railway, with a Soviet citizen as manager and a Chinese as chairman of the board of directors. In return, the Soviet negotiators agreed that the railway should revert to China after thirty years and that Soviet troops would leave Manchuria ninety days after the defeat of the Japanese.[67] With these agreements in mind, one of Chiang's first priorities was the resumption of control over Manchuria, a control which no Chinese national government had been able to impose since at least 1911. In particular, he wanted to acquire jurisdiction over Manchuria before the arrival of Chinese Communist troops in the region.

At about the same time the war ended. The atom bombs on Hiroshima and Nagasaki, combined with modifications of the Allied terms, brought about Japan's surrender within days of the Soviet declaration of war. The Soviet government thus did not have to send troops to Japan and could dispatch its best forces to Manchuria.

Meanwhile, to attain his twin objectives of occupying Manchuria and preventing any Chinese Communist influence there, Chiang enlisted the aid of the United States in moving some of his best troops to the north-east. He accused the Soviet Union of helping the Chinese Communists to occupy strategic locations in Manchuria and sought equivalent help from the Americans. On balance, this policy backfired. The Soviet leaders were apprehensive at the number of American troops in north China and were determined to keep them out of Manchuria. Thus, late in 1945, when American naval transports sought to dock in Dairen and land Nationalist troops, the Soviet forces guarding the port refused them permission on the grounds that Dairen was a commercial, not a military, port. The Soviet forces also took nine months, instead of the three months stipulated in the Sino-Soviet agreements, to withdraw from Manchuria. This was partly at the request of the Nationalists, who wished the Soviet army to guard the territory until they were ready to occupy it. Yet the Soviet troops still remained longer than necessary and allowed the Chinese Communist army to occupy most of northern Manchuria before their departure on 31 May 1946.

There is also no doubt that the Soviet Union attempted to profit from its control of Manchuria. Late in 1945, the Soviet government suggested to Chiang Kai-shek that it join with him in operating the bulk of the heavy industry in the province, a suggestion that Chiang's agents flatly rejected. Meanwhile, Soviet troops dismantled equipment from Japanese-owned factories and transported it to the Soviet Union as war booty. Much of the easily transportable wealth of the province was packed up and removed by Soviet troops. One American commission, appointed to investigate the damage, estimated that the Soviet forces confiscated approximately 900 million dollars' worth of industrial supplies. The Soviet leaders themselves claim that the figure was less than 100 million. They attribute the rest of the losses to Japanese and Nationalist depredations and to American bombing in the region.[68]

After the Soviet withdrawal in 1946, the Nationalists became even more committed to using the United States against the Soviet Union and the Chinese Communists. When their troops moved into Manchuria, they discovered that much of the north was already in Communist hands. They did not seek a rapprochement with the Communists; instead, they decided on a policy of extermination. Disavowing any interest in a coalition government, they relied on their own military strength, as well as on aid from the United States, to crush the Communists. Others have already recounted the story of the military and political deterioration of the Nationalists and their final collapse in 1949. Here we can only note their attempt to use one 'barbarian', the United States, against another, the Soviet Union, perhaps without realizing that the Chinese Communists had an indigenous appeal and strength and did not rely principally on Soviet assistance. Another factor that they overlooked was that though the United States furnished military and economic assistance for their efforts in Manchuria, it did not fight their battles for them. And their military prowess left much to be desired, so that, by the end of 1948, the Nationalist forces in Manchuria were finally destroyed. These losses tipped the strategic balance in favour of the Chinese Communist Party, which went on to expel the Nationalists from the Chinese mainland.

10 The Chinese Communists and Inner Asia

The Communist assumption of power in 1949 provided China with the first government since 1911 that ruled virtually all of the traditional territory of the Middle Kingdom. This is not the place to analyse the reasons for the Communists' success. It is, in any case, perhaps too early to attempt an objective evaluation. Similarly, it may be somewhat soon, less than a quarter of a century after their rise to power, to draw conclusions about the success of their efforts in Inner Asia. Despite the work of many observers, scholars, and journalists, information about the Communists' relations with the peoples and states of Inner Asia is fragmentary. Yet we can perceive the general pattern of their policies, and the Communists themselves occasionally offer a glimpse of their effectiveness in implementing their plans.

It is remarkable to note the similarities between the objectives of the Chinese Communists in Inner Asia and those of the Chinese dynasties. Like the Ming and the Ch'ing, they have perhaps been excessively concerned about their northern and north-western frontiers and about the security of their borders. Unlike those two dynasties, however, by the late 1950s they did not fear the non-Chinese peoples of Inner Asia but the Russians, their chief competitors for the allegiance of the people and for the use of the resources of the area. The extent of the territory under their control rivals that of the great Chinese dynasties of the past. They certainly govern Manchuria, Inner Mongolia, and much of Central Asia. Like so many of the dynasties in Chinese history, they have promoted Chinese colonization in Inner Asia. In Inner Mongolia and Manchuria, they have been extremely successful. It seems clear that they also intend to foster settlements in Sinkiang. It remains to be seen how successful their plans will be. Unlike the Ming and the Ch'ing, they have not had to worry about the attractiveness of Inner Asian life for their own peoples on the border. It is rather the fear that the non-Chinese peoples on their side of the frontier will join with the minorities on the Soviet side that has impelled them occasionally to limit the freedom of movement of the local peoples.

The Communists refer to the peoples of Inner Asia who live within the Chinese border as 'national minorities'. In this way, they acknowledge the impact of nationalism on the peoples of Inner Asia, distinguish between the Han, or Chinese peoples, and the other inhabitants of China, and have perhaps laid the foundations for different policies towards the latter. Yet by referring to the non-Chinese groups as 'minorities', they assert the Chinese right to govern these peoples. They have established autonomous regions for the various minorities of Inner Asia, but these have remained under the jurisdiction of the national government in Peking. As we have noted earlier, the peoples of Inner Asia had been influenced by nationalism in the early twentieth century, and some may have wished to establish their own national states in 1949. But they were surrounded by two great powers, China and the Soviet Union, which made it difficult to proclaim and maintain their national independence. Moreover, the Chinese Communists were conciliatory and appeared to offer more tangible benefits than the Chinese Nationalists, earlier Chinese governors such as Sheng Shih-ts'ai, and oppressive and corrupt indigenous leaders. The Chinese Communists' pledge of a more equitable distribution of income and political power also attracted a large number of the poor among the minorities.

The Communists have employed many devices to ensure the defence of their borders. They have attempted to prevent the unification of any nationalistic minorities which might prove troublesome. In Sinkiang, for example, they have established one administrative unit for the Uighurs and another for the Kazakhs. It seems natural that the Communists should use the same 'divide and rule' policy that had been so effective in the past. In earlier times, the Chinese had considered themselves superior because of their great Confucian civilization, their highly developed literary culture, their sedentary agriculture, and their cities. They offered the benefits of these to the peoples of Inner Asia if the latter desisted from attacks on Chinese soil. Now the Communists offer the benefits of a new ideology, Communism (emphasizing the tangible economic and social gains to be derived from it), as a means of attracting the support of the minorities. They appear to count on the acceptance of Communism as a tool in the possible assimilation of the non-Chinese peoples of Inner Asia. Their policy in their early years of power was to respect, within reason, the customs of the minorities. During the Cultural Revolution of 1966–69, they temporarily reversed this moderate approach, but for the first fifteen years of their rule, they recognized the need for compromise. They did not wish to risk alienating a large segment of the national minorities by a doctrinaire and rigid policy.

The Communists were also, no doubt, aware of the economic importance of the border regions, and, despite their denials, they attempted to profit from the resources available there. The Ming had denied the need for goods from Inner Asia, claiming that China was self-sufficient. Similarly, the present Chinese leadership has certainly been aware of the economic value of Inner Asia. The industrial base in Manchuria, the mineral resources of Sinkiang, and the animals and animal products of Inner Mongolia were not likely to be ignored by the Communists. Their desire for goods from these regions has undoubtedly influenced their policy. Like the Chinese dynasties, they scorn merchants, and this attitude, though derived from Marxist rather than from Confucian principles, has proved as beneficial to them as it did to their predecessors. For the Communist government has by and large excluded private merchants from most commercial transactions and holds a monopoly of trade both with Inner Asia and with foreign nations.

The benevolent and idealistic side of Communist policy towards Inner Asia ought not to be neglected. The Chinese leaders assert that they are motivated by a desire to improve the living conditions of the peoples of Inner Asia and to eliminate the oppression and exploitation which had been characteristic of the earlier Chinese and local rulers of the region. On the evidence of the fragmentary information available, it appears that the Communists have attempted to ensure an equitable distribution of goods, even though, in the process, they have challenged and, in some cases, prohibited certain customs and practices of the non-Chinese groups. Difficult as it sometimes is, however, to disregard the material and political aims which have partly motivated their overtly humanitarian policies, their idealism should not be discounted.

Another factor that has shaped Chinese Communist policy in Inner Asia has been relations with the Islamic countries. During most of their first twenty-five years of rule, the Communists have been interested in establishing good relations with the Muslim states in

Asia and Africa. Good treatment of the Inner Asian Muslims living in China would clearly make a favourable impression on their co-religionists in the Middle East and other areas. How much this consideration affected Communist policy and attitudes towards the Muslims of Sinkiang, for example, is, however, difficult to ascertain. So far, the Communists have encountered some obstacles in attaining their objectives. Their greatest success has been in Manchuria, where the non-Chinese minorities had been almost totally absorbed by the time the Republic of China was established (1912). In Inner Mongolia and in Sinkiang, where sizeable groups of non-Chinese peoples lived, the Communists were faced by serious difficulties which often forced them to abandon, or postpone, the implementation of their initial plans and policies. Perhaps one of the most formidable obstacles which they encountered in the region was the challenge of the Soviet Union. The Soviet government was at least as eager as the Chinese Communists to exert political influence over Inner Asia and to acquire goods from it. For about a decade after the Chinese Communist accession to power, the tensions between the Soviet and Chinese leaders were masked by common ideological bonds, but, since then, differing views and interests and contradictory territorial and economic claims have been made in public and have affected the course of Chinese-Inner Asian relations.

DIFFICULTIES IN MONGOLIA

In 1949, the Chinese Communists still wanted to play a role in the affairs of the Mongolian People's Republic, but their relative political and military weakness and Soviet dominance in the region dissuaded them from too rapid and too great an assertion of involvement in the political future of their neighbour. Having no plausible alternative, they at first accepted the status quo, confirming the Nationalist approval of independence for the Mongolian People's Republic. In February 1950, through a series of agreements with the Soviet Union, including a thirty-year Treaty of Friendship, Alliance, and Mutual Assistance, China recognized the autonomy of the Mongolian People's Republic and exchanged embassies with it. The republic was at this time in a deplorable state. It had contributed very heavily to the Soviet war effort without receiving much in return. Its own economy, which relied on imports of industrial products from the Soviet Union, was hard hit by the inability of the wartime Soviet government to transport most goods to Mongolia. By 1950, even after almost three decades of a Communist regime, the economy of the Mongolian People's Republic remained primarily pastoral, and the country's cultural, educational, and medical facilities were still barely adequate. At that time, the Mongol leadership, with the aid of the Soviet Union, started to transform the Mongol economy from pastoralism to a predominantly agricultural and industrial type. To do this, the Mongols first needed to improve their herding economy by such measures as the provision of winter shelter and extra feed for their animals, and the killing of wolves and pests. They also needed to rely more on crops, rather than exclusively on animal products, for their food and clothing.

Their most critical deficiencies were in men and capital. The Mongolian People's Republic was not only underpopulated but also lacked trained personnel for industry and mechanized agriculture. China, with its huge population, offered a vast source of labour, and by the economic agreement signed by the two Communist states in 1952 the first tentative steps towards co-operation were initiated. Later that year, the Soviet Union agreed to assist in the construction of a railway which would ultimately link Peking and Ulan Bator, yet another step promising increased collaboration between China and the Mongolian People's Republic. In 1954 the Inner Mongolian leader Ulanfu visited Ulan Bator to encourage more contacts, and, a year later, a second Sino-Mongol agreement was signed by which ten thousand Chinese labourers soon began to arrive to work in construction projects and factories.[1] In 1956, a further group of Chinese workers reached the Mongolian People's Republic. The arrival of the Chinese aid was accompanied by an increase in commerce between China and the republic. This increase inevitably resulted in a decrease in Soviet-Mongol commerce. It appeared that the Chinese might soon replace the Soviet Union as the Mongolian People's Republic's chief trading partner and might become the principal outside influence on that country.

The eruption of disputes between China and the Soviet Union in the late 1950s, however, dashed these prospects for the Chinese. From about 1957, with the first inkling of strife between the two states, the Soviet authorities began to reassert themselves in the Mongolian People's Republic. Khrushchev's secret speech in 1956 denouncing Stalin, and the revolt in Hungary and its subsequent suppression by Soviet troops, were preludes to other challenges to Soviet dominance in the Communist world. Ideological differences were crucial, but many states in the Soviet bloc also resented Soviet military and economic supremacy. China, being the largest of these states and having an independent-minded leadership, soon became embroiled in disputes with the Soviet leaders. In 1958, the Soviet Union refused to assist the Chinese in their efforts, which began in that year, to develop nuclear arms. Also, they were not sympathetic with the Chinese in boundary disagreements with India, they emphasized peaceful coexistence with the capitalist world in contrast to the Chinese insistence on confrontation and revolution, and they cultivated cordial relations with the established 'reactionary' regimes in Asia and Africa, while the Chinese courted and frequently assisted guerrilla organizations in the same states. All this friction finally led in 1960 to the abrupt withdrawal of most Soviet advisers to China, to the removal of some Soviet machinery, and to the curtailment of Soviet economic aid. From that time onwards, competition between the two states has been intense.[2]

Nowhere has the competition been more bitter than in the Mongolian People's Republic. The Soviet leaders had an ally in the Premier, Y. Tsedenbal, who had been educated in the Soviet Union. Though he signed a Treaty of Friendship and Mutual Assistance with China in the spring of 1960, thus obtaining a long-term loan, he also negotiated a more elaborate agreement with the Soviet Union by the end of the summer of that year. The Soviet Union promised to provide a much larger loan and to grant economic and technical assistance to the Mongolian People's Republic. The Soviet Union's economic power gave it a tremendous advantage over its Chinese rivals, and it is clear that by 1964 it had re-established itself as the leading patron of the Mongolian People's Republic. In June of that year, the republic asked for the recall of the Chinese workers in its territory.

Further evidence of the Sino-Soviet competition in the Mongolian People's Republic concerned their differing views of Mongol history, and in particular of the role of Chinggis Khan. As early as 1954, the Chinese announced plans to construct a tomb for Chinggis on the border between Inner Mongolia and the Mongolian People's Republic. Since then, they have praised Chinggis for ending tribal warfare, unifying the Mongols, developing a magnificent postal system across Asia, and encouraging beneficial contacts between East and West, though they have criticized him for his destructive raids, 'which disrupted production' in parts of China.[3] In conformity with this generally favourable view, the Chinese organized in 1962 a celebration of the eighth centenary of Chinggis' birthday. Ceremonies took place at Chinggis' 'tomb', and a scholarly conference was held in Inner Mongolia. Simultaneously, the Mongolian People's Republic conducted its own festivities to commemorate the birth of the first leader of the united Mongols. It too organized a conference of Mongol and foreign scholars at which Chinggis was lauded as 'an able statesman and a great general'. A stamp was issued in his honour, and a series of articles was published in order to 'rehabilitate' him.[4] The Soviet leaders, who had argued that the Mongol empire was destructive, regarded this campaign as a threat to their own position. After all, it was likely to arouse Mongol nationalism and Pan-Mongol sentiment which might stimulate an independence movement among the Mongols within the Soviet Union. The Soviet Union therefore launched a counter-attack against the nationalism of certain Mongol historians and officials and may have prompted the purge of these men by the government of the Mongolian People's Republic. The Soviet leaders denigrated Chinggis' achievements, insisting that his conquests damaged, rather than promoted, economic development in Asia and Europe. It may be that they feared that the Maoist dictum that 'the east wind will prevail over the west wind', exemplified by Chinggis, might challenge Soviet interests in Asia.

The Sino-Soviet conflict in the Mongolian People's Republic reached a critical stage in 1964. In that year, Mao Tse-tung told a group of visitors from the Japanese Socialist Party that he 'had asked Soviet leaders in 1954 to restore Mongolian independence'.[5] The Soviet leader, Nikita Khrushchev, replied that Mao had demanded Chinese control of the republic and that the Chinese leader had cited historical precedent for its inclusion in China. Khrushchev stated that 'the Chinese empires . . . had plundered much',[6] but that previous imperialistic domination of a region was no justification for current claims on it. Shortly afterwards, the government of the republic, perhaps under pressure from the Soviet Union, began to sever its economic ties with China. It accused the Chinese of planning to impose Chinese rule on the Mongolian People's Republic and of planning to colonize and overwhelm the Mongols of the republic as they had done in the case of the Mongols of Inner Mongolia. The government also launched a vitriolic attack on Chinese Communist ideology and territorial and economic aspirations, echoing, in general, the Soviet view on these matters.

The rupture between China and the Mongolian People's Republic in 1964 forced the Mongols into even greater reliance on the Soviet Union. It may be that this dispute with China harmed them even more than it harmed their neighbours to the south. The withdrawal of Chinese labour and capital led to almost total Mongol dependence on the Soviet Union. In 1966, the Soviet government negotiated a new commercial agreement with the republic, providing it with increased loans and credits to compensate for its loss of Chinese aid. Since then, the Chinese have repeatedly asserted that the Mongolian People's Republic is merely a colony of the Soviet Union, and at present they have sound reasons for this opinion. The Soviet government, for example, perhaps took advantage of the situation to help in the building of a new industrial centre in Darkhan, only fifty miles from the Soviet border but over one hundred and fifty miles from Ulan Bator, the most populous city in the republic. In 1972, ninety-nine per cent. of the Mongolian People's Republic's foreign trade was conducted with the Communist bloc in Eastern Europe and sixty-five per cent. with the Soviet Union. Such an economic arrangement created a balance of trade unfavourable to the Mongolian People's Republic, and although Soviet aid has erased the deficit,[7] it has rendered the Mongols even more dependent on and submissive to the Soviet Union. In return for economic assistance and for accepting Mongol students in its own universities, the Soviet Union has been granted the right to station troops in the republic, thus heightening Chinese fears and further aggravating the Sino-Soviet split. Soviet soldiers in the republic, it appears, considerably outnumber the whole Mongol army. Meanwhile the Sino-Mongol war of words continues unabated. Whether such total dependence on a foreign state is in the best interests of the Mongolian People's Republic is questionable.

In Inner Mongolia, the Chinese Communists did not face Soviet competition. And when they first assumed power, they did not impose Chinese authority over the Mongol inhabitants. Since it was founded in 1921, the Chinese Communist Party had attracted Mongols, some of whom had become ardent Communists by 1949. The Mongols of Inner Mongolia who joined the Communist Party came from diverse backgrounds. The first group to come to the Party in the 1920s was composed of young, urban, well-to-do intellectuals, not strongly tied to their own Mongol culture. Another group was composed of those who came to the Party during the time of the Long March of 1934–35 to north-western China and the years when its headquarters was in

269

Yenan in the late 1930s and early 1940s. They were generally illiterate, poor, and uninformed about Party doctrine. The Party took great pains to educate and train both groups, and by 1941 had established in Yenan an institute specifically designed for national minorities. By 1949, therefore, the Communists had trained a core of reliable and politically sensitive Mongols.[8] They selected the sinicized Mongol Ulanfu, described in one source as 'the most important non-Han member of the party',[9] as the chief executive of Inner Mongolia and permitted him much leeway in the handling of local affairs.

Until approximately 1958, the Chinese were extremely flexible in their treatment of Inner Mongolia. The very name of the area, the Inner Mongolian Autonomous Region, indicates that it enjoyed a measure of freedom from outside interference. Ulanfu himself was among the few Chinese provincial officials to be simultaneously the leading figure in the government, the secretary of the Communist Party, and the political commissar of the armed forces. He was also elected and appointed to high positions in the national government and in the national Party hierarchy. Moreover, the territory of the autonomous region grew. In 1952, the old province of Chahar was added to it, and its capital was moved from Kalgan westward to Kueisui (subsequently renamed Huhehot) in his newly acquired land. In 1954, the province of Suiyüan was incorporated into it, and in 1955, part of the old province of Jehol was brought under its jurisdiction.[10] As a result of these additions, it became the third largest administrative unit in China. The population of the region became increasingly Chinese, and by the mid-1950s Mongols comprised only fifteen per cent. of the total population of about 7.5 million. Despite this, four of the five Party secretaries were Mongols, and the Mongols were over-represented on all levels in the government and in the Party.

During this time, the Chinese Communist Party moved slowly to bring about political and economic changes in Inner Mongolia. Communist Party cadres and work teams were instructed not to alienate the Mongols. They were generally moderate both in their objectives and in their methods, and there were few complaints that they did not cater for minority needs. They limited and confiscated some of the wealth of the owners of lands and flocks, moneylenders, and the church, but they did not interfere in the daily life of the ordinary Mongol herdsman. They urged but did not force the Mongols to pool their livestock holdings and to form co-operatives, emphasizing the economic advantages of co-operation and offering some alluring inducements for those who organized co-operatives of their own accord. There was little pressure to transform the Mongols' economy from a pastoral to a more agricultural one, though agricultural settlements did, in fact, increase. Chinese pronouncements of the period repeatedly mention the unique characteristics of the Mongol minority and stress that it should receive special treatment. Chinese officials rarely imposed restrictions on the use of the Mongol language or interfered with Mongol culture during this time.

These moderate policies promoted the economic development of the region. The size of the herds increased, as more Mongols and Chinese stall-fed their animals and trained and employed veterinarians. The production of millet, oats, and kaoliang rose, and such new crops as sugar beet were introduced. Coal deposits were discovered, and new iron and steel plants were built, principally in the western city of Paotow. Railways and roads connecting the industrial cities of Paotow and Kalgan with the Mongolian People's Republic to the north and the province of Kansu to the west were also built. It seemed that the Communists were succeeding in fostering the economic development of the region.

The Great Leap Forward of 1958 reversed most of these policies. This dramatic change in direction has been attributed to many factors (the growing estrangement from the Soviet Union, the desire to make revolutionary changes in China's economy), but, whatever prompted it, it certainly led to radical changes in Inner Mongolia. The earlier emphasis on the uniqueness of the Mongols diminished, and the moderate and gradual approach that had prevailed since 1949 was now discarded. The national government apparently encouraged Chinese colonists to migrate into the region, thus alienating many of the Mongol inhabitants. Communist Party cadres pressed Mongol herdsmen into joining livestock communes, imposed limits on the number of animals owned by any single herdsman, and demanded an increase in the number of agricultural settlements. Most of the cadres who took part in the Great Leap Forward were not Mongols, but Chinese, and they grated on Mongol sensibilities. They were less concerned with the Mongol language and culture, and it seems that a larger percentage of Chinese and a smaller percentage of Mongols than before were now accepted as members of the Communist Party in Inner Mongolia. As in most other parts of China, the Great Leap Forward in Inner Mongolia did not fulfil the hopes of the Communist leadership. Indeed, it was positively disruptive. Many herdsmen resented the sudden imposition of communes and were apparently unwilling to renounce private ownership of their animals. Some even killed their own herds, and the total number of animals declined during the extreme phase of the Great Leap Forward. The experiments in agriculture often failed, alienating many of the Mongol herdsmen who had been forced into farming. They may also have resented the down-grading of Mongol culture and the sudden appearance of unsympathetic Chinese cadres.

By 1960, Ulanfu and other Mongol leaders recognized some of the failures of the Great Leap Forward. Ulanfu reorganized some of the communes, disbanded a few others, and placed fresh emphasis on livestock production as opposed to agriculture. He actively discouraged Chinese immigration into Inner Mongolia, hoping to prevent Mongol culture from being swamped. In his effort to preserve the culture, he himself studied the Mongol language and encouraged manifestations of the Mongol heritage.[11] He approved of and took part in the celebration of the eighth centenary of Chinggis Khan's birth and appears to have taken steps to bolster Mongol nationalism. He insisted that new Chinese cadres should learn Mongol before taking up their duties, in effect insisting on special treatment for the Mongols and, by inference, for the other national minorities. For the next six years, he pursued this moderate policy, which doubtless fostered Inner Mongolian nationalism and separation from China, and aligned himself with the 'return to normalcy' stance that followed the Great Leap Forward. In pursuing this policy, he apparently enjoyed the support of the Chinese Communist Party's national leaders.

The resurgence of the more radical elements at the outset of the Great Proletarian Cultural Revolution in 1966 was disastrous for these policies, and had a considerable impact on Inner Mongolia. Its proponents, primarily the Chinese, accused Ulanfu of stressing nationalism and of placing too little emphasis on the class struggle. They resented his support of a pastoral, as opposed to an agricultural, economy, his reassertion of the value of the Mongol language and culture, and his approval of Inner Mongolian nationalism. Knowing that he had studied in the Soviet Union in the 1920s, the Red Guards implied that he was acting in collusion with Soviet leaders in a plot to unite Inner Mongolia with the Mongolian People's Republic in an independent state under Soviet jurisdiction. One scholar has suggested that they may also have believed that his eulogizing of Chinggis Khan diverted attention from Mao Tse-tung.[12] Ulanfu was the perfect target for the Red Guards because of his domination of nearly all the major official positions in Inner Mongolia and because of his association with Liu Shao-ch'i, the former chief figure in the national government and a notable enemy of the Cultural Revolution. In the spring of 1967, armed clashes, virtually amounting to a civil war, broke out between the Chinese army and those troops who were loyal to Ulanfu. Within a short time, Ulanfu's forces were defeated by the People's Liberation Army. He was deprived of his government and Party posts and subjected to strong criticism by the Red Guards.

After Ulanfu's downfall, Chinese Communist policy in Inner Mongolia was to play down, if not ignore, national differences. This view was a reversion to Mao's maxim that 'national struggle is in the final analysis a question of class struggle',[13] and it was asserted that the Mongols should not be treated differently from the Chinese. It appears that pastoralism was down-graded, agriculture and industry were encouraged at its expense, and the Mongol language and culture declined. To facilitate this process, the Communist Party promoted further Chinese colonization of the region and gradually replaced Mongols with Chinese in some leading government and Party posts. They also stationed a large number of troops on the border, no doubt both to restrain Inner Mongolian nationalism and to combat any Soviet military threat through the Mongolian People's Republic. This military presence was apparently needed to ensure the proper implementation of these policies. Moreover, in 1969, the territory of Inner Mongolia was reduced. About 170,000 square miles in the east were returned to the provinces of Manchuria and about 65,000 square miles in the west were transferred to Kansu and to the Ninghsia Hui Autonomous Region. The territory of Inner Mongolia was thus reduced to half of its former size, and the population under its jurisdiction decreased from thirteen to nine million, of whom 600,000 were Mongols. The author of a recent study suggests that this reorganization was not politically motivated, pointing out that 'it made economic sense by reconnecting Inner Mongolian areas with adjacent provinces along lines of established transport routes and other economic linkages'.[14] That may be, but it seems hard to believe that the political difficulties of 1966–68 in Inner Mongolia did not influence those in the national leadership who made the decisions.

It is true, however, that, since the end of the Cultural Revolution, there have been signs of greater consideration being shown to Inner

273

Mongolian interests. The extreme phase of the Cultural Revolution has apparently passed, and the Mongol language and culture have survived. The eventual fate of the Inner Mongolian minority, nonetheless, is difficult to forecast.

The Mongols, formerly of Inner Mongolia, whose land was turned over to the Ninghsia Hui Autonomous Region in 1969 are in a minority among the Chinese Muslims (Hui) and Chinese in the region. In 1958, the government had created the Ninghsia Hui Autonomous Region out of several formerly autonomous districts. It apparently encouraged Chinese immigration into the area, for by 1969 less than one-third of the people were Chinese Muslims. The region could thus easily absorb the new Mongol population and still maintain a Chinese majority. How the culture of the Mongol and the Chinese Muslim minorities will fare in the Ninghsia region is almost impossible to foretell.

TROUBLES IN SINKIANG

The Chinese Communists also had eventually to dispatch troops to Sinkiang. Even as early as 1950, their position there was somewhat shaky. No Chinese national government had really governed the region since 1911. The people of Sinkiang had had closer political, military, and economic ties with the Soviet Union than with China from 1925 until 1949. Communications between Sinkiang and the Soviet Union were easier than between the former and China, and Sinkiang's trade reflected this. The choice of the Cyrillic alphabet in the 1940s for the transliteration of some of the languages of Sinkiang was another sign of Soviet influence. Soviet authority in the region was further bolstered by the accords signed as part of the general Sino-Soviet agreements of 1950. These accords stipulated that Sino-Soviet joint-stock companies would, for thirty years, co-operate to explore for oil and metals in Sinkiang; they also stipulated that the companies should provide facilities for air transport from Peking through Sinkiang to Alma-Ata (in the Soviet Union), and for the construction of a railway line from Lanchou through Hami and Urumchi to Alma-Ata. It seems unlikely that the Chinese volunteered such concessions (they smacked of imperialist exploitation of China's resources), but their military and economic weakness and their need for Soviet assistance in other areas prevented them from rejecting these demands when put to them by the Soviet government.

The Chinese also faced challenges from some of the national minorities in Sinkiang. In 1948, the Sinkiang League for the Protection of Peace and Democracy, a group composed of some of the most prominent nationalists who were opposed to Chinese rule, was founded and promised to threaten Chinese control of the region. Many of its leaders had suffered under the repressive regime of Sheng Shih-ts'ai and were not eager to be subject to Chinese authority again. Fortunately for the Communists, their principal opponents (those centred in the Ili region) died in the mysterious aeroplane crash in 1949; and Burhan and Saifudin, the two principal remaining leaders, allied themselves with the Communists to form the new province of Sinkiang. Burhan was appointed governor and Saifudin vice-governor of the province. Both also had posts in the North-west Military and Administrative Committee organized to govern Sinkiang, Kansu, Shensi, Ninghsia, and Tsinghai, in the Sinkiang military command, in the national government and Party hierarchy, and as envoys to foreign, particularly Muslim, lands. Having now found some support among the leaders of the minorities, the Chinese were still confronted with at least two styles of life in the province. The Kazakhs, Mongols, and Kirghiz generally pursued a pastoral economy, while the Uighurs were oasis-dwellers and farmers. The Communists were forced to devise different policies to cope with these disparate groups in Sinkiang.

All these problems forced on the Chinese an attitude of moderation towards and accommodation with the minority nationalities. As in Inner Mongolia, the Communists did not immediately attempt to alter the economic and political patterns of the region in order to impose their rule over the Kazakhs and Uighurs. They encountered many more difficulties however in Sinkiang (where the Chinese constituted a minority of the population) than in Inner Mongolia (where the Chinese outnumbered the Mongols). Cadres were instructed to move slowly, to recognize that the minorities ought to receive special treatment, and to co-operate with selected leaders of the non-Chinese groups in a kind of United Front arrangement. Communist pronouncements emphasized the doctrine that the development of a 'proletarian outlook' would eventually erase national and religious differences.

The government therefore permitted the leaders of Sinkiang a great deal of autonomy and power. In 1953, Burhan became the first president of the Chinese Islamic Association. In the following year,

275

the government founded the Ili Kazakh Autonomous *Chou* (District) within Sinkiang and permitted the old Kazakh leaders, many of whom were Soviet-oriented, to retain their powers. And in 1955, the Communists transformed the province into the Sinkiang Uighur Autonomous Region, a name which indicated a greater degree of independence for the territory. Saifudin, who by now had joined the Communist Party, replaced Burhan as chairman of the region. Burhan went on special assignments to Muslim countries. Like the Jurched envoy Isiha, who was sent repeatedly by the Ming court to improve relations with the Jurched, Burhan was employed by Communist China for motives of foreign policy.

The Uighurs constituted the largest section of the region's population. According to the 1953 census, there were 3.6 million Uighurs out of a total population of 4.9 million in Sinkiang. The Uighurs were concentrated in the oases, towns, and villages of southern Sinkiang in the Tarim River basin. Many of them lived in agricultural settlements close to the important towns of Kashgar, Aksu, and Khotan. In the 1950s, the government used the army to assist the Uighurs in irrigation and reclamation projects. The result was a striking increase in the output of crops traditionally grown in the region (wheat, corn, cotton, and rice) and the introduction of such crops as sugar beet. The Uighur farmers and town-dwellers at first posed fewer problems to the Chinese than did the largely nomadic Kazakhs and Kirghiz. The commune movement of 1958 gave rise to some Uighur opposition, but it was not as serious as that which developed among the Kazakhs. Also, the Uighurs were not faced with as large an influx of Chinese colonists as were the Kazakhs of Dzungaria in the north. They still constitute a majority in the Tarim River basin (with a population of about 4.5 million), and with the end of the Cultural Revolution, they no longer faced the same degree of Chinese pressure to become sinicized as they were subjected to in the late 1960s. Moreover, though their land has enough mineral resources for local use, it does not possess the vast reserves available in the Kazakh territories. Thus fewer Chinese industrial workers have arrived in the Tarim River basin than in northern Sinkiang.

The Chinese have concentrated on the Kazakh district in Sinkiang. It was in this area that much of Sinkiang's coal, iron, and petroleum resources were located. It was here too that the economy, based on pastoralism, posed the most serious threat to Communist objectives. Because of the nomadic style of life practised by the Kazakhs, it was often difficult for Communist cadres to reach the Kazakh herding areas, much less influence the Kazakh herdsmen. Yet the Communists did not initiate drastic reforms in their economic and social system. Instead they emphasized other solutions. They organized the Production-Construction Corps, composed of former Chinese Communist soldiers, to settle in the region. Members of the corps worked on state farms to produce wheat, cotton, and other agricultural products, founded state livestock farms, and served as models for the eventual transformation of the Kazakhs' way of life. But they did not use violent tactics to effect such a transformation. The state in fact provided high prices for Kazakh products and reduced the power only of the most obstreperous herdowners. It also hardly intruded on the rigid clan (*uru*) structure. The Communists apparently relied on the Production-Construction Corps to persuade the Kazakhs of the economic advantages of permanent livestock farms compared with persistent nomadism; little other pressure was used. With ready access to water in the summer and to pasture in the winter, the farms would naturally produce larger and better herds, and the Kazakhs quickly noticed this. Some began to settle down, and as they formed larger units, the old clan ties apparently weakened. More and more cooperative farms were established, and by 1959, it appeared that China might gradually attain its objectives in the region.[15]

There were nonetheless murmurs of discontent which eventually prompted a strong Chinese reaction. There existed a Kazakh national movement, which had not disappeared with the Communist takeover and sought greater autonomy, perhaps even the creation of an independent Kazakh state. Led by some of the few largely urban-based groups in the district, including many Communist cadres, the movement was strengthened by contact with the Kazakhs on the Soviet side of the border, which increased the Chinese distrust of the Soviet leadership. In 1957, the Chinese government issued public condemnations of the so-called anti-Communist, nationalistic group among the Kazakh cadres. It divested some of them of their power and appointed more Chinese cadres in the region. To hamper relations between the nationalists and the Soviet Kazakhs, it ordered the introduction of the Roman alphabet to replace the Cyrillic for the transliteration of Kazakh.[16]

But the policy that chiefly soured relations between the Communists and the Kazakhs was the initiation of the communes in 1958. Feeling threatened by Kazakh nationalism and wishing to hasten basic changes in the Kazakh economy and society, the Communists abandoned moderation and adopted a direct and radical path towards their objectives. As in Inner Mongolia, livestock communes were founded, the development of agriculture to accompany livestock production was emphasized, the creation of small industries was fostered, and the old clan loyalties were further undermined. This resulted in a decline in the livestock herds and caused other economic dislocations. The Communists encouraged Chinese colonists to migrate to the area in order to counter the anticipated opposition of some Kazakhs. Fortunately for the Party, the Lanchou to Hami railway was completed in 1959, and brought in its wake a large-scale influx of Chinese settlers.

This heightened Kazakh fears of sinicization and resulted in even greater opposition to Communist policies. The drive towards communization, together with the arrival of the Chinese colonists, alienated many Kazakhs. Some, who had contacts with or heard rumours about the Kazakhs on the Soviet side of the frontier, were attracted by the higher standard of living enjoyed by their compatriots across the border. In 1962, approximately sixty thousand Kazakhs fled to the Soviet Union.[17] The question that this raises is how did so many Kazakhs succeed in crossing the border in so short a time? The Chinese subsequently accused the Soviet Union of enticing the Kazakhs with propaganda broadcasts and of issuing false passports to facilitate their departure. Though the Chinese accusations were somewhat overstated, it is nonetheless true that the Soviet officials did admit the Kazakhs without questioning them or causing complications.

To understand the reasons for the Soviet action in 1962, one must examine earlier Sino-Soviet relations in Sinkiang. From 1950 to 1954, the two sides had been partners in joint-stock companies to develop some of the natural resources of the province, an arrangement that the Chinese resented. In 1954, a year after Stalin's death, the Soviet Union renounced its shares in the companies, and it seemed that this gesture might reduce the possibility of Sino-Soviet antagonism. Yet the Chinese still feared Soviet influence in Sinkiang, both in its cultural manifestation in the Kazakh use and knowledge of the Cyrillic alphabet and in the extensive Soviet commercial relations with the Kazakhs. The development of the communes in 1958 clearly aggravated tensions between the two states. In the Soviet view, the communes were an 'adventurist' and immoderate experiment. The Soviet leaders also resented the obvious attempt by the Chinese to limit Soviet influence in Sinkiang. It was their bitterness that prompted them to provide refuge for the Kazakhs of Sinkiang in 1962, and perhaps even to tempt that group into migrating. The Chinese reaction was not long in coming: they closed many of the Soviet consulates in the region and went to greater length than hitherto to prevent dealings between the Kazakhs on the Chinese and Soviet sides of the border. At the same time, they relaxed their policy towards the Kazakhs and Uighurs of Sinkiang. From 1962 until the Cultural Revolution in 1966, they moderated their demands for the immediate development of livestock communes and retreated somewhat in their plans for agriculture and industry in the Kazakh areas. Yet they continued to encourage Chinese to emigrate to Sinkiang, perhaps hoping to win the minorities over through assimilation. And the Chinese far outnumbered the Kazakhs in the Ili region by the mid-1960s. The Chinese population in Sinkiang numbered 2.6 million, many of them having settled in Kazakh lands, while the Kazakh population numbered about 500,000. By 1970, the total number of Chinese in the region was estimated to be four million.

Meanwhile Sino-Soviet competition in Sinkiang escalated dramatically. After all, Sinkiang was blessed with valuable natural resources and had become the centre for Chinese nuclear testing; it was a land well worth claiming. The Chinese have insisted that much territory in Central Asia now under Soviet control truly belongs to them, pointing out that the people in that area traditionally offered tribute and accepted Chinese suzerainty. They have claimed that the imperialist nations, including the Soviet Union, separated this territory from China in a series of treaties signed with the Ch'ing court. They have demanded Soviet acknowledgement that these were unequal treaties and have implied that they would not require the return of all this territory if the Soviet Union publicly admitted the correctness of the Chinese view. The Soviet leaders have replied that the presentation of tribute to the Chinese throne was not synonymous with the acceptance of Chinese rule. They have insisted that both traditional China and Tsarist Russia were guilty of imperialism; the unequal treaties were not the only instances of the exploitation of Central Asia. Finally, they have accused the Chinese Communists of imperialist designs on the minority nationalities and of attempts to sinicize and overwhelm the Kazakhs and the Uighurs. The controversy over territory in Central Asia thus continues unabated, and the number of troops on both sides of the border has increased. Border fighting has broken out several times, and the threat of war seems ever present.

Despite the presence of Chinese troops in Sinkiang, it appears that the Kazakhs and the Kirghiz are in a more favourable position than at any time since 1958. After the extreme phase of the Cultural Revolution passed in 1969, Chinese pressure on these nomadic peoples abated. It is difficult to predict Chinese policy towards the Kazakhs and the Kirghiz in the future, but their position along the strategic Sino-Soviet border may offer them some security. The Chinese will probably try to keep from alienating them.

The Chinese have been somewhat more successful in resolving border disputes with states in Central Asia than they have been in the case of the Soviet Union. In 1961, they signed a treaty with Nepal which delineated their common border line. In 1963, they negotiated frontier agreements with Pakistan and Afghanistan. Chinese negotiators readily resolved boundary disagreements with North Korea, North Vietnam, and Burma. And they have also concluded commercial and political treaties with most of these countries. The principal difficulty has involved China's borders with India. Both China and India claim the Aksai Chin area of Ladakh, the western section of their common boundary. The Chinese overrode Indian objections and built a road in the region in 1957. After a number of minor clashes, a border war between the Chinese and the Indians erupted in November 1962, in which the Chinese forces routed the Indian troops. The Chinese thus maintain control in this area. Their troops also advanced into the North-east Frontier Agency, the easternmost sector of the Sino-Indian boundary, but they subsequently withdrew without demanding concessions in this region.

RIVALRY IN MANCHURIA

In Manchuria, as in Central Asia, territorial and economic controversies have strained the Sino-Soviet relationship. Here, though, there were no problems of national minorities, for the bulk of the indigenous population had become assimilated with the Chinese. Nonetheless, despite the absence of a large minority group, the Chinese have had to face serious challenges in the region. Manchuria was a crucial area; it had valuable natural and mineral resources and ranked as the most important producer of industrial goods in China.

The Soviet Union, which had had some influence in Manchuria before the Japanese occupation, was eager to re-establish itself there after Japan's defeat in the Second World War. As early as 1949, there were indications that the Soviet leaders wanted to play a role in Manchuria. In July, the commander and political commissar of the North-east Military Region, Kao Kang, signed a trade agreement with the Soviet Union (possibly at the Soviet Union's request) by which Manchuria would provide agricultural products, including soybeans, to the Russians in exchange for such manufactured or processed goods as industrial equipment, textiles, paper, and oil.[18] The fact that this was the first such agreement to be signed by the Soviet Union and a Chinese Communist group indicates the great importance that both parties attached to the region. The future of Manchuria was also one of the key subjects of the overall Sino-Soviet agreements negotiated in 1950. As a result of these agreements, the Chinese Changchun Railway would be transferred to Chinese control by the end of 1952, Soviet troops would leave Port Arthur at about the same time, the Soviet Union would receive compensation for the equipment left in that port, and the port of Dairen would revert totally to China once a peace treaty with Japan had been signed. The property leased or owned by the Soviet Union in most of Manchuria was also to be handed over to the Chinese authorities.[19] The one problem that was apparently not discussed was the determination of the boundary between Manchuria and the territory in the Soviet Far East, an oversight that was to have extremely serious consequences later.

The Soviet Union had made major concessions to China, and it seemed probable that Sino-Soviet relations in Manchuria would now be reasonably stable. But this was not to be the case, for the Soviet leaders still hoped to profit from their strong position in Manchuria. They did not immediately withdraw their troops from Port Arthur and Dairen and procrastinated in the matter of handing over total control of the Chinese Changchun Railway. It may be that the outbreak of the Korean War in 1950, and the Chinese involvement in 1951, delayed the Soviet withdrawal. Manchuria was strategically located for the conveyance of supplies to the Chinese and North Korean troops in Korea from the Soviet Union. Even so, the Soviet government did not need to control these areas merely to transport supplies; the Chinese could easily have performed that task. Whether the Chinese complained to the Soviet Union about the continued presence of Soviet troops in Port Arthur and Dairen is not known. But after the death of Stalin in 1953 and the subsequent softening of the Soviet attitude in foreign relations, the new chairman of the

Soviet Communist Party, Nikita Khrushchev, finally transferred control over Dairen and Port Arthur to the Chinese.

Another early indication of the embryonic Sino-Soviet competition in Manchuria was provided by the case of Kao Kang. Kao had been the virtually all-powerful ruler of Manchuria since 1949. He held most of the important positions in the region and was able to appoint his protégés or friends to the remaining influential posts. In short, he had a strong base from which to influence national policy. And the Communist Chinese hierarchy later accused him of planning just such a challenge to the leaders then in office. Kao was charged with plotting to replace either Chou En-lai or Liu Shao-ch'i on the national level and to become the heir apparent to Mao Tse-tung. At some time in 1954, the central committee of the Communist Party decided that it could no longer tolerate the 'independent kingdom of Kao Kang'.[20] In their view, Manchuria ought not to be permitted to pursue too independent a course; the region was too important to be left outside the control of the central government. The stage was thus set for a confrontation between the officials in Peking and Kao and his men in Manchuria. In the clash, the national authorities defeated Kao, stripped him of his rank, and sacked his followers. Deprived of his power and perhaps threatened with more punishment, he committed suicide late in 1954. The intriguing aspect of the Kao Kang episode was the way in which it affected the Soviet Union. There are indications that Kao's principal sin was his effort to cultivate too close relations with the other great Communist power. He appeared much more eager than the other top-ranking Chinese Communist leaders to co-operate with the Soviet Union. He may have believed that such co-operation would lead to swifter progress in the Manchurian economy. But the senior Party officials, even at this stage, were apprehensive of Soviet intentions in Manchuria. Western scholars have uncovered several indirect references in Communist writings and speeches that seem to confirm that there was a conflict between Kao and the principal Party leaders over relations with the Soviet Union.[21]

The Soviet leaders apparently accepted their reduced role in Manchuria and concentrated on developments in Sinkiang and Mongolia in the late 1950s and early 1960s. Yet they were keenly aware of the need for a proper delineation of the border between Manchuria and the Soviet territory in the Far East. They witnessed the Chinese reaction to the frontier dispute with India, mentioned above, that erupted in the early 1960s, and duly noted the way in which the Chinese soundly defeated the Indian troops. The Soviet government had also noticed the amount of territory to which the Chinese laid claim. Tibet, for example, which had remained outside the Chinese orbit from 1911 to 1949, was now brought under Chinese control. And when the Tibetans rebelled in 1959, the Chinese expended vast resources to crush the revolt, even though there were few Chinese resident in Tibet.

Aware of these developments, the Soviet Union itself prepared to justify its claim to regions along the Amur River which had been granted to Russia by treaties signed with China in the seventeenth and nineteenth centuries. A plethora of books and articles appeared in the late 1960s, reviewing the history of Sino-Russian relations in the Amur area. One Western scholar has succinctly observed that 'as Russia's China policy has changed, so has her historiography'.[22] Material from the Russian archives has been published to support the Soviet position. As a *New York Times* dispatch, dated 18 November 1972, from Moscow notes, 'The Soviet Union, in an apparent attempt to bolster its negotiating position in stalemated border talks with the Chinese, has dug back into 300-year-old archives and come up with a documentary record of the first boundary pact concluded between Russia and China in the late 17th century. . . . The latest piece of evidence presented by the Soviet Union is the day-by-day account of Fyodor A. Golovin, a Czarist diplomat who headed the mission that negotiated the 1689 frontier agreement with the Chinese in the Siberian town of Nerchinsk.'[23]

The differing claims of the two parties came to a head in 1969. Two major clashes between Soviet and Chinese troops on the seemingly unimportant island in the Ussuri River known by the Chinese as Chen Pao and by the Russians as Damanski were reported in March that year. Each side claimed that it was on its own side of the border. The Chinese may have provoked the first incident. If they did, one plausible explanation is that the Chinese, thinking of the Soviet intervention in Czechoslovakia in August 1968, wished to assert their military power in the Ussuri River region in order to discourage a Soviet offensive policy in the Amur basin. Assuming that it was the Chinese who took the initiative, it was a disastrous move, since overwhelming Soviet military superiority was evident in the second battle, in which the Chinese casualties included eight hundred dead, whereas the Soviet troops suffered only sixty casualties in all. Frontier incidents in the Amur region, as well as along the border of Sinkiang, persisted throughout the spring and summer, and Soviet military power was made quite apparent on several of these occasions. The Chinese learned their lesson, for, since 1969, there have been no serious clashes along the Amur River up to the time of writing. Tensions, however, still exist on the border. It has been suggested, in fact, that the détente with the United States initiated by the Chinese in the spring of 1971 was in part prompted by the Chinese fear of a war with the Soviet Union. The Chinese needed allies, or at least fewer enemies, among the world powers, in order to withstand Soviet pressure and a possible Russian offensive.

CONCLUSION

The governments of the Ming and Ch'ing dynasties, and the present Communist Chinese leaders, have all pursued, in general, the same objectives in Inner Asia. They have all sought to defend their borders against incursions from Inner Asia, either by the indigenous peoples or by the great power in the region, Russia. They have all wished to profit from economic relations with Inner Asia, either through trade and tribute or through actual occupation of the area, and they have also wanted to control its natural and mineral resources. Yet each government, in one way or another, has denied having an economic interest in the area. The Ming and Ch'ing proclaimed their economic self-sufficiency and disclaimed the need for Inner Asian products, while the Communists insist that their concern for the region and its minority nationalities does not stem from a selfish desire to exploit its economic potential. Nonetheless, all three governments of China have attempted to control trade relations with Inner Asia for their own benefit. The Ming and Ch'ing regulated the activities of their merchants and imposed monopolies on certain products in order to obtain a better bargaining position in commercial transactions with the peoples of the region. The Communists have restricted trade between the Inner Asian groups under their control and other states, in particular the Soviet Union.

All the Chinese governments since 1400 have tried to prevent foreigners from intruding on China's territory and their own people from migrating across the border. Recognizing the attractions of the Inner Asian style of life for its own people, the Ming forbad Chinese to leave the country without official permission. It also prohibited the peoples of Inner Asia from entering China without authorization from the Chinese court, restricted the number of such foreigners permitted to enter China, and carefully regulated their activities during their stay in the country. The Ch'ing imposed the same regulations for a different reason. It wished to prevent its own merchants from travelling to Inner Asia to exploit the Mongols, the frontier Manchus, and the Muslims of Sinkiang, who were less sophisticated in commercial practices than were Chinese merchants. Since the beginning of their dispute with the Soviet Union, the Communists have maintained a close watch on the minority peoples along the Sino-Soviet border and have imposed strict controls on their activities. They have been particularly worried by the possibility that the minorities on the Soviet side of the border might entice those on the Chinese side to act in a way that would be contrary to Chinese interests and perhaps (as in 1962, when sixty thousand Kazakhs were lured across the border from the Chinese side) even establish independent states.

Despite such fears, the Chinese governments have often been willing to use Inner Asians residing in China for their own purposes. The Ming employed individual Jurched and Mongols as interpreters, translators, merchants, and horse-breeders, and occasionally as envoys to Manchuria and Mongolia. The Ch'ing followed the same policy, appointing some members of the local population to important government posts in the Inner Asian regions concerned. And the Communists have frequently called upon the Muslims and the Mongols in their domains to act as envoys or delegates to conferences in the Muslim and Mongol countries of Asia, and the Muslim countries of Africa. In seeking to make a favourable impression on these newly independent states, they have often used their 'good' treatment of the minorities to gain influence abroad.

Though they have denied it, the ultimate objective of every Chinese government since 1400 (except the early Ch'ing) has apparently been the sinicization of China's Inner Asian neighbours. The Ming court made no conscious effort to this end, but one of the tenets of the Confucian world view to which it subscribed was that a good government in China would induce the 'barbarians' to adopt the Chinese values, institutions, and language. The Manchus who conquered China in the seventeenth century eventually became sinicized, and in the late nineteenth century promoted Chinese colonization of Sinkiang, Mongolia, and Manchuria, with the intention that this should lead eventually to the assimilation of the less populous non-Chinese groups. And the Communists have encouraged Chinese to migrate to Inner

Mongolia and Sinkiang, no doubt thus accelerating the process of sinicization. To reduce the threat of a major attack by the unsinicized peoples in Inner Asia, the Chinese have traditionally employed the tactic of 'divide and rule'. They have sought by any means to prevent these peoples from unifying and thus posing a threat to China. The Chinese of the Ming, for example, remembered the humiliations which they had suffered at the hands of the Mongols and were determined not to submit to foreign rule again.

There was one essential difference between the policies of the Ming and those of the Ch'ing and the Communists. The Ming court chose not to occupy the lands of Inner Asia. Instead, it dealt with them through the tribute and trade system, and, in general, did not attempt either to govern them or to influence their choice of leaders. As the dynasty weakened and imposed restrictions on economic transactions with foreigners, it was harassed by upheavals and raids along its Inner Asian borders. The Ch'ing, on the other hand, conquered Sinkiang and Inner Mongolia and ruled Outer Mongolia and Manchuria. By 1760, they had occupied most of Inner Asia and were trying to govern this huge dominion. But they had constantly to deal with rebellions and other manifestations of anti-dynastic feelings in the late eighteenth century and in the nineteenth. In order to counter these insurrections, they sent large, well-supplied armies to subjugate the rebels, thus diverting valuable resources from coastal defence and allowing the Western powers and Japan to gain a foothold on the eastern coast of China. The Communists have followed the Ch'ing pattern and have attempted to rule much of Inner Asia. They no longer have the problem of a large minority group in Manchuria. It is in Inner Mongolia and Sinkiang that they face a large non-Chinese element, and here they have promoted Chinese colonization, hoping in this way to facilitate Chinese rule. The minorities in these two regions have not accepted this situation without resistance, and on several occasions the Communists have had to send in troops to suppress disturbances. It is difficult to determine whether the Communists were wise in deciding to impose direct control over these areas. As one recent student of Communist policy towards the various minority nationalities concluded: 'Minority problems in most societies have proven enormously resistant to easy or rapid "solutions", irrespective of the broad goals enunciated or the concrete policies applied. It is not yet clear that the People's Republic of China constitutes an exception.'[24]

Despite the remarkable continuity in the Ming, Ch'ing, and Communist policies towards Inner Asia, there are at least two notable differences between the present situation and earlier times. One is that Inner Asia is now surrounded and dominated by two powerful national states with conflicting claims in the region. The peoples of Inner Asia, even with their heightened awareness of their own unique national identities, cannot control their own destinies and are involved in a larger struggle between China and the Soviet Union. The second difference is that the policy of the Chinese Communists, unlike that of earlier governments, promises, according to Communist pronouncements, a better life for the average herdsman, farmer or town-dweller in Inner Asia. The Communists have contributed to the remarkable economic progress of these regions and have introduced into them a more equitable distribution of goods than existed earlier, while, on the other hand, making great efforts to sinicize the non-Chinese groups. These two major points of difference between the Chinese Communist government and its predecessors will no doubt shape future Chinese relations with Inner Asia.

China and Inner Asia have had a symbiotic relationship for the long period, about six hundred years in extent, that we have examined. The states and tribes of Inner Asia have repeatedly influenced Chinese economic and political policy, and China, in turn, has frequently determined the social, political, and economic structure of Inner Asia.

Notes to the text

PREFACE

1 For greater detail and for the citation of Oriental sources (which are omitted here) on the subjects treated in this book, I refer the reader to these writings. They include 'The Tea and Horse Trade with Inner Asia during the Ming', *Journal of Asian History*, IV, no. 2 (1970), pp. 136–68; 'Notes on Esen's Pride and Ming China's Prejudice', *Mongolia Society Bulletin*, IX, no. 2 (Autumn 1970), pp. 31–39; 'Ming China and Turfan, 1406-1517', *Central Asiatic Journal*, XVI, no. 3 (1972), pp. 206-25; 'Eunuch Power: The Role of Eunuchs in Ming Foreign Relations', *Monumenta Serica*, XXXI (1973); 'Cheng Ho and Timur: Any Relation?', *Oriens Extremus*, 20 (1973); 'Trade Routes in Inner Asia', in Denis Sinor, ed., *Cambridge History of Inner Asia* (London, forthcoming); 'The Jurchen in the Yüan and Ming', in Herbert Franke, ed., Chin Dynastic History Project (Seattle, forthcoming); 'Muslim Revolts in Late Ming China', in Frederic Wakeman, ed., *Conference on the Ming-Ch'ing Transition* (1974); and biographies of Ahmad, Aruqtai, Esen, Hajji Ali, Ibrahim, Isiha, Liu Yung-ch'eng, Mahmud, Mansur, and Tsong-kha-pa in L. C. Goodrich, ed., *Eminent Chinese of the Ming Period* (New York, forthcoming).

2 Even a cursory appraisal of the recently released Russian documents on early Sino-Russian relations might call for a volume of at least the present size. One of these collections is *Russko-kitaiskie otnosheniia v XVII veke: Materialy i dokumenty*, vol. I, ed. O. N. F. Demidova and V. S. Miasnikov (Moscow, 1969). For additional Soviet writings on early Sino-Russian relations, see Joseph F. Fletcher, 'V. A. Aleksandrov on Russo-Ch'ing Relations in the Seventeenth Century: Critique and Résumé', *Kritika: A Review of Current Soviet Books on Russian History*, VII, no. 3 (Spring 1971).

3 Denis Sinor, *Inner Asia: A Syllabus* (Bloomington and The Hague, 1969), p. 2.

INTRODUCTION

1 The two works are extant both in the official court chronicles (the *Ming Shih-lu*) and in several other editions. The report is entitled *Hsi-yü fan-kuo chih*, and the diary is called *Hsi-yü hsing-ch'eng chi*. Translations by Morris Rossabi of both works will be published

shortly. For a brief biography of Ch'en see L. C. Goodrich, 'Ch'en Ch'eng', in *Symposium in Honor of Dr Chiang Fu-tsung on his 70th Birthday: Bulletin, National Central Library* (Taipei, 1968), pp. 420-26.

2 Wolfgang Franke, *An Introduction to the Sources of Ming History* (Kuala Lumpur, 1968), p. 215.

3 David Farquhar, 'Oirat-Chinese Tribute Relations, 1408-1446', *Studia Altaica: Festschrift für Nikolaus Poppe* (Wiesbaden, 1957), pp. 61-62; Morris Rossabi, 'Ming China and Turfan, 1406-1517', *Central Asiatic Journal*, XVI, no. 3 (1972), p. 210; Henry Serruys, 'The Mongols in China: 1400-1450', *Monumenta Serica*, XXVII (1968), pp. 304-305; E. Bretschneider, *Mediaeval Researches from Eastern Asiatic Sources* (New York, reprint, 1967), II, pp. 184, 186, 193.

4 The Mongols were responsible for the excellent system of postal stations developed in China and Inner Asia. For this, see Peter Olbricht, *Das Postwesen in China unter der Mongolenherrschaft im 13. und 14. Jahrhundert* (Wiesbaden, 1954). For more detail on the guards and postal stations, see Morris Rossabi, 'Trade Routes in Inner Asia', in Denis Sinor, ed., *Cambridge History of Inner Asia* (London, forthcoming).

5 Jean Sauvaget, 'Caravansérails syriens du moyen-âge', *Ars Islamica*, 6, no. 1 (1939), pp. 48–55; 7, no. 1 (1940), pp. 1–19.

6 For a vivid description of the dangers of travel through Central Asia, see Arminius Vámbéry, *Sketches of Central Asia* (London, 1868), pp. 62–74.

7 Henry Serruys, 'Sino-Mongol Relations during the Ming: The Tribute System and Diplomatic Missions (1400–1600)', *Mélanges chinois et bouddhiques*, XIV (1967), pp. 539–40. The most famous of these emissaries, Cheng Ho, led seven expeditions to South-east Asia, the rim of the Indian Ocean, and the east coast of Africa. The most recent work on these missions is J. V. G. Mills, trans. and ed., *Ma Huan: Ying-yai Sheng-lan, The Overall Survey of the Ocean's Shores* (Cambridge, England, and New York, 1970).

8 There are several translations of this account, but the most accessible one is K. M. Maitra, trans., *A Persian Embassy to China* (New York, reprint, 1970). For a list of some other translations see Morris Rossabi, 'Ming China's Relations with Hami and Central Asia, 1404–1513: A Re-examination of Traditional Chinese Foreign Policy' (Columbia University Ph.D. dissertation, 1970), p. 11, f. 23.

9 K. M. Maitra, op. cit., p. 27.

10 K. M. Maitra, op. cit., pp. 52–56; John K. Fairbank and Ssu-yü Teng, *Ch'ing Administration: Three Studies* (Cambridge, Massachusetts, and London, 1961), pp. 141–5, describes the elaborate ceremonies arranged for foreign visitors to China.

11 K. M. Maitra, op. cit., p. 65. John Bell, a Scottish physician who travelled with a Russian embassy to China in the early eighteenth century, confirms that the rulers of China provided all the supplies for foreign embassies residing in Peking. See his *A Journey from St Petersburg to Pekin, 1719–22*, ed. J. L. Stevenson (Edinburgh, 1965), p. 106.

12 K. M. Maitra, op. cit., p. 108.

13 Owen Lattimore, *Inner Asian Frontiers of China* (Boston, paperback ed., 1962), pp. 545-6.

14 Ibid., pp. 37–39.
15 Ying-shih Yü, *Trade and Expansion in Han China* (Berkeley and London, 1967), pp. 14–16; Hans Bielenstein, 'The Restoration of the Han Dynasty, Vol. Three', *Bulletin of the Museum of Far Eastern Antiquities*, 39 (1967), pp. 88–91.
16 John K. Fairbank, *Trade and Diplomacy on the China Coast* (Cambridge, Massachusetts, and London, 1953), p. 27.
17 T. C. Lin, 'Manchuria Trade and Tribute in the Ming Dynasty: A Study of Chinese Theories and Methods of Control over Border Peoples', *Nankai Social and Economic Quarterly*, IX (1937), p. 857.
18 John K. Fairbank, op. cit., p. 29.
19 T. C. Lin, op. cit., p. 856. Note also Immanuel C. Y. Hsü's assertion in *China's Entrance into the Family of Nations: The Diplomatic Phase, 1858–1880* (Cambridge, Massachusetts, and London, 1960) that 'economically, the tributary practice was a loss to China' (p. 5).
20 Joseph F. Fletcher, 'China and Central Asia, 1368–1884', in John K. Fairbank, ed., *The Chinese World Order* (Cambridge, Massachusetts, and London, 1968), pp. 215-16.
21 Thomas A. Metzger, 'The Organizational Capabilities of the Ch'ing State in the Field of Commerce: The Liang-huai Salt Monopoly, 1740–1840,' in W. E. Willmott, ed., *Economic Organization in Chinese Society* (Stanford, 1972), p. 19.

CHAPTER ONE

1 K. M. Maitra, trans., *A Persian Embassy to China* (New York, reprint, 1970), p. 14.
2 From Morris Rossabi's translation of Ch'en's report on foreign lands (*Hsi-yü fan-kuo chih*), to be published shortly.
3 For additional information on Hami, see Morris Rossabi, 'Trade Routes in Inner Asia', in Denis Sinor, ed., *Cambridge History of Inner Asia* (London, forthcoming). A dated but useful work on Hami is M. C. Imbault-Huart, *Le pays de Hami ou Khamil* (Paris, 1892).
4 Henry Yule, *The Book of Ser Marco Polo the Venetian concerning the kingdoms and marvels of the East*, 3rd ed., rev. Henri Cordier (London, 1903), I, p. 210.
5 Jung-pang Lo, 'Policy Formulation and Decision-Making on Issues Respecting Peace and War', in Charles O. Hucker, ed., *Chinese Government in Ming Times: Seven Studies* (New York and London, 1969), p. 52.
6 Joseph F. Fletcher, 'China and Central Asia, 1368–1884', in John K. Fairbank, ed., *The Chinese World Order* (Cambridge, Massachusetts, and London, 1968), p. 209. For a translation of the letter recorded in the Chinese sources see E. Bretschneider, *Mediaeval Researches from Eastern Asiatic Sources* (New York, reprint, 1967), II, pp. 258–60.
7 On relations between Tamerlane and the Ming court, see Morris Rossabi, 'Cheng Ho and Timur: Any Relation?', *Oriens Extremus*, 20 (1973), pp. 129–36.
8 Yi-t'ung Wang, *Official Relations Between China and Japan, 1368–1549* (Cambridge, Massachusetts, and London, 1953), p. 35; Tilemann Grimm, 'Thailand in the Light of Official Chinese Historio-

graphy: A Chapter in the "History of the Ming Dynasty" ', *Journal of the Siam Society*, XLIV, pt 1 (July 1961), p. 6; Josef Kolmas, *Tibet and Imperial China* (Canberra, 1967), pp. 28–30.

9 For a description of the Ssu-i kuan, see Norman Wild, 'Materials for the Study of the Ssu I Kuan', *Bulletin of the School of Oriental and African Studies*, London University, XI (1943–46), pp. 617–640.

10 Henry Serruys, 'The Mongols in China During the Hung-wu Period (1368–1398)', *Mélanges chinois et bouddhiques*, XI (1959), p. 110.

11 Henry Serruys, 'The Mongols of Kansu During the Ming', *Mélanges chinois et bouddhiques*, X (1955), p. 295.

12 Morris Rossabi, 'Ming China's Relations with Hami and Central Asia, 1404–1513: a Re-examination of Traditional Chinese Foreign Policy' (Columbia University Ph.D. dissertation, 1970), pp. 84–86.

13 E. Bretschneider, op. cit., II, p. 180.

14 Guy Le Strange, trans., *Clavijo: Embassy to Tamerlane, 1403–1406* (London, 1928), pp. 222–3.

15 V. V. Barthold, *Four Studies on the History of Central Asia*, trans. V. and T. Minorsky (Leiden, 1963), II, pp. 50–51; Lucien Bouvat, *L'empire Mongol* (*2e phase*) (Paris, 1927), p. 65.

16 Joseph F. Fletcher, op. cit., p. 215.

17 Ibid., p. 213.

18 Ibid., p. 214.

19 Jung-pang Lo, op. cit., p. 59. On the disaster in Vietnam, see Alexander B. Woodside, 'Early Ming Expansionism (1406–1427): China's Abortive Conquest of

Vietnam', *Papers on China*, Harvard University, XVII (December, 1963), pp. 1–37; on the conclusion of the Cheng Ho expeditions, see Jung-pang Lo, 'The Decline of the Early Ming Navy', *Oriens Extremus*, V (1958–59), pp. 149–68.

20 Charles O. Hucker, *The Censorial System of Ming China* (Stanford, 1966), p. 76; Mark Elvin, *The Pattern of the Chinese Past* (Stanford and London, 1973), p. 100. See also Ray Huang, 'Military Expenditures in Sixteenth Century Ming China', *Oriens Extremus*, XVII, nos 1–2 (December 1970), pp. 40–47, for further examples of the deterioration of the Ming army.

21 David Farquhar, 'Oirat-Chinese Tribute Relations, 1408–1446', *Studia Altaica: Festschrift für Nikolaus Poppe* (Wiesbaden, 1957), pp. 66–67.

22 For more material on Esen, see Henry Serruys, 'Notes on a few Mongolian Rulers of the 15th Century', *Journal of the American Oriental Society*, 76 (1956), pp. 83–84; Louis Hambis, *Documents sur l'histoire des Mongols à l'époque des Ming* (Paris, 1969), pp. 97–104; C. R. Bawden, *The Mongol Chronicle Altan Tobči* (Wiesbaden, 1955), pp. 168–74; and the biography of him by Morris Rossabi in L. C. Goodrich, ed., *Eminent Chinese of the Ming Period* (New York, forthcoming).

23 See Morris Rossabi, 'Ming China and Turfan, 1406–1517', *Central Asiatic Journal*, XVI, no. 3 (1972), pp. 215–16.

24 René Grousset, *L'empire des steppes* (Paris, 1939), p. 573.

25 For brief accounts of some of these struggles, see V. V. Barthold, op. cit., II, pp. 164–75, and Percy

Sykes, *A History of Afghanistan* (London, 1940), I, pp. 269–72.

26 V. V. Barthold, op. cit., II, p. 112.

27 Morris Rossabi, 'Ming China's Relations with Hami and Central Asia, 1404–1513: a Re-examination of Traditional Chinese Foreign Policy' (Columbia University Ph.D. dissertation, 1970), pp. 207–208.

28 George A. Cheney, *The Pre-Revolutionary Culture of Outer Mongolia* (Bloomington, 1968), p. 13.

29 Owen Lattimore, *Inner Asian Frontiers of China* (Boston, paperback ed., 1962), p. 519.

30 Henry Serruys, 'Sino-Mongol Relations during the Ming: The Tribute System and Diplomatic Missions (1400–1600)', *Mélanges chinois et bouddhiques*, XIV (1967), pp. 245, 250.

31 Ibid., p. 30. Serruys notes in the same work that 'O. Lattimore makes the point that theoretically speaking the nomad could be self-sufficient, but so rarely does he do so that this selfsufficiency [*sic*] is hypothetical' (p. 29).

32 Henry Serruys, 'The Mongols in China: 1400–1450', *Monumenta Serica*, XXVII (1968), pp. 296–304.

33 Ibid., p. 244.

34 On these Mongol campaigns led by the Yung-lo emperor, see Wolfgang Franke's articles 'Yung-lo's Mongolei Feldzüge', *Sinologische Arbeiten*, III (1945), pp. 1–54, and 'Chinesische Feldzüge durch die Mongolei im frühen 15. Jahrhundert', *Sinologica*, III (1951–1953), pp. 81–88, also V. M. Kasakevich, 'Sources to the History of the Chinese Military Expeditions into Mongolia', trans. R. Loewenthal, *Monumenta Serica*, VIII (1943), pp. 328–31.

35 Henry Serruys, 'The Mongols in China During the Hung-wu Period (1368–1398)', *Mélanges chinois et bouddhiques*, X (1955), p. 260.

36 See Morris Rossabi's biography of Arugtai in L. C. Goodrich, ed., op. cit.

37 David Farquhar, op. cit., pp. 66–67.

38 Morris Rossabi, 'Notes on Esen's Pride and Ming China's Prejudice', *Mongolia Society Bulletin*, IX, no. 2 (Autumn 1970), pp. 34–36.

39 For an interesting study of the origin of the Oirats, see Ch'i-yü Wu, 'Who were the Oirats?', *The Yenching Journal of Social Studies*, III, no. 2 (August 1941), pp. 174–219.

40 Roy A. Miller, 'Biography of Batu Möngke' in L. C. Goodrich, ed., op. cit.

41 Ibid., p. 2. For additional material on Dayan Khan, see Hidehiro Okada, 'Life of Dayan Qayan', *Acta Asiatica*, 11 (1966), pp. 46–55, and Sei Wada, 'A Study of Dayan Khan', *Memoirs of the Research Department of the Toyo Bunko*, 19 (1960), pp. 1–42. Henry Serruys, *Genealogical Tables of the Descendants of Dayan-qan* (The Hague, 1958), provides detailed information on him and his heirs.

42 D. Pokotilov, 'History of the Eastern Mongols during the Ming Dynasty from 1368 to 1634', trans. R. Loewenthal, *Studia Serica*, ser. A, no. 1 (1947), pp. 101–103.

43 Henry Serruys, 'Four Documents Relating to the Sino-Mongol Peace of 1570–1571', *Monumenta Serica*, XIX (1960), p. 2.

44 Ibid., pp. 19–66, gives a translation of the principal agreements between Altan Khan and the Ming.

45 For differing views on Buddhism among the Mongols before Altan Khan's conversion, see on the one hand Sh. Natsagdorj, 'The Introduction of Buddhism into Mongolia', trans. John R. Krueger, *Mongolia Society Bulletin*, VII (1968), pp. 1–12, and on the other hand Henry Serruys' two articles: 'Remarks on the Introduction of Lamaism into Mongolia', *Mongolia Society Bulletin*, VII (1968), pp. 62–65, and 'Early Lamaism in Mongolia', *Oriens Extremus*, X (October 1963), pp. 181–216.
46 C. R. Bawden, *The Modern History of Mongolia* (New York and London, 1968), p. 31.
47 Henry Serruys, *Sino-Jürčed Relations during the Yung-lo Period (1403–1424)* (Wiesbaden, 1955), p. 22.
48 This section on the Jurched is based on Morris Rossabi, 'The Jurchen in the Yüan and Ming', in Herbert Franke, ed., Chin Dynastic History Project (Seattle, forthcoming). On Korea in Ming times, see the brief survey by Takashi Hatada, *A History of Korea* (Santa Barbara, 1969), pp. 61–78.
49 On this inscription, see E. G. Ravenstein, *The Russians on the Amur* (London, 1861), pp. 193–7; Louis Ligeti, 'Les inscriptions djurtchen de Tyr', *Acta Orientalia Academiae Scientarium Hungaricae*, 12, nos 1–3 (1961), pp. 5–25; Li Chi, 'Manchuria in History', *Chinese Social and Political Science Review*, XVI, no. 2 (July 1932), p. 251; Lucien Gibert, *Dictionnaire Historique et Géographique de la Mandchourie* (Hong Kong, 1934), p. 677; and Morris Rossabi's biography of Isiha in L. C. Goodrich, ed., op. cit.
50 See Morris Rossabi, 'The Jurchen in the Yüan and Ming', in

Herbert Franke, ed., Chin Dynastic History Project (Seattle, forthcoming), for a more detailed study of the two communities.
51 Henry Serruys, op. cit., pp. 44–46.
52 See Note 50 above.
53 For more material on this incident, see E-tu Zen Sun's biography of Wang Chih in L. C. Goodrich, ed., op. cit.
54 Wilhelm Grube, *Die Sprache und Schrift der Jučen* (Leipzig, 1896), pp. 106–45, translates twenty letters from Jurched envoys to the court. Nearly all of the missives contain lists of the tribute offerings and requests for specific gifts or ranks.
55 Arthur W. Hummel, ed., *Eminent Chinese of the Ch'ing Period* (Washington, D.C., 1943–1944), p. 450.
56 See, in particular, Arthur W. Hummel, op. cit., pp. 595–9, and Franz Michael, *The Origin of Manchu Rule in China* (Baltimore, 1942).

CHAPTER TWO

1 See the biography of Ma by Benjamin E. Wallacker in L. C. Goodrich, ed., *Eminent Chinese of the Ming Period* (New York, forthcoming).
2 John K. Fairbank and Ssu-yü Teng, *Ch'ing Administration: Three Studies* (Cambridge, Massachusetts, and London, 1961), pp. 115–23.
3 On the College of Interpreters, see Paul Pelliot, 'Le hoja et le Sayyid Husain de l'histoire des Ming', *T'oung Pao*, XXXVIII (1948), pp. 249–72, and Henry Serruys, 'Sino-Mongol Relations During the Ming: The Tribute System and Diplomatic Missions (1400–1600)', *Mélanges chinois et*

bouddhiques, XIV (1967), pp. 408–442. Compare the treatment of foreign envoys by the Chinese with that by their contemporaries in Europe: 'Since diplomatic service was sometimes dangerous, filled with hardships, time-consuming, and ill-paid, it was difficult to find qualified men of the higher ranks to fill diplomatic posts' (Donald Queller, *The Office of Ambassador in the Middle Ages*, Princeton and London, 1967, pp. 227–8).

4 Henry Serruys, op. cit., pp. 397–8.

5 See Angela Hsi, 'Social and Economic Status of the Merchant Class of the Ming Dynasty: 1368–1644' (University of Illinois Ph.D. dissertation, 1972), p. 200.

6 Morris Rossabi, 'The Tea and Horse Trade with Inner Asia during the Ming', *Journal of Asian History*, IV, no. 2 (1970), p. 145. Henry Yule, rev. Henri Cordier, *Cathay and the Way Thither* (London, 1915), I, p. 280.

7 Margaret Medley, 'Ching-te Chen and the Problem of the Imperial Kilns', *Bulletin of the School of Oriental and African Studies*, London University, XXIX, pt 2 (1966), pp. 326–8; Jung-pang Lo, 'Policy Formulation and Decision-making on Issues Respecting Peace and War', in Charles O. Hucker, ed., *Chinese Government in Ming Times: Seven Studies* (New York and London, 1969), pp. 61–62.

8 Berthold Laufer, 'Chinese Muhammadan Bronzes', *Ars Islamica*, I (1934), p. 135. For more material on the role of eunuchs in Ming foreign relations, see Morris Rossabi, 'Eunuch Power: The Role of Eunuchs in Ming Foreign Relations', *Monumenta Serica*, XXXI (1973).

9 Robert H. Van Gulik, *Sexual Life in Ancient China* (Leiden, 1961), p. 256.

CHAPTER THREE

1 Morris Rossabi, 'Ming China's Relations with Hami and Central Asia, 1404–1513: A Re-examination of Traditional Chinese Foreign Policy' (Columbia University Ph.D. dissertation, 1970), pp. 247–9.

2 Compare these gifts with those presented to the Mongols. See Henry Serruys, 'Sino-Mongol Relations During the Ming: The Tribute System and Diplomatic Missions (1400–1600)', *Mélanges chinois et bouddhiques*, XIV (1967), pp. 211–218.

3 These details are based on an official court list. See Morris Rossabi, op. cit., p. 254.

4 Henry Serruys, op. cit., pp. 433, 435.

5 Ray Huang, 'Fiscal Administration During the Ming Dynasty', in Charles O. Hucker, ed., *Chinese Government in Ming Times: Seven Studies* (New York and London, 1969), p. 110.

6 Edward Schafer, 'The Camel in China down to the Mongol Dynasty', *Sinologica*, II, no. 3 (1950), p. 165.

7 Sung Ying-hsing, *T'ien-kung k'ai-wu: Chinese Technology in the Seventeenth Century*, trans. E-tu Zen Sun and Shiou-chuan Sun (University Park, Pennsylvania, and London, 1966), p. 64, gives a brief description of the capture of some of the furry animals.

8 K. M. Maitra, trans., *A Persian Embassy to China* (New York, reprint, 1970), pp. 95–97; see also Edward Schafer, 'Falconry in T'ang Times', *T'oung Pao*, XLVI (1958),

pp. 293–338. For the medicinal uses of gerfalcons, see Bernard E. Read, *Chinese Materia Medica: VI, Avian Drugs* (Peiping, 1932), nos 311, 314.

9 Yi-t'ung Wang, *Official Relations between China and Japan, 1368–1549* (Cambridge, Massachusetts, and London, 1953), p. 97.

10 Berthold Laufer, *Jade: A Study in Chinese Archaeology and Religion* (Chicago, 1912), p. 5; Edward Schafer, *The Golden Peaches of Samarkand* (Berkeley and London, 1963), p. 224.

11 S. Howard Hansford, *Chinese Carved Jades* (London, 1968), pp. 89–90.

12 E. Bretschneider, *Botanicon Sinicum* (London, 1895), III, pp. 18–25; Maurice Kains, *Ginseng* (New York, 1916), pp. 130–31; M. Pomet, *A Complete History of Drugs* (London, 1748), II, pp. 194–5.

13 Bernard E. Read, op. cit., I (1931), no. 335.

14 Edward Schafer, op. cit., p. 218; Sung Ying-hsing, op. cit., p. 268; E. Bretschneider, op. cit., II, pp. 190, 243; Edward Schafer, 'Orpiment and Realgar in Chinese Technology and Tradition', *Journal of the American Oriental Society*, 75 (1955), pp. 73–87.

15 Edward Schafer, op. cit., p. 187; Berthold Laufer, *Sino-Iranica* (Chicago, 1919), pp. 341–2.

16 John K. Fairbank, *Trade and Diplomacy on the China Coast* (Cambridge, Massachusetts, and London, 1953), p. 29.

17 Ray Huang, op. cit., p. 106.

18 Henry Serruys, op. cit., p. 245.

19 Morris Rossabi, 'The Tea and Horse Trade with Inner Asia during the Ming', *Journal of Asian History*, IV, no. 2 (1970), p. 150.

20 John A. Pope, *Fourteenth-Century Blue and White: A Group of Chinese Porcelains in the Topkapu Sarayi Müzesi, Istanbul* (Washington, D.C., 1952), p. 18.

21 Basil Gray, 'Blue and White Vessels in Persian Miniatures of the 14th and 15th Centuries re-examined', *Transactions of the Oriental Ceramic Society*, 24 (1948–1949), p. 29.

22 Paul Kahle, 'Eine islamische Quelle über China um 1500. (Das Khitāynāme des 'Ali Ekber.)', *Acta Orientalia*, 12 (1934), pp. 91–110.

23 John A. Pope, *Chinese Porcelains from the Ardebil Shrine* (Washington, D.C., 1956), p. 20.

24 See Mitsutaka Tani, 'A Study on Horse Administration in the Ming Period', *Acta Asiatica*, 21 (1971), pp. 73–97, and Morris Rossabi, op. cit., pp. 136–68.

25 H. G. Creel, 'The Role of the Horse in Chinese History', *American Historical Review*, LXX (1965), pp. 655–6.

26 For the use of tea among present-day nomads, see George Cressey, *Land of the 500 Million* (New York and London, 1955), p. 302. Tea as a stimulant and as of medicinal value is discussed in William Ukers, *All About Tea* (New York, 1935), I, pp. 539, 556.

27 Morris Rossabi, op. cit., p. 141.

28 Ibid., p. 146.

29 For an interesting account of Esen's invasion, see Wolfgang Franke, 'Yü Ch'ien, Staatsmann und Kriegsminister, 1398–1457', *Monumenta Serica*, XI (1946), pp. 94–100.

30 On Yang, see Herbert Giles, *A Chinese Biographical Dictionary* (Shanghai, 1898), pp. 905–906, and Morris Rossabi, op. cit., pp. 155–7.

31 Sei Wada, 'A Study of Dayan Khan', *Memoirs of the Research Department of the Toyo Bunko*, 19

(1960), pp. 27–29; Morris Rossabi, 'Ming China and Turfan, 1406–1517', *Central Asiatic Journal*, XVI, no. 3 (1972), p. 223.

CHAPTER FOUR

1 John K. Fairbank and Ssu-yü Teng, *Ch'ing Administration: Three Studies* (Cambridge, Massachusetts, and London, 1961), p. 149.
2 C. R. Bawden, *The Modern History of Mongolia* (New York and London, 1968), p. 96.
3 Arthur W. Hummel, ed., *Eminent Chinese of the Ch'ing Period* (Washington, D.C., 1943–1944), p. 596.
4 Owen Lattimore, *Inner Asian Frontiers of China* (Boston, paperback ed., 1962), pp. 131–2.
5 Arthur W. Hummel, ed., op. cit., p. 596.
6 See, for example, Franz Michael's use of the concept 'Manchu Feudalism' in his *The Origin of Manchu Rule in China* (Baltimore, 1942), pp. 48–61.
7 Robert H. G. Lee, *The Manchurian Frontier in Ch'ing History* (Cambridge, Massachusetts, and London, 1970), pp. 24–25.
8 Ibid., pp. 29–30.
9 Arthur Hummel, ed., op. cit., p. 596.
10 David M. Farquhar, 'The Origins of the Manchus' Mongolian Policy', in John K. Fairbank, ed., *The Chinese World Order* (Cambridge, Massachusetts, and London, 1968), p. 201.
11 Ibid., p. 204.
12 Lucien Gibert, *Dictionnaire Historique et Géographique de la Mandchourie* (Hong Kong, 1934), pp. 680–81.
13 Yoshi Kuno, *Japanese Expansion on the Asiatic Continent* (Berkeley, 1937), I, pp. 61–178, and George Sansom, *A History of Japan, 1334–1615* (Stanford, 1961), pp. 352–62, provide adequate summaries of the Sino-Japanese War in Korea. Albert Chan, 'The Decline and Fall of the Ming Dynasty' (Harvard University Ph.D. dissertation, 1954), offers a detailed study of the internal problems of the late Ming.
14 James B. Parsons, *The Peasant Rebellions of the Late Ming Dynasty* (Tucson, 1970), p. 242.
15 Arthur W. Hummel, ed., op. cit., p. 107.
16 Robert H. G. Lee, op. cit., p. 40.
17 Ibid., pp. 64–65.
18 This system was virtually indistinguishable from that devised by the Ming to deal with the Jurched.
19 Robert H. G. Lee, op. cit., pp. 63–69.
20 Ibid., p. 75.
21 On the Russian drive to the East, see Robert Kerner, *The Urge to the Sea* (Berkeley, 1942).
22 Quoted in George V. Lantzeff, *Siberia in the Seventeenth Century* (Berkeley, 1943), p. 78.
23 Michael T. Florinsky, *Russia: A History and an Interpretation* (New York, 1947), I, p. 357.
24 Raymond H. Fisher, *The Russian Fur Trade, 1550–1700* (Berkeley, 1943), pp. 136–44.
25 Robert Kerner, op. cit., p. 166.
26 George V. Lantzeff, op. cit., p. 137. See also F. A. Golder, *Russian Expansion on the Pacific, 1641–1850* (Cleveland, 1914), p. 28.
27 George V. Lantzeff, op. cit., p. 18.
28 On the *prikaz* and *voevoda*, see Mark Mancall, *Russia and China: Their Diplomatic Relations to 1287*

(Cambridge, Massachusetts, and London, 1971), pp. 14–17.

29 George V. Lantzeff, op. cit., p. 95.

CHAPTER FIVE

1 A pioneering study of these early missions to the Amur region is E. G. Ravenstein, *The Russians on the Amur* (London, 1861). On the Poyarkov mission, see Mark Mancall, *Russia and China: Their Diplomatic Relations to 1728* (Cambridge, Massachusetts, and London, 1971), pp. 21–23, and Tien-fong Cheng, *A History of Sino-Russian Relations* (Washington, D.C., 1957), p. 15.

2 On Khabarov's exploits, see F. A. Golder, *Russian Expansion on the Pacific, 1640–1850* (Cleveland, 1914), pp. 40–50, and Vincent Chen, *Sino-Russian Relations in the Seventeenth Century* (The Hague, 1966), pp. 40–41.

3 Tien-fong Cheng, op. cit., p. 18.

4 O. Edmund Clubb, *China and Russia: The 'Great Game'* (New York and London, 1971), p. 25.

5 Lo-shu Fu, trans., *A Documentary Chronicle of Sino-Western Relations (1644–1820)* (Tucson, 1966), I, pp. 64–65.

6 Mark Mancall, op. cit., pp. 122–134, describes the encounters between Ch'ing and Russian forces along the Amur.

7 C. R. Bawden, *The Modern History of Mongolia* (New York and London, 1968), pp. 46–47.

8 About the Jebtsundamba Khutukhtus, see the fascinating translation by C. R. Bawden of *The Jebtsundamba Khutukhtus of Urga* (Wiesbaden, 1961).

9 C. R. Bawden, *The Modern History of Mongolia* (New York and London, 1968), pp. 59–60.

10 Robert A. Rupen, 'The City of Urga in the Manchu Period', in *Studia Altaica: Festschrift für Nikolaus Poppe* (Wiesbaden, 1957), p. 161.

11 One of the most important works on early Russian contacts in Mongolia is John F. Baddeley, *Russia, Mongolia, China* (2 vols, London, 1919).

12 O. Edmund Clubb, op. cit., p. 16.

13 On this subject, see Henry Serruys, 'Three Mongol Documents from 1635 in the Russian Archives', *Central Asiatic Journal*, VII, no. 1 (March 1962), pp. 1–41.

14 Joseph F. Fletcher, 'V. A. Aleksandrov on Russo-Ch'ing Relations in the Seventeenth Century: Critique and Résumé', *Kritika: A Review of Current Soviet Books on Russian History*, VII, no. 3 (Spring 1971), p. 146.

15 Joseph F. Fletcher, 'I. Ia. Zlatkin, *Istoriia Dzhungarskogo khanstva (1635–1758)*', *Kritika*, II, no. 3 (Spring 1966), pp. 21–23.

16 Li Tieh-tseng, *Tibet, Today and Yesterday* (New York and London, 1960), pp. 34–35.

17 Joseph F. Fletcher, 'China and Central Asia, 1368–1884', in John K. Fairbank, ed., *The Chinese World Order* (Cambridge, Massachusetts, 1968), p. 218.

18 Joseph F. Fletcher, 'I. Ia. Zlatkin, *Istoriia Dzhungarskogo khanstva (1635–1758)*', *Kritika*, II, no. 3 (Spring 1966), p. 24. On the Dzungars, see also Maurice Courant, *L'Asie Central aux xviie et xviiie Siècles: Empire Kalmouk ou Empire Mantchou?* (Paris, 1912); Paul Pelliot, *Notes critiques d'histoire kalmouke* (Paris, 1960),

297

basically a set of technical notes and supplements to John F. Baddeley, op. cit.

19 C. R. Bawden, op. cit., p. 67.

20 Arthur W. Hummel, ed., *Eminent Chinese of the Ch'ing Period* (Washington, D.C., 1943–44), p. 266.

21 Gaston Cahen, *Histoire des Relations de la Russie avec la Chine sous Pierre le Grand (1689–1730)* (Paris, 1911), pp. 11–12.

22 Vincent Chen, op. cit., p. 37.

23 On the Baikov embassy, see Mark Mancall, op. cit., pp. 44–53; John F. Baddeley, op. cit., II, pp. 133–53.

24 Vincent Chen, op. cit., pp. 55–58; O. Edmund Clubb, op. cit., p. 25.

25 Mark Mancall, op. cit., p. 63.

26 Ibid., p. 78; Vincent Chen, op. cit., pp. 63–64.

27 Harry Schwartz, *Tsars, Mandarins, and Commissars: A History of Chinese-Russian Relations* (New York, ed. of 1973), p. 27.

28 Michel N. Pavlovsky, *Chinese-Russian Relations* (New York, 1949), pp. 16–17.

29 Ibid., pp. 99–126, discusses this question in some detail.

30 See Joseph Sebes, *The Jesuits and the Sino-Russian Treaty of Nerchinsk (1689): The Diary of Thomas Pereira, S.J.* (Rome, 1961).

31 For the text of the treaty, see Mark Mancall, op. cit., pp. 280–86; for an examination of the various versions of the text, see Walter Fuchs, 'Der Russisch-Chinesische Vertrag von Nertschinsk von Jahre 1689', *Monumenta Serica*, IV, no. 2 (1939–40), pp. 546–91.

32 See his account as presented in E. Ysbrants Ides, *Three Years Travels from Moscow Overland to China* (London, 1706), and Adam Brand, *Relation du Voyage de Mr Evert Isbrand* (Amsterdam, 1699).

33 On these restrictions and on the E-lo-ssu kuan, see Ssu-ming Meng, 'The E-lo-ssu Kuan (Russian Hostel) in Peking', *Harvard Journal of Asiatic Studies*, 23 (1960–61), pp. 19–46.

34 One such study is Clifford M. Foust, *Muscovite and Mandarin: Russia's Trade with China and Its Setting, 1727–1805* (Chapel Hill, 1969), pp. 9–13.

35 A fine source of information on these caravans is Gaston Cahen, op. cit., pp. 39–50.

36 Mark Mancall, op. cit., p. 216.

37 Aitchen K. Wu, *China and the Soviet Union* (New York and London, 1950), pp. 16–19.

38 John Bell, *A Journey from St Petersburg to Pekin, 1719–22*, ed. J. L. Stevenson (Edinburgh, 1965), p. 52.

39 Ibid., pp. 131–8; O. Edmund Clubb, op. cit., pp. 41–42.

40 Mark Mancall, op. cit., p. 223.

41 Aitchen K. Wu, op. cit., pp. 21–22; Clifford M. Foust, op. cit., pp. 29–34.

42 O. Edmund Clubb, op. cit., p. 47.

43 The text of the Treaty of Kiakhta may be found in Mark Mancall, op. cit., pp. 302–10.

44 Eighteenth-century commercial relations between Russia and China are covered exhaustively in Clifford M. Foust, op. cit.

CHAPTER SIX

1 Owen Lattimore, *Inner Asian Frontiers of China* (Boston, paperback ed., 1962), p. xix.

2 Arthur W. Hummel, ed., *Eminent Chinese of the Ch'ing Period* (Washington, D.C., 1943–

1944), pp. 266–7. On Galdan's efforts to secure Russian assistance, see John R. Krueger, 'Three Oirat-Mongolian Diplomatic Documents of 1691', *Central Asiatic Journal*, XII, no. 4 (1969), pp. 292–4.
3 O. Edmund Clubb, *China and Russia: The 'Great Game'* (New York and London, 1971), p. 35.
4 Arthur W. Hummel, op. cit., p. 268.
5 O. Edmund Clubb, op. cit., p. 45.
6 On early Ch'ing-Tibetan relations, see Luciano Petech, *China and Tibet in the Early 18th Century: History of the Establishment of Chinese Protectorate in Tibet* (Leiden, 1950); Zahiruddin Ahmad, *Sino-Tibetan Relations in the Seventeenth Century* (Rome, 1970); and Giuseppe Tucci, *Tibetan Painted Scrolls* (Rome, 1949), vol. I.
7 Arthur W. Hummel, op. cit., p. 758.
8 As explained in the Preface, I cannot in this work deal at any length with Sino-Tibetan relations. For a recent work on the subject, though it is somewhat difficult to follow, see W. C. Shakabpa, *Tibet: A Political History* (New Haven and London, 1967).
9 Gavin Hambly, ed., *Central Asia* (New York and London, 1969), pp. 146–7; Michael Rywkin, *Russia in Central Asia* (New York and London, 1963), p. 17.
10 O. Edmund Clubb, op. cit., p. 39; Arthur W. Hummel, op. cit., pp. 785–6.
11 Translated by George Thomas Staunton as *Narrative of the Chinese Embassy to the Khan of the Tourgouth Tartars* (London, 1821). See also the recent Japanese translation of the text by Imanishi Shunjū (Tokyo, 1964).
12 John K. Fairbank, Edwin O. Reischauer, and Albert M. Craig, *East Asia: The Modern Transformation* (Boston, 1965), pp. 51–52.
13 Arthur W. Hummel, op. cit., p. 10. On the early Ch'ing-Dzungar campaigns, see Eva S. Kraft, *Zum Dsungarenkrieg im 18. Jahrhundert: Berichte des generals Funingga* (Leipzig, 1953).
14 Arthur W. Hummel, op. cit., pp. 10–11.
15 Clifford M. Foust, *Muscovite and Mandarin: Russia's Trade with China and its Setting, 1727–1805* (Chapel Hill, 1969), pp. 251–2; Agnes Fang-chih Chen, 'China's Northern Frontiers: Historical Background', *The Yenching Journal of Social Studies*, IV, no. 1 (August 1948), pp. 72–74.
16 O. Edmund Clubb, op. cit., p. 54.
17 John R. Krueger, 'The Ch'ien-Lung Inscriptions of 1755 and 1758 in Oirat-Mongolian', *Central Asiatic Journal*, XVI, no. 1 (1972), pp. 68–69.
18 Joseph F. Fletcher, 'China and Central Asia, 1368–1884', in John K. Fairbank, *The Chinese World Order* (Cambridge, Massachusetts, and London, 1968), p. 220.
19 Owen Lattimore, *Nationalism and Revolution in Mongolia* (New York and London, 1955), pp. 12–16.
20 Robert A. Rupen, 'The City of Urga in the Manchu Period', in *Studia Altaica: Festschrift für Nikolaus Poppe* (Wiesbaden, 1957), p. 159. For greater detail on the Ch'ing administrative system in Mongolia, see H. S. Brunnert and V. V. Hagelstrom, *Present Day Political Organization of China*, trans. A. Beltchenko and E. Moran (Shanghai, 1912), pp. 442–63.
21 C. R. Bawden, *The Modern*

NOTES TO THE TEXT

History of Mongolia (New York and London, 1968), p. 82.

22 C. R. Bawden, 'The Mongol Rebellion of 1756–1757', *Journal of Asian History*, 2, no. 1 (1968), p. 15.

23 See George G. S. Murphy, *Soviet Mongolia: A Study of the Oldest Political Satellite* (Berkeley and London, 1966), pp. 29–35, for a study of the Mongols during the Ch'ing period.

24 C. R. Bawden, op. cit., pp. 13–14.

25 The Chinese influence continued at least until 1921. See Owen Lattimore, *Nomads and Commissars: Mongolia Revisited* (New York and London, 1962), pp. 54–55.

26 On the economic power of the monasteries in Inner Mongolia, see Robert James Miller, *Monasteries and Culture in Inner Mongolia* (Wiesbaden, 1959), pp. 87–119.

27 C. R. Bawden, op. cit., p. 19.

28 C. R. Bawden, *The Modern History of Mongolia*, p. 121.

29 C. R. Bawden, 'The Mongol Rebellion of 1756–1757', p. 29.

30 Ibid., p. 31.

31 C. D. Barkman, 'The Return of the Torghuts from Russia to China', *Journal of Oriental Studies*, II (1955), pp. 95–99.

32 Their migration is recounted (somewhat inaccurately) by Thomas de Quincey in *The Revolt of the Tartars* (London, 1837).

33 John L. Mish, 'The Return of the Turgut', *Journal of Asian History*, IV, no. 1 (1970), p. 81.

34 See John R. Krueger, 'Toward greater utilization of the Ch'ien-lung pentaglot: The Mongolian Index', *Ural-Altaische Jahrbücher*, 35 (1963), pp. 228–40.

35 Ssu-ming Meng, *The Tsungli Yamen: Its Organization and Functions* (Cambridge, Massachusetts,

and London, 1970), pp. 9–11. On the Ch'ien-lung emperor, see the recent study by Harold L. Kahn, *Monarchy in the Emperor's Eyes* (Cambridge, Massachusetts, and London, 1971).

36 John Bell, *Travels from St Petersburg in Russia to Diverse Parts of Asia* (Glasgow, 1763), II, p. 183.

37 Vincent Chen, op. cit., pp. 67–72.

38 H. S. Brunnert and V. V. Hagelstrom, op. cit., pp. 160–66.

39 Ssu-ming Meng, 'The E-lo-ssu Kuan (Russian Hostel) in Peking', *Harvard Journal of Asiatic Studies*, 23 (1960–61), pp. 39–45.

40 Ibid., pp. 45–46.

41 John K. Fairbank and Ssu-yü Teng, *Ch'ing Administration: Three Studies* (Cambridge, Massachusetts, and London, 1961), pp. 13–17.

42 Thomas A. Metzger, 'The Organizational Capabilities of the Ch'ing State in the Field of Commerce: The Liang-huai Salt Monopoly, 1740–1840', in W. E. Willmott, ed., *Economic Organization in Chinese Society* (Stanford, 1972), p. 44.

43 John Bell, op. cit., p. 181.

44 Ibid., p. 138.

45 E. Bretschneider, *Botanicon Sinicum*, III, pp. 229–32. The medical encyclopedia is the *Pents'ao Kang-mu*, by Li Shih-chen.

46 John Gerarde, *The Herball or General Historie of Plantes*, rev. Thomas Johnson (London, 1633), pp. 392–5. On rhubarb as a purgative, see also John Parkinson, *Theatrum Botanicum: the Theater of Plantes* (London, 1640), p. 155, and Morris Rossabi, 'Rhubarb in China', a paper presented to the annual meeting of the American

Oriental Society (Cambridge, Massachusetts, 1971).
47 Clifford M. Foust, op. cit., pp. 181–5.

CHAPTER SEVEN

1 Immanuel C. Y. Hsü, 'The Great Policy Debate in China, 1874: Maritime Defense vs. Frontier Defense', *Harvard Journal of Asiatic Studies*, 25 (1964–65), p. 222.
2 Joseph F. Fletcher, 'China and Central Asia, 1368–1884', in John K. Fairbank, ed., *The Chinese World Order* (Cambridge, Massachusetts, and London, 1968), p. 220.
3 Wen-djang Chu, *The Moslem Rebellion in Northwest China, 1862–1878* (The Hague, 1966), p. 19.
4 Immanuel C. Y. Hsü, *The Ili Crisis: A Study of Sino-Russian Diplomacy, 1878–1881* (London and New York, 1965), p. 21.
5 Tsing Yüan, 'Yakub Beg (1820–1877) and the Moslem Rebellion in Chinese Turkestan', *Central Asiatic Journal*, VI, no. 2 (June 1961), p. 139.
6 Wen-djang Chu, op. cit., p. 5.
7 I have relied here on Joseph F. Fletcher's brilliant and as yet unpublished paper 'Central Asian Sufism and Ma Ming-hsin's New Teaching'.
8 For more information on the New Teaching rebellions, see Immanuel C. Y. Hsü, op. cit., pp. 22–24.
9 Saguchi Tōru, 'The Eastern Trade of the Khoqand Khanate', *Memoirs of the Research Department of the Toyo Bunko*, 24 (1965), p. 51.
10 For the development of the Khokand khanate, see Saguchi Tōru, 'The Revival of the White Mountain Khwajas, 1760 to 1820

(from Sarimsaq to Jihangir)', *Acta Asiatica*, 14 (1968), pp. 7–20.
11 Saguchi Tōru, 'The Eastern Trade of the Khoqand Khanate', p. 67.
12 Ibid., pp. 66–111.
13 Wen-djang Chu, 'The Immediate Cause of the Moslem Rebellion in Northwest China', *Central Asiatic Journal*, III, no. 4 (1958), pp. 315–16.
14 Tsing Yüan, op. cit., p. 145. For more material on Ya'qūb, see Demetrius Boulger, *The Life of Yakoob Beg* (London, 1878).
15 Tsing Yüan, op. cit., p. 149.
16 Wen-djang Chu, op. cit., pp. 81–82.
17 Russian dealings in Central Asia are described in Richard A. Pierce, *Russian Central Asia, 1867–1917: A Study in Colonial Rule* (Berkeley and London, 1966), and Seymour Becker, *Russia's Protectorates in Central Asia: Bukhara and Khiva, 1865–1924* (Cambridge, Massachusetts, and London, 1968).
18 Michael Rywkin, *Russia in Central Asia* (New York and London, 1963), pp. 29–31.
19 Immanuel C. Y. Hsü, op. cit., p. 18.
20 See, for example, N. Prejevalsky, *From Kulja Across the Tian Shan to Lob-Nor*, trans. E. Delmar Morgan (London, 1879). For a study of other explorers, see Jack Dabbs, *History of the Discovery and Exploration of Chinese Turkestan* (The Hague, 1963).
21 See Morris Rossabi, 'Trade Routes in Inner Asia', in Denis Sinor, ed., *Cambridge History of Inner Asia* (London, forthcoming).
22 Geoffrey Wheeler, *The Modern History of Soviet Central Asia* (London and New York, 1964), p.

80; Immanuel C. Y. Hsü, op. cit., pp. 30–32.

23 Gideon Chen, *Tso Tsung T'ang: Pioneer Promoter of the Modern Dockyard and Woolen Mill in China* (Peiping, 1938), pp. 49–76. On Tso's efforts to raise funds for his campaign, see Chung-li Chang and Stanley Spector, *Guide to the Memorials of Seven Leading Officials of Nineteenth-Century China* (Seattle, 1955), pp. 125, 135.

24 Wen-djang Chu, op. cit., pp. 156–61. On Tso's activities in the north-west, see the dated but still useful W. L. Bales, *Tso Tsung t'ang: Soldier and Statesman of Old China* (Shanghai, 1937), pp. 212–390.

25 Immanuel C. Y. Hsü, 'The Great Policy Debate in China, 1874: Maritime Defense vs. Frontier Defense', *Harvard Journal of Asiatic Studies*, 25 (1964–65), p. 220.

26 Robert B. Shaw, 'A Visit to Yarkand and Kashgar', *Proceedings of the Royal Geographical Society*, 14, no. 1 (February 1870), pp. 124–137.

27 Tsing Yüan, op. cit., p. 157.

28 On this episode, see Immanuel C. Y. Hsü, 'British Mediation of China's War with Yakub Beg, 1877', *Central Asiatic Journal*, IX, no. 2 (June 1964), pp. 142–9.

29 Tien-fong Cheng, *A History of Sino-Russian Relations* (Washington, D.C., 1957), pp. 45–46.

30 O. Edmund Clubb, *China and Russia: The 'Great Game'* (New York and London, 1971), p. 113.

31 On Gordon's visit and his suggestions, see Immanuel C. Y. Hsü, *The Ili Crisis: A Study of Sino-Russian Diplomacy, 1878–1881* (London and New York, 1965), pp. 122–38.

32 See ibid., pp. 153–88, on the protracted negotiations which led up to the Treaty of St Petersburg.

33 Immanuel C. Y. Hsü, 'The Late Ch'ing Reconquest of Sinkiang: A Reappraisal of Tso Tsung-t'ang's Role', *Central Asiatic Journal*, XII, no. 1 (1968), p. 62.

CHAPTER EIGHT

1 Robert H. G. Lee, *The Manchurian Frontier in Ch'ing History* (Cambridge, Massachusetts, and London, 1970), p. 80.

2 Kungtu C. Sun and Ralph W. Huenemann, *The Economic Development of Manchuria in the First Half of the Twentieth Century* (Cambridge, Massachusetts, and London, 1969), p. 11.

3 Aitchen K. Wu, *China and the Soviet Union* (New York and London, 1950), p. 62.

4 Tien-fong Cheng, *A History of Sino-Russian Relations* (Washington, D.C., 1957), pp. 32–33; A. Lobanov-Rostovsky, *Russia and Asia* (New York, 1933), pp. 137–42.

5 On Putiatin's mission, see R. K. I. Quested, *The Expansion of Russia in East Asia, 1857–1860* (Singapore, 1968), pp. 64–153.

6 David J. Dallin, *The Rise of Russia in Asia* (New Haven and London, 1949), p. 20; O. Edmund Clubb, *China and Russia: The 'Great Game'* (New York and London, 1971), p. 85.

7 On the Treaty of Tientsin, see Chien-nung Li, *The Political History of China, 1840–1928*, trans. S. Y. Teng and Jeremy Ingalls (Princeton and London, 1956), pp. 84–86.

8 On the Sino-Russian negotiations of 1858–60 and the Anglo-French occupation of Peking, see Masataka Banno, *China and the West, 1858–1861* (Cambridge,

Massachusetts, and London, 1964), pp. 127–71, and Hosea Ballou Morse, *The International Relations of the Chinese Empire* (London, 1910), I, pp. 593–608.

9 O. Edmund Clubb, op. cit., p. 88. Compare with the treaty signed by the French and the Chinese; see Henri Cordier, *Histoire des Relations de la Chine avec les puissances occidentales, 1860–1900* (Paris, 1901), pp. 3–7.

10 See Seymour Becker, *Russia's Protectorates in Central Asia: Bukhara and Khiva, 1865–1924* (Cambridge, Massachusetts, and London, 1968), pp. 136–7, 180–83.

11 Ibid., pp. 125–8; Ian Murray Matley, 'Industrialization', in Edward Allworth, ed., *Central Asia: A Century of Russian Rule* (New York and London, 1967), pp. 325–330.

12 B. A. Romanov, *Russia in Manchuria (1892–1906)*, trans. Susan Wilbur Jones (Ann Arbor, 1952), pp. 6–8. On Witte, see Sergei I. Witte, *The Memoirs of Count Witte*, trans. Abraham Yarmolinsky (Garden City, 1921).

13 Andrew Malozemoff, *Russian Far Eastern Policy, 1881–1904* (Berkeley and London, 1958), pp. 93–112.

14 Aitchen K. Wu, op. cit., p. 70.

15 O. Edmund Clubb, op. cit., p. 130.

16 Kungtu C. Sun and Ralph W. Huenemann, op. cit., p. 21.

17 Ibid., p. 26.

18 Robert H. G. Lee, op. cit., pp. 167–74.

19 For Japanese opinion before and during the Russo-Japanese War, see Shumpei Okamoto, *The Japanese Oligarchy and the Russo-Japanese War* (New York and London, 1970).

20 On Bezobrazov's demands on China, see Paul Hibbert Clyde, *International Rivalries in Manchuria, 1689–1922* (Columbus, Ohio, 1928), p. 104. On the negotiation of the Portsmouth Treaty, see John A. White, *The Diplomacy of the Russo-Japanese War* (Princeton, 1964), pp. 227–329. On Russian attitudes before the war, see George A. Lensen, *Revelations of a Russian Diplomat: The Memoirs of Dmitrii I. Abrikossow* (Seattle and London, 1964), p. 89.

21 Ernest Batson Price, *The Russo-Japanese Treaties of 1907–1916 Concerning Manchuria and Mongolia* (Baltimore, 1933), pp. 26–38.

22 Aitchen K. Wu, op. cit., pp. 89–95; Ernest Batson Price, op. cit., pp. 39–58.

23 C. R. Bawden, *The Modern History of Mongolia* (New York and London, 1968), pp. 155–7.

24 Robert A. Rupen, 'The City of Urga in the Manchu Period', in *Studia Altaica: Festschrift für Nikolaus Poppe* (Wiesbaden, 1957), p. 164.

25 Owen Lattimore, *Nomads and Commissars: Mongolia Revisited* (New York and London, 1962), p. 5.

26 George A. Cheney, *The Pre-Revolutionary Culture of Outer Mongolia* (Bloomington, 1968), pp. 41–42.

27 Robert A. Rupen, op. cit., pp. 167–8.

28 See N. Prejevalsky, *Mongolia, the Tangut Country, and the Solitude of Northern Tibet*, trans. E. Delmar Morgan (London, 1876), and A. M. Pozdneev, *Mongolia and the Mongols*, trans. John R. Shaw and Dale Plank, ed. Fred Adelman and John R. Krueger (Bloomington, 1971).

29 Robert A. Rupen, op. cit., p. 168.

30 C. R. Bawden, op. cit., p. 142.

31 Gerard M. Friters, *Outer Mongolia and its International Position* (Baltimore, 1949; London, 1951), p. 50.

32 Robert A. Rupen, op. cit., p. 167.

33 Walter Heissig, 'Some New Information on Peasant Revolts and People's Uprisings in Eastern (Inner) Mongolia in the 19th Century (1861–1901)', in John Hangin and Urgunge Onon, *Analecta Mongolica* (Bloomington, 1972), p. 95. On a secret society that opposed Chinese rule in Inner Mongolia, see Jean Chesneaux, *Secret Societies in China*, trans. Gillian Nettle (Ann Arbor, 1971), pp. 104–107.

34 Chien-nung Li, op. cit., p. 66.

35 On Tz'u-hsi, see Marina Warner, *The Dragon Empress* (London and New York, 1972), a popular but generally reliable work which contains excellent illustrations.

36 S. M. Meng, *The Tsungli Yamen: Its Organization and Functions* (Cambridge, Massachusetts, and London, 1970), p. 38.

37 Ibid., pp. 61–72.

38 Ibid., pp. 79–81.

39 On the T'ung-wen-kuan and several other educational institutions, see Knight Biggerstaff, *The Earliest Modern Government Schools in China* (Ithaca and London, 1961).

CHAPTER NINE

1 Richard Yang, 'Sinkiang Under the Administration of Governor Yang Tseng-hsin, 1911–1928', *Central Asiatic Journal*, VI, no. 4 (December 1961), p. 273.

2 Gavin Hambly, ed., *Central Asia* (New York and London, 1969), p. 306.

3 Jean Chesnaux, *Secret Societies in China*, trans. Gillian Nettle (Ann Arbor, 1971), pp. 43–47.

4 Richard Yang, op. cit., pp. 305–308.

5 Hélène Carrère d'Encausse, 'The Fall of the Czarist Empire', in Edward Allworth, ed., *Central Asia: A Century of Russian Rule* (New York and London, 1967), pp. 207–212; Geoffrey Wheeler, *The Modern History of Soviet Central Asia* (London and New York, 1964), pp. 92–94; Richard A. Pierce, *Russian Central Asia, 1867–1917: A Study in Colonial Rule* (Berkeley and London, 1966), pp. 268–95. For a study of these Central Asian groups, see Serge Zenkovsky, *Pan-Turkism and Islam in Russia* (Cambridge, Massachusetts, and London, 1960).

6 Richard Yang, op. cit., p. 308.

7 Gavin Hambly, ed., op. cit., pp. 228–30.

8 Michael Rywkin, *Russia in Central Asia* (New York, 1963), p. 49. On Soviet policy in Central Asia, see Alexander G. Park, *Bolshevism in Turkestan, 1917–1927* (New York and London, 1957).

9 See E. H. Carr, *The Bolshevik Revolution, 1917–1923* (Baltimore and London, 1966), I, pp. 334–43, for more details of the situation in Central Asia.

10 O. Edmund Clubb, *China and Russia: The 'Great Game'* (New York and London, 1971), pp. 172–3.

11 Ibid., pp. 192–4.

12 Richard Yang, op. cit., p. 313.

13 Michael Rywkin, op. cit., pp. 51–61.

14 Henry Wei, *China and Soviet Russia* (Princeton, 1956), pp. 124–6.

15 There are a great many works

dealing with the Soviet-Nationalist alliance. Some of the more interesting ones include Harold Isaacs, *The Tragedy of the Chinese Revolution* (Stanford and London, 1951); Benjamin Schwartz, *Chinese Communism and the Rise of Mao* (Cambridge, Massachusetts, and London, 1951); Conrad Brandt, *Stalin's Failure in China* (Cambridge, Massachusetts, and London, 1958); and Chiang Kai-shek, *Soviet Russia in China* (rev. ed., New York, 1957).

16 Aitchen K. Wu, in *Turkistan Tumult* (London, 1940), offers a first-hand account of developments in Sinkiang during this time.

17 Like Aitchen K. Wu, Sven Hedin, the Swedish explorer, presents an invaluable personal record of the trouble in Sinkiang in *The Flight of Big Horse*, trans. F. H. Lyon (New York and London, 1936).

18 Howard Boorman and Richard Howard, ed., *Biographical Dictionary of Republican China* (New York and London, 1968), II, p. 464.

19 Allen S. Whiting and Sheng Shih-ts'ai, *Sinkiang: Pawn or Pivot?* (East Lansing, Michigan, 1958), p. 29.

20 O. Edmund Clubb, op. cit., p. 322.

21 Ibid., p. 322. Clubb founded the American consulate in Urumchi in 1943 and certainly had intimate dealings with Sheng. He seems therefore to be a reliable source of information on the fate of Ma.

22 See his account of his journey in *Journey to Turkestan* (London, 1937).

23 Henry Wei, op. cit., pp. 139–148.

24 O. Edmund Clubb, op. cit., p. 310.

25 Gilbert Fook-lam Chan, 'Sinkiang under Sheng Shih-ts'ai (1933–1944)' (University of Hong Kong M.A. thesis, 1965), p. 236.

26 Owen Lattimore et al., *Pivot of Asia* (Boston, 1950), p. 81.

27 A. Doak Barnett, *China on the Eve of Communist Takeover* (New York and London, 1963), p. 247.

28 David J. Dallin, *Soviet Russia and the Far East* (New Haven, 1948), p. 366. Dallin's work must be read with caution, for he has a strong anti-Soviet bias.

29 On Chiang's failure in Sinkiang, see Owen Lattimore et al., op. cit., pp. 90–100.

30 O. Edmund Clubb, op. cit., pp. 368–9.

31 Howard Boorman and Richard Howard, ed., op. cit., I, p. 4.

32 Donald W. Klein and Anne B. Clark, *Biographic Dictionary of Chinese Communism, 1921–1965* (Cambridge, Massachusetts, and London, 1971), I, p. 7.

33 Michael Pavlovsky, *Chinese-Russian Relations* (New York, 1949), pp. 42–43, errs by two months on the date of the Mongol mission's arrival in Russia.

34 Peter S. H. Tang, *Russian and Soviet Policy in Manchuria and Outer Mongolia, 1911–1931* (Durham, North Carolina, 1959), pp. 303–304. On the period 1911–21, see C. R. Bawden, trans., 'A Contemporary Mongolian Account of the Period of Autonomy', *Mongolia Society Bulletin*, IX, no. 1 (Spring 1970), pp. 5–29.

35 O. Edmund Clubb, op. cit., p. 154.

36 Parshotam Mehra, 'The Mongol-Tibetan Treaty of January 11, 1913', *Journal of Asian History*, 3, no. 1. (1969), pp. 1–22.

37 C. R. Bawden, *The Modern*

History of Mongolia (New York and London, 1968), p. 197.

38 Robert A. Rupen, *Mongols of the Twentieth Century* (Bloomington, 1964), I, p. 68.

39 Gerard M. Friters, *Outer Mongolia and its International Position* (Baltimore, 1949; London, 1951), pp. 108–109.

40 Hilel Salomon, 'The Anfu Clique and China's Abrogation of Outer Mongolian Autonomy', *Mongolia Society Bulletin*, X, no. 1 (Spring 1971), pp. 74–75.

41 For more material on Hsü, see ibid., pp. 76–80, and Howard Boorman and Richard Howard, ed., op. cit., II, p. 144.

42 C. R. Bawden, op. cit., pp. 216, 234; Robert A. Rupen, op. cit., I, pp. 141, 192.

43 On Sukhe Bator, see Owen Lattimore, *Nationalism and Revolution in Mongolia* (New York and Leiden, 1955). For the agreement of 1921 between the Soviet Union and Mongolia, see Xenia Joukoff Eudin and Robert C. North, *Soviet Russia and the East, 1920–1927: A Documentary Survey* (Stanford, 1957), p. 126.

44 On events in Mongolia in the 1920s, see Ma Ho-t'ien, *Chinese Agent in Mongolia*, trans. John De Francis (Baltimore, 1949); V. A. Maslennikov, *Contemporary Mongolia*, trans. David C. Montgomery (Bloomington, 1964), pp. 15–22, a Soviet account; and Serge Wolff, 'Mongolian Educational Venture in Western Europe (1926–1929)', *Mongolia Society Bulletin*, IX, no. 2 (Autumn, 1970), pp. 40–100.

45 Owen Lattimore, *Studies in Frontier History: Collected Papers, 1928–1958* (London and New York, 1962), pp. 432–9.

46 Donald G. Gillin, *Warlord: Yen Hsi-shan in Shansi Province* (Princeton, 1967), pp. 211–15.

47 O. Edmund Clubb, op. cit., p. 296.

48 Alvin D. Coox, 'Changkufeng and the Japanese "threat" to Vladivostok, 1938', *Journal of Asian History*, 5, no. 2 (1971), pp. 119–39.

49 Larry W. Moses, 'Sino-Japanese Confrontation in Outer Mongolia: The Battle of Nomonhan-Khalkin Gol', *Journal of Asian History*, 1, no. 1 (1967), pp. 64–85.

50 Henry Wei, op. cit., pp. 150–54.

51 Larry W. Moses, op. cit., p. 82.

52 Charles B. McLane, *Soviet Policy and the Chinese Communists, 1931–1946* (New York and London, 1958), pp. 178–80.

53 Aitchen K. Wu, *China and the Soviet Union* (New York and London, 1950), p. 229.

54 On Ulanfu, see June Dreyer, 'Inner Mongolia: The Purge of Ulanfu', *Current Scene*, VI, no. 20 (15 November 1968), pp. 1–14; Paul V. Hyer, 'Ulanfu and Inner Mongolian Autonomy under the Chinese People's Republic', *Mongolia Society Bulletin*, VIII (1969), pp. 24–62.

55 S. M. Shirokogoroff, *Social Organization of the Manchus* (London, 1924), p. 137.

56 On this episode, see the excellent work of Carl F. Nathan, *Plague Prevention and Politics in Manchuria, 1910–1931* (Cambridge, Massachusetts, and London, 1967).

57 On the controversy surrounding the Karakhan Declaration, see Allen S. Whiting, *Soviet Policies in China, 1917–1924* (New York and London, 1954), pp. 30–33; Jane Degras, ed., *Soviet Documents on Foreign Policy* (London, 1951), I, pp. 158–61.

58 Aitchen K. Wu, op. cit., pp. 151–7.

59 On the struggle between Chang and Feng, see James E. Sheridan, *Chinese Warlord: the Career of Feng Yü-hsiang* (Stanford, 1966), pp. 170–76; O. Edmund Clubb, op. cit., pp. 218–19.

60 See C. Martin Wilbur and Julie Lien-ying How, ed., *Documents on Communism, Nationalism, and Soviet Advisers in China, 1918–1927* (New York and London, 1956).

61 Henry Wei, op. cit., pp. 87–89.

62 Peter S. H. Tang, op. cit., pp. 242–59.

63 On the Japanese invasion of Manchuria, see Sara R. Smith, *The Manchurian Crisis, 1931–32* (New York and London, 1948), and Takehiko Yoshihashi, *Conspiracy at Mukden* (New Haven and London, 1963). On the Sino-Soviet agreement of December 1932, see O. Edmund Clubb, op. cit., pp. 272–3.

64 Henry Wei, op. cit., p. 109.

65 On the Manchurian economy under Japanese control, see Kungtu C. Sun and Ralph W. Huenemann, *The Economic Development of Manchuria in the First Half of the Twentieth Century* (Cambridge, Massachusetts, and London, 1969), pp. 41–60, 75–88, and the dated but still partially useful E. B. Schumpeter, *The Industrialization of Japan and Manchukuo, 1930–1940* (New York, 1940), pp. 271–474.

66 Herbert Feis, *The China Tangle* (Princeton, 1953), pp. 249–50.

67 Aitchen K. Wu, *China and the Soviet Union* (New York and London, 1950), pp. 292–4.

68 For one point of view on the 'looting' of Manchuria, see O. Edmund Clubb, *Twentieth-Century China* (New York and London, 1964), pp. 274–5.

CHAPTER TEN

1 Larry W. Moses, 'Inner Asia in International Relations: The Role of Mongolia in Russo-Chinese Relations', *Mongolia Society Bulletin*, XI, no. 2 (Autumn 1972), p. 66.

2 Much has been written about the origins of the Sino-Soviet dispute. See especially Donald Zagoria, *The Sino-Soviet Conflict, 1956–61* (Princeton and London, 1962), William E. Griffith, *The Sino-Soviet Rift* (Cambridge, Massachusetts, and London, 1964), and Klaus Mehnert, *Peking and Moscow*, trans. Leila Vennewitz (New York, 1962), for differing views on the conflict.

3 See David M. Farquhar, 'Chinese Communist Assessments of a Foreign Conquest Dynasty', in Albert Feuerwerker, ed., *History in Communist China* (Cambridge, Massachusetts, and London, 1968), p. 180.

4 Paul Hyer, 'The Re-evaluation of Chinggis Khan: Its Role in the Sino-Soviet Dispute', *Asian Survey*, 6, no. 12 (December 1966), pp. 696–8.

5 M. T. Haggard, 'Mongolia: The Uneasy Buffer', *Asian Survey*, 5, no. 1 (January 1965), p. 19.

6 John Gittings, *Survey of the Sino-Soviet Dispute* (London, 1968), p. 167.

7 William Heaton, 'Mongolia: Troubled Satellite', *Asian Survey*, 13, no. 2 (February 1973), p. 247.

8 See June Dreyer, 'Traditional Minority Elites and the CPR Elite Engaged in Minority Nationalities Work', in Robert A. Scalapino, ed., *Elites in the People's Republic of*

China (Seattle and London, 1972), pp. 416–50.

9 Donald W. Klein and Anne B. Clark, *Biographic Dictionary of Chinese Communism, 1921–1965* (Cambridge, Massachusetts, and London, 1971), p. 883.

10 Paul V. Hyer, 'Ulanfu and Inner Mongolian Autonomy Under the Chinese People's Republic', *Mongolia Society Bulletin*, VIII (1969), p. 52.

11 William Heaton, 'Chinese Communist Administration and Local Nationalism in Inner Mongolia', *Mongolia Society Bulletin*, X, no. 1 (Spring 1971), p. 30.

12 June Dreyer, 'Inner Mongolia: The Purge of Ulanfu', *Current Scene*, VI, no. 20 (15 November 1968), pp. 11–14.

13 June Dreyer, 'Traditional Minority Elites and the CPR Elite Engaged in Minority Nationalities Work', in Robert A. Scalapino, ed., *Elites in the People's Republic of China* (Seattle and London, 1972), p. 447.

14 Theodore Shabad, *China's Changing Map: National and Regional Development, 1949–72* (New York and London, rev. ed. 1972), p. 280.

15 On the Production Construction Corps, see George Moseley, *A Sino-Soviet Frontier: The Ili Kazakh Autonomous Chou* (Cambridge, Massachusetts, and London, 1966), pp. 35–41.

16 For a lucid presentation of the language problem in Sinkiang and Central Asia, see Paul B. Henze, 'Politics and Alphabets in Inner Asia', *Journal of the Royal Central Asian Society*, XLIII (January 1956), pp. 29–51, and 'Alphabet Changes in Soviet Central Asia and Communist China', *Journal of the Royal Central Asian Society*, XLIV (April 1957), pp. 124–35.

17 George Moseley, op. cit., pp. 107–109.

18 O. Edmund Clubb, *Twentieth-Century China* (New York and London, 1964), pp. 379–80.

19 Aitchen K. Wu, *China and the Soviet Union* (New York and London, 1950), pp. 335–7.

20 O. Edmund Clubb, op. cit., p. 406.

21 Ibid., pp. 406–407.

22 Joseph F. Fletcher, 'V. A. Aleksandrov on Russo-Ch'ing Relations in the Seventeenth Century: Critique and Résumé', *Kritika: A Review of Current Soviet Books on Russian History*, VII, no. 3 (Spring 1971), p. 138.

23 Theodore Shabad, 'Soviet Publishes a Document On 1689 Treaty With China', *New York Times* (19 November 1972), p. 3.

24 June Dreyer, op. cit., p. 450.

Other works consulted

Note: I have excluded from this list works already cited in the 'Notes to the text' and have included only a selection of the more important studies consulted in the preparation of this book.

CHINA, RUSSIA, AND INNER ASIA, 1368–1689

Armstrong, Terence, *Russian Settlements in the North* (Cambridge, England, 1965)

Central Asiatic Journal (Wiesbaden, 1955–)

Chen, Agnes Fang-chih, 'Chinese Frontier Diplomacy: The Coming of the Russians and the Treaty of Nertchinsk', *Yenching Journal of Social Studies*, IV, no. 2 (February 1949), pp. 99–149

Crawford, Robert B., 'Eunuch Power in the Ming Dynasty', *T'oung Pao*, XLIX, no. 3 (1961), pp. 115–48

Grimm, Tilemann, *Erziehung und Politik im konfuzianischen China der Ming-Zeit (1368–1644)* (Hamburg, 1960)

Haidar, Muhammad, *A History of the Moghuls of Central Asia*, trans. E. Denison Ross, ed. Ney Elias (New York and London, reprint; 1970)

Hedin, Sven, *The Silk Road*, trans. F. H. Lyon (London and New York, 1938)

Heissig, Walther, *A Lost Civilization: The Mongols Rediscovered*, trans. D. J. S. Thomson (London and New York, 1966)

———, 'A Mongolian Source to the Lamaist Suppression of Shamanism in the 17th Century', *Anthropos*, 48 (1953): nos 1–2, pp. 1–29; nos 3–4, pp. 493–536

Herrmann, Albert, *An Historical Atlas of China*, ed. Norton S. Ginsburg (Chicago, rev. ed., 1966)

Kaschewsky, Rudolf, *Das Leben des lamaistischen Heiligen Tsongkhapa, Bzan-Grags-Pa* (2 vols, Wiesbaden, 1971)

Mitamura, Taisuke, *Chinese Eunuchs: The Structure of Intimate Politics*, trans. Charles A. Pomeroy (Rutland, Vermont, and Tokyo, 1970)

Natsagdorj, Sh., 'The Economic Basis of Feudalism in Mongolia', trans. Owen Lattimore, *Modern Asian Studies*, I, no. 3 (1967), pp. 265–81

Serruys, Henry, 'Were the Ming against the Mongols settling in North China?', *Oriens Extremus*, VI, no. 2 (December 1959), pp. 131–59

Sinor, Denis, *Introduction à l'étude de l'eurasie centrale* (Wiesbaden, 1963)

Teng Ssu-yü, 'Ming T'ai-tsu's Destructive and Constructive Work', *Chinese Culture*, VIII, no. 3 (September 1967), pp. 14–38

Vernadsky, George, *The Tsardom of Moscow, 1547–1682* (New Haven and London, 1969)

CHINA AND INNER ASIA, 1689–1900

Beveridge, Albert, *The Russian Advance* (New York and London, 1904)

Broomhall, Marshall, *Islam in China* (London and Philadelphia, 1910)

Chen, Agnes Fang-chih, 'Chinese Frontier Diplomacy: Kiakhta Boundary Treaties and Agreements', *Yenching Journal of Social Studies*, IV, no. 2 (February 1949), pp. 151–205

Curzon, George, *Russia in Central Asia in 1889 and the Anglo-Russian Question* (London and New York, 1889)

Demko, George, *The Russian Colonization of Kazakhstan (1896–1916)* (Bloomington and The Hague, 1969)

Haslund, Henning, *Men and Gods in Mongolia* (New York, 1935)

Ho Ping-ti, *Studies on the Population of China, 1368–1953* (Cambridge, Massachusetts, and London,1959)

Holdsworth, Mary, *Turkestan in the Nineteenth Century* (London, 1959)

Imbault-Huart, C., *Recueil de Documents sur l'Asie Centrale* (Amsterdam, reprint of 1970)

Lensen, George, ed., *Korea and Manchuria between Russia and Japan, 1895–1904: The Observations of Sir Ernest Satow* (Tallahassee, 1966)

Michael, Franz, *The Taiping Rebellion* (Seattle and London, 1966)

Piassetsky, P., *Russian Travellers in Mongolia and China*, trans. J. Gordon-Cumming (London, 1884)

Raeff, Marc, *Siberia and the Reforms of 1822* (Seattle and London, 1956)

Schuyler, Eugene, *Turkistan: Notes of a Journey in Russian Turkistan, Khokand, Bukhara, and Kuldja* (2 vols, New York and London, 1877)

Skrine, Francis Henry, and E.

Denison Ross, *The Heart of Asia* (London, 1899)

Widmer, Eric G., 'Archimandrite Palladius and Chinese Control of Barbarians in 1858', *Papers on China*, Harvard University, XIX (1965), pp. 55–84

Wright, Mary C., *The Last Stand of Chinese Conservatism: The T'ung-chih Restoration, 1862–1874* (Stanford, 1957)

CHINA AND INNER ASIA IN THE TWENTIETH CENTURY

Aberle, David F., *Chahar and Dagor Mongol Bureaucratic Administration, 1912–1945* (New Haven, 1962)

Bacon, Elizabeth E., *Central Asia under Russian Rule* (Ithaca and London, 1966)

Beloff, Max, *The Foreign Policy of Soviet Russia, 1929–1941* (2 vols, London and New York, 1947–49)

———, *Soviet Policy in the Far East, 1944–1951* (London and New York, 1953)

Cammann, Schuyler, *The Land of the Camel: Tents and Temples of Inner Mongolia* (New York, 1951)

Caroe, Olaf, *Soviet Empire: The Turks of Central Asia and Stalinism* (London and New York, 2nd ed., 1967)

Deutscher, Isaac, *Russia, China, and the West: A Contemporary Chronicle, 1953–1966* (London, 1970)

Doolin, Dennis, *Territorial Claims in the Sino-Soviet Conflict* (Stanford, 1965)

Gerasimovich, Ludmilla K., *History of Modern Mongolian Literature (1921–1964)*, trans. John R. Krueger *et al.* (Bloomington, 1970)

Ginsburgs, George, 'The Dynamics of the Sino-Soviet Territorial Dispute: The Case of the River Islands', in Jerome Cohen, ed., *The Dynamics of China's Foreign Relations* (Cambridge, Massachusetts, 1970)

Goldhagen, Erich, ed., *Ethnic Minorities in the Soviet Union* (New York, 1968)

Hinton, Harold, *The Bear at the Gate: Chinese Policymaking under Soviet Pressure* (Washington, D.C., 1971)

Jackson, W. A. Douglas, *Russo-Chinese Borderlands* (Princeton, 1962)

Kalb, Marvin, *Dragon in the Kremlin* (New York, 1961)

Kawakami, K. K., *Manchukuo: Child of Conflict* (New York, 1933)

Kolarz, Walter, *Russia and her Colonies* (New York and London, 1952)

Krader, Lawrence, *Peoples of Central Asia* (Bloomington and The Hague, 1963)

Lattimore, Owen, *Manchuria: Cradle of Conflict* (New York, 1932)

——, *The Mongols of Manchuria* (New York, 1934)

——, 'Religion and Revolution in Mongolia: A Review Article', *Modern Asian Studies*, I, no. 1 (1967), pp. 81–94

Mandel, William, *The Soviet Far East and Central Asia* (New York, 1944)

Moore, Harriet, *Soviet Far Eastern Policy* (Princeton, 1945)

Moseley, George, *The Party and the National Question in China* (Cambridge, Massachusetts, 1966)

North, Robert C., *Moscow and the Chinese Communists* (Stanford and London, 1953)

Ovdiyenko, Ivan, *Economic-Geographical Sketch of the Mongolian People's Republic*, trans. members of the Mongolia Society (Bloomington, 1965)

Phillips, G. D. R., *Russia, Japan, and Mongolia* (London, 1942)

Pierce, Richard A., ed., *Mission to Turkestan: Being the Memoirs of Count K. K. Pahlen, 1908–1909*, trans. N. J. Couriss (London, 1964)

Pipes, Richard A., *The Formation of the Soviet Union: Communism and Nationalism, 1917–1923* (Cambridge, Massachusetts, and London, 1954)

Rupen, Robert A., *The Mongolian People's Republic* (Stanford, 1966)

——, 'The Mongolian People's Republic and Sino-Soviet Competition', in A. Doak Barnett, ed., *Communist Strategies in Asia* (New York, 1963)

——, 'Cyben Žamcaranovič Žamcarano (1880–1940)', *Harvard Journal of Asiatic Studies*, XIX, nos 1–2 (June 1956), pp. 126–45

Sanders, A. J. K., *The People's Republic of Mongolia: A General Reference Guide* (London, 1968)

Vreeland, Herbert Harold, *Mongol Community and Kinship Structure* (New Haven, 1954)

Wiens, Herold, 'Geographical Limitations to Food Production in the Mongolian People's Republic', *Annals of the Association of American Geographers*, XLI, no. 4 (December 1951), pp. 348–69

Yakhontoff, V. A., *Russia and the Soviet Union in the Far East* (New York, 1931; London, 1932)

Glossary

茶馬司   Ch'a-ma ssu   崇厚   Ch'ung-hou

張學良   Chang Hsüeh-liang   馮御香   Feng Yü-hsiang

張作霖   Chang Tso-lin   傅安   Fu An

兆惠   Chao-hui   傅作義   Fu Tso-i

陳誠   Ch'en Ch'eng   海童   Hai-t'ung

陳鉞   Ch'en Yüeh   罕慎   Han-shen

鄭和   Cheng Ho   黑玉河   Hei-yü ho

蔣介石   Chiang Kai-shek   和親   ho-ch'in

斤   chin   新教   Hsin-chie

金樹仁   Chin Shu-jen   徐樹錚   Hsü Shu-cheng

景德鎮   Ching-te chen   胡桐   hu-t'ung

主客清吏司   Chu-k'o ch'ing-li ssu   會同館   Hui-t'ung kuan

洪武	Hung-wu	馬明心	Ma Ming-hsin
以夷制夷	i-i-chih-i	毛澤民	Mao Tse-min
奕山	I-shan	毛澤東	Mao Tse-tung
亦失哈	I-shih-ha	內閣	Nei-ko
異域錄	I-yü-lu	俄羅斯學	E-lo-ssu hsüeh
開中	k'ai-chung	俄羅斯館	E-lo-ssu kuan
高崗	Kao Kang	俄羅斯文館	E-lo-ssu wen-kuan
哥老會	Ko-lao-hui	白玉河	Po-yü ho
光祿寺	Kuang-lu ssu	盛世才	Sheng Shih-ts'ai
來化	lai-hua	四夷館	Ssu-i kuan
李成梁	Li Ch'eng-liang	蘇四十三	Su Ssu-shih-san
理藩院	Li-fan yüan	孫逸仙	Sun Yat-sen
李鴻章	Li Hung-chang	脫脫	T'o T'o
禮部	Li-pu	曾紀澤	Tseng Chi-tse
李達	Li Ta	左宗棠	Tso Tsung-t'ang
馬仲英	Ma Chung-ying	總理衙門	Tsungli yamen
馬化隆	Ma Hua-lung	通事	t'ung-shih

同文館	T'ung-wen kuan	楊一清	Yang I-ch'ing
慈禧	Tz'u-hsi	也先	Yeh-hsien
外務部	Wai-wu pu	閻錫山	Yen Hsi-shan
王振	Wang Chen	袁世凱	Yüan Shih-k'ai
衛	wei	永樂	Yung-lo

Index

Abahai 89–90
Ablin, Seitkul 126–7
Afghanistan 172, 236, 280
Africa 67, 265, 267, 285
argiculture: Chinese intensive 19, 24, 52-53, 193; Mongol 40–41, 46, 56, 86–87, 91, 118, 143, 263, 266; Russian 199, 231; Manchurian 203, 258; communes 270–2, 278
Ahmad (son of Yunus) 36
Aigun, Treaty of (1858) 196, 197, 198
Aksai Chin 280
Aksu 149, 187, 276
Albazin 107–110, 129–30; siege of 111
'Ali Akbar 68, 77
Alma-Ata 227, 231, 274
Altai 34, 147, 223, 231
Altan Khan 45–46, 47, 112; descendents of 113–17, 125
Amur River 51, 53, 93–94, 103, 166, 200; conflict over 106–109, 110–12, 117, 124, 126–30, 131, 189, 192, 194, 195, 197; Russian settlements on 199, 202, 283, 284
Amursana 147–8, 155–6, 239
Andijan 174
An-lo community 53
Argun River 107, 136-7, 200
Arugtai 42, 43
Astrakhan 95, 239
Ayuka, Prince 114, 145-6

Baikal, Lake 96, 130
Baikov, Fedor 126–7
Bakich (White Russian) 227
banner troops 85–86, 88, 90–91, 93–94, 161; decline of 167, 170, 194–5, 204
'barbarians': Chinese policy towards 20–22, 26, 28, 36, 59, 67, 80, 88, 145, 149, 184, 257, 285; China's knowledge of 61, 64, 65
Basmachi Muslims 227
Batu Möngke (Dayan Khan) 44–45
begs (Muslim chiefs) 170, 173
Bell, John 134, 163
Bezobrazov, Alexander 205
Bishbalik: see Urumchi
Black Mountain Khojas 120
Black Sea 196
Blagoveshchensk 202
Bodgo Ula Mountains 116

Bolsheviks 224–6, 227
Boshugtu Khan 119
Boxer Rebellion 202, 204, 205, 215
Buddhism 24, 35, 53, 120, 155, 172; Mongols and 40, 46–47, 112–14, 118, 140–141, 151, 248; 'Yellow' and 'Red' sects 50, 119, 121, 144
Buir Nor region 248
Bukhara 110, 119, 126, 127, 164, 173, 179; Russians and 180, 199, 226–7
Bura, Treaty of 136, 145
Burhan 236–7, 275–6
Burma 280
Buryat Mongols 95, 98, 120, 124, 238, 244
Buzurg Khan 177

Canton 186, 192, 228
caravanserai 14–15
Catherine II (the Great) 165
Caucasus Mountains 172
Chahar Mongols 90, 113, 117
Chahar Province 247–8, 270
Ch'a-ma ssu (Horse Trading Office) 79, 81, 82–83
Chang Hsüeh-liang 255, 257
Changkufeng 248–9
Chang Tso-lin 243, 252, 254–255, 256
Chao-hui, General 148–9
Ch'en Ch'eng, embassies of 13–16, 24, 31, 60–61, 67
Cheng Ho, Admiral 28, 32, 67
Ch'en I 243–4
Chen Pao (Damanski) 283
Ch'en Yüeh 56
Chiang Kai-shek 228, 232–3, 234, 235–6, 247, 248–51, 255–6, 257, 259–60
Chicherin, Georgi 253
Chien-chou (Jurched) 87
Ch'ien-lung (Chinese emperor) 147, 159, 185, 213
Chihli (Hopei) 203
chin (unit of weight) 79
Chin dynasty 50, 58, 88, 90
China: revolution of 1911 212, 219, 238, 265; Civil War 237; Communist government 220, 262–83 passim; Nationalist (Kuomintang) government 220–221, 228–30, 232–7, 247, 255–6, 259–61, 263; early republican policy 222, 238–243; see also Ch'ing dynasty, Ming dynasty
Chinese Changchun Railway 260, 281
Chinese Eastern Railway 201–2, 205, 206–7, 211, 225, 252–7, 259–60
Ch'ing (Manchu) dynasty 22, 57, 58, 97, 262; early

policy 84, 90–92; and Manchuria 93–94, 203–206; and Russia 103–9, 111–12, 128–30; trade 124–127, 132–3, 137; and Mongols 112–15, 118–24, 149–58, 212–13, 238, 245–246; treaties 128–30, 131, 138, 150, 152; and Dzungars 141–9, 150–52, 157–8, 166, 168; policies in Central Asia 160–65, 166–79 passim, 194; and Muslims 172–4, 181–3; and Sinkiang 189–91; compared to Ming 190, 215, 217, 262, 284, 286; decline and collapse 207, 219
Chinggis Khan 121, 139, 140, 267–8, 272
Ching-te Chen 67, 77
Chingunjav, General 155–6, 157
Chin Shu-jen 229–31
Choibalsang, Mount 116, 245
Christianity 101, 158, 202, 248
Chu-k'o ch'ing-li ssu 63
Ch'ung-hou 187–8, 189
Chungking 233, 234
Communists: Chinese 220, 228, 229, 233–4, 236–7, 251, 255, 260–1, 262–84 passim, 285, 287; Mongolian 245, 265
Confucian ethics 19, 52, 60, 68, 185, 263–4
corvée labour 66, 152, 153, 155, 157, 212, 221
Cossacks 95, 98, 101, 109, 110
Crimean War 180, 196
Customs duties 99
Cultural Revolution 264, 272, 273–4, 276, 279–280
Cyrillic alphabet 277, 278
Czechoslovakia 283

Dairen 202, 206, 252, 257–8, 259–60, 281–2
Dalai Lama 50, 112, 113–14, 118–19, 121, 141, 143–4, 213
Dalny: see Dairen
Damanski: see Chen Pao
Dambijantsan see Ja Lama
Darkhan 269
Daur (people) 107
Demchukdonggrub: see Te, Prince
Derbet Mongols 118
Diyā 'al-Dīn 172–3
Dolonnor 142, 150
Dorgon 90–91
Dungans (Chinese Muslims) 168

315